Approaches to Personality

An Introduction to People

Approaches to Personality

An Introduction to People

James Geiwitz

Janet Moursund
University of Oregon

Brooks/Cole Publishing Company
Monterey, California 93940
A Division of Wadsworth, Inc.

To Carol Jean and Donald Emil.
Two of the real people.
J.G.

To the other Three of the Gang of Four,
Janis, Maggie, and Nancy.
J.M.

Consulting Editor: Edward L. Walker
The University of Michigan

Printed in the United States of America

10 9 8 7 6 5 4 3 2 1

Library of Congress Cataloging in Publication Data

Geiwitz, P. James, 1938–
Approaches to personality.

Includes bibliographies and index.
1. Personality. 2. Personality—Philosophy.
I. Moursund, Janet, joint author. II. Title.
BF698.G416 155.2 78-25934
ISBN 0-8185-0291-6

Acquisition Editor: *Charles T. Hendrix*
Project-Development Editor: *Claire Verduin*
Production Editor: *Sally Schuman*
Interior and Cover Design: *Jamie Brooks*
Technical Art: *Kath Minerva*
Interior and Cover Illustrations: *Micah Sanger*
Typesetting: *Continental Graphics, Los Angeles, Calif.*

Preface

There's no getting around it—this is an unusual book. It is a book about personality theory. It is also a book about personality theorists. It is written for students who are interested—or willing to become interested—in how people tick, in why people behave as they do. It presents a lot of answers to that question; it does not present *the* answer, because we are not convinced that there is any one answer.

Personality theory is exciting to us, and we want to share that excitement with students. We have not merely listed theorist after theorist and concept after concept; we have tried, rather, to get *inside* each theorist, to portray the intellectual problems he or she was faced with and the struggles to solve these problems—the false starts as well as the acclaimed achievements. Things said by people you are personally acquainted with, people you know, stick in your mind. It would be hard to read this book and not feel acquainted with at least some of the theorists between its covers.

A personality theory is not a freestanding entity, born complete and whole and independent out of the mind of its creator. It has roots and tendrils. It emerges from an intellectual and social context, and it interacts with other ideas of its time. Students reading this book will be made aware of these contexts and interactions. They will be encouraged to compare and contrast different viewpoints, to argue, to take sides, to become involved. We have a great deal of faith in the students (and the teachers) who will use this book. We have faith that they will be able to handle difficult and complex ideas. (After all, personality itself is a difficult and complex idea. . . .)

This is truly an introductory text, and we have made no assumptions about previous coursework in psychology. Rather, we trust that the student will be open-minded, ready to entertain new ideas, willing to think about personality instead of simply memorizing a list of definitions in order to pass a test. We believe that the best way to engage students in this kind of thinking is to be as open and honest with them as possible: to share our own biases, to admit to not knowing, to pose the questions that hooked us on personality theory in the first place. Above all, we have tried to be real. The examples in this book come from our own lives and from those of our friends. The problems are problems faced by all of us. The book has no neat, pat answers, because we haven't seen many such answers that hold up very well for real people living real lives in a real world.

So what will this book do? It will introduce students to a variety of personality theories in a way that makes those theories meaningful and relevant to their lives. It will challenge students to integrate contrasting ideas, to pull together observations and information from a variety of settings, to master concepts and viewpoints espoused by some of the most creative personologists of our time. Most importantly, it will encourage students to form their *own* theory of personality, to become engaged in the never-ending process of grasping and groping after truth—to join the community of seekers who delight as much in the quest as in its fruits.

We are convinced that the only way to truly learn about personality theory is to become a personality theorist. This book is an invitation to begin to become one.

Acknowledgments

And now it's time to express our thanks. Our reviewers played an especially important role in the creation of this book, curbing our most outrageous excesses, encouraging our iconoclastic treatments, applauding our occasional insights. In fairness to them, it should be noted that we ignored most of their suggestions, except, of course, when they caught us in some hideous misinterpretation. Nevertheless, the changes they induced (both by positive reinforcement and by punishment) were many, and this book is much better because of them. Betty Chandler, Oscar Rose Junior College; Scot Gardiner; John McGuire, Florida Technological University; Norman Simonson, University of Massachusetts; Abigail J. Stewart, Boston University; and Richard Weigel, Colorado State University, reviewed the entire manuscript. Several reviewers commented on one or two chapters: John Barbour; G.S. Blum, University of California, Santa Barbara; Robert Borson; Roberta Klatzky, University of California, Santa Barbara; and Warren Norman, The University of Michigan. We thank them all.

A number of personality theorists were also especially helpful in providing us with information about themselves and their colleagues. We have neither time nor space to list all of those who have helped in this way, but our special thanks go to Albert Bandura, Herbert Lefcourt, David Martin, Neal Miller, Hobart Mowrer, and Herman Witkin.

Ed Walker, our consulting editor, watched over the development of the entire manuscript with patience, understanding, and care. At Brooks/Cole, Terry Hendrix had faith when the book was nothing but ideas and ambitions, and he kept the faith throughout the unusually painful periods of labor and delivery. We also thank our fine designer, Jamie Brooks, and our production editor, Sally Schuman. Finally, there is Claire Verduin, whose intensive and extensive efforts we could chronicle but won't; it's enough to say that, if not for Claire, this book probably would not have been published.

James Geiwitz
Janet Moursund

Contents

1

Introduction

There was once a small child who set out upon a long journey into a magical kingdom. It was magical because it was both real and not real; the people who lived in it were both strange and familiar, both frightening and comforting. And the child, continuing on the journey, was both wise and foolish, both brave and cowardly, both drawn to and repelled by the people and things along the way.

The study of personality theory cannot be a static thing in which you, the student, simply read and remember what is written in a textbook. To truly understand the nature of personality theory, and the enormous difficulties faced by the personality theorist, you must immerse yourself in the theorist's task. You must become a personality theorist yourself, wrestling with the contradictions, the mysteries, the inherent perversities of human behavior.

Here you have the beginnings of two introductions to this book. Both are true; both are trying to say the same thing. Together they illustrate (we hope) what we shall be trying to show over and over again: that the study of personality is a journey, a journey into *you,* a journey that can be taken *by* only you. It is not a safe journey, for you may be changed by it. As you learn about others, you are forced to see yourself in new ways; and, having had such new insights, you can never go back to the way you were before.

The study of human personality is a study of contradictions. People don't hold still the way rocks or chemicals or mathematical formulas do. They are many-faceted—they change, they grow, they shift. The patterns ripple and the colors blend. And we can never stop at just one person. Not to mention the fact that we, the observers, are people too, and our own people-ness is a part of the very phenomenon we are trying to understand.

But (another contradiction?) the very fact that understanding human personality is difficult—perhaps impossible—makes it fascinating. In this book, we want to infect you with that fascination. We want to hook you on people: the people who write the theories, the people about whom they are written, and the people who try to understand what they are saying—and that means us, as we start this journey together.

This is a very personal book. We don't think that we can truly share our excitement about personality theory with you if we stand off to one side and try to be "objective." We have tried to explain a variety of approaches to personality as we understand them, and that means mixing in our own excitements, our own enthusiasms, and sometimes our own biases. We've tried very hard to make it clear when a given theorist's viewpoint leaves off and our own reactions to that viewpoint begin. But we haven't hidden those reactions. We expect you will agree with some; we hope very much that you'll disagree with others. We invite you to argue with us, as well as with the theorists you'll be meeting. That's the excitement, you see; that's the involvement. That's where you get hooked.

At the end of every chapter, you will find two references sections. The first is a jumping-off place, an "appetizer." It tells you where to find out more about the things you may have found especially interesting in the chapter. The second is a more traditional referencing of our source materials, and you may want to use it to check up on us, or to do some in-depth studying in an area, or both.

You will meet a lot of theorists in this book. Although some have been dead for many years, all of them are very much alive. Some you will like, some dislike. You may see yourself in some of them; you may see the person you might have been or the person you may someday become. All have something to say. To you, and about you. You will meet them as people—people who make mistakes, people who laugh, people who wake up in the middle of the night and wonder "why?" None of them had all of the answers, but each of them tells part of "the answer." And the answer, of course, will not be the same answer for you and your teacher, or for you and your friend, or for you today and tomorrow. Answers change and grow, and shift and blend, too. Answers become questions. (We are back to the contradictions.)

In the end, you will ask your own questions and build your own answers. Out of the bits and pieces that you find—in this and other books, and in your own experiences. The process will be a living thing, growing and settling and occasionally surprising you. And this is what we, the authors of this book, would like to leave with you: some raw materials to help you in the never-ending excitement of building and growing and testing your questions and answers. We feel privileged to share with you in that process. We wish you well. We hope you do the same for us.

2

The Freudian Beginnings

If I cannot bend the gods above, then I will move the infernal regions.
Virgil

The time was one half hour past six in the early evening of May 6, 1856. It was a boy, and Jakob and Amalie were justly proud of their new baby. He was born in a caul, a part of the membrane that envelops the fetus and sometimes still covers the infant's head at birth. According to popular superstition, a caul was an omen, a sign that the baby would achieve fame for highly significant works. Jakob and Amalie were pleased. It was the first child of their year-old marriage. They named their son Sigmund. Sigmund Freud.

The boy grew strong and healthy. Handsome. Bright. He was at the top of his class in Vienna for seven years. At the age of 17, he entered the University. Eight years later, he took his degree as a Doctor of Medicine. In 1900, 44 years after his birth, he published a book entitled *The Interpretation of Dreams.*

So it all began. The scientific study of personality.

Hippocrates (400 B.C.) formulated a theory of personality. So did Aristotle (350 B.C.), and so have most other philosophers. Many of their ideas anticipated Freudian concepts. But Freud's was the first major theory of personality to be set forth after the beginnings of scientific psychology in general, a date set at 1879 with the founding of the first formal psychology laboratory in Leipzig, Germany. In addition, Freud's views on the "why" of human behavior represented such a large jump in the history of ideas that the break is almost "qualitative" rather than "quantitative." And, though it will not do to suggest that all later theories are direct descendants, there is no modern theory that has not been heavily influenced by his research and thought. If the word *beginning* is to have any meaning, therefore, it is appropriate here: the year is 1900, the public expression is the dream book, and the author is Sigmund Freud. But, like all beginnings, this one had a past.

In Search of a Riddle

The prophecy of the caul omen of Freud's birth was not only for great achievement but also for great happiness. The great achievements came, eventually, but the great happiness was not to be his, partly through character and partly through misfortune. Freud was to encounter scorn and ridicule because of his ideas, shattering dissension among his colleagues, a world war, a Nazi regime, and a painful cancer that finally took his life. Several of his closest associates were to die ugly deaths, mentally unbalanced and intensely hostile toward their "leader." These circumstances would have tried the good humor of the most cheerful and optimistic of persons. But by nature Freud was not that. He was a dedicated worker who forced himself to follow a life of the highest personal and scientific integrity. He considered life grim and painful and his accomplishments the result of hard work, not genius. He often complained that he lacked intellectual powers. There was no false modesty in this lament, for he truly believed that he made discoveries simply because he had the perseverance and the discipline to study what must have appeared to him to be elementary chains of thought. He saw himself as a determined plodder, successful only because of his stubbornness in the face of adversity and because of his dedication to "facts" wherever they might lead.

There was much truth in Freud's view of himself, but there was another side to the story, too. Freud had a dream, a fantasy of himself as a hero: "I am not really a man of science," he once said, "not an observer, not an experimenter, and not a thinker. I am nothing but by temperament a conquistador—an adventurer—with the curiosity, the boldness and the tenacity that belong to that type of being."[1] He dreamed of becoming famous. When he was a university student, he would often walk through the courtyard admiring the statues of great scholars. "Someday," thought the young Freud, ". . . someday *my* statue will be among them." He pictured the statue in his mind, with an inscription from Sophocles: "Who divined the famed riddle and was a man most mighty." That was his great goal in life, to solve a "riddle of the Sphinx." Whatever that riddle might turn out to be for an intellectual conquistador.

More practical problems faced this grim adventurer when he enrolled at the University of Vienna in 1873. He quickly made his first discovery: as a Jew he was expected to consider himself inferior. That he would not do, of course, but this early discovery made it somewhat easier for him to bear some of the later anti-Semitic attacks on his theory and its author. He was, however, forced to recognize that his career would be limited to the three professions open to a Viennese Jew: business, law, or medicine. Freud as a businessman is an inconceivable image. Throughout his life, his unwillingness or inability to deal with money matters was notorious, and many of his friends, and, later, his children, who offered to help out were shocked by the assortment of completely incompatible contracts he had signed (for example, for the foreign translations of his works). He briefly considered law, but in the end the lure of scientific investigation drew him into medicine, though he had no great desire to be a doctor. He worked in zoology, chemistry, and histology before deciding on a neurology specialty, where he would ultimately find his riddle of the Sphinx in the neuroses.

But that lay far in the future. For now, Freud was pursuing a general premedical course of studies and, in 1876, was awarded a grant to do his very first scientific research. On gonads of the eel. "No one has yet seen the testes of the eel," he wrote in his report, "in spite of innumerable efforts through the centuries."[2] (This was the "famed riddle"?!) In spite of his important and careful research, Freud was doomed to disappointment. He was not able to answer this burning question with definite proof that there is—or is not—a testicular organ in the male adult eel.

[1]From E. Jones' *The Life and Work of Sigmund Freud* (Vol. 1), New York: Basic Books, 1953, p. 348.

[2]From E. Jones' *The Life and Work of Sigmund Freud* (Vol. 1), p. 38.

He turned then to the University's Institute of Physiology, a physiological laboratory run by the great medical scientist Ernst Brücke. Brücke, totally committed to science, uncompromising, and ascetic, was a hero to the young research assistant. Freud was to work here off and on for some six years. He made several important contributions, including the development of some technical staining methods used in preparing nerve tissue for microscopic examination. He came close to discovering "neuron theory," the basis of modern physiology, but he failed to see the implications of his work. No riddles here.

But Freud's work at the Institute was to prove very important to the future course of his thought. From Brücke, he acquired discipline and a love of facts and one great assumption. This assumption of *absolute determinism,* which was a new and still controversial notion, held that nothing occurs without an identifiable "real" cause. No mystical "vital forces" or "free will." Freud accepted the assumption wholeheartedly and never deviated from it. It was both the basic assumption of his later theories and, in a sense, the creator of them. Someone not fully dedicated to this assumption would not have done what Freud was eventually to do—that is, see a behavior or hear of a mental experience and simply assume that there must be a "cause," something behind it, some reason.

And Freud made another discovery that was to loom large in his ultimate adventure. He was tracking nerve routes in the brain and found that, by studying the less complicated brain of a child, he could answer questions about the adult brain that could not be resolved by direct study of the fully developed organ. The study of recollected childhood experiences as a key to understanding adult behavior was to become one of the hallmarks of Freud's research approach.

This and much more Freud learned at the University, but the great and fame-producing discovery was not yet to be found. He took his medical degree in 1881 and then, on the questionable advice of Brücke, forsook his theoretical career to become a practicing physician, primarily because of his terrible financial situation. He became associated with the General Hospital in Vienna in a position resembling what is now called a "residency." But Freud's intellectual and theoretical desires were not to be suppressed, and he set out to become the world's expert on a part of the brain stem, the *medulla oblongata.* These studies did about as much for him as the eel gonads. He was still poor and was liking poverty less and less, so he broadened into the study of nervous diseases. He thought that perhaps he could become one of the few specialists in this field, building a reputation and a paying practice. What he later remembered of this period was, characteristically, his ignorance: telling some American physicians that a patient who was suffering from neurotic headaches had a brain disease. But that was a common diagnosis in those days, however inaccurate it may have been.

In 1884, Freud's quest for fame took a rather curious turn. He heard of a drug that had some anesthetic possibilities but had not been researched to any great degree. He decided to explore the possibilities. What makes this episode noteworthy is that the young Freud's interest in the drug was decidedly nonmedical. He tried it himself and found it to produce in him a joyous mood and a vitality that did not interfere with, but rather facilitated, his work. He gave some to a friend named Fleischl, who had been addicted to morphine, in hopes of allowing withdrawal. It was successful, in a sense, for Fleischl gave up morphine and took to the new drug "like a drowning man." The new drug was cocaine. And Fleischl died some years later, hopelessly dependent on the drug that was to have been his savior.

But in the early years Freud was cocaine's champion. He called it "the magic drug," and he himself took frequent "offerings" ("doses" he considered hardly appropriate for this magic drug). In a scientific essay, he talked of the "gorgeous excitement" it produced. To his future wife he wrote " . . . you shall see who is the stronger, a gentle little girl who doesn't eat enough or a big wild man who has cocaine in his body." He shared some with his fiancée and with his sisters. The possibility that cocaine might be addictive occurred to him, but then he ridiculed the idea: "Absolutely no craving for the further use of cocaine appears after the first, or even repeated, taking of the drug; one feels rather a certain curious aversion to it."[3]

Needless to say, what might have been "the great discovery" of Freud's career soon came skidding to an abrupt halt. Fleischl began having monstrous hallucinations under severe cocaine intoxication, and reports from around the world suggested that the drug was hardly as harmless as Freud had claimed. Freud lost a patient through an overdose. He stopped using the drug himself, and, after someone else had become famous for its medical use, he abandoned his advocacy of it. In the process of experimenting with cocaine, he had lost a patient, a friend, and considerable respect from scientific colleagues. In later years, Freud recalled this weird and traumatic period in uncharacteristically distorted fashion. He blamed Fleischl's problems on the use of a hypodermic needle, a somewhat bizarre explanation. And he blamed his wife for the fact that someone else got credit for the useful medical applications of cocaine, because he went to visit her during the time the truly important clinical discoveries were being made. Errors in dates and facts peppered his later accounts of this period, as if it were quite painful for him to think back. And, indeed, it must have been, for Freud was no abuser of drugs. It was, rather, his unbounded interest in new ideas and new techniques that led him into the cocaine trap.

The Origins of Psychoanalysis

In 1885, approximately one year after his first experiences with cocaine, Freud found another interest that was clearly better suited to his true professional direction. He received a fellowship to travel to Paris to study with the great French neurologist Jean Martin Charcot. Charcot was then involved with the study of hysteria, a category of medical illnesses marked by severe impairment of some bodily function, usually including paralysis. In his classes, Charcot demonstrated that subjects

[3]Freud's comments on cocaine are reported in Jones' *The Life and Work of Sigmund Freud* (Vol. 1), pp. 82–84.

under hypnosis could be made to exhibit hysterical symptoms and that some hysterical patients suffering paralysis could regain their mobility when hypnotized. Such demonstrations had a great impact on Freud, and he began to embrace hypnosis both as a technique and as a demonstration of what he would later call "unconscious forces."

But now let's go back in time some five years to an incident that did not involve Freud at all. At least, not at the time. But it was to lead to the very first steps toward psychoanalysis, and it can rightly be called one of the most important events in the history of psychology.

Anna O. and the "Talking Cure"

There was a young woman in Vienna by the name of Bertha Pappenheim, later known in print by the name of Anna O., who was suffering greatly from an unusual collection of symptoms including paralysis of three limbs, severe disturbances of sight and speech, and a nervous cough. An eminent Viennese physician, Josef Breuer, was called to treat the cough. Breuer was an experienced and knowledgeable doctor who kept up with the latest research, and he recognized at once the proper diagnosis: hysteria. To a medical doctor, this meant that the source of the symptoms was not organic, not physical, and therefore not susceptible to treatment by known means.

But Breuer took Bertha on as a patient anyway. The case seemed to intrigue him greatly, and he spent many long hours talking to his young, attractive, intelligent patient. That she was witty and pretty certainly did not inhibit his interest, but there was a certain feature of her illness that would have intrigued any serious scientist: Bertha had a double personality, flip-flopping from a fairly normal young woman to a naughty child as they talked together. Whatever his motives, Breuer worked with Bertha long enough to make a startling discovery.

Bertha, in the transition from one personality to the other, appeared to experience a state of self-induced hypnosis. During one of these hypnotic transition stages, she related to Breuer how one of her symptoms first appeared. (Most of them had originated in events surrounding the recent death of her father.) To Breuer's immense astonishment, the symptom she described disappeared completely, never again to trouble her. With no better means available, the thoughtful physician tried a similar technique on her other symptoms: hypnotizing her, probing the originating circumstances, getting her to "relive" these events. The procedure met with some success and was certainly better than doing nothing. Breuer was pleased. He called his method "the talking cure." Perhaps he had made an important discovery. Perhaps he would become famous (which he did). He must talk to his friend the young Dr. Freud about this. But not before further therapy. The proof of the treatment lay in her cure—Bertha must be cured. However, Breuer did not realize how deeply into the psyche he was getting. And he was totally unprepared for what happened next.

Breuer was quite unaware of how attached he had become to his young patient and she to him. But he talked of little else. His wife, however, was not impressed. She perceived something in the relationship other than pure scientific interest. She became jealous. *Very* jealous. Breuer was once more astounded, for she was reacting to an emotional attachment of which he was not conscious (though she was obviously correct in her perceptions). But, wounded and dignified and noble, he regretfully informed Bertha that he could no longer treat her. And, after all, she was, by now, much better anyway. Bertha, predictably for a true hysteric, became hysterical. Breuer rushed to her home, just in time to witness an unexpected event with frightening implications. Bertha was not having convulsions as he had been told; she was having a baby! She was going through labor and finally gave birth to a baby—Breuer's!—but all in her mind. A hysterical childbirth, completely imaginary but no less real in meaning and pain. Breuer, needless to say, was close to a nervous breakdown himself at that moment, but he managed to calm down long enough to quiet Bertha. He hypnotized her and told her that she would get a good night's sleep and be much better in the morning. Then he bolted from her house in a cold sweat. The next day Dr. and Mrs. Breuer left for Venice on a trip.

During this trip, a daughter (real) was conceived by the Breuers. This unfortunate child, created in the midst of the psychic turmoil that itself gave birth to Freud's psychoanalytic theory, later committed suicide.

And what of Bertha? She was in and out of mental institutions for the next few years, but eventually she became the first social worker in Germany and one of the first in the world. She devoted her life to women's emancipation and the care of children.

When Breuer returned from Venice, he told his friend Sigmund Freud about the case of "Anna O." (Bertha), who coincidentally happened to be a good friend of Freud's wife-to-be. Freud was quite as astonished as Breuer. The case made no sense to him at the time; it was a riddle. It was his riddle of the Sphinx, though he did not see that yet. But the puzzle was in Freud's mind as he went to Paris to study hysteria with Charcot.

Trauma, Transference, and Catharsis

Freud was as puzzled by Breuer's reaction to Bertha's plight as he was by Bertha's actions. As a scientist, a seeker of truth, a follower of facts, he could not understand how Breuer could so easily sever professional connections with a scientific challenge. To Freud, a mystery was a great find. The job of a scientist, in his view, was first to find the definite questions and then to seek reasonable explanations. Indeed, when Freud later experienced a similar event, his response was quite different. During the course of treatment, a female patient suddenly and unexpectedly threw her arms around Freud's neck, and only the entrance of a servant cooled this wanton display of affection. Freud later wrote "I was modest enough not to attribute the event to my own irresistible personal attraction."[4] He was, after all, a man of impeccable morality, integrity, and dignity. But no doubt the experience was one of great meaning for him.

[4]From *An Autobiographical Study,* translated and edited by James Strachey, New York: Norton, 1963.

It was a mystery and he knew it. Why on earth would she do such a thing? He did not try to escape the question; he tried to find a solution.

Freud knew that the feelings and emotions his patient displayed could not possibly be explained just by the therapist/patient relationship. There had to be more; some of the necessary facts lay elsewhere. So Freud formulated the concept called *transference.* The patient was transferring some feelings from a previous relationship onto the present one. Something from the past. The therapist was suddenly her father again or her brother, her husband, her boyfriend, or some other highly significant person in her past. Someone, or some combination of persons, had earned the love (and the hate) that boiled up in the course of treatment. And Freud, the therapist, was an available target when the emotions came to the surface.

But where did the emotions come from originally? If he could answer that, thought Freud, perhaps he would get a clue to the origin of her disturbance. From Charcot, Freud had learned that a *trauma,* a dramatic instance, was at the seat of hysterical symptoms. The daughter stays with her ailing father, falls asleep, wakes up to find her father dead. Traumatic event. Perhaps she has failed in her duty; perhaps she could have saved him. Her arm, over the chair and "asleep before her," is numb. It remains numb, paralyzed. The trauma has led to the paralysis, the hysteria. Could the design be reversed, the pattern retraced?

At first Freud did not see that transference provided a means by which the therapist could lead the patient back to the trauma. He was still under the influence of his friend and associate Breuer. So he used Breuer's method, the talking cure.

The talking cure was a great advance over previous methods (which included rest, massage, hydrotherapy, and electrical stimulation). In essence, the therapist used hypnosis to find out what the originating circumstances of the symptoms were; then the therapist asked the patient to relive the events in order to "relieve" the energy bound up in the original conflict. In many cases, this procedure met with some success. Freud called it *catharsis,* the releasing of restricted psychic energy.

From Hypnosis to Free Association

Over the years Freud's decision to specialize in neurology was bringing him more and more cases (such as hysterics) that could not be explained (or helped) by reference to some organic cause; the illnesses were clearly psychological. He noted that many cases of paralysis—of an arm, for example—had no basis in anatomical fact. In other words, if there were some organic damage to a nerve, the paralysis would take a certain form depending on the parts of the arm serviced by that nerve. Instead of this, however, the paralysis might affect the hand only as far as the wrist, for example, indicating an affliction based in the mind rather than in the body. To treat a "psychological" disease, new techniques had to be developed, and hypnosis and Breuer's cathartic method were the new techniques Freud turned to in the beginning.

But Freud was becoming dissatisfied with hypnosis. His developing awareness of transference was pushing him to explore in totally new directions. Transference brought out those strange emotions of love and hate in the therapy sessions. Hypnosis had some relationship to transference, too, but not in a helpful way. Treatment with hypnosis was itself rather intimate, and some patients "refused" to be hypnotized until they trusted or even "loved" the therapist. Sometimes the traumas discovered by hypnosis were of little use because the patient would forget them when he or she awoke. Or the patient would break off hypnotic treatment in a fit of (transferred) hostility. In short, the transference relations were in part responsible for the ability to be hypnotized, were capable of being explored through hypnosis but often with little benefit, and were obviously stronger than the hypnotic treatment itself. Why not, thought Freud, abandon hypnosis and try to use the disclosures of transference more directly? Explore them in the waking state, meet them head on. Maybe if he discovered the "real" object of this transferred hate or love, he could discover the trauma causing the disease, and discover it in a way that the conscious mind of the patient could accept.

But how?

Enter Elisabeth. In 1892, in the autumn of the year, she came to Freud for treatment. She was not susceptible to hypnosis, but Freud admitted her as a patient anyway, no doubt pleased to have an opportunity to try out his ideas for alternative treatments. And Freud did have some new ideas. First, he reasoned, if a symptom-producing trauma could be remembered under hypnosis, the memory must be somewhere in the mind, even if unavailable to consciousness at the moment. He would observe the transference to get some clues and then force the dastardly trauma out into the open. Somehow. He began by trying suggestion without the hypnotic trance. "Pressure" might be more apt than "suggestion": he made Elisabeth lie on a couch and close her eyes. He told her to concentrate on a symptom and to try to recall the moment of its origin. If she could not—which was usually the case—Freud would press his hand on her forehead and suggest that this act would cause an important memory to come to her mind. It was not black magic, this. It was common "demand instruction" typically used in hypnotic work but used here in a nontrance state.

Freud was on the brink of creation.

Birth of the New Science

At first, the technique failed miserably. But Freud, always a patient man, tried it again. And again. Finally, Elisabeth came out with something. But it was totally unrelated to the symptom or to any possible cause. Both Freud and Elisabeth were startled. And Elisabeth said "I could have told you that the first time, but I didn't think it was what you wanted."[5]

[5]This quote and more details on this episode can be found in Jones' *The Life and Work of Sigmund Freud* (Vol. 1), p. 243.

This is where Freud's absolute belief in absolute determination paid off. True, the statement seemed unrelated, but nothing happens for no reason. Freud sensed that the relationship between the statement and the symptom was more direct than it appeared. So he encouraged Elisabeth to continue, adding the demand that she stop censoring her thoughts for his benefit. She should say whatever came to her mind, no matter how irrelevant or trivial or disgusting it might seem. This requirement became the *fundamental rule* of the new technique.

Elisabeth was agreeable, but she wanted to add some demands of her own. She told Freud to stop asking so many ridiculous questions. And to please stop pressing on her forehead. It broke up her train of thought.

A lesser physician might well have taken offense. But Freud's great instincts perceived that she was telling him something important, that this technique would work if it were *free*. The associations coming to her mind had to be free to develop in their own direction, without interruption. *Free association*. In that moment in time when Freud was considering her request, a new science, along with the first scientific theory of personality, was born. It was to be named *psychoanalysis*.

How characteristic of Freudian discovery! The honest but bumbling efforts of the therapist were modified and clarified by the patient. Indeed, Freud was often disposed to think of himself as just that: a bumbling physician with a rather meager intellect who was lucky enough to have insightful patients. It was, after all, the patient Bertha (and not Breuer) who discovered the cathartic method, and now Elisabeth had discovered free association. This technique marks the first beginning of what can properly be called psychoanalysis. Of course Freud's judgment of himself is much too severe. He had observed something, he had the genius to recognize its value, and he had the character to persist, to develop an important new discovery. To be swayed by facts, as Freud was, is hardly the sign of a weak intellect; it is the hallmark of an enormous mind.

Freud now had a method, free association, for dredging up the hidden causes of a neurosis, and two concepts, transference and resistance, that described phenomena occurring in the treatment process. *Resistance* was an even earlier discovery than transference and free association and showed itself in the general unwillingness of a patient to talk or even think about unpleasant memories. Freud noted also that resistance was not always a deliberate unwillingness; the patient simply could not "will" himself or herself to remember. At first Freud talked of resistance as *defenses*, then later as *repression*. And he began thinking about the *unconscious*, an area of mental activity not known by the conscious waking mind.

In therapy, it was clear that most resistance marked points of conflict that were related to the illness, the way buoys mark hidden rocks at sea. Unacceptable thoughts were repressed and thereby became unconscious. But the "energy" of the thoughts remained and found outlet through *conversion*, converting itself to bodily symptoms such as paralysis of a limb, giving the clinical picture of hysteria. If one could find the conflicts behind the resistance and release the energy, the symptoms should disappear.

Freud saw that most unacceptable thoughts and desires arose from interpersonal relationships in the past and could often be seen, in distorted form, in the reactions of the patient to the therapist. In the transference. But whom is the patient really loving or hating? Father? Mother? Brother? Some combination of people? And is the love really love, or is it really hate in disguise? What happened to produce it? These questions, gleaned from the observations of resistance and transference, were "analyzed" through free association.

Though much knowledge and polishing of technique were yet to come, psychoanalysis now existed in all its essential features; Freud, at 36, was a father. Four years later, in 1896, he used the word *psychoanalysis* for the first time in print. He had made his great discovery. He was soon to become famous. Still, he did not grasp the import of his discovery. Nor did he foresee the personal consequences that were to befall one of those who "troubled the sleep of the world."

Toward a Theory of Personality

With the technical aspects of psychoanalysis slowly but surely developing, the elaboration of the associated theory of personality began in earnest. Notions of how transference and resistance functioned, of course, were crucial to the therapeutic technique, just as the technique was crucial in exploring the concepts. The theory and the technique, as in all science, depended on each other, fed on each other. The theory of unconscious processes and of repressing forces was also developing.

Two major obstacles now stood in Freud's path. The first was the notion of *trauma,* a term he took from Charcot. As Freud then viewed the neuroses, they were caused by some incident in childhood too terrible to mention or even think about—a trauma—that was repressed and therefore unconscious. But it was still active in unconscious memory. Freud found that many of these traumas were sexual in nature, such as the seduction of a child by a parent or relative. He saw children as innocent victims of these events. Many of the tales told by his patients were grotesque and ugly: incest, sodomy, and other perversions. Surely enough to make anyone hysterical!

But something didn't quite fit. His intuition—that famous intuition—told him that something was missing.

For one thing, many of the traumas were somehow related to the death of a parent. The death of a loved one is significant, to be sure, but it is not uncommon. Why did some children respond with neurosis and others not? Other "traumas" seemed even less likely candidates for "causes." Being frightened by a horse, for example. Freud sensed that, although the trauma was important, it was not the whole answer; a piece of the puzzle was still missing. He began to think that there must be something still deeper in the past, something that *predisposed* a person to overrespond to the trauma when it did occur. Freud used his new method, free association, to dig deeper, convinced that he would uncover some earlier experience that somehow made the trauma more threatening, more dangerous, more significant for this patient than for others.

Freud found that the associations of early childhood, surprisingly, remained sexual in nature. And he began to doubt the accepted view that children were innocent of sexual desires and innocent victims of sexual acts. Perhaps children were active participants, even in the traumatic events. Perhaps the so-called passive, innocent child who was raped by an uncle had actually done something to encourage the rape and—Heaven forbid!—had even wanted it! It was heady stuff in that Victorian age of morality and dignity, and there were few more dignified or moral than Sigmund Freud. But his views were changing. Instead of seeing the passively suffered trauma as sole cause of a neurosis, he was developing a more dynamic view: that many "causes" occur and develop, beginning in infancy, in which the child plays an active role. In early 1898, he published a paper containing his first statement on infantile sexuality: "We do wrong," he asserted, "entirely to ignore the sexual life of children. They are capable," he continued, "of all the thoughts and many of the physical acts of sex."[6]

While the obstacle presented by the old view of trauma was slowly crumbling, Freud came face to face with the second obstacle. This one almost brought his career down in ruins.

The Theory of Infantile Sexuality

Digging back into the past had fruitfully altered his theory about trauma, but it was also dredging up some real muck. The sexual thoughts and events of very early childhood were shocking enough; in addition, the horrified Freud was forced to listen to wild tales about traumas in back of traumas. He could understand, perhaps, why a father might seduce his beautiful 16-year-old daughter. But his 4-year-old daughter? And violation through the anus? Freud found these stories thoroughly repulsive, but he was a scientist and a healer. He stayed and listened, when less committed therapists might have left to relieve their own spreading nausea. Or would have dismissed the stories as the insane ramblings of a totally irresponsible crazy person. And, again, Freud began to sense something wrong, something missing. He knew personally many of the fathers and mothers who were being accused of these terrible things; he could not believe that all of them were guilty of such acts. He was slowly perceiving the truth: many of his patients were lying to him. The acts they described in such gory detail had never happened. They were, purely and simply, fantasies.

It is impossible to depict the force with which this revelation hit Freud. It very nearly destroyed him.

At this time in his life, Freud was gradually building a reputation for his theory and treatment of neuroses, especially hysteria. His work was his greatest comfort, and it earned him respect and some honor, as well as a living. His theory, of course, was based on the concept of trauma, which, he had asserted, usually meant childhood seductions. As evidence, he had untold numbers of patients recounting stories that

[6]From Jones' *The Life and Work of Sigmund Freud* (Vol. 1), p. 265.

"proved" this theory. These seduction stories were the entire factual basis for his theory. And now . . . now he understood for the first time that all his beloved "facts"—the evidence behind his theory—were not facts at all. Lies. Fantasies of sick minds. Nothing. The theory was obviously false. His reputation, he was sure, was about to disintegrate. He had been led up a blind alley. He felt hopeless, anxious, and bewildered. He wrote a letter to his friend Rudolph Fliess saying that his career had come to an end and gamely suggested that it might be rather peaceful to settle down and resign himself to the daily concerns of ordinary people. But not quite. For in that same letter to Fliess is a hint that Freud had not given up: ". . . But between you and me I have the feeling of a victory rather than a defeat." And well he might have such a feeling. He had just achieved insight into what was to become the greatest of all his theoretical achievements: the theory of infantile sexuality. It was one of the greatest single discoveries in the history of psychology.

Nonetheless, his depression was monumental, and it was not helped by the death of his father about this time. Freud became aware of strange emotions in himself concerning his father and his father's death—not quite appropriate and certainly not understood. Father dead, career halted, mind in a kind of paralysis—Freud considered himself in the throes of a full-blown neurosis, an assessment that was probably accurate. But there was a spirit inside him that would not let him quit. He began trying to pull the pieces of his life together.

He wrote to Fliess: "I believe I am in a cocoon, and God knows what kind of beast will creep out of it."[7]

The beast, it turns out, had already begun to creep out, and Freud was by no means enthralled by its appearance. As therapy for himself, he had prescribed hard work and self-analysis, the latter largely in order to understand his feelings toward his father. The self-analysis was destined to bring out the beast, his own unconscious.

But self-analysis is a difficult task, for it requires that a person be both therapist and patient. How can one be critical, as required of the therapist, and not critical, as required of the patient, at the same time? Freud's answer was a typical insight of genius: Freud as therapist would critically examine the dreams of Freud as patient.

The Theory of Psychosexual Development

As he traced his dreams and his associated memories back into his own childhood, he found much the same things as he had with other patients—a remarkable collection of thoughts about sexual desires for his mother and hatred for his father, who had (in Freud's memory) committed several atrocious acts. Amazed, he questioned his mother to get facts related to his memories. Surely he was not lying to himself. But he soon saw that it was true—he *was* lying. He saw that, although the events he "remembered" had not occurred in a real, physical sense, this was not an ordinary lie. His memories had a different kind of reality, an imagined

[7]From Jones' *The Life and Work of Sigmund Freud* (Vol. 1), p. 325.

Nonetheless, his depression was monumental, and it was not helped

reality, a fantastic truth. And he quickly discerned that the psychic "facts" were just as important, if not more so, than the "truth" or physical reality. It was another major breakthrough. His patients had not lied to him; that the horrible events they recalled had happened only in their minds did not detract from the essential truth of their assertions. His theory was not wrong. It had a basis in fact. It was a psychology.

Now the pieces of the puzzle began to fall into place. The nature of the romantic drama played out in early childhood, for example: The young boy has strong sexual desires; he is not innocent, as popular opinion would have us believe. His first love/sex object is his mother, who has been so close and warm and satisfying. But the father has the advantage—every night, he defeats the son and carries off the mother to the bedroom. The son's love is spurned. He blames it all on the father, whom he accuses—in his mind—of all sorts of vicious acts. From the Greek drama *Oedipus the King*, in which the son unknowingly kills his father and marries his mother, Freud gave the romantic drama of childhood a name. *The Oedipus complex*.

Freud now had the basic ingredients of his theory of personality: *infantile sexuality*, the sexual instinct's energy (called *libido*), the Oedipus complex, and the unconscious. Of course these and other concepts were continually elaborated and refined, some discarded, some added, from now (around 1900) until his death in 1939.

Freud's theory of *psychosexual stages* is a good example of a basic idea that underwent elaboration and refinement. With his insight into the nature of infantile sexuality and the importance of fantasized reality, Freud began to reconsider the implications of some of the stories told him by patients. Tales of sexual violation in infancy were certainly shocking enough, but an added jolt to Freud's moral beliefs had been the frequent description of sexual practices that did not involve the genital organs. Rather, the mouth and the anus were typically the orifices involved. From this (and from much additional evidence, of course), Freud formulated a theory of stages in the development and control of the sexual instinct.

According to this view, the first few years of life are crucial for the later development of one's personality. The important dynamic activities forming personality are centered around a particular area of the body, the area that is the primary mode of sexual response and gratification at the time. Thus, during the *oral stage*, which occurs in the very first year or so of life, the mouth is the center of attention: such activities as sucking, biting, taking in food, and sensing things with the lips are of primary importance. If there are disturbances at this stage, such as severe frustrations, the mouth may remain a perverted source of pleasure. It has been suggested that cigarette smoking, for some people, is related to such very early frustrations. Adult behavior may take more symbolic form, such as the extreme desire to "intake" knowledge or money or feelings of great hostility toward someone who cuts off one's "minimum daily requirement" of love or friendship.

The next stage is the *anal stage*, so called because the prominent region of sexual satisfaction is the anus. Expulsion of feces is a source of pleasure, if for no other reason than that it relieves discomfort. And, in this stage, toward the end of the second year of life and carrying on into the third, toilet training typically is begun and completed. From the child's point of view, and often from the parent's, this is an extremely important period. The child's first real "creation"—feces—is looked upon with scorn and disgust by the parents. They are concerned that the child postpone the pleasure of relief until he or she can get to a suitable contraption, something that's hard enough just to *sit* on. They expect to break the child's will—the will to do whatever he or she feels like, whenever—and the child often responds with a childlike independence. If this stage is not satisfactorily "passed," as may happen if the training parent is overly strict and requires too much too soon, the child may develop into an adult who becomes flustered and anxious in the face of demands from others. A man may fight his "symbolic mother"—the world—by refusing to "give in"—that is, by being stubborn for no good reason. A woman may become miserly, hoarding her money as she once did her feces. Under pressure, such people may become hostile and determined to "show them" by, say, keeping their desks at work as messy as possible in spite of repeated warnings from the boss.

Soon after toilet training is completed, sexual sensations center in their proper place, the genital organs. The stage is called the *phallic stage*, which is a clue that the theory (at least during this stage) applies primarily to personality development in males. However, the name of the stage is very descriptive: the young boy (from about 2 to 4 years of age, with related dynamics up to 6 years) has interest in nothing but his *own* genital organ, the phallus. When it feels pleasure, so does he, and he cares very little about anyone or anything else. He is "on the make," so to speak, and troubles at this stage might produce the kind of man who gives no thought to the feelings of his sexual partner as long as he is satisfied.

The phallic stage is noted most prominently as the stage when the Oedipus complex manifests itself. Our innocent Casanova picks as his object the one girl who appeals to him—his mother. But soon he discovers that his father is a formidable rival, superior in both strength and size of penis. He hates his father—and loves him, for other reasons, at the same time—and wishes him to leave, or die, or something, so that he can be alone with his beloved. Then he begins to think of the less fortunate aspects of rivalry with his father. What if his father got mad at him for fighting over the mother/wife? Why, his father would surely cut off his little penis! This fear of castration, called *castration anxiety*, causes the boy to forget (repress) his sexual urgings toward his mother and his hostility toward his father. Instead, he sees his father in a new light, as a person of great power. Seeking the same power for himself, he begins to identify with the father. And with the male role. He may even decide that "girls are no good for anything."

For the young girl, this stage must obviously be formulated differently. She lacks the one thing required for the playing out of the Oedipus conflict and resolution: she has no penis. Does this matter—in an intellectual sense, in terms of the theory? Freud, at the beginning, thought not. He formulated the notion of the Oedipal drama for males and largely from clinical experience with men; the general psychic forces, he assumed, would apply to women in roughly parallel fashion. He later admitted that he was wrong.

Freud did formulate a comparable theory for females, involving what is sometimes called the *Electra complex*. It has always been less certain, with less basis in actual clinical observation, and more subject to dispute, but it runs something like this: Castration anxiety, for the female, cannot take the form of a fear that one's penis will be removed, since she has no penis in the first place. Instead the girl feels that she has already had it cut off, she is "wounded" and "deficient," and somebody is responsible for this terrible act. Who? Who else but the person she has loved throughout the early psychosexual stages: her mother! She begins to hate her mother (while loving her, for other reasons, at the same time), and she loves her father more than before. This greater love consists largely of envy (*penis envy*). A new "daddy's girl" is born. And, unlike the boy, who loves the mother but begins to identify with the father out of extreme fear, the girl—having already lost her penis (what more can they do?)—continues in this stage for a longer period. She is resentful of her mother but gradually recognizes their common mutilization. She loves her father and seeks the male role (a "tomboy") but gradually recognizes the impossibility of acquiring a new organ by association and resents her father's "preference" for the mother. Identity becomes an increasing problem, and this feeling of having lost early in the game (inferiority) creates an adult woman who wants a husband and a baby, preferably male, for "fulfillment." Needless to say, these notions of female psychosexual development have come under heavy criticism. Many people have suggested that, in our male-dominated world, "privilege envy" would describe the situation better than "penis envy." In any case, female psychosexual development is by any standards explained less well by Freudian theory than is that of males.

All stage theories of personality development have a final stage, and in Freudian theory it's called the *genital stage*. In a way, this stage describes perfection in sexual relationships, in which concern for the other person and for the realities of life in both a social and a biological sense are fully developed and mature. Love in the purest sense, unselfish relationships, selection of a mate, propagation of the race. The individual strives throughout his or her lifetime to attain this "perfect" stage. It is the great learning task of any individual to become as nearly "genital" as possible.

Freud believed that the genital stage is preceded by a period of *latency*, in which the sexual impulses are relatively quiescent or adequately repressed. This period runs roughly from the resolution of the Oedipus complex (around age 6) to the beginning of puberty, when the intensity of sexual desires is affected. The theoretical importance of this latency period lies primarily in the idea that the great increase in sexual desire (at puberty) occurs after a quiescent period in which the child has learned relatively little about the proper control of sexual impulses. The onset of puberty, therefore, is frightening. Strong impulses, inexplicable and unpredictable, and no new means of controlling them. *Regression*, or retreat to earlier, childlike solutions, is common. It is a difficult end to childhood. How the now-young-adult handles these impulses has great bearing on his or her future personality. And poor adjustment at the oral, anal, or phallic stage now becomes crystal clear. It is a time when dormant neuroses begin to bloom.

Although this conceptualization of psychosexual stages developed gradually over the years and in fact is still being refined today, it is a good example of how Freud looked at what his patients said and did and then formulated a systematic theory to make sense of what he saw. Such representation, in a systematic and coherent way, of a mass of observation is the basic function of any theory. And it represents accurately the work remaining for Freud. He now had the technique (free association) and some basic concepts (sexual libido, the unconscious, resistance, transference). For the rest of his life, in a continuous series of publications, Freud polished this technique and elaborated the general theory of personality, of which the theory of psychosexual stages is only one part.

The Interpretation of Dreams

The very first book on psychoanalysis appeared on November 4, 1899; the publisher put the date 1900 on it. It was called *The Interpretation of Dreams*, and its sources were Freud's hard clinical work and his self-analysis during the preceding years. Its appearance marked the public beginning of psychoanalysis and of scientific personality theory in general. Even today, the book is the undisputed flagship of Freud's enormous collection of writings. Freud himself was disposed to think of it as his only real contribution. It was a first, a great first.

But not exactly an instant success. In the first eight years, *The Interpretation of Dreams* sold a grand total of 600 copies. With few exceptions, book reviewers and psychiatrists ignored it. And most of those exceptions thought it was a terrible, worthless book: Freud was called a mystic and an artist (a very insulting term, at the time, when applied to a scientist). Seldom has such an important book elicited such a miniscule response. Freud continued his work in isolation.

Relative isolation, at least. There were some young men in Vienna interested enough in Freud's ideas to form in 1902 what they called the Vienna Psychoanalytic Society, a rather grandiose title for a group of five men. Freud was among them, and one of the other four was named Alfred Adler, of whom we will hear more later. Freud, by now, was in good spirits; he seemed to sense his greatness, his future fame, even if the world was not equally convinced.

The Interpretation of Dreams, viewed from our vantage point, was truly a marvelous book, a tour de force of a great mind. Broadly viewed, it started with a review of the scientific literature on dreams up to that time, modestly pointing out how ridiculous most theories were. Freud then described his theory of dreams (as wish fulfillments) and his methods (free association and interpretation) of uncovering their true meaning for the individual patient. In a final and most important chapter, he described "the psychology of the dream-process." Throughout the book he stressed the "wish" or instinctual desire behind the dream and the energy of the instinct demanding satisfaction; the "unacceptable" nature of the wish, leading to distortions (in most cases—children's dreams are typically freer of distortions because children have yet to learn how "unacceptable" their desires are); and, finally, the fact that dreams are hardly a special case, since both neurotic symptoms and everyday-life "Freudian slips" operate on essentially the same principles. Several important concepts, including the unconscious and repression and the primary and secondary processes (to be discussed later) were introduced. A magnificent work of science and insight. But almost no one read it.

Troubling the Sleep of the World: The Case of Dora

Between 1900 and 1905, important things were happening elsewhere in the world. In 1902, a child was born in Oak Park, Illinois, and was called Carl Rogers. Two years later, B. F. Skinner was born in Pennsylvania. One year after that, a child named Raymond Cattell was born in Staffordshire, England. All were to become famous personality theorists, each challenging Freud in his own way. A Russian named Ivan Pavlov received the Nobel Prize in 1904 for his work on digestive secretions. In 1903, the University of Chicago awarded its very first Ph.D. in psychology, to a man named John B. Watson. In the same year, the Wright brothers put a vehicle into the air for 59 seconds. Portents of things to come.

But Freud knew little of this. He was thinking and writing. In 1905, he hit the world with two blockbusters. The first was a book entitled *Three Essays on the Theory of Sexuality*, in which he put forward in detail his ideas of infantile sexuality. The second was a case history with an innocent-enough title, "Fragment of an Analysis of a Case of Hysteria," that described his treatment of a young girl who had bizarre sexual experiences and even more bizarre sexual fantasies. Although he changed the names (she was called Dora), the case history was published without her permission.

Thus, in 1905, Freud became the "dirty old man" of psychology. His dream book of 1900 had not been well received. One critic had said earlier that "the imaginative thoughts of an artist had triumphed over the scientific investigator." Another had accused him of listening to the worthless statements of sick people in order to "fill his pockets adequately." But now! Now he had really gone too far. Suggesting that innocent children have sexual desires of a most perverted kind, and that these desires are directed toward honest, upright parents. Publishing the most intimate details of a young woman's life without her consent. Suggesting that she had nasty, twisted sexual impulses. His critics had considered Freud a little nutty; now he was evil, obscene, unethical, and, worst of all, dangerous.

The reaction was not a surprise to Freud. He knew fairly well by this time that his ideas were bound to elicit outraged criticism and personal vilification; his own theory would predict such responses. His critics felt personally attacked; his ideas aroused their defenses against recognition of their own sexuality. Anticipation, however, did little to make the criticism more pleasant.

To appreciate the force and intensity of the criticism, imagine that you are a respectable European scholar in 1905, reading Freud's account of Dora. Freud describes the treatment of a young and beautiful teenage girl. She relates how a family friend, Mr. K., "attacked" her when she was 14. Freud writes:

> He . . . suddenly clasped the girl to him and pressed a kiss upon her lips. This was surely just the situation to call up a distinct feeling of sexual excitement in a girl of fourteen who had never before been approached. But Dora had at that moment a violent feeling of disgust. . . . In this scene . . . the behavior of this child of fourteen was already entirely and completely hysterical. I should without question consider a person hysterical in whom an occasion for sexual excitement elicited feelings that were preponderantly or exclusively unpleasurable . . . there has also been a displacement of sensation. Instead of the genital sensation which would certainly have been felt by a healthy girl in such circumstances, Dora was overcome by the unpleasurable feeling which is proper to the tract of mucous membrane at the entrance to the alimentary canal—that is by disgust.[8]

Freud also interprets another of Dora's hysterical symptoms, a nervous cough. He relates it to her jealousy of her father's relationship with Mrs. K., the wife of her "attacker." She knows (or thinks) that her father is impotent, but she still asserts that he is having a sexual affair with Mrs. K. Freud asks how this is possible if her father is impotent. And he writes:

> Her answer showed that she had no need to admit the contradiction. She knew very well, she said, that there was more than one way of obtaining sexual gratification . . . she must be thinking of precisely those parts of the body which in her case were in a state of irritation—the throat and the oral cavity . . . the conclusion was inevitable that with her spasmodic cough, which, as is usual, was referred for its exciting cause to a tickling in her throat, she pictured to herself a scene of sexual gratification . . . between the two people whose love-affair occupied her mind so incessantly. . . . So it is not to be wondered at that this hysterical girl of nineteen, who had heard of the occurrence of such a method of sexual intercourse (sucking at the male organ), should have developed an unconscious fantasy of this sort and should have given it expression by an irritation in her throat and by coughing.

Freud interprets the case as a whole in terms of Dora's sexually based love for her father and for Mr. K. and for *Mrs.* K.! And for a few others, both male and female. And, if he needed more, she masturbated and wet her bed!

[8]This and all other quotations about the case of "Dora" are from "Fragments of an Analysis of a Case of Hysteria," by S. Freud. In *Collected Papers of Sigmund Freud*, Volume 3. Copyright 1959 by Basic Books, Inc., Publishers. Reprinted by permission.

That these selections about Dora have been chosen and edited to represent the most sensational parts of the work, completely out of context, is obvious. But, even in context, these events and interpretations were strong enough to unsettle the stomachs of most crusty scholars at that time, and these are just the kind of passages that one offended scholar would read to others, who in turn were scandalized. Freud was not popular.

But Freud cared more about truth than about popularity. His interpretations of any given case or of a particular symptom might be wrong, as he would be the first to admit, but he knew too much about the sexuality of children to hold back his ideas or to disguise them in nonprofessional euphemisms. The sex in the case history bothered him less than his agonizing decision to publish the case history without Dora's permission. He waited five years before making it public and satisfied himself that the history had been disguised enough to preclude the slightest possibility of Dora's true identity becoming known. In the end, he published the account because he was a scientist. He had a theory based on clinical observation, and he knew that, without presenting the data from which he formed his theory, the theory could not be acceptable. In fact, the Dora case is famous not for its sensationalism but because—as is obvious to anyone who bothers to read the study—it relies heavily on the interpretation of two dreams. In other words, Freud saw it as a practical illustration or application of the principles set down in his previous book, *The Interpretation of Dreams*.

"A Man Most Mighty"

After the publication of *The Interpretation of Dreams*, the Dora analysis, and *Three Essays*, Freud's professional life became considerably more exciting. On the one hand, he was now "worthy" of the most critical attacks by other professionals, and the attacks were indeed "most critical." On the other hand, then as now, sex repulsed some people but it attracted others, especially the young scientists with less vested interest in the old traditions and more (vested) interest in new directions. Freud's early colleagues were mostly Jewish, for reasons having to do with the relative freedom of Jewish inquiry in those days and also the particular form of European bigotry practiced then. Freud was distressed by his lack of non-Jewish associates. He was much relieved when a very respectable Christian by the name of Carl Jung wrote to him. Jung, a brilliant young Swiss physician, became a "regular" in 1906 and, in the bargain, was deemed the "fair-haired boy" and "heir apparent." Freud was overjoyed. With emphasis on "over-." In his scramble to please his number-one Christian, Freud alienated many of his closer and earlier associates. But in 1913 Freud and Jung were to break off both professional and personal relations.

At the time, though, it was a good time. Freud had friends and colleagues to insulate him from the attacks of his critics. There was an excitement of newness and of truth. In 1906, on his 50th birthday, Freud was honored by his friends and associates. The Vienna Psychoanalytic

Society presented him with a medallion. On it was his portrait and the inscribed words: "Who divined the famed riddle and was a man most mighty."

Freud became pale when he read the inscription, almost fainting. He had never told anyone of these dreams before, of his walks through the courtyard of famous statues at the University of Vienna, of imagining himself among them, a statue with the very same inscription engraved on the medallion. He was shaken, as by a mystical experience.

Freud was at his absolute peak. It is good that he enjoyed the period, for he was not destined to experience much happiness in his remaining years. Antagonism was already developing among his followers, first between the Viennese and those outside Vienna. Five years later, Alfred Adler, one of the charter members of the Psychoanalytic Society, quit the group and set up his own psychology. Two years after that blow, the much-favored Jung split in acrimonious dispute. About the same time, an Austrian archduke was assassinated in Serbia, and all of Europe plunged into total war. World War I. The wild inflation following the war was to wipe out Freud's savings. Then a growth appeared inside his mouth; it was cancer. No less than 16 painful years later, the cancer was to kill Freud. Almost at the same moment, England, where Freud was living, declared war on Germany and Austria, the homeland he had fled to escape the Nazis. World War II began as he died. It was not a pleasant period for Freud. It was not a pleasant period for the world.

But these painful years were not unproductive. During this time Freud was to develop his theory further, including his conceptualizations of the id, the ego, and the superego and of the aggressive instinct. Ahead lay the applications of Freudian theory to literature, religion, and society. The great discoveries had been made. The basic concepts had been developed, but the later works would prove no less important.

Theoretical Refinements: New Answers to the Riddle

So, if we draw on both early and later works, what do we have as the Freudian image of the human animal? A creature with instincts or basic motives that have an energy associated with them, an energy striving for release in one form or another. From the standpoint of neurosis or of personality in general, the sexual instinct is the most important. Unlike the need for food or water or air, the need for sex and love can be suppressed (by society) and/or repressed (by the individual). Often it is. But the energy remains, the thoughts and desires remain, in the unconscious mind. And the energy and the thoughts show themselves eventually, in slips of the tongue or pen, in dreams, or in neurotic symptoms. Sometimes the energy is diverted into more socially acceptable channels, a benevolent defense called *sublimation*. The artist paints; the executive works; the scholar reads. "If you can't get a date," says the student, "you might as well study."

The road to maturity is blocked by the obstacles the child must somehow overcome if he or she is to achieve a reasonable balance between personal desires and the dictates of society. Among the most nearly universal learning tasks, according to Freud, are those associated with sucking and weaning—the oral stage, in which the infant must come to grips with the fact that dependency on the mother (and her nipples) must come to an end. Then the child must meet the demands of the anal stage, in which toilet training is the major achievement test and a passing grade is encouraged, even demanded, by a bewildering parental assault on the child's capabilities. And in the phallic stage, which includes the Oedipus drama and castration anxiety, the young egotist must learn to defer personal desires in order to get along with other people. Should one of these obstacles be dealt with in an unsatisfactory manner, a "scar" (sometimes called a *fixation*) may result, and it is quite probable that, later, the adult will return to the scene of the earlier "failure." Symbolically, of course. Infantile responses that really stem from an early deficiency have a name: *regression.*

Whether we talk of mature adults or infantile children, infantile adults or mature kids, we need some terminology to describe the basic structure of personality. In Freud's early theory, the personality was a two-part structure, divided into a conscious mind and an unconscious mind. Most unacceptable urges and thoughts and emotions were in the unconscious, fighting the conscious for control of behavior. In this conflict, neurosis was often the compromise solution. The early theory worked reasonably well, especially for understanding hysterical patients.

Soon, however, problems developed. Primarily problems of logic. New patients appeared, with obsessions, compulsions, and depressions, and it was clear that many of these patients were not "converting" the energy of unconscious desires into physical symptoms (as in hysteria). Instead they were using unconscious defense mechanisms (resistances) to keep repressed material from coming into consciousness. *Unconscious* resistance to the *unconscious*. Logically, such a formulation leaves much to be desired; one can't really have "conflict" between two structures that are identical. And, to top it off, Freud was running into some patients whose main problem was an exaggerated sense of guilt—also unconscious! The "unconscious" conscious had warded off unconscious desires but had, in the bargain, been attacked from the other side by an unconscious guilt. If that sentence doesn't make sense to you, you are perhaps experiencing what Freud felt as he tried to bend the conscious/unconscious theme to fit these events. Fate should be so unkind to a lowly theoretician! The unconscious fighting the unconscious for the sake of the unconscious. Something had to be done.

Id, Ego, and Superego

The result was the emergence of a theoretical concept of personality as a three-part structure, in which the *id,* the *ego,* and the *superego* represented the three primary systems active in personality in general and in most behavior. The *id* is the most basic. It is the "power system" of the personality, providing the sexual and aggressive impetus for behavior. It operates on the sole principle that what is pleasurable is good, regardless of the consequences—the *pleasure principle.* The id does not tolerate delay of gratification. In the thought process, the pleasure principle is translated into the *primary process:* thinking that is totally uninhibited by everyday restrictions like logic, planning, or even probability (a bizarre dream is a good example). If the id wants an apple, it wants it *now* and will try to get it; if that desire is frustrated, it will think (or hallucinate) an apple.

Hallucination of an apple, however, will not do much to stop a stomach's growling. Eventually, from the primitive personality organization that is essentially all id, a new system develops. The *ego.* Unlike the id, the ego operates on a *reality principle.* If we need an apple, let's see—what must we do to get one? Where is the apple? How can we get it? Is it too green, so that the momentary pleasure of eating it will be followed by great pain later? The ego is entirely pragmatic and totally amoral. Like a great general of an army, it accepts its duty and sets out on the most logical course of action to achieve the desired objective. The ego is the strategist of the personality. In the thought process, the ego encourages realistic, rational thinking: the *secondary process.* It engages continually in *reality testing.*

But the ego, master tactician though it may be, is really no more than a servant of the id. The impulsive id cannot achieve its aims, precisely because it *is* impulsive. The ego sets out to accomplish what the id cannot. And its Machiavellian drives soon encounter another master: The *superego.* The moralist. That part of us that tells us we've been "good" when we do something that society says is good and reprimands us when we do otherwise. The superego is composed of one part *ego-ideal*—rewarding those actions that are approved—and one part *conscience*—punishing those actions that are condemned. The superego develops from the moral values of society, as transmitted largely through the parents. "Don't steal!" (Theft, after all, is one good way to get an apple.) "Help someone in need." (Which, of course, the ego would not do unless it had guarantees of an ample return favor.)

Needless to say, the demands and desires of these three systems often conflict. Imagine a sex-starved hedonist, a black-frock-coated Puritan minister, and a totally humorless computer scientist chained together and turned loose in the world, and you have a good approximation of what Freud was trying to show us about the personality.

Because they are chained together, the id, ego, and superego cannot decide to go their separate ways. They have no alternative but to adjust to one another. And the result, for better or for worse, is the adult human personality.

Now Freud's division of personality into the conscious and unconscious was, as we have seen, becoming cumbersome. The concepts of id, ego, and superego were redefined and placed in a position of prominence. But where did they come from, these concepts? Whatever possessed Freud to describe the structure of human personality this way?

Personality as Drama

Essentially, Freud was dividing personality into three categories: (1) "I want"—the natural desires and needs of the individual; (2) "I can"—not in an abstract sense but in the context of an environment, both social and physical; and (3) "I should"—the effects of culture, past, present, and future, with all its traditions and moral standards. The id, the ego, and the superego, respectively. But Freud was a dramatist. Drama excited him. He loved good literature, and he was an avid theater-goer. He was a fan of classical Greek plays. And his way of conceptualizing human experience was mightily influenced by the insights of dramatic literature. The Oedipus complex is a prime example of this influence. So was his somewhat naive acceptance of the early tales of parental seduction and, more directly, his early focus on the *one* event, the trauma, as the cause of neurosis. Often he referred to the trauma as "the dramatic instance." Contemporary psychologist Jerome Bruner has similarly called transference a "play within a play."

Calling Freud's concepts "inspired imagery," Bruner thinks they provide a major clue to his ideological power.

> Freud's is a theory peopled with actors. The characters are from life: the blind, energetic pleasure-seeking id; the priggish and punitive superego; the ego, battling for its being by diverting the energy of the others to its own use. The drama has an economy and a terseness. The ego develops canny mechanisms for dealing with the threat of id impulses: denial, projection, and the rest. Balances are struck between the actors, and in the balance is character and neurosis. Freud was using the dramatic technique of decomposition, the play whose actors are part of a single life. . . . [9]

Personality as an ongoing drama. The roles are all played by you, or different aspects of you. You as id; you as the hero, or ego; you as superego. In some dramas, the id is powerful—the libertine; in others, the superego dominates the action—a story of guilt. When these roles are balanced—when the hero acts to satisfy personal desires in accordance with the restrictions of reality and with the moral dictates of society—the drama is "normal." What drama are you acting out now? That is the basic question of psychoanalysis.

With the appearance of these new concepts, the division of personality into the conscious and the unconscious undergoes some changes. No longer is the ego conscious and the id unconscious. Parts of the ego and parts of the superego are unconscious, too. Repressed material is unconscious, as before, but not all unconscious material is repressed; for example, the ego's defense mechanisms are not. This major theoretical change, made public in 1923, was speedily accepted.

Other things were happening, too. Freud had just witnessed World War I. Two years after the surrender of Germany (and not coincidentally), Freud put out a book entitled *Beyond the Pleasure Principle.* In it, he suggested that perhaps another major source of energy (besides sexual) needed to be conceptualized: an aggressive instinct. A death force to go with the life force.

Life. Death. Aggression. To understand these concepts in Freudian theory, it is important to recognize that Freud categorized certain behaviors and attributed to them a motive force—the instinct. Or *instincts*. There

[9]From Bruner's article "Freud and the Image of Man," *American Psychologist,* 1956, *11,* 463–466.

are many motives, many instincts. They may be broad or specific, basic or derivative. But they can be classified as belonging to one or the other (or both) of two primary camps: those seeking life (survival, reproduction, love) and those seeking death. The first have been called erotic or sexual, with energy called *libido,* but words like *love* and *life* are more accurately descriptive than *sex.* The other class of instincts works in the opposite direction. Freud, the dramatist, called them *Thanatos*, the death instincts, as opposed to *Eros,* the life/love instincts.

One of the greatest Freudian scholars, David Rapaport, asserted that Freud was more involved with the *nature* of drives and how they affected behavior than he was with describing or listing specific drives.[10] From his early theoretical reliance on sexual impulses, Freud had shown that many behaviors thought to be nonsexual were in fact basically sexual. And, in so doing, he contributed greatly to our understanding of how a basic drive gets diverted or transformed. But the impact of the war—Freud was a pacifist—forced him to consider more closely the behaviors we call aggressive and violent. Aggression in patients (notably in cases of sadistic sexuality) was giving therapists some thorny interpretation problems. But change was not easy. Simply positing an aggressive instinct would have been unthinkable. Too many cases of aggression and violence had already been explained well by the libido theory. And Freud was never one to change just for the sake of change. It had to be reasoned, rational.

So. Drawing on numerous examples from the biology of lower organisms, Freud very tentatively proposed that there is a basic force or impetus in human beings to achieve the most primitive state possible: inorganic matter. In other words, an instinct to die or to destroy one's own life. Aggression—pure aggression, at least—is always directed toward oneself. But aggression toward the self conflicts directly with the basic instinct to live and to love, to preserve life. And so the aggression is turned away from its real object (the self) and toward others. In a passionate moment, it may result in impulsive violence; at quieter times, it is "used" by the ego to gain some desired end (to best a rival, for example, or to "aggressively" fight for promotion).

It's an interesting concept. What Freud was saying is that destruction and violence in the world are the result *not* of the death instinct, which seeks to destroy only the individual life, but of the presumed "good" instincts, self-preservation and self-love, which force the darker instinct outward to find its expression.

The notion of a death instinct has not received wide acceptance. Not that it is inaccurate or ineffective theoretically; rather, most theorists view the notion as simply unnecessary. Looking back, it appears that the violence of the war influenced Freud to begin a deeper consideration of aggression. Natural enough. But his true course was a theoretical one: he was still troubled by the question of what was fighting with what in the individual personality. Where, exactly, were the beginnings of the

[10]From D. Rapaport's "The Structure of Psychoanalytic Theory: A Systematizing Attempt," in S. Koch (Ed.), *Psychology: A Study of a Science* (Vol. 3). New York: McGraw-Hill, 1959.

conflict that ended in neurosis? His early theory had the sexual instincts pitted against the ego instincts—the unconscious versus the conscious. But Freud's encounters with self-love *(narcissism)* in patients had weakened that formulation. Love of self—clearly an ego instinct—could not logically be seen as antagonistic to love in general (sexual instincts). Love versus love. The same kind of logic problem he had faced with the unconscious.

To resolve this problem, Freud apparently investigated in two directions at the same time, one leading to the id, ego, and superego, the other leading to the death instinct. His purpose was to conceptualize a conflict, to find a *new* conceptualization to take the place of one that no longer worked. Love versus love and unconscious versus unconscious—these had to go. Instead, Freud postulated the conflict between the life instinct and the death instinct. Or between the ego and the id. Two possible solutions to the problem. The ego/id team won the minds of Freud's followers; it was easier to use and made more sense than Eros versus Thanatos. According to this strengthened and elaborated view, the ego not only had unconscious aspects but also could generate its own special desires, including the desire to remain intact, to love itself. The problem of narcissism was solved.

Let's digress for a moment. We shall see throughout this book that theorists are often faced with "facts" that require a change in theory. Often they have a choice, as Freud did, among several new concepts adequate to the task. Which alternative they choose is a matter of no small importance; their decision will profoundly affect the development of later thought, the discovery of new facts, the "success" of the theory by whatever measure is relevant (cure rate, heuristic value, and so on), and many other significant events. Freud's ego/id formulation was accepted over the life/death notion and found many applications in art, literature, history, and sociology. But stop and consider what the results would have been had the life/death concept been accepted. What directions would psychoanalysis have taken? What would the implications be? We won't attempt to answer such questions here, but take pause and think for a bit. It's a virgin area.

Anxiety, Threat, and Defense

Throughout the history of psychoanalysis, through various theoretical transformations, the concept of *anxiety* has played a role. Anxiety was first conceived as a sort of "leakage" in the system, as some of the energy of repressed instincts slipping through the defenses, just enough to cause nervousness and discouragement but not enough to allow recognition of its source. In Freud's last major (psychological) book, *The Problem of Anxiety,* he updates the concept so that it "fits" better with other theoretical changes, especially with the id/ego/superego change. He describes anxiety as primarily a function or device of the ego, used by the ego to warn itself of impending danger. The ego, in the middle of all the action, experiences threats from three sources. The first is the real environment, which may threaten to injure the person or frustrate a plan. The resulting anxiety is termed *reality anxiety,* the type most closely approximating what we would call real fear. The second source of danger to the ego is the id, with its strong impulses always threatening to break through and take control of behavior. The resulting anxiety is termed *neurotic anxiety,* since this feeling is often associated with strong personality conflicts. Finally, the superego is also a threat, always attempting to influence or control behavior. *Moral anxiety* is a warning that the powerful weapons of the superego (like guilt) are coming into play and will continue unless the behavior is altered or the ego defenses against guilt are reinforced.

As the individual matures the ego takes on greater power, greater responsibility. It coordinates id, superego, and environment. It develops its own resources and methods to protect the often fragile organization of the personality. As a "slave" with new powers, it seeks to preserve itself against the wishes of the "master" id and to subvert the "unrealistic" demands of the superego. Its most powerful weapons are called *defense mechanisms,* a term we have already encountered. They can be broad, as in repression, or specific, as in *reaction formation* (turning an emotion and its associated behavior into their opposite). An example of reaction formation is a show of tender loving care for a parent toward whom the underlying feelings are resentment and hostility. Reaction formation is doubly blessed as a defense, of course, since it inhibits the destructive id impulses and earns the praise of the superego at the same time. Some defense mechanisms are socially productive—for example, *sublimation,* where the energy of the instincts is not blocked but is instead converted to desires to work hard, to paint well, to be a great scientist, and so on. Though Freud often discussed the separate mechanisms, it was his brilliant daughter, Anna Freud, who collected them into a complete exposition of defenses. And that comes later in our story and represents what was to occur among later psychoanalysts: a much greater interest in the ego. Freud was primarily an "id" man. That was the great discovery, the great riddle; that was his genius.

From Death to Immortality

And what of the rest of our genius' life? He had achieved fame throughout the world. His theories had become an integral part not only of psychiatry and the scientific world but also of the intellectual history of humankind. His concepts were appropriate to art, religion, and society, and so they were applied, often by Freud himself (for example, in *Moses and Monotheism* and *Civilization and Its Discontents*). He met and became friends with great physicians and the greats of all fields: Thomas Mann, for example, and Albert Einstein. (He was even asked to write an article for *Cosmopolitan* magazine. He declined.)

But there were blacker moments. Adler split, then Jung, then Otto Rank, and finally even his greatest friend, Sandor Ferenczi. The latter two died insane, still hostile toward Freud. But others took their place: Karl Abraham, Ernest Jones, and others, who disagreed often enough with Freud but never lost their love and respect for the great old man. Jones arranged for Freud's escape from Vienna when the Nazis entered, and Freud went to London. He had, of course, the continuing pain of his jaw cancer during these last years. Operations removed much of his jaw, and he was forced to wear a clumsy and painful artificial device in order to speak or eat.

The end was not a pleasant one. The cancer was growing rapidly, and death was clearly approaching. Although he was in extreme pain, Freud continued to refuse drugs, wanting even at age 83 to continue writing. (His last book, *An Outline of Psychoanalysis,* was published after his death.) He was even seeing patients.

Then, in August of 1939, he began to fail rapidly. The pain of his cancerous wound was great, but perhaps the greater pain was knowing the burden his infirmity placed on his loved ones—on Anna, his daughter, in particular, always by his side. The cancer was now giving off an unpleasant odor. Freud's faithful dog, a chow, kept him company. Freud had always loved animals and was rarely without a pet; he seemed to gain considerable strength from loving and caring for them and receiving their affection in return. The chow knew something was wrong; she came into Freud's room, to be near him. But the smell of the cancer was too strong. She retreated to a corner of the room and sat in silence, quietly guarding her master from the unknown enemy that was not to be defeated. Freud looked at his dog. He realized that hope was at an end. He asked for morphine for the first time. The next day he died.

On February 4, 1955, long after his death, a statue of Freud—with the inscription he dreamed of—was unveiled in the courtyard of the University of Vienna.

Summary Outline of Freud's Theory

Structure

I. *The id.* The most basic and the earliest of the "mental provinces," describing everything that is inherited, present at birth, or fixed in the individual's constitution—above all, therefore, the instincts.

  A. *Pleasure principle.* The principle by which the id operates. Whenever tension builds, the id acts to reduce the tension (that is, pleasure equals tension reduction). In practice, this means that the id strives for immediate satisfaction of its desires, which stem from instincts.

  B. *Primary process.* The process of thought used by the id, not concerned with logic or reality. Bizarre sequences of thought are often the result, as in dreams, but the sequences are bizarre only from the standpoint of logic or reality; in terms of achieving a goal—for example, thoughts of a gigantic breast giving sweet milk on request—they make sense.

II. *The ego*. The "intermediary" between the id and the external world. Developed in the course of later experience, organized from parts of the original id, the ego attempts to achieve the goals of the id by considering the requirements of the external reality. Delay of gratification is often necessary.

   A. *Reality principle*. The principle by which the ego operates. By logically planning a realistic course of action designed to satisfy the instinctive desires, the ego is able to reduce tension by finding a suitable goal-object.

   B. *Secondary process*. The thought associated with ego activity. Close to the common view of thinking as planful, logical, and goal oriented.

III. *The superego*. The last major part of the personality to be developed. The internalized representation of the values and moral standards of society.

   A. *The conscience*. That aspect of the superego that punishes (by producing guilt) unacceptable actions or thoughts.

   B. *The ego-ideal*. That aspect of the superego that rewards (by producing pride) actions or thoughts supporting societal values.

Dynamics

I. *Instinct*. The psychological counterpart of a bodily need—hence the psychological energy representing physical demands. The basic life (sexual) instinct, from which more specific instincts emerge, is called *libido*. Each instinct has four aspects: a *source* (physical need), an *aim* or goal (reducing sexual tension, for example), an *object* (all objects and behaviors that aid in achieving the aim), and an *impetus* (the strength or degree of desire). Freud was most interested in the distortions that occur between an instinct's aim and its object. For example, the aim may be sexual gratification, the object may turn out to be religious fanaticism, and how did that happen?

II. *The conscious and the unconscious*. That of which we are aware and the vast reservoir of which we are unaware. The conscious mind includes the *preconscious*, those mental facts that can be brought into awareness by focusing attention on them. The unconscious cannot be recalled even though it influences behavior. Most, if not all, of the id is unconscious, and most of the ego and superego is conscious (or preconscious). But some important aspects of the latter two are unconscious, including the unconscious *defense mechanisms* that the ego uses to *repress* the strivings of the id and the anxiety caused by the superego. In other words, the conscious/unconscious distinction applies to thoughts in general, whether their source be id, ego, or superego.

III. *The psychosexual stages*. A theory of the development and control of the sexual (life) instinct.

   A. *The oral stage*. The stage at which the primary aim of instincts is gratification of hunger needs through eating and sucking.

   B. *The anal stage*. The stage at which the elimination of food through the anus becomes important, partly due to the maturation of motor capabilities that make toilet training both possible and probable.

C. *The phallic stage.* The stage at which pleasure centers in the genitals. For males the sex/love object is the mother. The *Oedipus complex* describes the desire of the young boy to keep the mother for his own gratification and somehow to eliminate the father as a rival. Imagined fears of reprisal from the stronger father lead to *castration anxiety,* which causes repression of the original desires and a resulting identification with the father as a representation of power. For females, the stage involves the less clearly formulated working out of a feeling of deficiency called *penis envy.*

D. *The latent stage.* A period in which the sexual desires (oral, anal, and phallic in representation) have been brought under some degree of control. The latent stage ends at puberty, when the increasing strength of the sexual instincts illuminates weaknesses in infantile development and requires that new defenses be developed. *Regression* to earlier modes of behavior is common, and latent neuroses often show themselves.

E. *The genital stage.* The perfect solution to accommodation between instinctive urges and societal demands. Strived for but never completely achieved. Relationships between people in this stage are characterized by honest affection, with concern for the individuals and for the nature of their interdependence.

IV. *Anxiety.* A feeling of "unpleasure" caused by signals from the ego; used to warn of impending danger, either from the external world (reality anxiety), from the id and its instinctive urges (neurotic anxiety), or from the superego (moral anxiety).

Technique

I. *Free association.* A therapeutic technique in which the patient tries to associate symbols (as from dreams), symptoms, and actions with their originating cause or causes by thinking about the thing to be understood and saying whatever comes to mind, no matter how trivial or disgusting those associations might be (the *fundamental rule*). The therapist tries to make sense of these associations by interpreting them on the basis of general knowledge and experience and by using additional information gained from observation of resistances and transferences in the therapeutic relationship.

II. *Resistance.* An unwillingness, not usually conscious, to discuss painful memories. Usually seen in lapses in memory or pauses in conversation and sometimes disguised by hostility toward the therapist and/or the therapist's approach. And in many other ways. The theoretical counterparts of this technical concept are repression and defense mechanisms; that is, a resistance usually means that some painful memory has been repressed and defenses are being used to keep it that way.

III. *Transference.* Emotions and actions directed toward the therapist beyond those that could reasonably be expected, indicating that feelings are being transferred from some relationship in the past. The nature of these feelings and their original object are clues to important events of the past. The therapist, incidentally, must recognize that he or she, too, can play this game—call it countertransference —and must be on guard lest his or her own unresolved conflicts interfere with the treatment of the patient.

Suggested Readings

Perhaps the best introduction to Freud is to let Freud himself speak to you in his own way and in his own words. The best source, in this sense, in his book of lectures to medical students entitled *A General Introduction to Psychoanalysis.* (In some editions it's entitled *Introductory Lectures on Psychoanalysis.*) The problem with starting with this book is that it predates the id/ego/superego "discovery." But you can pick that up later, by reading, for example, *The Ego and the Id.* Both are available in inexpensive paperback editions.

The life of Freud is described with loving attentiveness by Ernest Jones in a three-volume biography called *The Life and Work of Sigmund Freud* (Basic Books). An expertly abridged version is available in paperback from Doubleday-Anchor.

Secondary sources include Gerald S. Blum's *Psychoanalytic Theories of Personality,* published by McGraw-Hill, and *Psychodynamics: The Science of Unconscious Mental Forces,* published by Brooks/Cole; C. S. Hall's *Primer of Freudian Psychology,* published by World; and the chapters on Freud in Hall and Lindzey's *Theories of Personality,* published by Wiley.

Comments on more detailed inquiry can be read in the Notes and References for this chapter.

Notes and References

The major reference sources for this chapter were the writings of Freud and, for biographical data especially, the three-volume opus by Ernest Jones, *The Life and Work of Sigmund Freud* (New York: Basic Books, 1953, 1955, 1957). *An Autobiographical Study* (of Freud), translated and edited by James Strachey (Norton, 1963), was also useful in this regard. The primary substantive sources were Freud's books: *The Interpretation of Dreams; Three Essays on Sexuality; A General Introduction to Psychoanalysis* (also called *Introductory Lectures on Psychoanalysis)*; *Beyond the Pleasure Principle; The Ego and the Id; The Problem of Anxiety* (also called *Inhibitions, Symptoms, and Anxiety*); *New Introductory Lectures on Psychoanalysis;* and *An Outline of Psychoanalysis.*

Among the most important papers are: "Fragments of an Analysis of a Case of Hysteria," "Formulations regarding the Two Principles in Mental Functioning," and "Instincts and Their Vicissitudes." These and many other important papers by Freud are available in *The Collected Papers of Sigmund Freud* (Basic Books, 1959). The books are available in several forms, from paperbacks to the most accurately translated collection, *The Standard Edition of the Complete Psychological Works,* translated and edited by James Strachey and published in London by Hogarth over several years beginning in 1953.

Apart from Jones and Freud, it is impossible to trace the source of some of the information gained over many years of study, but these two works certainly account for much of it: Otto Fenichel's *The Psychoanalytic Theory of Neurosis* (New York: Norton, 1945) and David Rapaport's "The Structure of Psychoanalytic Theory: A Systematizing Attempt," in *Psychology: A Study of a Science* (Vol. 3), edited by S. Koch (New York: McGraw-Hill, 1959). Gerald S. Blum, both as writer (*Psychoanalytic Theories of Personality,* New York: McGraw-Hill, 1953, and *Psychodynamics: The Science of Unconscious Mental Processes,* Monterey, Calif.: Brooks/Cole, 1966) and a patient teacher, has contributed in ways that cannot be satisfactorily described and referenced in words alone.

3

The Early Dissenters

But you can say anything, you know. One can say that a church spire is a phallic symbol, but what is it when you dream of a penis? You know what a man has said, one of the orthodox men . . . ? His explanation was that in this case the censor had not functioned. You call that a scientific explanation?

Carl Jung[1]

A theory is a sometime thing. Sometimes it works well, even brilliantly, neatly fitting the known facts and pointing to others that would not have been noticed otherwise. Sometimes it works less than well, and unanswered questions spill out from the framework of its construction. It leads nowhere, or, worse, it misleads. When weaknesses are discovered, theorists may attempt to alter the theory so that it will fit the new facts and answer the unanswered questions. Without, of course, losing its power to handle the old material.

Freud's theory was no exception. It had its strengths and its weaknesses, and Freud and his associates were constantly trying to improve and elaborate on it—to take psychoanalysis in new directions and into unexplored areas. Some of Freud's associates, however, went so far in new directions that they were forced to dissociate themselves from the "orthodox" dogma of psychoanalysis. They found not an improved psychoanalytic theory but a new theory altogether. The difference between their new ideas and the most basic tenets of Freudian theory was too great (at the time) to be resolved. And these theoretical splits led to personal problems with Freud, as often happens when strong and brilliant people clash; the intellectual dissociation becomes personal dissociation as well, often with less than friendly feelings. Disappointment. Anger. Even hatred.

Understand that Freud was not one to stifle dissent. In fact, he encouraged it, never forgetting how easily his authority could suppress budding insights. But some dissent went so far as to undermine the absolute essentials of psychoanalysis: the libido (sexual) theory; transference and resistance, the keystones of his technique; the unconscious and the notion of repression; and the Oedipus complex, which came more and more to be the most basic fixture in his view of personality development. These were foundation stones. To remove them would bring the whole structure down. That it might be necessary to do so and to rebuild his theory slowly and painfully on a new and altered foundation was something Freud considered. When a key belief was attacked, he did not respond in haste but tried valiantly to judge if his idea could be wrong. But if Freud ultimately judged the dissident concept to be less sound theoretically, and therefore a threat, the dissenter would have to leave, no longer a true psychoanalyst. And so Adler, Jung, and Rank left, for they attacked foundation stones and would not, as Jung put it, "recant."

[1]From *Conversations with Carl Jung,* by R. I. Evans. New York: Van Nostrand, 1964.

Adler was the first to go, Jung the second, and Otto Rank—later—the third. There were others, but these three were the most important dissenters. Three new theories. Each man accepted much from Freud; their theories were all analytic. But they all differed so profoundly in important respects that Freud asked the dissenters not to use his trademark, *psychoanalysis.* Adler's approach became known as *individual psychology,* Jung's is known as *analytic psychology,* and Rank's is often called the *theory of birth trauma,* although *will psychology* is really more appropriate. All attacked certain basic parts of psychoanalysis. This chapter will focus on those points of attack. There is a surprising similarity among the dissenters—in what they saw as the weaknesses of Freud's theory, at least, if not entirely in their proposed revisions.

Cast of Characters: Adler, Jung, and Rank

Adler

Alfred Adler was born in a suburb of Vienna in 1870. In 1895, he earned his degree in medicine from the University of Vienna. Born Jewish, he converted to Christianity early in life, an indication of the personal independence that characterized this man throughout his life. Another indication of that independence came in 1900 when Freud's new book, *The Interpretation of Dreams,* received a hostile review in the local newspaper. Adler shot off a heated letter vigorously defending Freud's ideas. Impressed and touched, Freud wrote to Adler to thank him and also to ask him if he would care to join a small group of men meeting regularly to discuss Freud's theory. Adler accepted and thus became a charter member of the group that became the Vienna Psychoanalytic Society. In 1911, Adler resigned as president of the Society and also as a member. Association and separation, now complete.

If Adler were living his college years today, in all likelihood he would be a pugnacious radical. He was certainly a rebel, even then, and he had an abiding interest in social and political issues and a radical concern for the underprivileged. His Russian wife was an ardent Socialist and a friend of Trotsky's, but Adler was too rebellious to submit to the discipline of organized political parties—even those he clearly admired and supported as a sympathetic nonmember. More to his liking were the informal debating societies that met in the cafés in Vienna; here he could be found night after night aggressively championing his personal views on politics or skillfully poking holes in the unrealistic and corrupt ideas of his opponents. He was an able and informed debater. He was also inclined to write stinging letters to people who were wrong, and, if no clear target could be found, he wrote pamphlets correcting the world at large. One of his pamphlets, *The Health of Tailors,* depicted the inhuman working conditions in Viennese shops. This highly controversial tract has been given much credit for several meaningful changes in local labor laws—primarily because it filled the Viennese Establishment with an unholy fear of contracting some dread disease from their new clothes!

Adler loved dispute. He did not like to lose an argument—and rarely did—but there were some notable standoffs. The most notable came within Freud's circle, one of the few arenas in which Adler could find his equals in intelligence, knowledge, and verbal abilities. Here the fights were staged between giants. Not accustomed to the heat and intensity of café debates, however, most Freudians found Adler acrimonious, stubborn, and divisive. They suggested that he was suffering from an inflated desire to be number one. Heaven forbid! As it turned out, however, Adler's theory was to be compatible briefly with Freud's (hence the association) but would eventually become so divergent as to make a split inevitable. (Even had his ideas remained Freudian, it seems likely that he would have broken away out of pure rebellion and individuality.) When the break with Freud finally came, Adler set up a rival organization with a name reflecting his natural pugnacity: The Society for Free Psychoanalysis! Later, when his anger had cooled, he retitled his new movement; we now know it as individual psychology.

Jung

Carl Jung was about as different from Adler as id is from superego, and they were not what one could call bosom pals; their relationship at its best was one of latent hostility. Adler, the combative social thinker, found it difficult to understand how anyone could be so totally unaware of politics as Jung was. A good example of Jung's pervasive naiveté was his acceptance of the presidency of Hitler's International General Medical Society for Psychotherapy, a society based on the "essential truths" in *Mein Kampf* and commissioned to discriminate between "true" Aryan psychologies and "false" Jewish propaganda. Jung was apparently trying to stem the anti-Semitic tide and to keep some semblance of scientific respectability in the organization, for he gave several speeches that, had anyone been able to understand his highly abstract thinking, would have landed him in the gas chamber; he consistently praised Freud and the contributions of Jewish thinkers. But the prestige he gave to the Nazi group just by allowing them to use his name was the visible evil, and Jung was severely criticized, perhaps fairly. On the other hand, it should also be noted that, if one wanted to destroy a Nazi organization, among the best methods imaginable would be to make Jung its president: Jung had a constitutional aversion to order and efficiency and seemed to believe that good, truth, and beauty could best be obtained through chaos. Years before, in 1910, when the International Psychoanalytic Association was founded, Jung was made its first president and very nearly destroyed the organization before it got started; he allowed it to become a slipshod forum for petty bickering.

Jung's disorganized mind was just as apparent in his writings and talks as it was in his executive abilities. Disorganization plus a predilection for high abstraction: a combination requiring genius on the part of the listener or reader to understand him. Freud, of course, was such a genius, and their styles complemented each other nicely. Freud was the systematic theorist and Jung the excitable catalyst, his strikingly brilliant ideas flowing in a dozen different directions at once. Freud was thrilled by the brainstorming sessions with Jung, and Jung, in turn, was amazed at Freud's ability to sit and listen to his rambling ideas for hours, and then efficiently summarize everything he'd said. Until their break in 1913, Jung was a favored member of Freud's circle—"heir apparent" in Freud's own words. But the break was just as inevitable as that between Freud and Adler.

Jung said later that sexuality was the issue that caused the split, but that was just another way of saying that the cause was the lack of spirituality in Freudian theory. As befitted the son of a pastor, Jung's interest in spirituality continued throughout his life. That life was a long one, spanning some 85 years from 1875 to 1961. He was 25 years old when he read *The Interpretation of Dreams.* It was an assignment: he was to review the book for staff members of the Psychiatric Clinic of Zurich. And he was greatly impressed, mainly because Freud presented a solution to a problem that had been puzzling Jung: why patients hesitated with some words in his word-association test. In 1906, he began to write to Freud regularly; soon they met, and by 1910 Jung was the first president of the new International Psychoanalytic Association. But the sexuality/spirituality debate was already drawing them apart, and three years after his election Jung and Freud were no longer close.

Rank

Otto Rank was born in Vienna in 1884. In 1906, he joined the Vienna Psychoanalytic Society with a dual introduction: an acquaintance with Adler and a manuscript on the psychoanalytic interpretation of art and artists, a field of much interest to the cultured Freud. Because of the group's encouragement (and, some have said, with Freud's financial assistance), Rank went to the University to pursue the nonmedical side of psychoanalytic investigation; that is, he specialized in art, ethics, philosophy, and anthropology, rather than in medicine. He was the first "lay" (nonmedical) analyst, and he brought to Freud and the group a different point of view. Throughout some 20 years of association, Rank functioned largely as a proponent of the search for psychoanalytic truth in nonmedical areas and also as a faithful and hardworking aide. He had chief responsibility not only for secretarial duties in the Society but also for the creation, publication, and maintenance of several journals and books.

Rank's break with Freud was more physical than ideological, at least compared with how Adler and Jung left. Rank considered himself a devoted follower, not a leader. He had ideas, of course, and some great insights, but up until the break he considered them only as contributions to Freud. Gifts from the student to the Master. In a book (with Ferenczi) called *The Development of Psychoanalysis,* he explored the relationship of theory to therapy. Among other things, he had (like many others) become concerned about the prohibitive length of psychoanalytic treatment, and so he explored possible ways to shorten it. One way was to put a time limit on treatment—specify the end at the beginning—an idea that Freud himself had often pondered. And he wrote a book, *The Trauma of Birth,* exploring another Freudian idea: that birth—when the child is forced out of its warm and quiet womb to face a bewildering array of intense and rather unpleasant stimuli—is the prototype for anxiety. The child cries, and anguish is born too. But Rank explored a little too deeply, and Freud and other loyalists began to wonder if he was not suggesting that the mother/child relationship was more important than the father/child conflict (the Oedipus complex). By 1926, the question had been resolved against Rank, and he left, somewhat bewildered, to develop the new approach he had had no desire to create.

The King Must Die: Oedipus Attacked

Ralph Waldo Emerson once told young Oliver Wendell Holmes, who had just written a college essay criticizing Plato, "When you shoot at a king, you must kill him."[2] Adler, Jung, and Rank took their shots at Freud. They left him bloodied but very much alive, and so they were exiled. Freud the King was too strong, too wily to be destroyed. But Oedipus the King was considerably more vulnerable. And the King must die.

According to Freud, the male child from 3 to 5 years of age becomes interested in monopolizing the attention of his mother. His competition is his (very large and very strong) father. Freud suggested that both the child's desire for the mother and his feelings of competition with the father are sexual in nature and that the child's thinking runs something like this: I want my mother all to myself. To do that, I'll have to get rid of Daddy. But he's probably thinking of ways to beat me out, too, and he's pretty strong. I'm frightened that he'll cut off my penis.

But here logic runs out, because the logical conclusion is too frightening. The child's desire for the mother is repressed, and admiration of his father's strength becomes the chief determinant in his further development. The child has become a young man. A social role is born.

The Oedipus complex and the accompanying anxiety determine not only the sex role of the boy but also (in part) his future attitudes toward females, his response to authority figures, and a number of other important features of his personality. It is an extremely significant stage of development, one on which a large portion of both Freud's theory of neurosis and his general theory of personality rest. An attack here was not a matter to be taken lightly. But attack here they did.

The Striving for Superiority

First, Adler. He had done some work (and had written a book) on *organ inferiority,* in which he explored how people with physical disabilities or weaknesses face up to their physical inferiority. How do they

[2]From C.D. Bowen's *Yankee from Olympus.* New York: Bantam, 1960, p. 118.

compensate? He found that typically they deal with the natural disadvantage by, very simply, trying harder. Demosthenes became famous as an orator in spite of (because of?) a speech impediment; he practiced talking near the ocean's roar with rocks in his mouth.

Despite the biological bent of his early work, Adler's socialistic orientation was clearly pushing him to consider "inferiority" more as a social phenomenon. He began to see that psychological disability was more important than physical disability; in fact, even an organ deficiency would not produce an impulse toward compensation unless the person suffering from it *felt* it to be a weakness. Anyone who felt inferior, therefore, for *any* reason, would strive to overcome the inferiority—would attempt to make a "plus" out of a "minus." In line with the common cultural designation of weakness as feminine and strength as masculine, Adler called the compensatory striving *masculine protest* (against the feminine weakness, or inferiority). He postulated an *aggressive instinct* to account for the energy fueling the protest. Later he reformulated the instinct to that of power—Nietszche's *will to power*—because aggression seemed to suggest an intention to cause pain. And still later the will to power became even more general: the *striving for superiority*. I will do better; tomorrow's me will be superior to the me of today.

What then of Oedipus? Adler said that, in his opinion, the Oedipus complex was not sexual in nature at all. It merely exhibited the early attempts of a child, who is biologically inferior, to assert superiority. Castration anxiety? A fear of being inferior. And penis envy? Woman's own masculine protest. Privilege envy.

Freud was not amused. Adler left.

Archetypes and the Collective Unconscious

Soon thereafter Freud received a letter from his heir apparent, Carl Jung. Jung was pleased to report that he had made a surprising discovery: if you avoid discussing intimate sexual details, it is much easier to gain acceptance from both patients and lecture audiences. Freud was horrified. Of course it is easier, he snorted, and it would be easier still if we abandoned the unconscious and repression and all the other disturbing features of the theory. But Jung's mind was taking wing. He had never been comfortable with the pervading sexuality in Freud's theory. And, although he was influential in the formulation of the Oedipus complex—the idea of a *complex*, an integrated *collection* of thoughts, emotions, and images, was his contribution—there was something in the Freudian view that was too specific, too . . . personal? Jung saw in the Oedipal notion something mythical, universal, transpersonal. Not so sexual.

A desexualized Oedipus complex? Freud was not happy. He said to Jung, with passion, "Promise me never to abandon the sexual theory. . . . We must make a dogma of it, an unshakeable bulwark."

Astonished, the young Swiss asked "A bulwark—against what?" And then he left to find the "real" answer to the Oedipus riddle.

Jung looked at his own dreams and imaginings and found in them ideas and feelings great and majestic, beautiful but frightening. Though he was well educated in Freud's methods of dream interpretation, he found those methods inadequate, not "occult" enough somehow. He felt almost as if someone were trying to communicate with him, through his dreams, someone from another world. He was puzzled and not a little anxious.

As he investigated more closely, he noticed that some of the images in his dreams bore a strong resemblance to symbols used in rituals: the chalice, the figure of the father, and the suffering hero are some of these figures found in Christianity. But he was not only finding symbols of Western culture. He traveled to foreign lands, like Africa and India, and he found the same symbols. He dusted off the books of ancient philosophers and alchemists, and there they were again. And, eventually, he put forth his answer.

The images *were* communication from another world. Not from little green men on Venus, though. From Earth, from the past, back to and including the animals from which humans evolved. The communications come in the form of *archetypes,* meaning "an original form of something." Archetypes include thoughts, feelings, and images related to an object (a mother, for example) or an event (such as being faced with danger). They are all things that have been encountered repeatedly before—that is, by one's ancestors—and those ancestral experiences have left their mark, a deposit, an engraving, that is passed on genetically. They make it easier to think, feel, and imagine in certain ways (and harder to do so in others). Part of the strange sensation called *déjà vu* that people sometimes experience—that feeling that they have been somewhere before or done something before, even though they know it cannot be so—comes from the activation of an archetype. Perhaps even feelings of reincarnation, of having lived previous lives, can be so explained. And fantastic experiences under the influence of drugs, like those reported by Aldous Huxley and Timothy Leary—archetypes?

The archetypes reside in the *collective unconscious,* called collective because it is essentially the same in all people, universal rather than personal. Attempts to describe or define these archetypes result in pictorial representations, called symbols, that are universally meaningful. Sometimes they are pictured in human form (the madonna) and sometimes not (the mandala or magic circle, the universal symbol of unity). The sense of awe that accompanies recognition of an archetype makes it likely that religious feelings will be directed toward these external representations—Jesus may be associated with the symbol for the ideal self, for example.

The Oedipus complex? . . . is an archetype! A universal drama played out largely in response to ancient thoughts and feelings and images that are triggered by the same family situation that our ancestors have faced throughout the ages, the typical (archetypical!) conflict between dependence and independence in the relation of young to old. A touch of incestual desire, perhaps. We need not always live out this drama as it was lived out in the past, of course; archetypes influence, but they do not control. But it is much easier to repeat the actions of our ancestors because our body and brain have been "programmed" to do it that way.

So there you are, Freudians. The Oedipus complex is just one of many archetypes, not the structure on which all of personality is based. Sexual desires, furthermore, although they may be present, are more or less incidental to the true archetypal significance of the Oedipal drama. This is Jung's contribution.

The Freudians thought Jung was stark, raving mad! Jung left.

Mother, Child, and Birth Trauma

Things stayed calm in the house of psychoanalysis (after Jung's departure) for several years. About ten, to be exact. It was 1923 before the next attack was launched, and this one came from an unexpected quarter. Not good old faithful Otto Rank?! Yes, good old Otto. First there was his book called *The Development of Psychoanalysis,* co authored by Ferenczi. It contained some disturbing assertions about the methods of analysis. Disturbing. But then came Rank's *The Trauma of Birth.* That was devastating.

In the latter book, Rank explored the implications of an idea Freud touched on briefly—that the bewildering influx of sensations that a child experiences at birth might be a prototype of anxiety felt later in life. Such an exploration led inevitably to a closer look at the mother/child relationship, not only at birth but later as well. What could be more natural, more biologically primary, than the mother/child bond? Nothing. What could be more frightening than separation of the child from its support system, its mother, at birth? Even after birth? Nothing. And Rank went on and on, to the point of viewing this relationship as not simply the first, not simply the most basic relationship, but as the key to understanding all human interaction.

Mother and child? How about father and child, where the Oedipus complex starts? Sorry. With his lifetime interest in anthropology, Rank saw this "strong father" interpretation as a misleading cultural artifact based largely on the authoritarian character of European families. He felt also that the emphasis on the relationship of the child and the father was a reversal of the natural biological order. The Oedipus doctrine was a screen, hiding the truly important data about relationships conditioned by mother/child interaction.

Although Rank, unlike Adler and Jung, had no real desire to go off on his own and create an alternative to psychoanalysis, he soon found that he had no choice. Freud and the regulars could hardly accept his views. Of the three dissident theories, Rank's was perhaps the most direct threat to the essence of the Oedipus complex.

Rank was very vulnerable. As one of the few analysts with no medical degree, he was bound to suffer by a separation from Freud; his credentials would not bring eager scouts from hospitals and universities knocking at his door. But now he was out. And still not sure why. Hadn't he dedicated his birth-trauma book to Freud?

Shaking the Foundation: Sexuality, Biology, Transference, and Resistance

On their own now, the three dissenters worked on their own approaches. Although they would always retain elements of orthodox Freudian dogma, away from direct Freudian influence all three men significantly altered their thinking on many Freudian tenets, and new concepts like that of archetypes developed apace.

They continued to chip away at some of the "foundation stones" of Freud's theory.

Sexuality

Jung had never been happy with the basic energy drive of psychoanalysis, the sexual libido. His break with Freud was directly related to his increasing tendency to view energy as general "life force," not necessarily sexual at all. Psychic energy, period. Adler, too, gave up on sexuality, turning instead to the striving for superiority. Rank began to speak of a desexualized and generalized "impulse" and also of "will," a higher form of energy, more human and more spiritual.

None of course denied the sexual instinct. What they denied was its primacy. Adler's position is a good example: There is a sex drive, and there are drives to obtain food and to avoid pain—all kinds of drives. There is heredity, and there is experience. But none of these are direct causes of behavior. They are merely elements to be taken into account and "used" by the *creative self* to reach its goal, which is superiority. Or, to phrase the goal another way—to redefine superiority—the direction of striving is toward a fictional *ideal self.* Sexuality is not the most important consideration.

Jung took a different approach. (Jung usually did.) He posited an archetype called the *shadow*, within which could be found most of the animal/sexual characteristics influencing behavior. In part, the shadow represents our heritage from our animal ancestors and the more animal-like experiences of our human predecessors. Something like Herman Hesse's *Steppenwolf.* Most of the time the shadow stays in the dark, in the unconscious. But it is always there—whispering, influencing—and sometimes it leaps to the foreground, taking control, involving us in animal things like sex. (The devil made me do it!)

So sex did not disappear from the dissident theories. Not at all. It lost its position of prominence, however, and became just one of many influences. Perhaps the most significant change was the feeling that animal desires were not all bad—that they could be positive forces. Sex to Adler was like fire: a force, pure and simple, that could be used well or poorly. The results, good or bad, of its use would be determined by something quite different from the force itself. By the creative self. Similarly, Jung saw sex as essentially neutral (natural). He felt that it was not an uncommon experience for people to go overboard with sex, but this also happened with other natural tendencies—the tendency toward mystical spirituality, for instance. And in such an instance, the balancing realism of the animal desires kept the ship of the soul on a straight course. (In Rank's theory, sexuality wasn't talked about much. Rank assigned it a minor role, without even offering an explanation for doing so.)

Biological Basis

Most psychoanalysts were (and are) trained in medicine; they could be considered applied biologists. One of the reasons Freud's emphasis on sex eventually found acceptance was that biologists found it difficult to reconcile their knowledge of the biological sex instinct with the apparent lack of sexual feelings in some people. Freud's theory of sexuality was clearly biological at its base. Quite openly, it was constituted and defended on biological grounds, and Freud yearned for the day when biology could explain all of his insights with a more comprehensive theory of physiological activities in the body and in the brain. At the beginning, the dissenters shared this hope. Even Rank, the only nonphysician, began his dissent by studying birth, and you can't get much more biological than that. Adler began with a study of physical disability. Jung became interested in dreams. Are dreams biological? Anyhow, over the years and without exception, all the new theories showed a clear trend away from biology, not just in the deemphasis of sexuality but in all aspects of personality.

The clearest evidence of this trend is in the nature of the "facts" each theorist used to support his theoretical speculations. Freud became somewhat less reliant on biological support for his theory as it developed (although certainly he didn't move as far away as Adler, Jung, and Rank did), but he usually found that acceptance of his speculations was closely related to the degree to which they could be justified biologically. Take the death instinct. It was not widely accepted, largely because the psychoanalysts could not integrate it with their biological understanding of life. This was true, even though Freud tried his best to drag in every bit of biology (and even botany!) that he could amass. Adler became convinced, on the other hand (and Rank was with him on this), that society and social organization explained personality best. Biology mattered but not that much. More and more, support for their theories came from sociology and anthropology. Psychology for its own sake, not as imperfect biology. Jung, too, though for different reasons, used a lot of anthropological data: he was looking for the universal archetypes and symbols in various cultures.

The result of all this development was the formulation of the new psychoanalytic concepts in nonbiological terms. *Instinct*, for example, all but vanished from the later writings of the dissidents. Sex was demoted and replaced by terms like *self* and *will*. And, perhaps most important of all, the notion that personality can be described in terms of electrons coursing through the brain and spine (*reductionism*) came to be seen as a misleading idea. It may be possible that the creative self or the will or an archetype will eventually be isolated in brain structure or chemistry. But that is not what really mattered to Jung and Adler and Rank—the concepts themselves were more important.

Transference and Resistance

If you observe the interaction between a therapist and a patient, you cannot miss seeing the behaviors that Freud labeled *transference* and *resistance*. Resistance is just that, a "resisting," seen in passive forms like forgetting and long pauses in conversation or in active forms like hostile denials of perfectly logical suppositions. Transference is manifest in the emotions and feelings of the patient toward the therapist—very strong feelings that seem to be unwarranted, both love and hate. Since the strength of feelings in transference is not justified by the relationship between therapist and patient, Freud suggested that the emotions were being *transferred* to the present situation from another situation in the past. The intensity of feeling suggested that the past experiences were of great psychological importance. Freud therefore began to use these behaviors to get to the heart of the patient's psychological conflict. Through transference a conflict could be brought out into the open, where the therapist could see how the patient felt about his or her father or mother or whomever the conflict enveloped. Resistance gave clues to the identity of the "conflict person," and transference gave clues to the thoughts that were being resisted.

No one can deny the existence of transference and resistance, just as no one can entirely dismiss the importance of sexuality. The dissenting theories did, however, modify Freud's view of what was going on when these behaviors were taking place. Jung, as you might imagine, agreed with Freud that transference involved a transferring of past experience—but there is considerable doubt whether Freud agreed with Jung that the past experiences could include those of someone's great-great-grandfather 150 years ago or of some prehuman anthropoid leaping out of a tree. As for resistance—well, Jung did not agree that "resistance" was really resistance—at least not always. The poor patient, said Jung, simply cannot put into words the thoughts and images triggered by the archetype. So while Freud sought the "truth" behind the resistance, Jung had his patients draw pictures, hoping to see in symbols the conflicts that could not be verbalized.

Adler was by now looking at behavior through the social/psychological tint of his new theory. Behavior in therapy came into focus this way: therapeutic interactions, like any other, were power struggles. Transference was an attempt by the patient to assert superiority over the therapist by the usual everyday means—hating and loving. Hate is a misguided attempt to dominate; and love—well, that's the same as hate, really. It's just an inverted or submissive form of the same striving.

Note that Adler was suggesting that emotions can be and often are *used,* for social purposes. A tricky little change in emphasis but one destined for further development by other, later theorists. Not only were the more nearly pure emotions of Freudian fame being discarded, but also those emotions were conceptualized as instruments, tools, to be used in a controlled and semirational form. Not emotions boiling up chaotically from the id, you see, but emotions in the service of the ego. Adler claimed the same role for anxiety, asserting that anxiety was used by the ego to warn the psyche of impending danger—a revolutionary view that Freud later accepted as his own.

Meanwhile, back on Adler's couch, love and hate were still fighting it out. But something was wrong with the theory. There was a maladjustment someplace. True superiority, said Adler, is not dominance, not at all; it's more like becoming the best (most competent) person you can possibly be. But the problem is that the average person for average reasons often mistakes dominance for competence, and the will to power is not checked (as it should be) by *social interest* (innate) and the *natural* tendency to *cooperate* for social good. Selfishness replaces selfhood. To reach for the stars (the ideal self) is not an easy task or a clearly defined one, so often we find the embryonic version instead, a simple grasping for the more immediate dominance-type superiority. The task of analysis, therefore, as Adler sees it, is to recognize selfishness as basically good, an active striving for superiority, and to *keep* it and add to it. Add to it the social interest necessary for truly human development.

Adler adds the warning that it will not be an easy task. Neurosis is best defined, he said, as the exploitation of weakness. You, the patient, have come for help because your innate social interest cannot be denied, and there is inner conflict between that and your overt selfishness. But you will not easily relinquish an illness (your neurosis) that has enabled you to avoid the heavy responsibilities of working with rather than against others.

Adler's view of resistance follows similar lines of interpretation. It is part and parcel of the same old power struggle. Who will be the boss, the leader, the superior figure in the analyst/patient relationship? No need for a conflict person from the past; the here-and-now has plenty of conflict to offer.

Like Adler, Rank was impressed by resistance and saw it as a basically positive force that has become just a little misguided. He built his whole theory out of the facts of transference and resistance. For him, resistance was *will* expressed in its most primitive form: saying "no!" The task of the therapist should be to turn this negative will into a "yes!" Movement toward fulfillment rather than away from it.

Transference in its essence is a *dynamic relationship,* and, for Rank, if anything was being transferred from the past, its most significant analogue was—you guessed it!—the birth trauma. A reenactment of the fears about separation (*fear of life*) and the fears about staying in union (*fear of death*). This is the real conflict. We as patients want to strike out, to become independent, to become real individuals, but we are afraid of losing the comfort and support that come with our illness. At the same time, we fear that same comfort and support because we know, deep down, that we must grow or die. It is the story of life itself, said Rank. Separation, union, separation . . . from each union take a little, separate and experiment, unite and consolidate, then move on again. The dialectic: wholeness out of disintegration, repeated in endless cycles. Not an easy scenario to play out. But that's life. There is no other way.

One thing that comes across in the writings of Rank more than in the works of Adler and Jung is the tremendous respect he has for the person, even a person in trouble. The person has will, and, if this will can be freed from self-limiting aims, the patient will bring about his or her own cure. This respect represented another significant change in emphasis, and it had a great destiny. It was to be the basis for the client-centered therapies of later years, and Rank was the theoretical father of Carl Rogers.

The concept of will (which derived from the observation of resistance) is clearly central to Rank's theory and therapy. It is the patient's own will that heals, not the skills of the therapist. The therapist helps as much as possible, mostly by being a sympathetic listener and by trying to unleash the patient's own creative self-renewal. That is why Rank's approach eventually acquired the label "patient-centered." And, in practice, a number of differences from Freudian therapy developed, the most notable being the response to transference: the Freudians "interpreted" transference as a key to past conflicts, whereas Rank "experienced" transference, empathized with it, tried to sense the movement of the patient's will, tried to let it come out without pressure or fear. He did not interpret it. To him, it was simply the life force, active, struggling to redirect itself. If the theory stresses the patient's own abilities, this is a result of Rank's conviction that powerful drives and abilities toward betterment do exist, and the overall view is one of a human potential for greatness. Quite unlike the Freudian view: potential for disaster.

Let's look a bit longer at transference and resistance as conceptualized by Freud and by the three dissenters. Logically enough, the theoretical significance of the behaviors called "transference" and "resistance" varies according to the theory being used. Freud and Jung emphasized the "transferring," whereas Adler and Rank tended to dismiss the past and to emphasize the present situation and the here-and-now personality. The latter approach had the obvious advantage of shortening therapy, since less time was "wasted" in digging up historical facts. In Rank and Adler we also find more concern for the future: "Don't tell me how you got into this mess; tell me what you intend to do about it!" Simply put, for Freud transference was a replaying of a previous interpersonal conflict; for Jung it was a demonstration of archetypes in action; for Adler it was a simple power struggle; and, in Rank's theory, it was the "relationship" reenacted, the fear-of-life/fear-of-death playlet seen first when the baby is separated from its mother's body.

To Freud, resistance signaled points of conflict. It was related to repression: the patient could not speak because the thoughts or feelings had been repressed and now resided in the unconscious. Jung attributed the patient's inability to express himself or herself to a different cause: mere words could not convey what the patient was trying to express.

Rank and Adler saw resistance as a generally beneficial but misdirected life force at work: the striving for superiority (Adler) or the will (Rank).

Beyond Freud: The Dissenters in Their Own Right

In contrast to Freudian theory, the single most striking quality of the dissenters' views was their immensely more *positive* quality. Because of his unique position in the history of psychology, Freud had to focus on the less pleasant aspects of personality, infantile sexuality, perversions, and selfish motives. The sexuality of children, in particular, had not been acknowledged before. Freud discovered the animal in humans; that was his great contribution. The id was his baby. And, as a consequence, the more positive aspects of the psyche got less than their fair share of attention. Had Freud asserted the goodness and rationality of humans, we would never have heard of him; everyone of Freud's generation knew that people were good and rational. But his failure to explore the positive side of personality *was* a weakness, and even Freud knew it. In his later works, he turned more and more toward the strengths and away from the deficiencies of the personality; and he did it, as he had always done, properly, in order, in due time. One cannot formulate the ego until the id is well in hand.

But the negativism of psychoanalysis stuck in the craw of the dissenters. Adler, the social thinker, was concerned about the good person harnessed by an inhuman government. Jung, the religious mystic, saw in people's awkward and fumbling activities, a drive toward spiritual fulfillment. Rank, at heart an artist, could not believe that art was nothing but the smearing of feces on a canvas. When they broke from Freud, they could do what he did not: explore the highest levels of human achievement and potential. Let's look at where their explorations took them.

The Creative Self

Start with Adler. The *striving for superiority,* tempered by an innate *social interest* and a desire to *cooperate*. The result is a sense of and a striving for an *ideal self,* the best self possible. (The "unconscious," according to Adler, is largely the lack of knowledge about what our own personal ideals are.) As the individual struggles through life toward this ideal, he or she develops a *style of life*, an organization and a consistency, that characterizes a unique personality. (It is the style of life, according to Adler, that is the primary drive behind behavior—not the sex drive or the aggressive drive, which are nothing but tools in the drive toward the ideal self.) This process is described by Adler's integrative concept *the creative self*: the creative self strives for superiority or toward the ideal self, which is judged on the basis of social interest and cooperation, and, over the years, forms a distinctive style of life. That's Adler's theory in one sentence! A positive picture.

In its drive to become Captain Wonderful, the creative self faces three primary adjustments: to work, to love (usually spouse and family), and to social contacts (people encountered in the journey of life). These adjustments are *responsibilities*, and, in Adler's theory, the best way to meet a responsibility is to be *cooperative*: to work together for the best that can be had. A very positive picture.

It sounds very nice, but we all know that life is not without its ugly side. Dictators, parasites and cowards exist like blots on the beauty of the grand picture. Adler knew this, and, in his typically pugnacious style, he called them not "poor misunderstood humans with a need for help" but dictators, parasites, and cowards. We've already met Adler's "coward" in the neurotic personality. Unwilling to accept responsibility, the coward exploits an "illness" in order to survive while doing nothing. The "parasite" also refuses responsibility but does it in a more socially acceptable manner. The "dictator" is more active and industrious but is misled; dictators confuse their own goal—superiority—with simple dominance.

But such people represent failures of the creative self. They are hindered by an *inferiority complex*, a reaction to the stresses of continually trying to be superior. But Adler believed that, even in failure, the picture of what a person could be or accomplish was always there. It's a positive view, and it was offered at a time when the only positive thing that Freud was offering was sublimation—"distorting" animal sexual impulses into useful activities. Optimist versus pessimist.

The Balanced Self

Now take Jung. A mystic, a true believer. Jung really believed in archetypes, and he was therefore a traditionalist, glorying in human achievements over the centuries. Like Adler, Jung stressed the tendency (life force) in humans to better themselves, to overcome bondage, to move beyond their animal instincts to something higher and more spiritual. But most significantly, Jung insisted that the elements of the unconscious were not negative and destructive determinants of behavior. The most prominent feature of his theory had always been a sense of *balance*. The ego (the conscious mind) and the unconscious (personal and collective) must be in balance; one or the other must not dominate, or there will be hell to pay. Unconscious forces are no more and no less beneficial than ego impulses. The shadow can drive us to rape, but it can also impel us to eat, to avoid danger, and to solve problems. Mental illness, in this view, is *exaggeration* of *either* of these two naturally opposing tendencies. Being too rational is just as neurotic as being too irrational. Always the sense of balance.

This approach has a striking implication—that we can learn from our non-sense and that even severe psychosis may be a healing process. If life tasks become too confusing or too distressing, the unconscious in its wisdom will work for our psychological survival. In the collective unconscious, after all, in the archetypes, there is the wisdom of the ages. Many psychiatrists have noted that their patients, when "cured," are not just "well" but are better than before, as if the journey into the neurosis or psychosis was an educational trip. Valuable. And the opinion is gaining ground that it may be a mistake for therapists to fight the illness. Instead, they should let it develop, and run its full course, for the benefit of the patient. The works of R. D. Laing represent a present form of this thinking, and Jung is a kind of intellectual godfather of this movement.

Jung had a name for this balance: he called it *the self.* Unlike other theorists who treat the self as a concept roughly equivalent to the ego, Jung considered the self to be an *integration* of ego and unconscious. This balancing of opposing forces produces a personality organization—the self—that is the prime mover. Much like Adler's creative self and style of life.

According to Jung, when you first meet someone, what you initially encounter is the *persona,* the "mask" of behaviors designed for public consumption, different from the private personality. A weak and anxious individual may mask inner doubts with a public display of bravado and confidence. And there is nothing wrong with a mask, as long as you remember that you are wearing it and that you are out in public, on display, at the workaday masquerade. When there is lack of balance or exaggeration, however, the mask begins to grow into your face until it cannot be removed even in the privacy of your own mind. The "he-man" begins to believe that he has no feminine tendencies (which he probably equates with homosexuality). He can no longer be tender and sensitive; he may even be driven to suicide because he cannot reconcile the "womanish" feelings that explode in him at times of crisis.

But where there is imbalance, there is always movement toward balance: the man feels pressure to recognize his feminine attributes, and the woman feels an urge to come to terms with her "maleness." Archetypes play a role in this balancing, of course, because all of our ancestors have had experience with males and females. The *anima* is the archetype of the female in men, and the *animus* is the male in women. When the he-man's *persona* finally crumbles, his anima may take control—it was so long denied—and he may weep. Then gradually comes the integration, which is health. A man who is "all man" is neurotic; so is a woman who is "all woman." Always the sense of balance, of integration.

In the United States and in many Western societies, there is strong differentiation between "masculine" and "feminine." Men are not supposed to weep, be sensitive, or show too much affection to other men; women are not supposed to be aggressive or too intelligent. In other words, there is imbalance. In many respects, contemporary Western society is much like that of Freud and Jung: male dominated and authoritarian. But Jung saw things differently than Freud did. Castration anxiety, for example, is really a man's fear of unleasing his anima. Penis envy in women is a desire to unleash the animus, to become more masculine. Both the male fear and the female desire are basically unhealthy, according to Jung, because they are exaggerations, caricatures, rather than integrations.

Relations between men and women are also troubled by unbalanced archetypes. Love at first sight, for example. What does it mean? Ever see a friend fall in love with someone you thought particularly unattractive? Jung suggested that a good deal of intersexual attraction is influenced by sexual archetypes. A young man may fall in love, maybe "at first sight," because the loved one corresponds to his anima. But she loves him not. Alas! How can he compete with her animus? He is not her ideal man. Even in marriage, the discrepancy between real and ideal, however small, is enough to provoke not a few moments of anger and hostility. "I will never understand men" may mean "I don't understand why he is not like my animus."

But we digress. The *positive* features of Jung's general theory of balance are two-fold. First, there is a clear message that the less conscious aspects of personality are not only a necessary part of growth but are also creative contributions. The femininity in a man, if accepted, will make him a better human being, and a woman's masculinity cannot be denied (unless, of course, we want a world peopled by men and their slaves). Second, in Jung's emphasis on balance and integration, there is a sense of a whole that is greater than its parts. Out of the ego and the unconscious, something new and beautiful is formed, something more: a *self*. Freud said, "Let us take the whole and break it down so we can look at the parts." That's analysis. Jung said "Let us take the parts and see if we can build a new whole." That's synthesis.

Art versus Neurosis

Like Jung, Otto Rank was impressed by humankind's cultural achievements, especially in the field of art. There is no getting around the fact (much oversimplified, of course, but still a fact) that Freud viewed the artist as a "useful" neurotic. Rank tried but could not accept this view. How was an artist different from a neurotic? Both are original—that's for sure. They may do crazy things, say things we don't understand, or draw weird pictures. All artists are eccentric by social definition; the stereotype has a kernel of truth. Pondering this issue, Rank conceptualized three basic forces in the human personality: (1) *impulse* (sometimes called "blind" impulse); (2) *will*, that distinctly human power to use blind impulse for its own purpose (much like the creative self of Adler); and (3) *inhibition*, the slowing or obstructing of positive will. As we have seen, will is the central concept. Impulse is a kind of infantile will, and inhibition is like negative will.

Now suppose one or another of the three basic forces becomes predominant. What type of person results? When impulse predominates, the result is the *antisocial personality*, or psychopath, who grabs for what he or she wants, with no concern for others. If inhibition reigns, out of fear or whatever, the result is the *neurotic*. The *artist* develops when healthy will is allowed to flourish. The artist is not neurotic, you see; the artist is the exact opposite of the neurotic. Art is positive and creative; neurosis is negative and limiting. Rank now had the distinction he was looking for.

But notice that he had, in the process, elevated the status of the poor unfortunate neurotic just as much as that of the artist. The neurotic is really an artist except for one problem: the will is turned against creativity instead of allied with it. Turn the nay-saying of the neurotic around and you find the yea-saying of the artist. Maybe that's why Rank developed such respect for the mentally ill: he viewed them all as potential artists. Even the psychopath has the potential, if only the impulse can be elevated to will. A blooming, burgeoning world filled with creative people. It's possible. Otto Rank dared to dream of the possibility.

Up from the depths. Positive versus negative. In the most general terms, that is the difference between Freud and his early dissenters. This primary difference necessarily had diverse theoretical implications. The emphasis on integration, as opposed to the Freudian stress on analysis, is one example. In turn, the emphasis on integration, on synthesis, led to different practices in therapy. Less interest in childhood experiences, for instance, and more emphasis on contemporary situations and more on the future—what are you going to do next? The value of certain concepts, like the id and instinct, decreased, and the value of others, like the ego and the self, increased. The dissenters forecast a similar trend in orthodox Freudian theory, known today as the new "ego psychology." And there was a "wholeness" in the dissident views not found in Freud's theory, a belief that the most important feature of personality is its wholeness. One does not study a symphony by looking at harps and drums. A positive synthetic view. Call it "holism" (we will see this term again later). And more emphasis, in therapy, on contemporary, environmental crises.

Contemporary. Environment. That's more social psychology than personality, isn't it?

Socializing Freud

If you look at the history of personality theory since the 19th century, probably the clearest trend you will find is in the development of social concepts—that is, concepts that have to do with the relationship of the individual to society. Today it has become almost impossible to distinguish between personality and social psychology, a fact recognized by the American Psychological Association when it created one journal for the two disciplines: the *Journal of Personality and Social Psychology*. The early dissenters began this trend, and Adler and (in particular) Rank would be as appropriately found in a history of social psychology as they are here. Even the asocial Jung was pushed in this direction.

Introversion and Extraversion

Jung distinguished between two opposing orientations of the individual toward the world, and these popular concepts have become part of our everyday language: *introversion* and *extraversion*. Introversion is turning away from the world, toward the inner experience and the subjective aspects of self. Extraversion is turning toward the world, toward the outer and objective. If the attitudes are extreme, we have a type—an introvert or an extravert. The first is quiet and reflective, and the second is outgoing and gregarious. The bookworm versus the publicity hound. Jung considered this distinction a basic dimension of personality, and he is not alone in his belief. A British scientist named Hans Eysenck has presented experimental data largely supporting Jung's view. (We'll be properly introduced to Eysenck in Chapter 4.) Certainly the concepts have been highly significant in personality theories and in the common language, albeit in somewhat distorted fashion.

In Jung's system, the orientation that fails to dominate in the conscious ego goes into the unconscious, still active and often highly compelling. Even in extreme cases, or perhaps we should say *especially* in extreme cases, extraverts must come to grips with their need for introversion, and, conversely, introvert types must adjust to their powerful extravert tendencies. Here there must be balance. And just as the male may be controlled by his anima in a time of crisis, or the female by her animus, Jung cautions us to look for the emerging introvert in the anxious extravert. Integrate your ego and your unconscious, says Jung, and make a "self." A good self will not be surprised or anxious when the unconscious takes control. It will benefit from the experience.

Responsibility and the Family Constellation

Adler's theory is clearly social. It depends on such things as cooperation and an innate social interest, and actions are judged on the basis of social validity. Adler was critical of asocial or antisocial personalities, calling them cowardly or irresponsible, almost as a high government official might call an inefficient worker a slacker. Many theorists who support Adler's basic assumptions nevertheless claim that he failed to see clearly when the failure to perform duties represented intelligent resistance to unacceptable social demands. But even this debate produced progress, and Adler produced the debate.

Among Adler's most important contributions were his ideas on the *family constellation.* Aware as he was of the effect of social structure on personality, he looked at the family as a mini-society and speculated about what he saw. The first child, for example, is born into a different "society" than the later-born. As an older child, you tend more toward authoritarian behaviors simply because you are oldest—or, to put it more positively, older children are more responsible because they have more responsibility. Younger children can be more rebellious—perhaps they must be—but they can also be more creative. Because they have less responsibility. If you are the very youngest, you may be spoiled (the baby of the family) because you have more people to spoil you. Or you may be the most successful personality, unencumbered by responsibility or the need to rebel. Again, like Jung's extraversion and introversion, these early concepts have become very important in modern theories, and birth order continues to be an important part of personality research.

Union and Separation

Rank had no such catchy phrases, no well-named concepts that became part of our everyday vocabulary. But Rank's theory also moved in a clearly social direction: the concept of interpersonal relationship was central. Rank saw the individual as a social being, one who needed a

"Thou" in order to be an "I." The relationship *I and Thou* is a *union*—coming together, integrating, consolidating. But anxiety is always present: the fear of death through union. And the fear of *separation*—pulling apart, striking out in new directions, free and independent. But there is always the dread of lack of support: the fear of life.

One of Rank's major concerns was the relationship of theory to therapy. When he was still in the Freudian fold, he was very distressed by the fact that psychoanalysis took so long and cost so much. Was there no way to shorten therapy? Was all this therapy necessary? His distress was amplified by the observation that, as psychoanalytic theory grew in scope, psychoanalytic therapy grew in length. Freud's theory and therapy were so closely related that one often didn't know whether he was talking about a theoretical construct or a practical technique (transference and resistance are two good examples of this). In Rank's opinion, such close correspondence between the theory and the therapy was not wise; in many cases, it led to unnecessary therapy—overexamination of childhood experiences, for example—that served to illuminate the theory, but not to cure the patient. Freud, too, was concerned about the length of therapy, but he was unwilling to inhibit deep exploration of the past. He had, after all, made his discoveries in the course of such explorations, and he had seen seemingly insignificant events turn out to be crucial to understanding a patient's symptoms. And, as several recent scholars have pointed out (for example, Rychlak), Freud was not above using patients to gather data, for his basic motives were more scholarly than they were curative.

One possible way to shorten therapy, suggested by both Freud and Rank, was to set a time limit. The time limit would depend on the illness, of course, but for any given case there would be a definite deadline at which the patient would leave the care of the therapist. A time limit, obviously, limits time. To accept this as technique, however, requires a belief that something good and valuable will be accomplished by the limit, other than just the time and money savings. Freud considered it as a technique but then dismissed it. Rank found a rationale for the time limit and therefore used it. The rationale was decidedly social.

Back we go to Rank's basic view of relationships: union, separation, union, separation . . . on to individuality. Therapy is a union, a coming together of a person who needs help and one who offers it. Sooner or later union is followed by separation, and especially in this case: the *goal* of the therapist is to lose the patient. If, at the beginning of therapy, a time limit is set, the separation that is to come takes on a reality, a meaning it did not have before. The future comes into the present. The time of separation and the resulting problems—the fear of life—can be dealt with before they become insurmountable threats. The therapist can say "I can help you, but eventually I will not be around when you need me. I will be gone, and you will have no one but yourself. You must therefore build you own inner resources; you must become strong." If this instruction reminds you of what a mother might say to her child, remember that this is Otto Rank, who based his theory on the union (in the womb) and separation (at birth) of mother and child. Therapy is rebirth.

The Legacy of Dissent

There are theorists today who call themselves Rankian. There are also Jungians and Adlerians. Compared to the Freudians, their number is small (even though the strict Freudians themselves are a vanishing breed). But that does not mean that the influence of Rank, Jung, and Adler is not with us. Inferiority complex. Birth-order effects. Extraversion and introversion. These and other concepts live on. The ideas live on, in the ego psychologies of today, in the emphasis on social determinants of behavior, in the stress on goals rather than causes. Rank is reborn in Carl Rogers, whom we will meet later. Adler kicked social psychology in its foundation stone and got it moving. Jung's influence may be growing too, in an age that respects the study of *I Ching,* which Jung also studied in fascination.

One does not detract from the genius of Freud by saying that Adler, Jung, and Rank put forward necessary dissents. Freud told us that people are animals, and in psychology, it was perhaps the first time we had been told this in a way that made us understand and believe it. The dissenters reminded us that, however awe inspiring Freud's discovery, people are *people,* too. Animals, sure, but something more also. Even should a person fail in his or her strivings and remain only an animal, there is at least the *potential* there for a greatness that no other animal can achieve or even dream of. And some of us may achieve that greatness.

Self-actualization. The greatness *can be,* if we *will.* That's the story of this chapter, and the struggle for that greatness exists today as a complement to the struggles of the Freudian personality. Carl Rogers has espoused it; so have Maslow and Murray and Allport. It started here, with the "minor" geniuses who had the gift of sensing flaws, if not that of creating whole new systems.

It was the second beginning.

Chapter Summary

Table 3-1 may help you tie together the basic ideas of the three theorists we have talked about in this chapter. Like all such tables, it's an oversimplification. Take it with a grain of salt. The really important considerations are these: *Adler* introduced a social concern into personality theory and got us thinking about the effects of social relationships. *Jung* convinced us that people are spiritual as well as animal, and his ideas about balance raised new and important issues. *Rank* got us to turn our attention away from the skills of the therapist and toward the potential of the patient. All three theorists accentuated the positive, even if they did not entirely eliminate the negative. Overall, as a result of the work of these three men, we now look on the individual as more conscious and rational, more social and capable. The good in people—their creativity, their spirituality, their artistry—these are now all with us, and they are in no small part the legacy of Adler, Jung, and Rank.

Table 3-1.

	Adler	*Jung*	*Rank*
Drives (Innate)	Aggression Will to power Striving for superiority	Nonspecific psychic energy (life force)	Will Impulse (infantile will) Inhibition (negative will)
Other Innate Components	Social interest Cooperation	Archetypes (collective unconscious)	
Key Social Concepts	Family constellation	Attitudes of extraversion/introversion	Relationship, based on mother/child; cycles of union and separation
Positive Results	Creative self Style of life The cooperative type	The self Balance	The artist (free will)
Major Therapy Contribution	Social/environment emphasis	Interpretation of archetypal symbols	Time limit; philosophy of empathy rather than interpretation
Deviations	The coward, dictator, and parasite	Exaggeration or imbalance	The antisocial or asocial personality; the neurotic Impulse or inhibition (negative will) predominant

Suggested Readings

If you'd like to pursue the ideas discussed in this chapter, we would suggest the following books:

Ansbacher, H., and Ansbacher, R. (Eds.). *The Individual Psychology of Alfred Adler.* New York: Basic Books, 1956.

Jung, C.G. *The Collected Works of Carl G. Jung.* Princeton, N.J.: Princeton University Press, 1953– . Especially Vols. 7, 8, and 9.

Hall, C.S., and Lindzey, G. *Theories of Personality* (2nd ed.). New York: Wiley, 1970. Good for Jung and fair for Adler.

Karpf, F.B. *The Psychology and Psychotherapy of Otto Rank.* New York: Philosophical Library, 1953. A good place to start.

Munroe, R.L. *Schools of Psychoanalytic Thought.* New York: Dryden, 1955. Good for Jung and Rank and fair for Adler.

Notes and References

Our sources for the information in this chapter include many books that we have read over the years. *The Collected Works of Carl G. Jung* (Princeton, N.J.: Princeton University Press, 1953–) certainly serves as a major reference, especially Volumes 7, 8, and 9. Also important are Jung's "autobiography," *Memories, Dreams, Reflections* (New York: Pantheon, 1961) and *Conversations with Carl Jung* (New York: Van Nostrand, 1964), a series of dialogues with R.I. Evans.

Perhaps the single best collection of Adler's ideas is *The Individual Psychology of Alfred Adler,* edited by Heinz and Rowena Ansbacher (New York: Basic Books, 1956). Rank is best described by his own books, *The Trauma of Birth* and *Will Therapy,* both available in several types of reprints, and we found Fay B. Karpf's little summary, *The Psychology and Psychotherapy of Otto Rank* (New York: Philosophical Library, 1953), a very useful guide.

Secondary sources include Hall and Lindzey's *Theories of Personality* (New York: Wiley, 1970), which offers a very sympathetic treatment of Jung's approach; P. Bottome's biography, *Alfred Adler* (New York: Vanguard, 1957); and Ruth Munroe's masterful *Schools of Psychoanalytic Thought* (New York: Dryden, 1955), which is especially noteworthy for its comments on Jung and Rank.

E.V. Weigart wrote an important article about Adler and Jung in relationship to Freud: "Dissent in the Early History of Psychoanalysis," *Psychiatry,* 1942, *5,* 349–359. And anyone interested in the trivia of Jung's Nazi inclinations should read E. Harms' "Carl Gustav Jung—Defender of Freud and the Jews," *Psychoanalytic Quarterly,* 1946, *20,* 199–230.

J.F. Rychlak's *A Philosophy of Science for Personality Theory* (Boston: Houghton Mifflin, 1968) is a brilliant treatment of the philosophies and motives guiding personality theorists, including Freud. Freud is shown to have scholarly motivations, as opposed to the ethical drives that characterize Adler, Jung, and Rank. Eysenck's experimental work on Jung's extraversion/introversion dimension is documented in *Dimensions of Personality* (London: Routledge and Kegan Paul, 1947).

The Freudian view of dissent, along with much biographical material on the dissenters, is comprehensively discussed in Ernest Jones' *The Life and Work of Sigmund Freud* (New York: Basic Books, 1953–1957).

4

Evolution and Individual Differences

The art of statistical reporting is that of picking out plums!
Winston Churchill

The year was 1859. Charles Darwin stunned the world with an incredible theory of evolution put forth in his book *Origin of Species.* In the United States, however, people didn't hear much about the book. Their newspapers were full of accounts of events much closer to home: John Brown had attacked Harpers Ferry! Now there was no way to avoid it, this dreaded civil war!

No war has a single, pure and simple cause, but John Brown did: he believed that all human beings were equal, and he wanted to free the slaves. Equality. Isn't this the basic principle on which our nation was founded? Isn't it the teaching of the Good Book? Yes. And equality certainly is not an assumption any intelligent evolutionist would deny, if by equality we mean equality of *rights* or equality of *opportunity.* But it is ironic that John Brown was attacking Harpers Ferry in the name of equality at the same time that Darwin was asserting the basic principle of evolution: *all specimens are unequal.* Evolution through natural selection could not happen unless there were *individual differences* from which to naturally select. A fertile new field of inquiry for psychology was opened. The individual-differences approach.

The Size of Intellect: Measuring Intelligence

Francis Galton's "Mental Test"

Charles Darwin had a cousin named Francis Galton. He was a fascinating character whose greatest fault was an insatiable curiosity that prevented him from studying only one subject for any length of time. He was intrigued now by fingerprints, now by the geographical distribution of female beauty, until he finally reached his peak: he announced to a totally disinterested world that prayer was ineffective because he had been unable to control the weather with it. In a more serious enterprise, Galton tried to apply Darwin's principles to psychology, and, in 1869, he published a book called *Hereditary Genius.* In this book, he tried to show that genius runs in families and therefore can be considered inherited. If only the more intelligent members of the race are allowed to reproduce, he argued, the quality of the race would rapidly improve. He campaigned for a national program of *eugenics*—a term he coined—for the English, the people he wanted to improve first.

There was a glaring flaw in Galton's project, a flaw he was the first to recognize. There was no way to identify the truly gifted. There were, of course, a few people whose genius was publicly apparent and generally acknowledged, but just these few would be hard put to populate the entire island, and, besides, they were too busy with their music and their writing. So Galton decided to create a test of intellectual abilities that would screen candidates for reproduction in his utopian empire. The task took him almost 15 years, partly because he couldn't concentrate on one topic but mostly because nobody knew what such a test ought to be like. In 1883, he published his long-awaited "mental test"—the first of its kind.

It may well be the worst such test ever constructed. The test takers were asked to lift two weights and say which was heavier. They were also asked to demonstrate their ability to see well, to hear well, and to smell well. The logic of the test was not bad: ideation and intelligence come from sense experience—that is, ideas grow from sensations that reach the brain through the eyes, ears, and nose—and therefore those people with the best perceptual skills must be the most intelligent as well. Such an assumption was not inconsistent with the strongly empirical orientation of British philosophy at that time. But today the thought of generating a population of good seers, hearers, and sniffers in the hopes of improving the quality of the race is mind boggling.

Testing Individual Differences

The same year Galton published his mental test, a feisty young American named J. McKeen Cattell turned up on the doorstep of Wilhelm Wundt's laboratory in Leipzig, Germany. Wundt was an imposing figure, more interested in experimental psychology than in personality theory, and he had gained the title "Father of Scientific Psychology" when he established the first psychology laboratory some four years earlier. The story goes that Cattell brashly informed Wundt that the lab was sorely in need of a good assistant and that he, Cattell, was willing to sacrifice himself in order to take the job. Such audacity could not go unrewarded, and soon Cattell was puttering around the lab doing almost everything except assisting Wundt. He was interested mostly in individual differences in ability and did some classic experiments on reaction times. Finally Cattell returned to the United States and founded his own laboratory at the University of Pennsylvania. In 1891, he moved to Columbia University and began promoting mental tests as standardized estimates of "important" individual differences. Five years later, he published results from tests of incoming Columbia undergraduates, the first "entrance exams." He was a vigorous proponent of the study of individual differences and the use of mental tests. He was also a vigorous *opponent* of war, and pacifist sentiment was not well accepted by World-War-I society. In 1917, he was fired from Columbia (for his pacifism and for other reasons). It was, of course, the end of his academic career.

Cattell could have been the "father" of intelligence tests, but he was not. Like Galton, he relied too much on perceptual tasks—the eye, ear, and nose examinations, as they're sometimes called—and too little on the verbal/cultural tasks that are probably more accurate reflections of true "intelligence."

The First "Intelligence Test"

Enter our next hero: Alfred Binet. This dapper Frenchman was simply not interested in why or how fast a person punched a button after a signal light turned green. How people play chess—that was much more interesting. And, as Binet saw it, more scientifically valuable, because it involved higher mental processes. In 1904, the French Minister of Public Instruction was interested in finding a way to distinguish between students of low ability and students of high ability but low motivation. Binet created a mental test that resembled Galton's and Cattell's in form (a series of brief tasks) but that differed greatly in content. It was full of verbal material. Instead of lifting weights, distinguish between "tomorrow" and "yesterday." Instead of discriminating smells, show me where your nose is. The test was a huge success. From its inception through several revisions (the last in 1911, the year of Binet's death), Binet's became the test to beat. Binet became the true father of today's intelligence test as his brainchild began to be used outside France. In the United States, Lewis M. Terman at Stanford developed a translated and revised version and called it the Stanford-Binet; in only slightly modified form, the Stanford-Binet is still one of the two most commonly used individual tests of intelligence.

The Shape of Id: Measuring Personality

The Rorschach Test

While the mind testers were taking impressive steps toward understanding intelligence, other researchers were struggling to unlock the secrets of the id. Jung, for example, had done some research (before 1900) on the word-association test; he was especially interested by the idea that slow or confused responses might be clues to areas of personal conflict. In 1921, another Swiss psychiatrist, Hermann Rorschach, published a weird-looking collection of inkblots that he claimed were a test. Most psychologists, now well into the intelligence-test methods, had a good laugh and relegated poor Rorschach to the nutpile (which seemed to include a lot of Swiss, including Jung).

Rorschach was unconcerned with ridicule. His test was as much a test as any other—a standardized situation in which people are asked to respond to something they don't encounter in everyday life. He wanted an instrument that would aid in the diagnosis of mental patients, and psychoanalysis had suggested the answer. If the stimulus is ambiguous, as it is in the inkblots, the patient will *project* his or her own personality onto the stimulus; the patient has to supply the organization, for there is little in the blot. Some people will see an animal, some will see a snowflake, and others will complain about "all these dirty pictures." At the very least, said Rorschach, it can easily be demonstrated that responses to the blots vary considerably—there are marked individual differences—and we might do well to investigate the relationship of these variations to psychiatric difficulties. So Rorschach presented his test to already diagnosed patients and found that patients with different diagnoses saw different things in the inkblots. Other psychologists, notably those with psychoanalytic training, were intrigued and soon were using the test, but the emphasis shifted from psychiatric classification to an attempt to understand individual personality dynamics. Its popularity continued to grow until today the Rorschach inkblot test is probably the most widely used *projective test.*

The Rorschach test cannot claim to be the first real personality test, however, even if Jung's word-association test is disregarded. Such a claim would be difficult to establish for any test, since many of the early intelligence tests included items that now would be considered measurements of personality. Galton, for example, played around with some questionnaires that could be termed personality tests. And, if one includes the "interview," personality tests date back to the first time a father questioned his daughter's prospective fiancé about his moral character.

The Woodworth Personal Data Sheet

A more recent example of an attempt to measure personality, and a more significant one in the development of modern tests, was the Woodworth Personal Data Sheet. When the United States entered World War I, the Army asked psychologist Robert Woodworth to devise a simple test for screening out the mentally disturbed, and the Personal Data Sheet was the result. Woodworth first listed the symptoms that *might* indicate psychiatric disorder and then developed a questionnaire that asked the test takers to indicate whether they had such symptoms. The eager young patriot of that time came off the farm, stood in a long line to enlist, left his home on a train while the high school band played and the mayor spoke and his girlfriend cried—his parents were so proud!—only to enter a large room where they gave him a pencil and a questionnaire that asked him "Do you wet your bed?" and similar questions. Recruits who answered "yes" to such questions were given more complete examinations by Army psychiatrists. As naive as the questionnaire might seem today, it was better than nothing; individual examination of every soldier was out of the question.

The MMPI

Psychological tests have changed considerably since World War I, although we still might find questions like "Do you wet your bed?" Today's more sophisticated tests have ways of telling if you are lying, if you don't understand the items, if you don't care about your answer, or if you are deceiving yourself. Such a test is the MMPI—the Minnesota Multiphasic Personality Inventory—developed by Starke Hathaway and J. C. McKinley and published in 1942. The interesting thing about this inventory is the manner in which it was developed. The content of the items was not really too important; the goal was simply to gather a number of items (the MMPI is a true/false test, with an "undecided" category for those who refuse to answer a question) and administer the test to two groups, one "normal" and one "different." The "different" groups consisted of people who had received various psychiatric diagnoses: schizophrenic, paranoid, depressed, psychopathic, and so on. Each such group was compared with a normal group to see if the answers of the "diseased" subjects differed in any consistent way from those of the "normal" groups. If 90% of the schizophrenics answered "true" to item 367 and only 10% of the so-called normals did so, the item was retained and a "true" answer was scored as one point for the diagnosis "schizophrenia." Over the final list of 550 items, the MMPI gave scores for nine clinical categories. Later research has added a tenth category and a number of scales for detecting the cheaters, the inept, and other people not doing it right.

Test Methodology: Empirical versus Theoretical

The method of test construction used in developing the MMPI—the empirical method—is only one of two possible methods. The second—the theoretical method—proceeds in the opposite way. The content of the items is of utmost importance and typically is derived from a theory. For example, Sarnoff and Martha Mednick wanted to test creativity. Instead of finding one group of normal people and another of highly creative people and comparing their responses to test items (the MMPI method), they began by trying to decide what creativity is. In a somewhat oversimplified theory, they claimed that creativity was the ability to see unusual relationships. Now, how to construct a test from this theory? Their way was to develop test items that would be answered correctly by subjects who were able to see unusual relationships and incorrectly by subjects who were not. The result was the Remote Associates Test, or RAT, as it is more affectionately called. A typical item presents three words and asks for a response word that can be associated with all three. For example: *calm, southern, station.* The correct answer is *comfort.* To calm is to comfort; Southern Comfort is a brand-name alcoholic beverage; and a comfort station is a rest room.

When a test is constructed in this manner, the test designer still must offer evidence that the test measures what it's supposed to measure. In the case of the RAT, the test might be given to a group of "normals" and a group of "creatives," to show that their average scores are different (the designers hope that the creative group will score higher). But note the difference between the MMPI method (the *empirical* method), and the RAT method (the *theoretical* method). The first takes existing examples of what is being estimated, such as schizophrenia and "normality," notes differences in responses to certain items, and uses those items for the test. It may then proceed to an attempt to explain these differences in theoretical terms. The second method starts with items suggested by theory: these items comprise the test. The test makers *must* then proceed to provide evidence that the items really work—that different groups of people do respond to them in different ways.

The empirical method held sway for many years, but the theoretical method is becoming more and more common. In the early days of mental testing, the immediate interest was in tests to discriminate between groups, as we have seen. Low intelligence versus low motivation. Bad soldiers versus good soldiers. Sanity versus insanity. The empirical method is more effective in making such discriminations. It also fit well with the behavioristic bias that pervaded North American psychology from about 1910 to 1950, for it concerned itself little with theory and lots with simple, observable behaviors: checking these, rather than those, answers on a test form. Who cares *why* Jane Doe chose her answers? The test works; that's enough. But, over the years, somewhat decreasing needs for psychiatric diagnosis, suspicion about the assumptions and value of strict behaviorism, and the desire to have instruments that could be used to test important theoretical concepts all converged to increase the trend toward the theoretical method.

The Beginnings of Trait Theory

Obviously, many—perhaps most—personality tests can be used in either an empirical or a theoretical way. An empiricist looks at the test results and says "Because fat people score higher on this test than thin people do, the test must be measuring something related to the tendency to gain weight." The theoretician looks at the items on the test and says "These items all relate, in one way or another, to attitudes and feelings typical of the oral stage of psychosexual development. Therefore the test measures the degree of fixation at the oral stage." Both—or neither—may be right; the difference lies in the approach, the focus on either the instrument or the people being tested. The empiricist starts with *people's responses* and infers what is being measured from these response patterns. The theoretician starts with the *questions being asked* and infers what is being measured from these question patterns.

In either case, there is inference. The tester inevitably draws conclusions from the actual data about what is important to know in order to understand behavior. And these conclusions group behaviors or feelings in a general way; they say "These things tend to work together" or "If a person does this, then he or she is likely also to do that." Such groupings are called *traits*—relatively broad categories of behavior, presumably influencing lots of specific activities and presumably remaining rather stable over time. We use the trait notion all the time in everyday speech: she's shy; he has a terrible temper; she's very bright; he has great willpower.

The point here is that *tests tend to measure traits.* Using a test to measure intelligence, assertiveness, or willpower implies that we believe that such things really exist. This assumption is so pervasive and so subtle in our test-taking culture that it is seldom challenged. We won't challenge it in this chapter—quite the contrary! We'll go along with it, to see just how far it can take us toward our goal of understanding, predicting, and/or controlling behavior. But you should be aware that the assumption can be and has been challenged—that the trait approach is not the only possible path to knowledge of human behavior.

One of the first questions to ask, once we decide to pursue the trait idea, is "How many traits are there?" How can we tell which personal characteristics or qualities are traits and which are not?

One way to answer is to make the simple assumption that, if a quality or attribute of personality can be used as an adjective, then it is a trait. Peter is an *anxious* man. Sarah is a *dominant* woman. If the adjective is important enough to be used for description, it will be in the dictionary. All we have to do is go through an unabridged dictionary and pick out all the words that might possibly be used to describe a person. There are approximately 18,000 such terms. (Yes, indeed—two dedicated scientists, Allport and Odbert, actually performed this eyesight-destroying task!)[1] Of the 18,000 terms, however, many can be eliminated on the grounds that they do not represent attributes of an individual; instead, they describe activities or temporary states (for example, running) and the like. The remaining terms number around 4500. Let us say, then, that there are 4500 words in the English language that describe more or less permanent characteristics of an individual's personality. Only 4500 traits! All we need are 4500 good tests!

Clearly, something had to be done at this point. People have trouble holding 10 independent characteristics in mind at one time, let alone 4500. Fortunately (or unfortunately, depending upon your point of view), mathematics was able to come to the rescue. Mathematics provides a technique for combining those thousands of traits and boiling them down to a much more manageable number. In order to understand something about that process, we are going to have to grit our teeth and wade into a topic that some people find quite frightening. That topic is statistics.

Statistics

Or "sadistics." Some of us called it that. We were the ones who went through statistics courses hating every minute and learning as little as possible. Others—we could never quite understand why—seemed actually to enjoy manipulating those numbers. They loved the clarity of a problem that had only one right answer, and some of them even had computers for friends.

Like it or not, though, the study of statistics seems to be here to stay. Some questions *do* have only one right answer, and that can't be changed, even by majority rule. The ratio of a circle's circumference to its diameter, for instance, is always the same. This ratio is called pi, and it turns out to be a very awkward number indeed: 3.14 (rounded off to two places) or 3.1416 (rounded off to four places). It never comes out even, no matter how many decimal places you carry it out to. In 1897, about the time Freud was working out his theory of dreams, a well-intentioned politician introduced a bill in the Indiana state legislature to set the exact value of pi once and for all (no exact number was suggested). But whoever was responsible for referring bills for committee

[1]The Allport-Odbert collection of trait names can be found in *Psychological Monographs,* 1936, *47* (whole no. 211).

study must have been not only perceptive but also rather prankish. The bill was given to the Committee on Swamp Lands. They apparently noticed the "error" and gave it to the Education Committee, from whence it was delivered to the full house of representatives with a recommendation for approval. It was passed without a single dissenting vote! On to the state senate for final approval, where it was referred to the Committee on Temperance, another magnificent choice. Concerned scholars, unfortunately, had by this time heard of the bill and quietly told the senators that an exact determination of pi, however desirable, could not be accomplished by the geometric tricks proposed in the bill. The bill never came to a vote in the senate. Legalized pi was dead.[2]

Many statistical procedures are still evolving. New techniques are created every day. They won't determine pi, but they can do a surprising number of other things. They will be influenced by theory, of course, and they will in turn influence later theories, just as the statistics of mental and personality testing have facilitated (and been facilitated by) the trait approach.

The Correlation Coefficient

The man who thought he created the correlation coefficient was one Carl Spearman. As a young student in the late 1800s, Spearman had found academic philosophy courses sterile and frustrating. He was a philosopher at heart, however, so he decided to take up "practical philosophy," which he felt could best be pursued by making a career out of military service. (Times, they are a-changing!) After several fruitless years, Spearman returned to the academic life and began his psychological studies. In 1901, we find him in a small English school looking at the abilities "commonly taken to be intellectual" among the students. To his great surprise (it was an era of belief in specialized intelligence, rather than in one "general" intelligence), he discovered that students who did well in one subject exhibited a strong tendency to do well in others also. Spearman sensed that he was on to something, a factor of general intelligence. But how could it be studied and demonstrated?

The first step was to create a measure that would demonstrate statistically what he had already surmised—that, if you did well at task *A*, you also did well at task *B*. A measure of relatedness was needed, and Spearman developed the *correlation coefficient.* Two perfectly related things would be assigned a coefficient value of 1.00; two totally unrelated things would receive the value 0.00; and two partially related things could range from 0.01 to 0.99. Obviously, the higher the coefficient value, the higher the degree of relatedness. In addition, the relatedness can be positive (+)—as one thing increases, so does the other, such as a baseball player's batting average and his salary—or negative (–)—as one variable decreases, the other increases, such as a pitcher's earned-run average and his salary.

Once Spearman had finished work on his correlation coefficient, he was ready to present his great discovery to the world. Unfortunately

[2]The story of pi is taken from M. H. Greenblatt's account in *American Scientist,* 1965, *53,* 427A–432A.

for him, Galton and one of Galton's students, Karl Pearson, had already done so several years before. Communication of results was not then what it is now, and Spearman was not what you would call "up" on the latest reports.

So Spearman went back to his correlation studies of intelligence. In 1904, he published a paper on general intelligence proposing what has been called *the theory of two factors.* In every task, said Spearman, there are two factors determining skill. One factor is very specific to the task itself (*s* for specific), and the other is general intelligence (*g* for general). We all have lots of *s* factors, one for every kind of task, but only one *g* factor. Remember that the idea of a general intelligence was very controversial. Spearman not only claimed that a general factor existed (indicated by positive correlations among tasks) but also suggested ways to estimate the degree to which an individual possessed that factor. One of the easiest ways, he claimed, was simply to take an average of all the tasks; the specific factors could be high or low, and therefore they would cancel each other out over many tasks. Nowadays, students are so accustomed to such averages (such as the grade-point average) and their use as an indication of general intelligence or ability that it is strange to realize that such measures came into being only recently.

Alfred Binet's intelligence test, published in 1905, used an average score over many little tests to measure a student's general level of intelligence. With the success of Binet's test, the success of Spearman's concept of general intelligence was similarly guaranteed.

The unfortunate Spearman did not get the credit for developing the correlation coefficient, but his use of correlations in his search for the general factor of intelligence led him to another, more complex procedure for which he did get the credit—and rightly so. That procedure is called *factor analysis.*

The Search for a General Factor

In his correlation studies, Spearman found a positive relationship between a student's ability in one subject and his or her ability in others. As we have seen, he argued that this relationship was evidence of two factors in any intelligence task, one general (*g*) and the other specific (*s*). There are as many specific factors as there are tasks, but there is only one general factor, consistent across all tasks. Since specific factors, as he defined them, were uncorrelated across tasks, positive correlations "proved" the general factor. There was no question that Spearman had demonstrated some kind of factor common to the positively correlated tests; there is no way to get a consistent correlation of above 0.00 unless something affecting performance in one test also influences performance in the other. Similarly, since the correlations were not perfect (not 1.00), there must be factors *not* in common: that's the only way you can get a coefficient much less than 1.00. A correlation above 0.00, therefore, always indicates at least two factors (three, really—one common to the two things being correlated and two specific factors, one for each task).

What these factors *are,* of course, is a different question. The common factor may be trivial; a correlation between two paper-and-pencil tests might indicate nothing more than a common factor of "ability to write," not necessarily anything so lofty as general intelligence. Or it might be that both tests were taken in overheated rooms, and some students respond poorly to high temperatures. They therefore do poorly in both tests, producing a positive correlation.

So how could Spearman find out what the common factor was? The answer was simple enough. Look at more tests or tasks. Suppose two tests are given, both in hot rooms, and they correlate +.60. Intelligence level or prickly heat? Give another test at normal temperature. If general intelligence is at work, the first two tests will correlate around +.60 with the third one; if temperature disability was the *only* common factor between the first two, the third will not be correlated (0.00) with the others.

Now consider another possibility. Suppose the first two tests correlated +.60 with each other but only +.30 with the third. What does this suggest? That not one but *two* common factors are present. Maybe one is general intelligence, which would produce a correlation of around +.30 between any two intellectual tests; maybe the second is temperature disability that is shared by the two "hot" tests, doubling that correlation, but not by the third or normal test. Interpreting (naming) the factor is always difficult, and it can be done confidently only by looking at more and more tests, of widely varied types, taken under different conditions, and so on.

Now a note of caution about the danger of oversimplification. It is clear enough that a score on an intelligence test is affected by millions of things—everything from general intelligence to hard spots on your pencil lead. Many of these influences are so minor and/or so fleeting that they are impossible to control and would not be worth the time and expense even if control were possible. Psychometricians—people who specialize in measuring psychological characteristics—tend to lump most of these influences into a category they call "error" (meaning lack of knowledge), and they call that error "random" (meaning that, eventually, the truth will be known, because random errors are here today, gone tomorrow). In practice, this means simply that correlations between the same two tests will vary from day to day, often considerably. Tuesday's correlation might be +.53, Wednesday's +.79, and Thursday's +.42. Wednesday's testing must have had a larger collection of transient common factors (maybe it was very hot Wednesday). But never fear. Statisticians have some very neat procedures for estimating error, and such variations, in the long run, can be easily handled.

Factor Analysis

Factor analysis is a procedure for taking the correlations between tests and finding the important factors. There are three kinds of factors: *general* (common to all tests, such as general intelligence), *group* (common to not all but to a sizable grouping of tests, as our temperature-disability example was common to hot tests but not to all), and *specific or unique* (found on only one test). Then there are the "errors" (error factors), which are unique and thus turn up only now and then even in the same test. If 200 people took a test, and then took the exact same test a week later, you might predict that the correlation would be 1.00, since all general, group, and specific factors are identical. However, something may have changed during the week, and maybe that change influences performance: four students had the flu a week ago and gave it to seven others who have it now; last week was final-exam week; this week's test giver has bad breath; the coffee machine broke down; a bird is chirping outside. These factors all can produce variations in an individual's score and variations in the correlation coefficient. We cannot take every little thing into account; the best we can do is to keep the conditions of test taking as similar as possible.

Once Spearman had developed the basic statistical procedures, he put factor analysis to use in his search for *g*. Sure enough, *g* turned up consistently—*g* and all the little *s*'s. The evidence was quite impressive, especially to those psychologists who didn't understand the mathematics involved. However, there was a young American named L. L. Thurstone who did understand those mathematics. He knew that Spearman's mathematics were *designed* to pick up general factors; Spearman's factor analysis *assumed* a general factor and had great power to highlight it. Maybe too much power. Maybe it created a general factor when there was none.

About the time Spearman was presenting his theory of two factors in intelligence, Thurstone had his first scientific publication: a plan for preserving the beauty of Niagara Falls, which was threatened by the ecology-destroying hydroelectric companies. After earning a degree in mechanical engineering, Thurstone worked with Thomas Edison and then returned to the University of Chicago to study psychology. He had gotten interested in the mathematics of learning. "I recall one of my first impressions of graduate students," he wrote later. "When they were asked a question, they would start talking fluently, even when they obviously knew nothing about the subject." The scorn of an engineer-mathematician! His memory of the first year is dominated by his learning how to carry five soup plates at once (he worked as a waiter). But, if Thurstone doubted the substance of his peers, they thought he was somewhat odd as well. He was studying Indian ragas (melodies) for a master's thesis; he was interested in "pitch excursions." In 1915, before he got his Ph.D., he was hired by Carnegie Tech for a new department focused on applied psychology, and one of the main reasons he was hired was because the department head shared his interest in Indian ragas!

Multiple Factor Analysis

In his new role as applied psychologist, Thurstone plunged headlong into tests and test procedures. Numbers, scores, averages, correlations—it was a perfect home for the creative mathematician. With World War I, interest in test construction increased, Thurstone was on his way. It was natural to concentrate on intelligence tests, and he did. Among other diversions, he used his mathematical prowess to figure out the nature of the relationship between intelligence and age, and extrapolate that relationship back to the point of "zero" intelligence (indicated by zero variability), which, he concluded, represented the beginnings of intelligent thinking in the human—several months before birth. The findings were not what one would call "universally accepted"; many psychologists, remembering Galton's study of the effectiveness of prayer, simply took the research as another example of the "mathematical personality." But Thurstone was unconcerned.

He was concerned with intelligence, however, and with intelligence tests and factors and factor analysis and Spearman's theory of two factors, as any good applied psychologist would be. There was a difference between his views and Spearman's, and it was this: Spearman would look at correlations and ask whether or not they supported his notion of a general-intelligence factor, whereas Thurstone looked at the same correlations and asked, simply, how many factors were necessary to account for these data. The seemingly trivial difference in how the question was asked made for a large discrepancy in how the question was answered. Thurstone was seeking group factors, not general factors, although, if a general factor did exist, it would show up. He called his method *multiple factor analysis,* and technically (but not spiritually) he was the father of modern factor analysis. His method was eventually accepted over Spearman's.

Orexis Unbound: The Structure of Personality

Spearman was interested in intelligence or, to put it in broader terms, in cognitive activities. "Feelings and strivings," which he called *orexis* (after Aristotle) and which we might call emotion and motivation, were recognized as important aspects of human behavior but "logically posterior" (which translates roughly as "only an ass would study them first"). But soon a doctoral student by the name of Webb came to him and asked if he might make "oretic" processes the topic of his dissertation. Spearman gave the OK; he wanted to see how his new mathematical technique, factor analysis, worked on a new field (the desire of all true mathematicians). Webb obtained ratings on the emotionality and activity of a number of people, correlated the ratings, and factor-analyzed the results. Spearman's method, which was designed to accent general factors, turned up a new one in this new field; it was *will (w).* It looked very much like a general personality factor of self-control. Orexis unbound, the debate began, and it followed lines very similar to the debate in the area of intelligence. Was there a general factor in personality? Were there major group factors? How many factors were there in all? Even the result of the debate was the same, with most scholars accepting in essence a hierarchical organization of personality. An example of this view is contained in Figure 4-1. This pictorial view is particularly instructive—forget for the moment the question of whether the arrangement is true or false.

It describes a view of personality and behavior that pervades all approaches to personality today, at least in its use of four levels of organization: the *type,* the *trait,* the *habit* (habitual response), and the *specific response.* Types are very broad personality classifications, such as "feminine" or "introvert." Traits we have already met. Habits, as in ordinary English, are defined as groups of responses typically made in some general kind of situation. And specific responses are single responses that are made only and specifically in one particular situation. There is and always has been considerable debate as to what level is best for study. Many personality theorists (perhaps the majority) favor the trait level. In theory, the trait level should be broad enough to be worthy of intensive study but narrow enough to be of use. But there is a large and vocal minority who feel that traits are still too general for any significant use; habits and even specific responses must be studied in order for a theory to have any real use for predicting or controlling behavior, especially when applied to an individual. And others believe that the most parsimonious theory—that is, the one requiring the fewest explanatory factors—is the most promising one. They are interested in major types. We will see more of this controversy.

What we must recognize now is that the particular *kind* of factor analysis we use will play a large part in determining whether we end up focusing on lots of relatively narrow traits or on a few very broad ones. Some researchers go one way, some another. We're going to take a closer look at two theorists who have made opposite choices. It is appropriate that we turn our attention first to the man who, more than any other, is associated with factor-analytic theory.

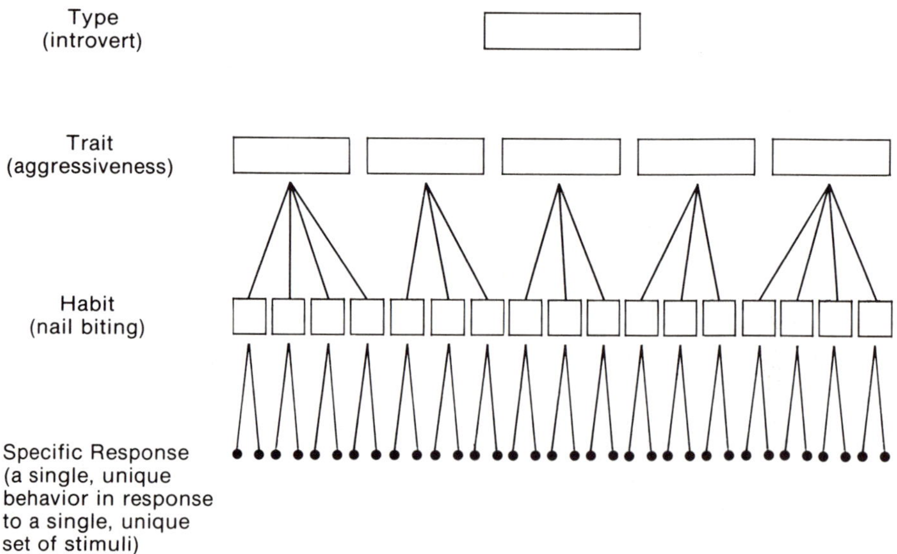

Figure 4-1. Eysenck's four levels of personality: types, traits, habits, and specific responses. (From *Dimensions of Personality,* by H. J. Eysenck. Copyright 1947 by Routledge & Kegan Paul, Ltd., London. Reprinted by permission.)

Raymond B. Cattell, Mr. Factor Analysis

If there is a Mr. Factor Analysis in any meaningful sense, he is Raymond B. Cattell. Prior to the publication in 1966 of a handbook on the use of factor analysis in experimental psychology, one reviewer made the comment "It's loaded with Cattell's work. Over 25% of the book is pure Cattell. But that's O.K. because Cattell has done over 25% of the work in the field." Born in England in 1905, Raymond B. Cattell earned his Ph.D. from the University of London in 1929, working with both Spearman and Cyril Burt, another pioneer in the mathematics of psychology. In 1937, he came to the United States, eventually moving to the University of Illinois (1944), where he set up an empire from whence he issued periodic reports for three decades. By 1964, the unofficial count had him down for 22 books, a number of tests, and well over 200 articles. The years after 1964 have shown no slackening of output.

Clearly, if one does this much, one has very little free time to do things that might be interesting in a biographical sketch. Anecdotes about Cattell all concern work or work-related matters. For example, one young graduate student who worked with Cattell told of his first meeting with the man. As Cattell was showing him around his laboratory, the two of them came upon a table with copies of all Cattell's books. The student picked up a copy of one and expressed interest. Cattell asked, smiling, if he would like a copy. The student answered quickly "Of course, of course!" "That'll be $7.95," replied Cattell. We have no way of knowing if this story is true, but it fits the image Cattell has generated. Scientific, hard-working, orderly, and make sure that students stay on their toes.

People who have tried to read Cattell's books know him as an important figure in psychology and also as one who writes in an impenetrable style that makes one think he is desperately trying to get every fact in print before he meets an untimely death. In his books, he spends very little time with trivia (such as whatever possessed him to study a given problem), quickly focusing instead on the facts. A polite hello, then the measurements and their analysis, and down to business: what are the building blocks of personality? That is Cattell's quest, and everything else pales to insignificance. And so the reports, the articles, the books continue to emerge, and the reader is first overwhelmed and then numbed by the flood of information.

Source Traits

All personality theorists, whether they will admit it or not, are in some sense ultimately trying to devise a system that will allow them to predict and possibly control human behavior. Cattell is no exception—au contraire! The prediction and control of behavior is his explicit and proud goal. But Cattell was not satisfied with a theory that merely "works." After all, the theories built on the notion that the sun revolves around the earth "worked" very well in explaining astronomical events. They just didn't happen to be *right;* they didn't square with reality. Many psychological theories, Cattell believed, are the same. Cattell wanted to get the facts, to discover what personality *is,* not how it seems to be or what it's analogous to.

Factor analysis led Cattell to believe that about 15 or 16 basic traits account for all of the variability covered by the thousands of adjectives that can be used to describe people. These traits are, then, the *source* of all that variability, of all the richness of everyday human interactions. Let's call them *source traits.* But what do we do with these source traits once we've identified them?

For a thoroughgoing scientist like Cattell, the answer is obvious: the first step is to nail them down, define them precisely, and measure them objectively. Factor analysis should be the ideal tool for this task, because, in the process of extracting the source traits from the welter of descriptive adjectives, factor analysis also specifies which adjectives contribute to each trait and how strongly each one contributes. For example, there is a source trait called ego strength. It comes from ratings of people by other people. If I rate you as emotionally stable, realistic about life, steadfast, calm, thorough, and dependable, you will get a high score on ego strength. If I rate you as emotional, dissatisfied, hypochondriacal, evasive, and careless, you will get a low score. In other words, these "people-descriptions" tend to go together—they are highly correlated—so that, if I say you are calm, I am also likely to say you are stable. And I'm not likely to see you as dissatisfied or careless. To measure your ego strength, I can have people rate your calmness, your emotional stability, and so on and add up those ratings. Once I have scores for all of the clusters of adjectives or characteristics that make up the various source traits, I will have a *profile* (a numerical picture) that will tell me what kind of person you are.

The 16 P-F Questionnaire

Cattell devised a psychological test that did exactly what we've described, with one small difference: instead of asking other people to rate the individual whose profile is being prepared, that individual is asked to rate himself or herself. Cattell assumed, as most of us would, that the source traits identified by *self-ratings* would be the same as those identified by other people's ratings. After all, what difference does it make if I'm describing *your* behavior or *my* behavior? Won't I use the same words? Approximately? The answer seems to be yes. The statistical matching of factors from two different types of data (ratings by others and self-ratings) presents some mathematical questions, and there is a lot of controversy about it, but most studies do suggest that the primary factors in self-ratings are the same as those in ratings by others.

The end product of all this work is one of the best known of all personality tests: the 16 P-F Questionnaire (16 *P*ersonality *F*actors). The factors measured on the 16 P-F are shown in Table 4-1. As you can see, each factor is a dichotomy—that is, each represents an either/or kind of quality. You've got to be one or the other; you can't be both. Nobody is both reserved and outgoing or both trusting and suspicious. But you can be *extremely* reserved, or *extremely* outgoing, or somewhere in the middle between the two extremes. That's what the numerical score for each factor tells you: not just which category someone falls into but also how strongly his or her personality is "tuned" in that direction. And the total profile is thought to describe the whole personality. Completely.

Table 4-1. One dozen personality factors found in both Q data and L data; also 12 of the 16 Personality Factors in the 16 P-F Questionnaire.

Factor Label	*Low Score*	*Versus*	*High Score*
A	Reserved		Outgoing
B	Dumb		Smart
C	Emotional		Stable
E	Submissive		Dominant
F	Sober		Happy-go-lucky
G	Expedient		Conscientious
H	Shy		Venturesome
I	Tough-minded		Tender-minded
L	Trusting		Suspicious
M	Practical		Imaginative
N	Naive		Shrewd
O	Assured		Guilt-prone

Here are the other 4 in the 16 P-F. They are Q-data factors but could not be matched to L-data factors.

		Versus	
Q1	Conservative		Radical
Q2	Conforming		Self-sufficient
Q3	Casual		Controlled
Q4	Relaxed		Tense

This table was adapted from R. B. Cattell's *The Scientific Analysis of Personality,* p. 365; the names of factors in some cases have been changed.

Now Cattell, being nobody's fool, was aware of one major flaw, or possible flaw, in this method of describing the personality. Whether someone describes himself or herself on a questionnaire (*Q* data) or is rated by an observer (Cattell calls this *L* data, for *L*ife observation), what we end up with is opinions. *Q* data come from your opinions about you, while *L* data come from somebody else's opinions about you. And opinions aren't necessarily true; the rater might be misinformed, biased, or even a downright liar. Wouldn't it be fine if we could get facts instead of opinions? If we could measure how people really *are* on these important characteristics? Cattell thought so, and he set about building *objective* tests to measure how people actually are on various dimensions—tests that should really tell us what people are like.

Maybe.

The sad truth seemed to be that the source traits that emerge from *T* (for objective *T*est) data don't look anything like the *Q*- and *L*-data source traits.

This kind of setback might have caused some people to give up in despair. Not Cattell! He simply worked harder. Technical papers on procedure. Proposals for the standardization of procedures and results. Periodic reports on the most commonly found (and replicated) factors from each kind of data. Considerable thought about the ways in which these factors could be related to other theoretical constructs and about the very goals of factor analysis—the ways in which it can handle the genuine issues of personality theory. Cattell was persistent, and, for that quality alone, he came to be a powerful figure in psychology.

Second-Order Traits

He also solved the problem, at least partially. He found that the basic source traits do appear both in *Q* and *L* data and in *T* data, but they're grouped differently. One *T*-data trait, for example, may correlate with *two L*-data traits or vice versa. And a *primary* source trait in *T* data may match a *second-order* trait in other data.

But what is a "second-order trait"? Technically, a second-order factor comes from the factor analysis of *factors*. Think of it this way: if we took a number of measures from the body, intercorrelated them, and factor-analyzed them, we might extract several main factors as basic descriptors of the body—height, weight, blood pressure, and the like. But height and weight are themselves correlated; a tall person usually weighs more than a short one. Correlation suggests something in common, and that is the definition of a factor. The *primary* factors are height and weight, but you can go a step further and extract the *secondary* factor—what do height and weight have in common? Do you want to call it . . . size? Whatever.

If we factor-analyze the source traits that emerge from *Q* and *L* data, we come up with some second-order factors. Similarly, we can get second-order factors from factor-analyzing the source traits from *T* data. And there do seem to be important matches between some of the second-order factors of the *T* data and the primary source traits of *Q* and *L* data and, similarly, between the second-order *Q* and *L* factors and the primary source traits of *T* data. But why? Why should we have to play such complicated mathematical games to get the different sets of data to agree?

Another way of asking that question is to ask how *Q* and *L* data are similar to each other and different from *T* data. First, as we mentioned earlier, *Q* and *L* rest on opinions rather than on objective measurement. They are also more dependent on language than *T* is. And they tend to be assessments of average behavior over some period of time, whereas *T* data reflect what is, here and now. All of these differences, and perhaps some others as well, may contribute to the mismatches among *L, Q,* and *T* source traits.

Cattell and his co-workers have begun to bring some order out of this confusion. The notion of primary traits and second-order traits helps a lot. But there's still a long way to go, and in the meantime how do we decide which factors from which analysis represent the *real* basic dimensions of personality? Cattell said in 1957

> A . . . new world of personality structure . . . has become visible. . . . On the foundation of measurable functions, the psychology of the second half of the twentieth century may proceed to build its laws and theories of personality, as the first half did on the cloudy shapes glimpsed by the superbly perceptive eye of Freud.[3]

[3]From R. B. Cattell's *Personality and Motivation Structure and Measurement,* Harcourt, Brace & World, 1957, p. 281.

That vision of an orderly world is still only a vision. We just aren't there yet.

There are some psychologists, in fact, who say that we will never get there. That Cattell's 15 or 16 basic dimensions of personality are illusions, wishful thinking, a case of building into the data what we want to believe is there. It is an uncomfortable truth that factor analysis doesn't always yield consistent answers to a given problem. Depending on who sets up the analysis, and what method of factor analysis that person subscribes to, the result may be a few factors, or lots of factors, or a constant number of factors that are based on different groups of characteristics.

Hans Eysenck, who was a fellow student of Cattell's under Cyril Burt, decided that the best way out of this dilemma was to shoot for the smallest number of basic factors or traits that would still describe the personality. Let's travel back from Urbana, Illinois (the kingdom of Raymond Cattell), to Maudsley University in London and see how Eysenck's strategy has worked.

Hans Eysenck, the Bridge Builder

Hans J. Eysenck, the theorist/evangelist. Not content with publishing books and articles for the edification of his colleagues and textbooks for the edification of his students, he has written numerous "popular" books for the edification of the general public. For Eysenck, the issues of psychology in general, and of the structure of personality in particular, are of burning interest, even though his first intellectual love and career choice was physics. In Eysenck's office hang two pictures: one of Ivan Pavlov, the other of Sir Francis Galton. Eysenck has spent the better part of his career building bridges between these two giants, from the mathematical, descriptive Galton to the behavioristic, experimentally oriented Pavlov. To no small degree, he has succeeded. In his work Eysenck has successfully combined the strengths of learning theory with personality theory, of mathematical theorizing with experimental observation. Let's see if we can distill out some of what he has to tell us.

For Eysenck, the first principle of scientific research and discovery is parsimony. "Don't use two where one will do" or "Get the most possible from the least possible" could easily be his motto. Not for Eysenck the laborious listing of 4500 distinct traits. His goal is to explain (predict) as much of the detail of human behavior as possible using the fewest possible concepts. Factor analysis is a useful tool in the initial extraction of these basic concepts, but it is only a tool and should be left behind (in favor of enlightened experimentation) as quickly as possible. Moreover, factor analysis should be used to confirm or disconfirm theoretically based hunches, rather than to generate theory all by itself. First comes the theory, says Eysenck, then the mathematical check to see if the theory fits the data, and then the empirical testing of the implications of that (mathematically checked-out) theory in the real world of human interactions.

The Four Humors

Eysenck begins most of his discussions of the dimensions of personality by pointing out the threads of consistency that run through much of the literature in this area for hundreds of years. Galen, who died around 200 A.D., proposed that people fell into one of four personality categories—melancholic, choleric, phlegmatic, and sanguine—depending on the relative proportions of certain fluids in their blood. This typology was adopted by Kant, in the 1700s, and by Wundt, the first true experimental psychologist, in the mid-1800s. Looking at the kinds of people who typically fall into these categories, says Eysenck, there seem to be two major dimensions involved. "Choleric" and "melancholic" people appear to be highly emotional and "short fused" and less stable than "sanguine" and "phlegmatic" folks. "Choleric" and "sanguine" people are extraverted and outgoing, while "melancholic" and "phlegmatic" individuals tend to be introverted or withdrawn. We can show these relationships diagrammatically, as in Figure 4-2; here Eysenck has added a set of trait adjectives to give a better notion, in nontechnical terms, of the personality characteristics associated with the various types and dimensions.

Emotionality and Introversion/Extraversion

Eysenck's message is that "his" two dimensions, emotionality (stability or neuroticism) and extraversion/introversion, account for an enormous amount of the personality diversity that we see among people. They are not the only dimensions of personality, but they are certainly the most important. Eysenck believes that a third basic dimension of personality, "psychoticism," may be necessary to account for some kinds of extremely abnormal behavior. Because this dimension is of only minor importance in differentiating among "normal" personalities, it will not be included in the present discussion.

But where did these two dimensions come from? Why did Eysenck begin looking for them in the first place? According to his own accounts, they have been around for quite a while. Not as long as Galen's four types, to be sure, but they have been exciting the interest and imagination of psychologists for at least 50 years (and, as personality theory goes, that's a long time). In the 1920s, when psychological test making was just beginning to hit its stride, lots of tests for "neuroticism" were kicking around. As we mentioned earlier, the whole problem of screening potential soldiers for service in World War I focused attention on how to identify potential neurotics quickly and accurately. Also, around that same time, people began to take an interest in what that strange Swiss fellow Jung was saying about introverts and extraverts; it was only natural that tests for introversion/extraversion would begin to appear on the scene. We should recognize, of course, that the notion of introversion (defined and described in various ways) had been around for some 200 years, and it's quite impossible to trace back to the time when scholars, philosophers, and doctors first characterized people as "emotional" or "unstable." Rather, the 1920s saw the happy conjoining of ongoing, taken-for-

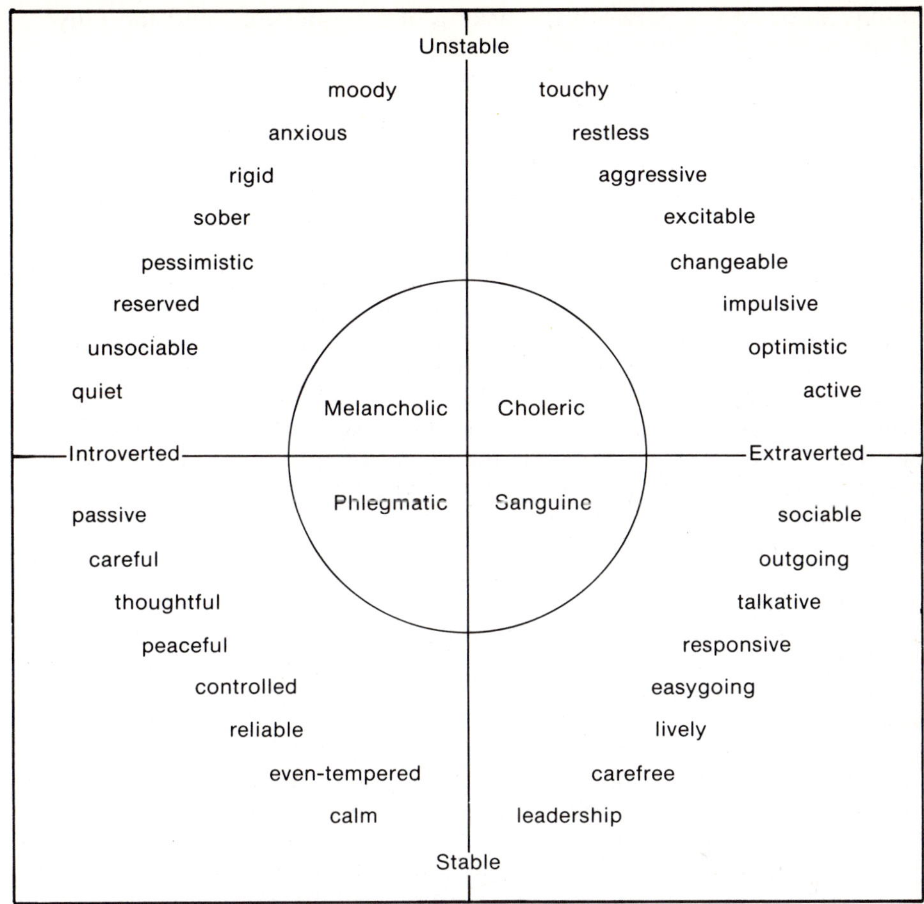

Figure 4–2. Personality in two dimensions: varying the combinations of strengths of the four traits yields a wide range of descriptions.

granted ideas with a new theoretical impetus (Jung's) and with a new scientific tool (the psychological test).

So tests were built and used, data accumulated, business was good, and everybody was happy. Everybody except . . . in this case, it was a few critics who made everyone uncomfortable by pointing out (". . . but the Emperor has no clothes on!") that all of those tests that were supposed to be measuring the same thing didn't agree with each other. Now, if Joe Smith and Sara Stokes each take two tests of "neuroticism," and Joe scores very high on the first and very low on the second, while Sara scores very low on the first and very high on the second, there is certainly reason to suppose that something may be very wrong somewhere. Gradually, reluctantly, kicking and screaming all the way, the test-makers were forced to agree that something was indeed wrong. The tests, though theoretically sound, simply didn't measure what they were supposed to be measuring. They should be (they asked all the right questions), but they didn't. Somewhere, between the asking of the questions and the tallying of the scores, something was haywire.

One answer, of course, was that people who take tests don't always answer the questions truthfully. There are dozens of reasons why anyone might not want to admit having some thought or habit or fear or desire; and it's not unreasonable to assume that highly emotional or unstable people might have even more reason to be less than honest (with the test-giver, or even with themselves). The questions on the tests were indeed right, but some of the answers were wrong. Not all—just some—and there was no way to tell which were which. Time to back up and start over. We can't assume that the answers given on a test are "true." But that doesn't mean that the dimensions we are trying to measure are wrong. They exist. So let's sort people on the basis of how they fall on those dimensions. We can use expert and intuitive judgments for that, evaluations based on long hours of interactions with the individuals being evaluated, and then ask each of them lots of questions and see if any pattern emerges. That is, forget about whether the answers are "true" and concentrate on finding questions that discriminate among the various groups we have identified.

Thus we meet again the *empirical* method of test construction. As we already know, it spawned myriad tests. It was now possible to construct a test for every dimension on which people could be sorted. No theory needed! Instant measurement! Suddenly we had tests for every possible personality characteristic imaginable and a few that were virtually unimaginable.

Eysenck, however, was not to be diverted. He had started out to look at the two dimensions that kept popping up through the history of psychology with too much persistence to be ignored, and he was going to use this new method to continue to investigate these two dimensions. And investigate them he has, to the tune of more than 30 books and an enormous number of articles. (What is there about factor-analytic theorists that makes them so prolific? Is this a basic personality trait?) Having asked thousands of questions of thousands of research subjects and having run the answers to those questions through a variety of complicated mathematical analyses (one of which, of course, is our old friend factor analysis), Eysenck remains convinced that introversion/extraversion and emotionality/nonemotionality account for the great majority of individual personality differences. The mathematical tool has, for him, proven the theoretical belief.

Eysenck's Two Factors and Behavior

Eysenck continues to explore the implications of his two-factor theory for other aspects of psychology. People are different from each other, his argument runs. Because they are different, they behave in different ways. They respond to a given situation in different ways. But experimental psychology has been reluctant to recognize these differences. The experimental psychologist typically looks at people *qua* people, assigning them randomly to some set of experimental conditions and attempting to predict how they will respond. "Wrong!" says Eysenck. If introverts respond one way and extraverts another, then lumping them together will make it look as if there's no consistent response at all. Suppose one is interested in determining, for instance, what happens to a fact or an idea—a learned item of information—during the first few minutes or hours after it has been committed to memory. That is, does one remember it better after a while (memory consolidation), or does the memory begin to fade (forgetting)? To determine what happens, we get a group of subjects to memorize some nonsense syllables (things like "lak" and "pir" and "gog"), and then we test them at intervals after they've finished the memorization. Some are tested almost immediately, some after one minute, others after five minutes, still others after half an hour, and so on. And we find that there isn't much difference in the average amount recalled at these different intervals. Can we conclude that, during the time immediately after memorization, memory is relatively stable? That's the conclusion that this research would lead us to—and, according to Eysenck, it's entirely wrong. Extraverts, he says, consolidate their learning very quickly, and then the amount retained begins to fall off. Introverts, in contrast, consolidate more slowly, so that the the amount they can remember continues to increase for some time after the initial learning period. Failing to take individual personality differences into account will distort and may hide altogether the truth of what is happening in learning situations and many other situations.

Behavior and Physiology

More recently, Eysenck has gone beyond positing two major personality factors or dimensions and exploring their implications for various kinds of behavior. Humans are biological creatures, he argues. If there is consistency in a person's behavior, it must be based on consistency in that person's physiology. Eysenck set about exploring possible biological characteristics that could account for introverted/extraverted behavior patterns.

He found one such characteristic that seems to do the job very nicely. People appear to vary in their general level of *cortical arousal;* some people tend to be more aroused, more receptive to stimuli, than others. Such people don't need massive doses of stimulation or excitement to keep them interested; it is as if for them everything is already magnified and larger than life. Other people tend to be just the opposite. Small stimuli go unnoticed; ideas must be loud and vivid and bold to be of interest. Differences on this dimension can be measured physiologically in terms of the electrical activity in the outer layer of the brain. And differences in this electrical activity (more precisely, in the *excitatory* and *inhibitory potentials* of the cortex) correspond rather neatly to differences on the introvert/extravert continuum, as shown in test scores. Introverts have high excitatory potentials and low inhibitory potentials. They don't need a great deal of stimulation from the outside; a little goes a long way. Extraverts, in contrast, have low excitatory and high inhibitory potentials. They seek the stimulation of conversation, excitement, broad splashes of color and sound.

What we have presented here is only a sample of Eysenck's theory and research. But even in this overview we can see a clear progression from abstract theorizing (the four "types" of Galen and Kant and Wundt), to data collection and mathematical analysis (from which Eysenck's two major dimensions are extracted), to experimental testing (studies of individual differences and learning), to the physiological basis for individual differences. Because personality has its basis in neurophysiology, Eysenck believes, all personality theory must eventually make a similar journey. Personality tests as we know them, and the mathematics that help us to understand test results, are only partial solutions—only signposts on the road to a true, objective understanding of why people are as they are.

Some Criticisms of Factor Analysis

It all sounds very neat, doesn't it? Maybe too neat. For, despite the enthusiasm and optimism of both Cattell and Eysenck and of the many other factor-analytic theorists around the world, the inescapable fact is that factor theories still don't predict behavior with the precision that they ought to have. Ought to, that is, if they worked as well in the real world as they do on paper or in carefully controlled laboratory situations.

That doesn't mean, of course, that the factor theories are wrong. Quite the contrary—they are probably right. All of them. Even the ones that contradict each other. But they are only partially right. They have hold of only one chunk of truth; they help us to look clearly at human behavior but from only one perspective.

Critics of the factor-analytic approach have pointed out some specific problems in the method. First, some say, there are still unknown, as yet undiscovered factors. These unknowns clog up the machinery and get in the way of unambiguous prediction of what a given individual will do in a given situation. Second, the critics find fault with the *kinds* of factors being talked about: the factors are "too static," "too general," "too specific," "too meaningless." Finally, it has been pointed out that factor-analytic theory does not take sufficient notice of the fact that many people behave as they do at a given moment because their environment pushes them into that sort of behavior. (People are quiet in church not because they have quiet natures but because quiet is expected of them and they know it.)

Especially in the last two criticisms, we can hear echoes of our earlier point: factor-analytic theory addresses itself to only part of the truth, to one facet of a multifaceted organism/environment interaction. Other approaches on other facets, each one its own bit of truth. As we have seen. And shall see further.

We have chronicled the beginnings of the individual-differences, testing, factor-analysis line in the history of personality theories, from

Darwin to Raymond Cattell and Eysenck. The factor-analytic theories reached a peak in the 1950s and early 1960s, and it is at this peak that our story ends. This is not to say that theory construction ended or that research stopped or that personality tests were discredited, for life goes on for test creators and analyzers, as for us all. But unfulfilled promises and criticisms that hit the mark took their toll, with the result that life among the testers lately has been one of reevaluation, reconstruction, and reformation. Regrouping. The global personality theories, which were so numerous a decade or two ago, appear infrequently now.

In the place of global theories, we find more intensive studies of particular instruments (like the MMPI) and particular theoretical dimensions (like introversion/extraversion) and a lot of soul-searching about "test bias" (against disadvantaged minority groups, for example) and "test abuse" (using tests in invalid ways). There is a lot of research and theory on the underlying mechanics of test construction and statistical prediction. Some assessment psychologists are proposing that personality traits are not characteristics of a person but are, rather, conceptual categories or screens we use to perceive people. (If this idea is unclear, wait until you've met George Kelly in Chapter 11.) Others are trying to understand the relationship of traits to language: do the traits call forth the adjectives to describe them? Or does the language determine what we will look for and therefore find?

The march goes on. But the beat is perhaps less clear and less insistent than it has been in the past.

Chapter Summary

The genealogy of factor analysis is fairly direct. We begin with Darwin, with the notion of individual differences. From there to the desire to create a better race, or at least to be able to select individuals who are high or low on some characteristics. The development of statistics to help with the measurement problem: the correlation coefficient and its friends. And then we arrive—factor analysis, with a host of variations and legions of enthusiastic supporters.

But the important story has to do with the beginnings of an orientation to personality called the "individual-differences approach." The reliance from the beginning on tests—diagnostic devices really—was a reasonable strategy for discriminating among people, for picking up differences among them. A test can get you in or keep you out of a university, a mental institution, a prison, an honors program, a job, or the Army. Tests are used for prediction—to guess whether or not you will succeed, commit suicide, or do well as a subject in a university professor's ingenious research project.

Tests and their mathematical ghosts, the factors, are also used in theory construction. When they are so used, they almost invariably result in a trait theory. Factors, which (supposedly) point to traits, are *things.* Oh, they can change, to be sure; people do grow and learn. But it is certainly easier to handle the measurement of something that stands still, and the great temptation is therefore to treat traits as if they were static and unchanging. So we have theories full of static things. The trait approach.

The individual-differences/trait approach historically has been based on discrimination and, from Darwin, has always had a tint of evolutionary fervor. Almost all of the "scientific" racism of this century has developed out of this approach: Blacks score lower on our tests; therefore they are inferior and should not be allowed to reproduce. (Contrast this with the learning-theory approach presented in Chapter 5, in which individual differences are sometimes so muted that one might think that a rat and Albert Einstein could both learn the same thing, given the proper "training.") Certainly racism is a perversion of the individual-differences/trait approach, but it is an illustrative perversion. The underlying principle is the same as that used by people who seek to "identify" slow learners or culturally disadvantaged children so they can be given special treatment. The basic idea is that there are differences—real and important differences—among people. Because the differences are real and important, they lead to action, to treating some people in different ways than others. That's a basic assumption.

We're not being generous, perhaps, in asserting that the individual-differences/trait approach is potentially racist and portrays people as composed of static things. But our criticisms are offered as one offers them to an old friend, an old friend who nevertheless has some character faults. Or perhaps we feel a touch of scorn for the front-runner—this approach has been *the* approach in personality theory and research for so long that one wonders what the alternative might be. Freudian theory held sway for maybe 30 years, but then the trait approach took over. It is still holding the fort, though its grasp may be weakening. (Even psychoanalytic theory has been affected. Originally a dynamic theory, psychoanalysis has become more and more structural. The ego became a thing. You can find a test today to measure primitive thinking—imagine! The primary *process* as a thing! A process as a structure. What next?)

But is that so bad? Isn't the trait approach productive, effective, superior to the rater's clumsy judgment? It works. Pretty well. But it should work better. Make it work better.

A reasonable request. The factor theorists are working on it.

And remember this. The individual-differences approach does not necessarily limit itself to the study of differences among individuals. How about differences within a single individual over time? They're working on this, too. The factor analysis of temporary states and the like. And much, much more.

The trait-approach team is the team to beat.

Perhaps that's why it's difficult to understand why R.B. Cattell and H.J. Eysenck are not the most important theorists in the area of personality. Did Freud have too much charisma? Are psychologists too mathematically unsophisticated? Or are Cattell and Eysenck the *reductio ad absurdum* of the trait approach, the disproof of its basic assumption by showing how absurd it is when carried to its logical conclusion? Or perhaps their fundamental disagreement with each other makes each of them less than completely convincing.

Whatever the answer, the factor-analytic techniques have produced mountains of data in raw and purified form that deserve our attention: the general personality factors in three dresses—*L* data, *Q* data, and *T* data—data that match and data that don't, the biological correlates of factor differences and their relationship to a variety of behaviors, and more.

And then there are the people involved. Eccentrics, prickly, lovable, irritating mathematicians all, like Galton, Spearman, Thurstone, Eysenck, and Cattell. They worked hard; they and their followers are working still. And in this computer age, they've got more than ever to do.

What will come of it?

Suggested Readings

Cattell writes hard, and it's hard reading. The mathematical aspects make it even harder. But his paperback *The Scientific Analysis of Personality* (Penguin, 1965) is a good introduction, and he attempts to write at a level we can understand. His major book, *Personality and Motivation Structure and Measurement* (Harcourt, Brace & World, 1957), is good for more detailed comments, but don't try to read it all at once.

Eysenck is easier, if not so precise. His *Sense and Nonsense in Psychology* and *Fact and Fiction in Psychology* (Penguin, 1957 and 1965) both have sections that introduce you to his factor-analytic style and to a number of other topics about which he evangelizes in entertaining fashion.

A good textbook on all aspects of testing, including brief descriptions of the process and results of factor analysis, is L.J. Cronbach's *Essentials of Psychological Testing,* now in its third edition (Harper & Row, 1970).

For quite a different picture of Cattell—of Cattell the philosopher and concerned world citizen—you might like to sample his *A New Morality from Science: Beyondism* (Pergamon Press, 1972).

And, for a picture of the modern scene, with all its poking and probing and reshuffling and reexamining, there is a magnificent book by Jerry Wiggins, entitled *Personality and Prediction* (Addison-Wesley, 1973). No doubt one day all these efforts will result in new global personality theories. Indeed, the attempts have already begun; the initial skirmishes can be glimpsed in Leona Tyler's book, *Individuality* (Jossey-Bass, 1978), or in *Individual Differences* (Gardner Press, 1976) by A.R. Buss and W. Poley.

Notes and References

Most of the material on Galton, J.M. Cattell, Binet, and Spearman came from history books, especially E.G. Boring's *A History of Experimental Psychology* (2nd ed.) (Appleton-Century-Crofts, 1950) and J.C. Flügel's *A Hundred Years of Psychology, 1833–1933* (Macmillan, 1945). Boring is good on facts and philosophy; Flügel is lighter and picks up the fascinating tidbits. Spearman's most important book is *Abilities of*

Man: Their Nature and Measurement (Macmillan, 1927). The five-volume (so far) series *A History of Psychology in Autobiography* has Spearman's autobiography in Volume I and those of Cyril Burt and L. L. Thurstone in Volume IV. (The Churchill quote at the opening of this chapter comes from Burt's autobiography, p. 67.) A good textbook for information on tests, their validation, and essential factor analysis is L.J. Cronbach's *Essentials of Psychological Testing* (Harper & Row, 1970).

H.J. Eysenck's major factor-analytic work can be found in four books: *Dimensions of Personality* (London: Routledge & Kegan Paul, 1948), *The Scientific Study of Personality,* (London: Routledge & Kegan Paul, 1952), *The Structure of Human Personality* (New York: Wiley, 1953), and *The Biological Basis of Personality* (Springfield, Ill.: Thomas Publishing Co., 1967).

One of the most complete and important of Cattell's book is *Personality and Motivation Structure and Measurement* (Harcourt, Brace & World, 1957). A 1966 handbook edited by Cattell and containing much of his work is the *Handbook of Multivariate Experimental Psychology* (Rand McNally, 1966). It is fairly technical. *Personality and Mood by Questionnaire* (Jossey-Bass, 1973) and *Handbook of Modern Personality Theory,* edited by Cattell with R.M. Dreger (Wiley, 1976), continue and update the 1966 *Handbook* and are also fairly technical. Finally, you might look into *Motivation and Dynamic Structures,* with D. Child (Halsted Press, 1975).

5

Intelligent Animals

Man is a biped without feathers.

Plato

Before Darwin, the prevailing view of nature was that humans were human and animals were animals. Different, but how? Well, humans had souls, they were intelligent, and they were rational, whereas animals, being without souls, were like robots, responding to their environment in a more or less automatic way. A philosopher named Descartes was the hero (or villain) of this approach. It's probably good that he didn't live to be 250 years old—Darwin would have utterly appalled him. Though parts of Descartes' philosophy live on, his assumptions about the relationship of human to animal were in for a rude jolt.

Descartes had a strange mind, given to dreaming in mathematical forms. Once, as a young soldier asleep on the banks of the Danube, he dreamed of analytic geometry, which was odd, since analytic geometry had not yet been invented. He died in 1650 from pneumonia he contracted when trying to explain to Queen Christina of Sweden what he meant by "I think, therefore I am." Not from the frustration of the teaching, but from the chilly room where the Queen had her lessons, at 5 o'clock in the ice-cold Swedish morning, three times a week. Some 200 years later, Darwin would destroy his philosophy with his assertion that "humans are animals, too."

Darwin's theory of evolution contained three assumptions that were crucial for psychology, and we can identify three main lines of personality theory and research with these three Darwinian assumptions. All three follow from Darwin's basic discovery that humans evolved from lower animals, that this relationship of human to animal is one of continuity through the ages, and that humans and animals have much in common with each other, as well as sharing common ancestors. The continuity between man and animals as a scientific belief forces one to consider several things. First, maybe there is a lot of the animal in humans—dark, hidden impulses that rational people may not be willing to admit. Base instincts like sexual drives. Freud picked up this line. Second, for evolution to occur, there must be individual differences from which to select. Galton picked up this line. Now we can explore the third line, the possibility that there might be a lot of humanity in animals. Are animals intelligent? Nobody really thought to ask the question before. Why do animals behave the way they do? For the first time, the answer seemed relevant to an understanding of people as well as of animals, and the new relevance ushered in a burgeoning new field of psychology. Animal research. Almost from the beginning, this new field focused on *learning.*

We must begin our examination with an apology, for we will not do justice to all the vital concerns of those who labor long and hard in the area we are about to describe. This is not a chapter on learning theory and research; it is a chapter on the *impact* of learning theory on personality. Some learning theorists have been more influential than others, and we will concentrate on them and the aspects of their work that are pertinent to understanding the human personality. Learning as a psychological discipline is not accurately portrayed here, for the field has many legitimate concerns that have not been found useful by the personologist, a psychologist involved in personality theory and research. We will discuss here the broad, general issues that apply to the changing behavior of humans in (broad) terms that students of personality can handle.

Edward L. Thorndike: An Effective Start

For our purposes, the search for humanity in animals began during the last few years of the 19th century, when a Harvard graduate student named Edward Lee Thorndike was refused permission to continue his experiments on the extrasensory perception (ESP) of young children (he was sure that unconscious facial gestures were clues to their ESP). His experiments were considered unethical; the prevailing view (at that time) was that children should not be used as subjects for *any* research. So Thorndike proposed to study the "intelligence" of chickens instead and was given the go-ahead.

Was given the go-ahead, that is, by his academic advisers, but his landlady had different ideas. There weren't many psychological laboratories in those days, so Thorndike kept his chickens (and ran his experiments) in his rented room. His landlady pointed out that there was nothing in his lease about a dozen dirty chickens and politely dumped Thorndike (and his chickens) out on the streets. The kindly philosopher/psychologist William James took pity and offered the use of his basement, where neither Thorndike nor his chickens did much except lay eggs.

After two years at Harvard, Thorndike applied for a scholarship from Columbia and won it. After his parents had almost kicked him out of the family home because his animals didn't smell good, he went to New York with a basket containing his two brightest chickens, which he hoped to breed. At Columbia, James McKeen Cattell was in charge, and he gave Thorndike an attic to work in. Thorndike was moving up in the world.

Animal Intelligence

Thorndike's research dealt with the intelligence of animals, including some fish, his beloved chickens, cats, dogs, and a few monkeys. Intelligence in animals, as we have mentioned, became a fertile area of interest after Darwin, although for many years the interest seemed to be limited to a collection of anecdotes about animals doing seemingly intelligent things. Pet stories. Thorndike saw clearly that anecdotal evidence wasn't sufficient and that, in most cases, the stories simply related an act that *seemed* intelligent. But how did the animal come to perform that act? How was it learned? How fast? Was there insight? Thorndike phrased the question of animal intelligence in terms of learning ability, and there the question remained.

Thorndike didn't think animals were very intelligent, at least not as bright as the pet stories suggested. Take his cat experiments. He rounded up a gang of tough New York alley cats and put them, one at a time, in a "puzzle box" of his own design. They had to learn to get out in order to get the food he had placed outside the box. He set up simple escapes: step on the lever on the floor and the cage door will open. Could a cat learn this simple task?

Yes, they could. But Thorndike thought they learned it in a rather stupid way. First the cat in the puzzle box tried to claw the box to pieces (which seems quite logical). Finally, after a lot of nervous pacing and clawing, it might bump the lever with its tail, and the door would open. Insight? Not much evidence of that. The next time, the cat would pace and claw again and then bump the lever again, as if by accident. Gradually, *very* gradually, the ineffective behaviors dropped out, and the effective response was made more directly. Even then, the cat might continue its solution of flicking the lever with its tail instead of pushing it with its paw, a much easier maneuver. Thorndike was unimpressed. (Knowing cats, we suspect they were just showing contempt for Thorndike by refusing to do it the way he wanted.)

The year was now 1898, two years before publication of Freud's *Interpretation of Dreams* and the same year that Lt. Col. Theodore Roosevelt was doing some rough riding up San Juan Hill. Thorndike published a monograph with the ironic title *Animal Intelligence,* in which he expressed his contempt for the little creatures. Their learning, he said, was hit or miss, a laborious trial-and-error process. (He seemed to be about to exhume Descartes.)

The Law of Effect

Then Thorndike made a frightful discovery. Human subjects presented with tasks similar to those he gave his cats solved the puzzle using approximately the same slow, trial-and-error method. Are we all stupid? Is there no intelligence? Or are we all smart and just defining "intelligence" incorrectly? These questions didn't interest Thorndike one bit. He forgot about measuring intelligence in animals and ignorance in humans and began to study learning. Period. And, after many studies, he presented his important *law of effect.*

The law of effect, as it was originally proposed, had two parts, both concentrating on the effect of the consequences of an action. There is a stimulus (S) and a response (R), and between the S and the R is a connection or bond. The strength of this bond is the degree of learning; it is the probability that a particular R will occur when S occurs. The *law of effect* stated that, if a particular S precedes a particular R and R is, in turn, followed by a "satisfying state of affairs," the bond will be strengthened. However, if the R is followed by an "annoying state of affairs," the bond will be weakened. To counter the criticism of the growing behaviorist movement that satisfaction and annoyance were subjective and mentalistic terms not suitable for use in a true science, Thorndike defined them precisely: a satisfying state is one that the animal will approach and make efforts to maintain or renew, and an annoying state is one that the animal will avoid, withdraw from, and make attempts to eliminate.

Maybe this law of effect doesn't sound like much. If you do something and get a prize, you are likely to do it again; if you do something and get a punch in the jaw, the probability of a repeat performance goes down. Common sense? Well, yes and no. There were some issues in learning theory that were controversial, and the law of effect was one of them: many scholars at that time did not believe that the consequences of an act had any effect at all. Hard to believe? Perhaps. But what seems obvious to us today was not so obvious several generations ago.

S-R Theory Revised

More important, perhaps, than the law of effect itself was the way the law was phrased—in S-R terms, a mechanistic system that consciously avoided subjectivity. The theory inspired a lot of research, and that's good. As a matter of fact, the research it inspired destroyed the theory itself—at least part of it, as even Thorndike admitted. He later revised the law of effect, omitting those parts that didn't correspond to the actual behavior of his research animals. But this was not a defeat for Thorndike; rather, it was a victory. If any theory or law or hypothesis is precise enough to be proven wrong, that's progress. That's science: precision, measurability, testability. How unlike much of earlier theorizing! You could argue about the validity of a Freudian hypothesis, for instance, and, if you disagreed with Freud, you could split off and form your own school, be an Adlerian or a Jungian. But, unlike the Thorndike hypotheses, you could never *prove* Freud wrong, not by a definitive experimental procedure with outcomes that are observable to anyone.

It was in the early 1930s that Thorndike changed several of his original ideas. He originally believed that, in addition to his law of effect, there was also a *law of exercise,* meaning that simple *repetition* of a response also strengthened the S-R bond. By 1932, evidence was mounting against such a hypothesis, and he admitted he had been wrong. There had to be a reward following. And the law of effect was truncated: the part about the bond being weakened when the response is followed by an annoying state of affairs was dropped. Experimentally, punishment did not decrease the probability of a repeated response. The "truncated law of effect," therefore, stated only that reward strengthens the S-R bond.

Simple repetition does nothing. Reward strengthens. Punishment does little or nothing. These were the first laws of learning from S-R theory and research. Of course, Thorndike's conclusions were not accepted as "laws" in the true sense, and even today these issues remain a matter of substantial controversy. But being objective, scientific, and mechanistic, using the term *S-R,* using operational definitions, studying human and animal behavior experimentally, focusing on learning—all this started with Thorndike. The idea that one could understand the *human* by studying the animal was gaining ground. Another beginning with Thorndike. And two others—a man named Watson and a man named Pavlov.

The Elementary John B. Watson

John Broadus Watson was born near Greenville, South Carolina, in 1878. After a less than distinguished school record and a couple of adolescent arrests, he ended up with the first Ph.D. in psychology ever awarded from the University of Chicago, in 1903. He was ten years away from what may have been the single most important article ever published in psychology.

The Introspective Approach

Since this chapter began with Thorndike and his S-R approach, you might assume that Thorndike was the dominant figure in experimental psychology at this time. Not true. Thorndike was significant, and he foreshadowed what was to come, but the era was still dominated by an approach some have called "mental chemistry." Wilhelm Wundt, the father of experimental psychology, and, in the United States, E. B. Titchener were among its chief advocates. Based on theory from the physical sciences, these psychologists had begun a search for the "atoms" of psychology, and they also advocated the philosophical notion that thinking is composed of ideas that come originally from sensations. They began an intense study of the sensory processes and their effect on ideas (the *introspective* approach). Aren't sensations food and fuel for thought, and isn't thinking the key to understanding human behavior?

Experimentally, however, the study of ideas was a hard nut to crack. How do you observe something going on inside my head? Well, I can observe it myself. Perhaps I can tell you what I observe. And my words are certainly "observable"; they are data and can be treated objectively, like any other kind of data. The main thrust of the *introspective* ("looking inward") movement was its emphasis on the internal events of consciousness, the notion that one can only learn about psychology by looking at one's own thought processes. (The procedure did not produce a lot of useful information, but who could argue with the rationale?) But we're getting ahead of ourselves.

"Psychology as the Behaviorist Views It"

Watson, as a new Ph.D., was born into this era of research. But he was uncomfortable using human subjects; he was shy, embarrassed, and awkward. He felt more comfortable with animals, so he tried to extend the "mental chemistry" approach to animals. He published a paper on the white rat learning to run through a maze and focused on the probable sensations the rat experienced at each decision point; he interpreted those sensations in terms of the animal's "consciousness." Writing in this manner was a heavy burden for the young Watson; he thought the approach confining, unproductive, and unnecessary. For one thing, he was genuinely interested in the behavior of the rat for its own sake. He disliked having to write in terms of consciousness and then to qualify everything with the ridiculous addendum: ". . . if the rat has consciousness at all." And he had a sneaking suspicion that somehow, by just watching animal behavior, he could discover everything that other researchers discovered listening to their human subjects. He suggested the same to his colleagues at the University of Chicago, but they gave him very little encouragement.

In 1908, Watson moved to Johns Hopkins University and found more fertile ground for his ideas. Still five years away from his great publication, however, he continued to use Titchener's experimental manuals in his teaching. Finally, in 1913, he published the paper that changed forever the direction of American psychology: "Psychology as the Behaviorist Views It." It was a bombshell.

> Psychology as the behaviorist views it is a purely objective experimental branch of natural science. Its theoretical goal is the prediction and control of behavior. Introspection forms no essential part of its methods, nor is the scientific value of its data dependent upon the readiness with which they lend themselves to interpretation in terms of consciousness. The behaviorist, in his efforts to get a unitary scheme of animal response, recognizes no dividing line between man and brute.[1]

These were the first four sentences. Each was an attack and each a clarion call. Psychology objective and experimental? The best-known theories of the time were subjective (mental chemistry and psychoanalysis), and Freudian theory was certainly not experimentally based. The goal is "prediction and control of behavior"? The goal had been the understanding of mind. Introspection and consciousness are not essential? Incredible!

The main theme of the paper was that behavior, because it is observable and public, is the only proper object for a science to study. We can never know what people think; we can know how they behave. Isn't that really why we want to know their minds? To predict and understand behavior? We can get answers by studying behavior alone and by observing the conditions in which certain behaviors occur. Understanding the mind is unnecessary, maybe impossible, and certainly not scientific.

Powerful words, indeed. But psychology in America, for many reasons, was ready for Watson; he was in the right place at the right time. In fact, many of his arguments made little sense. Introspection was criticized for not being behavioral (although it most certainly was—verbal reports are behavior). But introspection and mental chemistry did not seem to be leading anywhere or producing much of use. Edward Thorndike had developed something of use, and that something fit easily into the behavioral mold. Stimuli and responses are observable. Satisfaction and annoyance were defined in terms of observable events, like approach

[1]From "Psychology as the Behaviorist Views It," *Psychological Review*, 1913, *20*, p. 158.

and avoidance. These were useful, operational definitions. The important fact was that introspection was not working, and Thorndike's approach was working. And now Watson offered psychologists the creed and the cause. The psychological world was enthused.

And then the Behaviorist movement got still another unexpected boost—from a man named Pavlov in Russia.

Ivan Pavlov

Pavlov was a physiologist who earned his medical degree two years after Sigmund Freud received his. He had hoped to be a priest, but as it turned out, he began (oddly enough) to study the secretions of the body instead. By 1904, he had been awarded the Nobel Prize. He began to study the secretions involved in digestion, and he did so by a simple procedure. He put the secretions into test tubes where they could be measured more accurately. He inserted a tube into the secreting ducts of his research animals (dogs, usually) and rerouted the fluids outside, to his test tubes. He did this, in particular, to study salivation.

When Pavlov had his dogs rigged to salivate into his measuring device, he noticed something peculiar. The dogs were "anticipating"; that is, the flow of saliva began before the meal was served, so to speak. It began when the dog saw the food coming in the door or even (what's this?) at the sight of the experimenter. Pavlov was scientist enough to know that he was observing an important phenomenon. He began to study it in more detail. Food elicits salivation naturally; why were the dogs salivating at the sight of Pavlov? Pavlov figured that stimuli *associated* with food had taken on a new power, heretofore reserved for food alone; the new stimuli had a kind of equivalence to food; the new stimuli had "become" food in a sense. A more systematic exploration was needed.

For example, take a stimulus unrelated to salivation, like a buzzing sound. Test it to make sure; sound the buzzer and watch the tubes. No saliva. Good. Now sound the buzzer just before presenting the food. Saliva, of course, stimulated by the food. But Pavlov found that, if he sounded the buzzer and presented the food together enough times, soon the dogs would salivate when they heard the buzzer alone, without food. Pavlov called the procedure *conditioning,* which was a very nice term to use because it put the emphasis where Pavlov wanted it: on the *conditions* or observable environmental events that could be manipulated for the purpose of controlling behavior. The new stimulus (the buzzer, in this experiment) became the *conditioned stimulus,* and the response was called the *conditioned response* because it was not elicited by the buzzer before Pavlov manipulated the conditions. And Pavlov explored the conditions meticulously. A buzzer that sounded before food was presented became conditioned; if it was sounded after food, it did not. Presenting a conditioned stimulus without the food for a long period eventually "de-conditioned" the light or buzzer, reducing it to its original, neutral status. This de-conditioning of a response was called *extinction.*

It was a beautiful series of studies, probably unmatched in rigor and productivity until B. F. Skinner came along. Its real beauty, and its real impact came from the way Pavlov put it all together into a theory of learning. Learning, association, anticipation—mental events! And studied without recourse to what was going on in the mind. Anyone could hear a buzzer, and the response could be measured. Watson had *said* that one could study important problems in psychology without referring to consciousness; Pavlov was *doing* it.

For many years, researchers in the U. S. were ignorant of Pavlov's work. It was physiology, and it was published in Russian. But it was too important to escape notice forever: Watson learned of it from his vast network of colleagues. Pavlov was proclaimed the next hero of the behaviorist revolution, second only to Watson. Behaviorists were given the facts ("the ammunition") with which they could destroy the "muddle-headed" introspectionists. Which they proceeded to do. As in any conflict, the introduction of a new and powerful weapon on one side (in this case, Pavlov's work) results in a rapid shift of power. By 1920, the introspectionists were in full retreat.

Behaviorism versus Psychoanalysis

The S-R approach now held sway and would likely have swept the field had it not been for the psychoanalysts. They were the superior politicians, never stating anything precisely enough to be attacked or destroyed. Attacking psychoanalysis was like stabbing a bowl of jello with a sword; it doesn't resist, but as soon as the sword is removed, the whole somehow globs together again as if there had been no attack at all. The Freudians said "We have to treat real human beings in trouble; what use is it to know that a dog can be trained to salivate to a buzzer?" "But our approach is more scientific!" said the behaviorists. "O.K.," said the Freudians, "you sit there with a man whose consuming desire in life is to kill his mother. What do you want us to do? Tell him to come back in 50 years when we have scientifically discovered the conditions leading to matricide?"

The upshot of this debate was a severe split between the applied psychologists (like psychotherapists) and the "experimentalists," the pure and basic psychological researchers. For many years, the split was to produce two camps with little or no interaction or communication, each with its own body of theory and its own collection of relevant research. The experimentalists could have learned much from the problems faced by practitioners, and the practitioners could have learned much from the discoveries of the experimentalists. But they weren't speaking to one another.

It was a stalemate, but there were people on both sides who refused to accept it. Watson, in particular, was looking for evidence that Pavlov's work could be applied to important human problems. If he could find that evidence, the psychoanalysts would have to accept the behavioral approach. But Watson found no such evidence; he would have to create it himself. He would, he decided, apply Pavlovian techniques to the study of emotions in the human child. Then, he thought, he would gain the final victory.

He proceeded on that assumption. First, he observed infants for a long time and noted that fear was an emotion that could be easily "defined" by behavior: avoidance, crying, and similar activities. More significantly, he noticed that fear in infants was a natural (unconditioned) response to certain stimuli or events, such as loud noises or sudden loss of support. A fear response is to loud noise as salivation is to food. A perfect arena for battle. Watson would show that fear could be "learned" in the Pavlovian manner.

Little Albert

So Watson set up his experiment. He found the perfect subject in Albert B., age 11 months. Response to loud noise: puckers lips, raises arms, whimpers, displays avoidance behaviors. The proposed conditioned stimulus was a white rat. Albert's initial response to the rat was approach; he attempted to grasp and touch it. Albert clearly did not fear the rat; he loved it. Perfect. So the experiment began. The rat was brought in. Albert reached for the animal, and, just as he touched it, Watson's research assistant, a young woman named Rosalie Rayner, whanged a steel bar with a hammer. Albert exhibited fear. The procedure was repeated once more, and Albert showed the same response.

A week later, Albert's behavior indicated that he had learned a lesson. He exhibited avoidance when the rat was brought in. After five more hammer blows, Albert was in mortal terror of the rat. What had previously been attractive was now terrifying. The response of fear had been conditioned to the stimulus of the white rat. Watson found that Albert responded with fear to other stimuli that resembled the rat: a white rabbit, a dog, and even a fur coat. Watson worried for a time that Albert had been made afraid of *everything*, but he stopped worrying when he saw that Albert appeared to love his building blocks as much as before.

The account of the Albert experiment was published in 1920,[2] and it was another blockbuster. At the end of the report, Watson made his attack on psychoanalysis. Twenty years from now, he said, some analyst is going to meet a man named Albert with a fur-coat phobia. This well-meaning analyst, he said, will probably provoke Albert to remember a dream or two "proving" that he once pulled his mother's hair and was scolded and thus developed an unnatural dread of furry objects. Such are the pitfalls of a nonscientific, introspective approach.

But Watson's attack had little effect. Watson had sorely underestimated not only the strength of the psychoanalytic position, but also the emotional intensity of the response to his research. Watson had deliberately taught an infant to fear animals, even dogs. He had said it was "unfortunate" that Albert was removed from his control before the fear response could be scientifically extinguished. And, in the same year, he had divorced his wife of 17 years and married his research assistant, Rosalie Rayner. Divorce was scandalous in those days; personal relationships with students were considered highly unethical; research of any kind with children was taboo; and this—teaching fear, with no remedy—was by far the worst of all. Watson had made a fatal mistake, and it would destroy his career. He was front-page news for a year. He was,

[2]See Watson and Rayner's article "Conditioned Emotional Responses" in *The Journal of Experimental Psychology*, 1920, *3*, 1–14.

of course, fired from Johns Hopkins and found a job with the J. Walter Thompson advertising agency promoting Yuban coffee. He wrote some but nothing of much interest. An article he wrote for *Cosmopolitan* was noteworthy only because they got Watson to contribute the article after Sigmund Freud had refused. Academically speaking, Watson was dead. (He was, however, an enormous success in advertising.)

If Watson was dead, though, the behaviorist movement was very far from it. Watson had, after all, demonstrated what he had set out to show: that human emotional responses could be conditioned in just the same way that a dog's physical responses can be conditioned. He had shown that animal research was relevant to human behavior. His research had undermined the psychoanalytic position severely, and, although he had lost the battle, it was now inevitable that the analysts would lose the war. He was accused of degrading science, but he had inspired it, too. It was just a matter of time.

The Principled Clark Hull

The behaviorist movement, after Watson left its ranks, went quietly back to work. The public's attention was on the "talking" motion picture and what Adolf Hitler was up to in Europe, not to mention the stock-market crash and the depression that followed. The behaviorists continued to make progress, especially in the fields of learning and motivation, and they were building their mazes and their puzzle boxes by the gross. The white rat came to be very much in demand as an experimental subject. Sequestered in their labs, scientists were watching the rat choose and run and learn, and they were learning by watching. They did not repeat Watson's mistakes; aware of ethics and of the public sensibility, they patiently strove to build a body of knowledge and facts that could not be disputed.

The two decades after Watson's demise were relatively quiet but not without great advances. Thorndike was refining his law of effect, and a man named E. R. Guthrie was keeping up interest in theoretical issues. Pavlov's works were translated and studied intensely. A young man named B. F. Skinner began his studies of a "new type" of conditioning called instrumental or operant, resembling Thorndike's, in which the reward (following the response) is more significant than the stimulus (preceding the response). E. C. Tolman was opening up the restrictive assumptions of behaviorism by showing how, if one were very careful about grounding theoretical concepts in observable behavior, one could extend the theory to nonobservable phenomena. A lot of research was being done, and techniques and equipment were being refined.

Principles of Behavior

By 1940, the time was ripe for the behavioral learning theorists. In 1943, a very significant book entitled *Principles of Behavior* was published. The author was a Yale psychologist named Clark Hull.

Hull's theory certainly did not spring full-grown from his head like Athena from the head of Zeus; many years of research and discussion preceded its appearance. And although Hull was the prime mover behind the theory, he was far from alone: research and comments from both supporters and critics contributed to its development. But the dream was Hull's. Perhaps it is every scientist's goal to formulate the consummate theory—the grand design—that puts all the bits and pieces of research into place, that takes isolated facts and meshes them into an organized whole. Clark Hull's dream was to formulate a psychological theory of the magnitude of the great theories in physics and chemistry, to make a scientific advance as significant as Newton's or Einstein's, and for a while it looked like he might succeed.

From 1930 to 1960, Hull was the most important learning theorist, the most important *psychologist* of any breed, in the world. Almost everything said, written, or done in the field of psychology was either in support of his ideas or in criticism of them. In the decade from 1941 to 1950, the peak period of his influence, nearly three-fourths of all articles on learning and motivation in the two leading psychology journals referred to Hull at least once. A survey of articles in the leading journal on abnormal psychology and personality showed that, from 1949 to 1952, Hull's *Principles of Behavior* was easily the most frequently cited book—cited more than four times as often as the second-place book. And this, remember, was in the area of personality! It was an incredible era.

Hull's Mathematico-Deductive Theory

Principles of Behavior began modestly enough with the statement that it could "be regarded as a general introduction to the theory of all the behavioral (social) sciences." It presented, in exceptionally precise and rigorous terms (for that time), a *mathematico-deductive theory of behavior.* Simply put, the theory went something like this: a stimulus from the environment (observable) impinges on the organism and then a response (observable) is made. Good old S-R stuff. Between the stimulus and the response, something is going on inside the organism. The stimulus is transformed into a neural code of some sort and has certain effects, and eventually the system produces an output—a response. If human or animal physiology were adequate to the task, we could describe the internal process in terms of that science, but physiology was not (and is not) up to the job. So Hull used conceptual terms—not physiological but not incompatible with physiology. The important terms were *habit strength,* written as ${}_SH_R$, meaning the strength of the "bond" between stimulus and response or, in other words, the degree of learning; *drive* (*D*), the motivational concept; and *reaction potential* (${}_SE_R$), a fancy term for the final stage, the potential response (reaction) about to become a real (observable) response. Essentially, reaction potential = habit strength × drive (${}_SE_R = {}_SH_R \times D$), meaning that performance depends on learning and motivation.

Hull also developed a concept known as *I,* for *inhibition,* which had to do with the fact that one's performance of a task can get worse rather than better if one works at it too long and too hard. New learning can inhibit previous learning and can even inhibit future learning. Inhibition became a very important concept for a number of personality theorists. It was linked to the superego, to the development of conscience. It also was to become important in some of the theoretical underpinnings of a new kind of psychotherapy called behavior modification.

Needless to say, the idea that behavior was a function of learning and motivation was *not* the feature of Hull's theory that made him so important. Lots of people had been saying that for years. But how does an external stimulus affect the body? How does a stimulus become associated with the response to form a habit? How is drive produced? What else besides habit strength and drive affects performance? These were the kinds of questions that Hull came to grips with.

He took two approaches to answering them. First, he made his best guess from available evidence about what happened during each step of the process between stimulus and response. These guesses were called *postulates;* Hull formulated 16 postulates in all. And second, he "anchored" each postulate in observable data (characteristics of stimuli or responses) by means of precise mathematical formulations. Let's take an example. Say X is some hypothesized thing that mediates between stimulus and response. The stimulus (S) and the response (R) are observable and measurable. If we *postulate* that $X = 2S$ and that $R = 2X$, where the units of S and R are defined and standardized, then we can calculate the value of X from the observable data (the stimuli) and use X to predict exactly what R will be. Add another theoretical concept: $X = 2S$; $Y = 2X$; $R = 2Y$ or $X = 2S$; $Y = 1.5S$; $R = X + Y$. If we know the value of S, we can predict R exactly.

What the theory proposed, then, was a series of assumptions called postulates that related each theoretical concept to observable data ($X = 2S$) or to another theoretical concept ($Y = 2X$) with mathematical exactitude. From these postulates, one could deduce the response that would occur. In addition, one could deduce theorems, scientific hypotheses about behavior.

Here is a nonpsychological example of this kind of deduction: Mickey's wife is pregnant (postulate 1); Mickey is sterile (postulate 2); hence (theorem), Mickey didn't do it; hence (theorem), there must be another man involved. Such a system, you see, is very heuristic—it promotes search and research. If there is no other man, maybe the postulate is in error. Is she really pregnant? Is Mickey really sterile? The beauty of the whole system was the tightness of logic—postulates could be proved wrong. In Hull's case, thousands of psychologists ran to their laboratories to prove his postulates wrong . . . or right. When he was "proved" wrong, he changed the postulate, and that set off a new flurry of studies.

This example of deduction was taken (with only slight changes) from a popular soap opera, but equally interesting illustrations could be excerpted from a Sherlock Holmes novel or other such drama. Deduction is drama; it's exciting and satisfying, just as much to critics as it is to supporters. Hull gave us this drama in psychology. But unlike the theory of Freud and others, Hull's theory was mathematically precise.

Let's look at just one example, Postulate 4, which states his belief about the way habit strength builds up.

> Whenever an effector activity ($r \rightarrow R$) and a receptor activity ($S \rightarrow s$) occur in close temporal contiguity (${}_{\dot{s}}C_r$) and this ${}_{\dot{s}}C_r$ is closely associated with the diminution of a need (G), or with a stimulus that has been closely and consistently associated with the diminution of a need ($\dot{G}$), there will result an increment to a tendency (${}_{\Delta S}H_R$) for that afferent impulse on later occasions to evoke that reaction. The increments from successive reinforcements summate in a manner which yields a combined habit strength (${}_SH_R$) which is a simple positive growth function of the number of reinforcements (N). The upper limit (m) of this curve of learning is the product of (1) a positive growth function of the magnitude of need reduction which is involved in primary, or which is associated with secondary, reinforcement; (2) a negative function of the delay (t) in reinforcement; and (3) (a) a negative growth function of the degree of asynchronism (t') of $\dot{S}$ and R when both are of brief duration, or (b), in case the action of $\dot{S}$ is prolonged so as to overlap the beginning of R, a negative growth function of the duration (t'') of the continuous action of $\dot{S}$ on the receptor when R begins.[3]

You probably don't understand the postulate, because not all of the terms have been defined here. But the important thing for you to understand is the rigorous precision that this methodology brought to psychology.

You have read merely the verbal form of the postulate. All the mathematical terms such as *negative growth function* were put down in their precise mathematical dress: ${}_SH_R = M(1-e^{-kw})e^{-jt}e^{-ut'}(1-e^{-iN})$, for example, which is roughly equivalent to our example, $X = 2S$. Let's explore this equation further. All the numbers and letters before the last set of parentheses, for a given situation, form one quantity. Let's call it A. It does not vary. We've seen that ${}_SH_R$ is habit strength—the amount of learning. So ${}_SH_R = A(1-e^{-iN})$, but Hull said that e equals 10, and everyone believed him, and e^{-iN} means $\frac{1}{e^{iN}}$, so ${}_SH_R = A(1-\frac{1}{10^{iN}})$. The value of i is constant. It's always the same for a particular organism (a rat, a pigeon, Lucy Smith, or Eddie Jones). Hull introduced quite a few constants; that's how he got around the problem of individual differences later—now back to the equation. A is a number that does not vary in this experiment, and i is always the same for any particular learner. The only thing that varies is N, and that refers to the number of trials that are reinforced. The equation says, then, that, for a given animal in a given environment, the habit strength goes up as the number of reinforced trials goes up. Or, roughly, practice makes perfect (if each practice leads to reward). Not an earth-shaking discovery, but it is the precision and the rigor that were so exciting.

Criticisms of Hull's Theory

Hull died in 1952, the year in which the latest revision of his theory was published. Many of the postulates had changed, based on experimental data gathered after his first book came out. The latest revision triggered a new wave of research as psychologists tried out the revised

[3]From Hull's *Principles of Behavior,* Appleton-Century-Crofts, 1943, p. 178.

formulae for size. But the book was to be Hull's last gasp. His dream was not to be realized.

As so often happens, the reasons Hull's theory enjoyed such a meteoric rise to the top of the psychological world were the same as the reasons for its collapse. It's a grand theory, said Hull. We're not ready for a grand theory, said the critics. Hull was too much, too soon.

Critics said that the theory was both too narrow and too broad—they couldn't accept a scientific postulate that contained such specialized information as the number of days a rat can go without food and that was also supposed to apply to all behavior. In some ways, the theory was too integrated: some of the theoretical constructs could not carry their weight in explaining behavior but were necessary parts of the theory as a whole. And it was too unintegrated: some important concepts were not adequately related to others. The theory was obstructing valuable research by forcing studies in certain directions; the assumptions about reinforcement, for example, were too precise for an issue that was so highly controversial, and attempts to estimate mathematical constants in a relationship that had not been proven to exist were a waste of time. So said the critics. For a long time, B. F. Skinner had been asking "If $X = 2S$ and $R = 2X$, why not say $R = 4S$ and eliminate the step in the middle? Is the theory really necessary?" And now he was being heard.

But, whatever the critics said, a major underlying factor in the demise of Hull's theory was the fact that psychology was becoming more and more specialized. Psychologists were interested in perception or sensory psychology or cognitive development. In each specialized area, miniature theories (dealing with only one aspect of behavior) sprang up, and they worked better (in their own area) than did Hull's. His theory disappeared from the pages of introductory psychology textbooks and even from the learning texts; more and more, his book was regarded as an interesting bit of history.

Hull's Theoretical Legacy

To say that Hull's theory is dead, however, is not to say that it had no effect. Many of Hull's postulates were demoted to the status of hypotheses, but, as such, they remain viable today. His general approach has affected psychology to such a degree that it is difficult to relate pre-Hull concepts to post-Hull concepts, so different are the two in form and in their relationship to behavior. Hull, like Freud, has become part of the spirit of psychology. In personality research and theory, Hull had a tremendous effect. Most directly, a theory of personality evolved from his thought (Dollard and Miller's). More generally, the spirit of his work is clearly present in certain basic assumptions and certain basic orientations.

Reinforcement and Motivation. Largely because of Hull, personologists are very concerned about reinforcement and its effects. The term *reinforcement* opened up areas for research, though Hull did not coin the word. Reinforcement means strengthening. Of a bond (Thorndike). Of habit strength (Hull). In practice, it usually means a reward, and a reward of some sort is what most people think of when they hear the term. But it can be the removal of an obnoxious state of affairs, too, and, in that sense, includes some events not typically thought of as rewards. Reinforcement is the more technical term, and now it is commonly used, thanks in no small part to Clark Hull.

Hull asked, "What reinforces?" Answer (postulate): whatever reduces drive or drive stimuli. For example, food reduces hunger—a drive—or it reduces stimuli associated with hunger—drive stimuli—like hunger pangs. Food is therefore reinforcing for a hungry animal, water is reinforcing for a thirsty animal, and the reduction of pain is reinforcing for an animal experiencing it. Such an interpretation had the effect of turning the focus of research to studies of motivation or drives, since drives now had two purposes: a drive that needed to be reduced (reinforcement) had to be present in order for learning (increase in habit strength) to occur; and drive, of course, had the function of energizing behavior (that is, ${}_SE_R = {}_SH_R \times D$, or performance equals habit strength times drive).

Hull's interest in drives attracted the interest of the personologists. One of the problems of relating animal studies to human behavior has always been the simplicity of animal motivation. In animals, four basic drives have been the usual focus of study: hunger, thirst, sex, and pain avoidance. But it's nearly impossible to explain human behavior in these terms alone. (You may be reading this book because you are hungry, but food reinforcement will probably be a long time coming: you gain knowledge, you get a better job, you make more money, you buy food, and then you eat.) Freud based his theory on sex, a primary drive, but he based his explanations of behavior on secondary drives or learned motivations. For example, we are motivated to seek approval; we have learned that approval is desirable because it has, at some time, been associated with sexual satisfaction.

Secondary Motivation. Hull, as well as other learning theorists, had to come to grips with this same issue. Hull did so by conceptualizing two secondary processes, *secondary motivation* and *secondary reinforcement.* These were not new concepts, obviously, but they were interesting because of the way they were handled by Hull's very rigorous and mechanistic theory.

To understand secondary motivation, think of little Albert B., Watson's subject. Fear, an emotion that can be seen as part of the primary pain-avoidance drive, was induced by associating a previously neutral stimulus—the white rat—with the drive, which was elicited by the loud noise. Neal Miller, one of Hull's adherents, did a lot of similar research on animals. In the classic experiment, rats were given electric shocks when they were in the white portion of a two-colored box and no shock when they were in the black portion.[4] Soon the rats showed fear of the white portion, even when no shock was administered. To prove that this learned drive was motivating, Miller asked a simple question: Would these rats work to learn a response that would do nothing more than let them

[4]Miller's account of this experiment can be found in *The Journal of Experimental Psychology,* 1948, *38,* pp. 89–101.

enter the black portion of the box? (Remember, no more shocks were being administered in the white portion; only the whiteness was evoking the fear.) The answer was clearly yes.

Note the result of this experiment: rats are placed in the white portion of the box, where they work very hard trying to get to the black portion. Seeing this for the first time, one might well ask why the rats have a drive toward black; one might not realize that an untrained rat would likely stay all day in the white box. The rats who work to get out are trying to avoid pain; by Miller's ingenious manipulations, that primary drive has been translated into an attempt to avoid white—a secondary motivation. Consider all the people who work so hard and long to get some green slips of paper called money. Is there a green-approach drive in humans? No. Then what is the drive? The human case is much more complex, but some have suggested that lack of money causes fear and anxiety because, in the past, it has led to pain. So our human examples work to avoid pain (avoid the absence of green slips of paper). The drive to make money probably does help to avoid pain. The lack of money can be associated with hunger, thirst, physical pain, lack of sexual satisfaction, and many other things. Hull gave us a glimpse into how these multiple associations are made.

Secondary Reinforcement. Secondary reinforcement is closely related to secondary motivation. When a primary drive is reduced, this occurrence is called primary reinforcement. Now suppose that there is a neutral stimulus frequently or always associated with the primary reinforcement. For example, every time a food pellet is delivered to a rat, a soft, clicking sound is made. Soon the click will become reinforcing; that is, it will cause an increase in habit strength, as indicated by the increased probability of response, even if no food is delivered at all. The sound has become a secondary reinforcer. Any stimulus associated with the primary reinforcement will do. Miller's frightened rats worked for blackness; "black" had become a secondary reinforcer.

Secondary reinforcement is a substitute for the real thing, of course; rats cannot live long on a diet of clicking sounds. If food never again follows the click, the click will lose its power to reinforce. But the real importance of secondary reinforcers is not that they are effective; it is their greater flexibility.

Consider, for example, money as a secondary reinforcer. People work for money because money is associated with the reduction of many primary drives: it can buy food and drink, a sexy dress, and drugs to relieve pain. Should it lose this power, however, as sometimes happens in countries experiencing wild inflation, people stop working for the pieces of paper. As long as it continues to be reinforcing, it's much easier to use than a primary reinforcer would be. The point is flexibility. Money is flexible in the sense that it can be delivered quickly and efficiently when and where and in whatever quantity you want it. And it doesn't have to be "consumed" right away. Best of all, it can substitute for whatever primary reinforcer is most valuable to the person receiving it.

Hull also found evidence that, if there were a gap of more than a few seconds between the response to be learned and the primary reinforcement, no learning would occur. But a principle like that complicates efforts to explain learning in both humans and rats. A rat runs a long maze and gets food at the end. It learns the maze; that is, its time to reach the goal box decreases. Why? Because it gets food—primary reinforcement—at the end, right? Wrong. This principle may explain why the rat takes the last step into the goal box, but why did it learn the second-to-last step? Why, when it reached the first decision point in the maze, did it take the correct path? It takes the correct path and, seven minutes later, gets food. Does getting food—primary reinforcement—"stamp in" the habit of taking the correct turn, even though the reinforcement is given seven minutes later? No. Hull's evidence showed that primary reinforcement can't even affect a response made ten seconds ago; how can it affect one made seven minutes ago? There must be a bridge of some type. Here's where secondary reinforcement comes in.

Hull considered it the crowning achievement of his theory that he could answer this question to his satisfaction. Here is how he did it.

When the rat reaches the goal box and eats the food, there are stimuli present that are associated with the primary reinforcement. These stimuli become secondary or learned reinforcers because of that association. Some of these stimuli are "in" the organism (the rat) rather than in the environs of the goal box. Hull focused on those internal stimuli produced by the goal response itself: if the consummatory response is eating, that behavior produces certain stimulation in the body—perhaps muscle tension in the jaw. Jaw tension becomes a secondary reinforcer.

Now, the real goal response becomes associated with several stimuli by means of the primary reinforcement in the goal box, but some of these stimuli are present elsewhere, like the color of the maze or the internal body stimulation, such as hunger pangs, caused by the drive. Hull suggested that, because of these associations, the goal response (or some part of it) would begin to be made before the goal box was reached; the hungry rat would learn to make eating motions before it reached the goal box—anticipatory responses. These anticipatory responses would again produce bodily sensations (jaw tenseness), which are now enforcing. So the early responses in the maze, like choosing the correct path seven minutes before reaching the food, would get reinforced, stamped in by the secondary reinforcement. This is Hull's crowning achievement.

Psychologists had often before spoken of "goals" and "purpose," but how to conceptualize such "anticipatory responses" had been a real problem; Hull gave the answer. Psychologists began again to think in terms of the goals and purpose of behavior, and that by itself was remarkable in a behavioristic era.

The concepts of secondary motivation and secondary reinforcement were especially important to personality theorists. In human behavior, there is not much evidence of action motivated by purely animal drives or reward by primary reinforcement. Hull's theory explained certain human behaviors—working all day to earn money, for example—in a way that was more consistent with the complexities of human experience.

Generalization. There was one concept in Hull's theory that threw psychologists off the track for a while. That concept was *generalization.* It was postulated by Hull, with plenty of good evidence, that, if a response were learned to one stimulus, that response could also be elicited by a similar stimulus, although with slightly decreased intensity or probability. If you learn to make a certain response to a bright light, then a slightly dimmer light will evoke the same response. You have generalized your response, and the more similar the new stimulus is to the original stimulus, the stronger your response will be. Personologists used this principle for a long time to explain "displacement" actions, behavior intended for one target but displaced to another because the primary target was not accessible. You wish to beat the daylights (*R*) out of your father (*S*) because he has made you mad; you don't do it, because you know that he won't take kindly to such treatment; so instead you attack a "father figure" (a stimulus similar to your real father), like a priest (or the church) or a policeman (or the establishment). They are similar to your father on the authority dimension.

A fine theory for explaining aggression. But it doesn't usually work. We shall see why in a later chapter, but here is just one example. If this theory of displacement of aggression is correct, then why was aggression so often displaced on minority groups? Why did young Whites, angry at their fathers, attack Blacks? The reason can't be that Blacks resemble their fathers. Rather, they were taught that Blacks were an acceptable object of aggression, directly, not by simple generalization. Read this sentence and see if it makes sense: I have *generalized* my aggression to a group of people I want to *discriminate* against. Generalization and discrimination are contradictory terms. Even so, for a long time, personologists thought about discrimination and prejudice in terms of generalization. But the explanation was too simple. Evidence came pouring in suggesting that other forces and processes were involved, but only recently have personologists been willing to foresake the safety of Hull's approach.

Behavior Relevance. So there was the bad with the good. Perhaps that is an inevitable feature of theories. Perhaps the most significant contribution was the *form* of the theory. Not that it was mathematical, not that it was deductive, but that it was behavioristic and objective and not "mentalistic." Hull showed that Watson's philosophy could be translated into a meaningful theory of behavior, one that dealt with meaningful concepts. Hull's approach put the focus on prediction and experimentation. His assumptions could be proved wrong by experimental evidence. That fact was exciting.

The letter of Hull's theory may be gone, but its spirit continues. After Hull, psychologists had to relate their theoretical statements to observable behavior. The psychological world would never again accept theories that were not *behavior relevant.* The age of armchair theories was over, and psychologists, including personologists, moved into the laboratory. They took a permanent lease.

B. F. Skinner

While Hull was dominating the pages of the scientific journals, there was always a pesky voice in the background, the voice of a rebel and a gadfly. Burrhus F. Skinner. In the end, Skinner would win out over

Hull; if there were an award for the greatest learning theorist of the first hundred years of psychology, it would have to go to Skinner. But this is odd, because Skinner was not a theorist in the usual sense of the word. He claimed to hate theories, he stopped using them, and he said that they were the first step on the road to speculation addiction. Here is Skinner's story, from its beginnings in a quiet town in Pennsylvania to the height of his reknown, when *Life* magazine proclaimed the man and his ideas "a corruption of an impulse."

After a quiet childhood, marked by his failure to build a perpetual-motion machine, Skinner went to Hamilton College with hopes of becoming a serious writer. Here is a sample from his efforts:

> An old man, sowing in a field,
> Walks with a slow, uneasy rhythm.
> He tears handfuls of seed from his vitals,
> Caressing the wind with the sweep of his hand.
> At night he stops, breathless,
> Murmuring to his earthly consort,
> "Love exhausts me!"[5]

He sent three stories to Robert Frost, who encouraged his literary efforts. Skinner decided to make writing his career, so, when he graduated from college, he set up a study in the attic of his parents' house, where he read books, built model ships, listened to the radio, and thought about seeing a psychiatrist. Typical first year of a writer. Finally he wrote a book. It was called *A Digest of Decisions of the Anthracite Board of Conciliation,* which is not a bad title; but, unfortunately, the title accurately reflected the contents. He had been hired by a coal-mining company to write the book.

Needless to say, *A Digest* was not Skinner's idea of great literature (nor anyone else's), so he went to New York and lived in Greenwich Village to stimulate his creativity. He lived "a bohemian life," which most psychologists, knowing only the quiet and refined Skinner of later years, still find hard to imagine. Not hard to believe, mind you, just hard to imagine. Skinner admits to having indulged in prohibition gin. But he was beginning to understand something about himself–that his interest in writing was more an interest in human behavior than in literature as an art form.

> I failed as a writer because I had nothing important to say, but I could not accept that explanation. It was literature which must be at fault. [I learned of] Chesterton's remark about a character of Thackeray's: 'Thackeray didn't know it but she drank.' I generalized the principle to all literature. A writer might portray human behavior accurately, but he did not therefore understand it. I was to remain interested in human behavior, but the literary method failed me.[6]

[5]From *A History of Psychology in Autobiography* (Vol. 5), p. 534. Reprinted by permission.

[6]From *A History of Psychology in Autobiography* (Vol. 5), p. 395.

From Bohemian to Behaviorist

Skinner then enrolled at Harvard. His area of concentration was to be psychology, though he knew very little about what he was getting into. He had read Pavlov and Watson before entering Harvard, and he had seen a troupe of performing pigeons at a county fair. And that was all he knew about psychology.

Psychology wasn't at all like that. It was sensation and perception and a little psychoanalysis. Skinner ended up spending most of his time with physiology professors; they, at least, knew about Pavlov. But he got his Ph.D. Now he was on his own.

Skinner's interest in behavior intensified. He wanted to know what caused behavior, that's all. He had grown thoroughly dissatisfied with literary explanations like "The world was too much for him," and he found "the conflict of id and ego" equally inadequate. Behavior. Behavior! Watson said it could and should be done, and Skinner believed him. Forget the mind. Psychology is the science of behavior. But how should he study behavior? Thorndike had given some simple demonstrations. Pavlov, however, gave him the answer: control your conditions and you will control behavior.

Control of Conditions

Skinner liked the idea of controlling conditions. To him, it meant building something by design, and he had always been a builder. For example, he built a puzzle box like Thorndike's, but the architectural engineering was much better. He used all kinds of measuring devices, such as kymographs, those circular gizmos with a pen attached that jumps and jerks and jots a crooked line on paper showing when and how much something happened. He became a kind of apparatus king; against his will, his puzzle box gained the name "Skinner box" and became widely used for the study of learning. In more sophisticated form, his kymograph also began to be widely used, and the *cumulative record*—which is essentially what a kymograph produces—became the basic raw data of many learning experiments.

Skinner believed that a good experiment starts with good apparatus. Stick in something for the animal to do—a lever for it to press, for example—and attach that lever to an electronic kymograph to produce a record of the animal's responses. And put in a food-delivery system so that, when the lever is pressed, a food pellet comes out. You hardly need a human scientist around. But you do need a hungry animal.

Responses and Reinforcement

Skinner's first major discovery was that a hungry rat will press a bar in order to get food. Maybe that doesn't sound like an earth-shattering discovery, and by itself it wasn't. Thorndike had already shown that animals would do all kinds of things to get food. But in his major book, *The Behavior of Organisms* (1938), Skinner shed new, and significant, light on this phenomenon. He proposed that there are two classes of response. One is *respondent*—responses *elicited* by stimuli—as salivation is elicited by food. The other class is more important. These responses are called *operant* because their purpose is to "operate" on the environment in order to attain a goal. They are *emitted* rather than *elicited*. What is important for the understanding of a respondent response is the stimulus that *precedes* it, but what is important for the understanding of an operant response is the stimulus that *follows* it—the reinforcement, in other words. Most behavior is operant.

Simple enough. But Skinner's simple words turned the attention of psychology in a different direction. S-R psychology became S-R-S psychology, and the era of reinforcement had begun. "If the occurrence of an operant is followed by presentation of a reinforcing stimulus, the strength is increased."[7] It was Thorndike's law of effect, but now it was Skinner's.

From the beginning, Skinner refused to speculate about what was going on inside the organism, and so he became known as a radical behaviorist. At best, he said, theories are unnecessary, and at worst they are misleading; it is not the purpose of the science to do anything other than propose analyses of behavior—to identify the conditions that produce different behaviors. Why is that dog sitting up? Because you are holding a morsel of food above its head. Does it "want" the food? Skinner wasn't interested in that kind of question.

The result of nonspeculative thinking is invariably dry and colorless. No habits or drives or seething emotions or conflicts or anxieties. No love, no hate, no poetry. Just behavior and its controlling environment. Skinner was accused of dealing with an "empty organism" or a "black box," but that was unfair. He simply was not interested in speculating about what went on "inside" while learning was taking place.

Skinner's book elicited a brief flurry of positive response, then a long flurry of criticism, and most learning theorists and researchers turned happily to Clark Hull's book when it appeared five years later. Probably most people felt that Skinner's approach could not work and would not be productive in the long run. It was too sterile. It would exist for a generation and then die out for lack of progeny, for lack of new ideas. How could you advance if you refused to speculate?

Skinner's "Scientific Method" and Reinforcement Schedules

Many years later, a retrospective Skinner suggested some answers. For example, apparatus sometimes breaks down—he proposed this as a major principle of the scientific method! His food-delivery system jammed, and he discovered *extinction*—the decrease in probability of response when the reinforcement no longer follows the operant response. Another proposed principle of the scientific method was that one might

[7]From Skinner's *The Behavior of Organisms*, Appleton-Century-Crofts, 1938, p. 21.

learn a lot from being lazy. Because he built most of his own devices, at least in the beginning, he had to make his own food pellets for his delivery system. He squeezed them out one by one from a small pill machine he copied from the one used by his friendly neighborhood pharmacist. "One pleasant Saturday afternoon," he recalls, "I surveyed my supply of dry pellets and, appealing to certain elemental theorems in arithmetic, deduced that unless I spent the rest of that afternoon and evening at the pill machine, the supply would be exhausted by 10:30 Monday morning."[8] Ah, such a beautiful day! And it's the weekend. So many more pleasant things to do. "Is there any reason I should reinforce every response?" he thought. "They will be happy enough with one pellet every minute; rats don't need to be fat." He computed the life span of his pellet supply at the rate of one per minute and found that it would last through the next week. He made the necessary adjustments on his apparatus and went off to frolic in the sunshine.

But on Monday, he returned to find his rats doing funny things, not at all the behaviors of his one-response, one-pellet subjects. Skinner convinced himself that these perverted cumulative records had some scientific value. (Since no theory had been used to gather the new data, his thinking went, the scientific value must be tremendous. And since the scientific value is tremendous, the theory about no theories must be correct.) Skinner had discovered *intermittent reinforcement.* One reward every minute. Or every 2 minutes, or 6, or 10. Reinforcement on schedule. Fix an interval of time, and then deliver a food pellet for the first response following the end of that fixed interval. Call this family of schedules *fixed-interval* schedules. The number of kinds of schedule is nearly infinite; it's possible to experiment for years and never use a theory.

Skinner would never say it this way, but what happened with fixed intervals was that the rats learned the schedule and used it to their advantage. For example, there is a rat which is on a fixed-interval schedule of 15 minutes between food pellets. It has to press the bar for a while to determine what the interval is. But soon it figures out that it will have to wait a while for the next pellet, regardless of what it does. Now a fool would keep punching away mindlessly and get fed every 15 minutes. The rat, however, gets one pellet, sits and rests until it "thinks" 15 minutes have passed, and then goes back to the bar and presses it. What's the use of wasting energy? Rats unfortunately have a lousy time sense; they think 15 minutes pass in about 1 or 2, so they still waste a lot of time punching away without effect. But their logic is sound.

Skinner may have liked lazy scientists, but he disliked lazy rats. He knew they were outsmarting him, so he devised a plan to challenge their intelligence further. He would reinforce a rat after 3 minutes, then after 5, then after 7, then after 6. The interval would vary; it would not be fixed. The average interval could be determined, but the next interval couldn't be predicted. The *variable-interval schedule* was born.

Other concepts were born too: the *fixed-ratio schedule,* according to which the rat was rewarded a fixed percent of the time and the

[8]The lazy Saturday when Skinner discovered intermittent reinforcement is described in *Psychology: A Study of a Science* (Vol. 2), p. 368.

variable-ratio schedule, in which the percent varied over the course of learning.

Skinner succeeded in his plan. The variable schedules were too much for the rat; it fell into a hopelessly constant rate of responding. The constant response rate was somewhat higher for variable-ratio schedules than for variable-interval schedules, as if the rat's fevered brain could differentiate between an interval of time and a number of responses but could not make more complex differentiations. Skinner soon had the rats making up to three responses per second over long periods of time. No more sluggards there.

Now Skinner had six schedules, or families of schedules: continuous, extinction, fixed-interval, fixed-ratio, variable-interval, and variable-ratio. Other schedules immediately came to mind—Skinner lists 13 in his 1957 book on schedules—like the "alternative schedule." In this schedule, there is a fixed ratio (for example, 60 responses per reinforcement) and a fixed interval (for example, one minute before reinforcement). The reward is delivered when either one or the other schedule is satisfied. If the animal makes 60 responses before the minute is up, it gets the food; if one minute passes before the 60th response, it gets the food then. You might call this the "warranty" schedule—"5 years or 50,000 miles, whichever comes first." Like many of the other new schedules, it is a combination of two of the original six.

Skinner's Theory and Human Behavior

Skinner was in clover. He had a number of different, objectively defined reinforcement schedules that were easy to program into the Skinner-box apparatus. They could be compared, and the kymographic cumulative recorder would trace their effect on behavior. Outstandingly scientific! Which one produces the fastest rate of response or the slowest or the most constant? All these things could be determined. Was it practical information? Enormously so. Take the owners of a gambling casino. They obviously do not want to reinforce every response made at the slot machines, but they would love a constant, high response rate. Skinner could tell them which schedule to use. Louis Cassels gives the following advice to preachers about delivering sermons: "When you make your point, stop—even if you've been preaching only five minutes. Anti-climax is even deadlier in speaking than in writing. *Besides, an occasional very short sermon will condition your congregation to listen attentively from the very outset, instead of assuming they have 20 minutes in which to tune you in.*"[9] (Emphasis ours.) Clearly this is a suggestion to use the variable-interval schedule in order to elicit a constant rate of attention responses. And it is quite sound advice at that.

The idea of schedules of reinforcement can be used not only to train animals (including humans) but also to understand behavior. Take

[9]From Cassels' article "A Little Advice for Preachers," *San Francisco Chronicle,* April 3, 1971.

the example of a child who has frequent temper tantrums. If you observe the child and his or her father in daily life, you might discover that the father has placed the child on a schedule of reinforcement that naturally leads to increasingly frequent tantrums. One such schedule—not an uncommon one—is a basic fixed-interval schedule with an overlay of a fixed-ratio schedule for high-intensity responses. In other words, the father plans to work from 9 A.M. to noon, at which time he plans to stop work to play with his child. The interval is thus fixed at three hours, and attention-seeking responses before the end of that interval are ignored. But high-intensity responses—screaming, shouting, and breaking things—cannot be easily ignored. They are on a ratio schedule, and the ratio is generally small: one or two tantrums is enough for the father to stop his work and pay attention. Attention, even if not entirely loving, is the reward. Any child on this schedule would soon learn that a few well-timed tantrums get results. And the "problem child" is created.

Learning Theory Meets Personality Theory

Schedules of reinforcement brought learning "theory" into the domain of personality with a flourish. Child training. Gambling behavior. Criminal behavior. The whole legal system in this country can be seen as a reinforcement schedule. Is "society" itself a reinforcement schedule? Certainly, in part. Skinner's theory is now being accepted by most psychologists as a bona fide theory of personality. In addition, it has given rise to a new branch of psychotherapy called *behavior therapy,* which in essence seeks to determine and correct the reinforcement schedules that develop and/or maintain undesirable behaviors (tantrums, fear of snakes or sexual intercourse, or "general behavior disorders" such as psychosis or neurosis). Treatment consists of changing the schedule so as to develop and maintain desirable alternatives. The evidence suggests that behavior therapy is quite often effective.

Like Hull, Skinner relied heavily on the concept of *secondary reinforcement* to explain much of human behavior. Skinner, of course, offered no theory about the nature of secondary reinforcement; he simply described how to set it up. Repeatedly present a stimulus in conjunction with primary reinforcement. This stimulus will then become reinforcing by itself; that is, if it follows a response, the probability of that response will increase.

Skinner Applied: Teaching Sam to Dance

Establishing a Secondary Reinforcer. Several years ago, an introductory-psychology class at the University of Michigan wanted to study certain learning principles, and so they liberated a rat from the animal labs. Their first task was to establish a secondary reinforcer. For this purpose, they used the clacking sound made by a little frog-like metal toy that made a sharp clack when squeezed. For hours, a few members of the class sat around with the rat, whom they called Samuel. They clacked, and then they dropped in a food pellet. They clacked again, and they dropped in another food pellet. Over and over, many times, until finally Samuel got the idea. The clack became a secondary reinforcer.

The reason the students had to establish the secondary reinforcer was that the primary reinforcer (food) would not be useful for the demonstration they wanted. It was too slow, and it required Samuel to be looking at the food dish. Now they had a fast, clear, and distinct substitute—the clack—and it could be heard no matter what Samuel was doing at the time. They were ready for the classroom demonstration, and Samuel was brought on to center stage. "What should we teach him?" asked the naive professor. At that time, a crazy new dance called the Twist was just coming in. "Teach him to do the Twist!" someone said. OK, the Twist it is.

Rewarding Successive Approximations. Now you can't exactly wait for a rat to do the Twist and then reinforce it, because very few rats have been known to do the Twist in public. But luckily Skinner had already spelled out how to proceed: the trainer must *shape* the behavior by reinforcing *successive approximations* of the final desired result. First, therefore, the students had to get Samuel up on his back feet. So whenever he raised his head, even slightly, they clacked. The first thing this procedure demonstrated was the tremendous power of a single reinforcement. Samuel absentmindedly looked up toward the ceiling of his cage—clack. He ran to his food dish (the students didn't want to extinguish their secondary reinforcer), and then he ran back to where he was before and raised his head again—almost like one-trial learning. But now the standards had risen. The students didn't make the sound again until Samuel had lifted his head a little higher than before. Then they required still greater elevation of the head, until Samuel was standing up on his hind legs, trying to get his head higher and higher. Samuel looked disdainful, but he was willing to go along with the gag to get the food.

Once Samuel was standing up, the students stopped reinforcing vertical movement and looked for lateral movement. One step to the right—clack. Now two steps to the right—clack. Now three. Three to the right and one to the left. Finally three to the right, three to the left, and CLACK. It was an impressive demonstration. Here was this rat who had never danced before in his life, and now, in 15 minutes, he was shuffling three to the right and three to the left, doing the Twist better than many of the students.

Using Discriminative Stimuli. Then the class decided to teach Samuel to discriminate proper social customs. Skinner, you remember, had proposed that the stimulus (reinforcement) following the response was most important, but he did not disregard the importance of stimuli preceding the response, even in operant conditioning. These preceding stimuli could function as *discriminative stimuli,* indications of whether or not a response was going to get its reward. Not causes of responses but cues as to what, if anything, would follow the response. The class taught Samuel, therefore, to dance only when music was playing. They reinforced him only when a Chubby Checker record was playing (that's Twist music), and they withheld the reward when it was not playing.

He learned this quickly, too, and now the class had a rat who sat and waited until the music (the discriminative stimulus) came on and then got up and did a vigorous Twist.

The ease with which animals can be trained once a good secondary reinforcer is established is truly impressive. In the same class hour in which Samuel was taught to Twist, he was also taught to climb to the top of his cage to ring a bell. And then, with plenty of time left, he learned to play basketball—that is, to drop a Ping-Pong ball through a small hoop made from a paper clip. This skill turned out to be short-lived, however, because Samuel ate the Ping-Pong ball after his first success (demonstrating nicely that, although training techniques are powerful, so are instinctive reactions). Samuel's eventual fate, after having served valiantly as classroom subject, was to demonstrate that still another psychological phenomenon, prejudice, can be shaped by an appropriate reinforcement schedule. Among those prejudiced against rats, cats and people rank high, but, after two classroom performances, a young woman student fell in love with Samuel and took him home as a pet, where he lived happily ever after with her and her cat. (The cat had also come from the psychology department; it had been raised in total darkness, for a perception experiment, and now seemed to think that Samuel was its mother.)

Reinforcement versus Punishment

Reinforcement, of course, is Skinner's key concept. It is defined by observable effect: increase in response probability. Increased probability is brought about in one of two ways: by *presenting* a stimulus after the response—presenting food, for example, to a hungry rat—or by *removing* a stimulus after the response—shutting off an electric shock, for example. A *positive reinforcer* is one that reinforces when it is presented; a *negative reinforcer* is one that reinforces when it is removed. Note that, when the descriptions are reversed (removing a positive reinforcer like food or presenting a negative reinforcer like shock), you have the definition of *punishment.* Punishment, in the Skinnerian scheme, is a procedure. And, unlike reinforcement, which is defined in terms of its effect (increased response probability), the effects of punishment must be determined by experiments. One might assume that the effects are the opposite, since the procedures are opposite, but this does not seem to be the case. In reality, punishment is not the opposite of reinforcement. It is, rather, *extinction* (no reinforcement) that decreases the probability of response. Punishment has unusual effects, and hearty controversy surrounds investigation of those effects.

Effects of Punishment. Although it is not yet possible to specify the effects of punishment, the issue is of such great importance to personology that we cannot let it slip by without some discussion. People who want to control or influence the behavior of others will often resort to punishment to "eliminate" undesirable actions. Parents spank children, courts impose fines on citizens, and countries drop bombs on other countries. In most cases, the undesirable behavior does indeed disappear . . .

but not for long. Soon the child is abusing the family pet again, the thief is back on the street picking pockets, and the bombed country is planning retaliatory measures. The evidence strongly suggests that punishment *suppresses* behavior for a time but does not *weaken* the tendency to respond in that undesirable fashion.

One characteristic of punishment is that it produces a response itself, often an intense response. If you take candy from a baby (remove a positive reinforcer), the baby will probably howl. If you take candy from a large man, he may break your body into little bits. If you spank a baby (present a negative reinforcer), the baby will cry and cringe. If you spank a large man, he might put your little finger in a pencil sharpener. Fear and aggression are two common responses to punishment. Why, you might ask, does punishment have an immediate deterrent effect? One answer is that punishment elicits a response that is incompatible with the response we want to eliminate. If you drop bombs on an enemy soldier, he will run for cover, and that is incompatible with making an attack. His inclination to attack, however, is undiminished—it may even be increased (by rage)—and, when the stimuli (empty skies) indicate that bombing is over, he will strike again.

Punishment as Stimulus: Good and Bad Effects. Punishment in and of itself results in a lot of stimuli, many of which come from inside the person being punished. You hit me and it hurts—that's stimuli—and I become fearful, with sweaty hands and dry throat—that's a response. But it can also be stimuli for my next behavior. From my point of view, these are bad stimuli; they make me feel bad. I am experiencing all these bad stimuli at the same time as I am engaging in the "undesirable" behavior. The bad stimuli (feelings) can get attached to some event and apparently do so. But to what? The simplest way of answering this question is to distinguish between the cases in which the bad feelings become attached to something that happens *before* the punished response and those in which the feelings are associated with something that happens *after* that response. If I think of doing something awful and feel bad just thinking about it, I probably won't do it. But, if I think of doing something awful and don't feel bad until after I've done it, I will do it but feel "guilty" afterwards. The first case is obviously preferable from the standpoint of the controller of my behavior. But the second case is the more common one, which is unfortunate because nobody wins. I get no pleasure from my act (just guilt feelings), and yet the act is performed, which gives you no pleasure either.

Since my tendency to perform the undesired act is undiminished, even though I have been punished, I either experience conflict (if the bad feelings come before the act) or become aware of personal guilt (after the act). I experience pain either way. And often the pain carries over into situations to which it was not meant to apply. In the past, people in many Western societies were taught that sex before marriage was wrong, but they were expected to enjoy it after marriage. But sexual responses—even sexual thoughts—were subject to severe reprimand (a secondary punishment), so that, when many people married, their sexual activity was either preceded by bad feelings (impotence and frigidity) or followed by guilt and loss of pleasure.

Punishment, on the other hand, is not always a villain. In many instances, the immediate effect, the suppression of behavior, is both valuable and effective. If a child is about to run into a busy street or stick a hand through a glass door, the behavior must be suppressed immediately or there may be no long term to worry about. Suppression of behavior, in general, also allows for other, more desirable responses to occur, and these can be reinforced so that, in the future, the same situation is more likely to produce the desirable response. You come upon your daughter, for example, throwing rocks at the neighbor's window. You tell her to stop and administer a little stern disapproval and maybe a whack or two. This will suppress rock throwing for a while, and, in the interval, she may pick up a bat and ball and find that the national pastime is great fun. Later she will go out to play ball instead of throwing rocks; everybody's happy (except perhaps the neighbor, who can't see much difference between a window broken by a rock and one broken by a baseball).

But, in the overall picture, punishment cannot be said to be a good or an effective training procedure. The bad effects generally outweigh the good. And there are nearly always alternative training procedures. The best way to eliminate bad behavior is to stop reinforcing it—extinguish it. Don't pick up a cranky child simply because he or she is whimpering; ignore the noise and soon it will stop. If you can't control the reinforcement—you can't make a thrown rock not reach its target—try reinforcing a different, incompatible response. Don't run out and hit your kid when she throws a rock at the neighbor's window; go out and start a game of ball. Encourage her, reward her. Christian theory confirmed by Skinner: positive reinforcement (such as love) works better than punishment.

Freedom or Control: Social Implications of Skinner's Theory

We'll talk more about punishment later, but now we should turn to other aspects of Skinner's theory. Using Skinner's methods, one can exert astounding control over the behavior of animals (including humans) in the laboratory. It stands to reason, then, that such control could be applied to human behavior in the real world. The thought of humans not being "free" but being controlled and manipulated inspired great fear and rage, and a lot of it was directed toward B. F. Skinner.

Most scientists work under the assumption that events are determined, not capricious. Scientifically, the personal responsibility of humans for their own behavior makes no sense; *free will* and *free choice* are not terms in the language system of science. Consider, for example, a scientist, like a psychiatrist on a witness stand being asked whether or not a defendant was responsible for his or her behavior. In scientific terms, there is only one answer: the defendant was not responsible, because all behavior is determined. What the court should ask is whether the crime was committed in a situation so unusual that the chances of its recurring are slight and it is therefore safe to let the defendant back on the streets. (Most good courtroom psychiatrists probably translate the original question into those terms anyway.) The point is that two major language systems exist side by side—that of science, based on prediction and control and determinism, and that of free will and personal responsibility, on which society in general is founded. The two systems are not necessarily incompatible. They come into conflict because, in science, "freedom" is a dirty word—it means random, unpredictable behavior, outside the realm of study. And in society's view, "determinism" and "control" are taboo because they represent loss of freedom and liberty.

The conflict is more apparent than real, however, because the comparisions are made between two languages, not within one. But there is no question that Skinner's ideas have terrified more than a few readers, for he has always tried to apply his findings to problems in the real world. He wrote a book (an unspent response tendency from his youth) called *Walden Two,* a utopian novel in which he describes the "perfect" society in light of his behavioral discoveries. His influential book *Beyond Freedom and Dignity* deals directly with societal applications of rat and pigeon research, in government, religion, and business. His applications range from the explanation of simple superstitions to the design of world cultures. No arena of human behavior escapes his scrutiny or his advice.

But there are many sides to this "frightening" prospect that human behavior may be controlled and manipulated. There are times, for example, when you want behavior (your own or that of others) to be controlled, and you are upset if it is not. We pay good money to psychotherapists in the hopes of changing our behavior in some way; if the psychotherapist fails, nobody glories in the triumph of freedom over control. We pay to be educated or to have our children educated; failure is not welcomed. We pay to have our streets safe at night; we're not pleased by a mugging. Take the welfare "problem," and look at it as a behavioral problem. For many years, in many parts of the United States, people on welfare have been given money if they had no job. If they got a job, even a part-time job, their earnings were subtracted from their welfare check. This situation left them an interesting choice: do nothing and receive a certain amount of money, or work and get the same amount (or less). You don't need Skinner to tell you the probable results of such a schedule of reinforcement.

And, still, the fear remains that, if someone knows all these techniques of behavior control, we can be manipulated against our will. Think of the advertising industry, striving mightily to elicit a buying response for everything from toothpaste to presidents. The sales representative who makes you think you're a bad person because you don't have a set of encyclopedias for your child or because you're unwilling to help him or her win a scholarship. Sex as a sales tool. Use Brand A on your hair, Brand B on your teeth, Brand C on your underarms, Brand D on your genitals, Brand E on your feet, and Brand F all over your body, and you can't miss. Give lavish praise because people like it. Buy a gift for someone from whom you want something. Do it our way, and we'll see that you're happy.

Skinner might call our attention to the words of Francesco Lana, a 17th-century scientist who pondered the possibility of a "ship" that could float on air instead of water. It might not work, he said, for there is the possibility "that God will never suffer this Invention to take effect, because of the many consequences which may disturb the Civil Government of men. For who sees not, that no City can be secure against attack, since our Ship may at any time be placed directly over it, and descending down may discharge Souldiers; the same would happen to private Houses, and Ships on the Sea: for our Ship descending out of the Air to the sails of Sea-Ships, it may cut their Ropes, yea without descending by casting Grapples it may over-set them, kill their men, burn their Ships by artificial Fire works and Fire-balls. And this they may do not only to Ships but to great Buildings, Castles, Cities, with such security that they which cast these things down from a height out of Gun-shot, cannot on the other side be offended by those below."[10]

The airplane was invented, and, God's disfavor notwithstanding, has often been used in the horrible fashion Lana so accurately forecast. Similarly, Skinner says, behavior technology is possible, it has been "invented," and it is being and will be used, for good and for bad. By itself it is neither good nor bad. We cannot ignore it. It will not ignore us.

Chapter Summary

In this chapter, we've presented a partial history of learning theory and research and attempted to show the influences of learning theory on personality theory and research. Some of these influences were subtle: a spirit, a general approach, a demonstration of effective procedure, and a new enthusiasm for rigor and precision. In the era of Thorndike, Watson, Pavlov, Hull, and Skinner, all of psychology including personology became behavioristic: objective, empirical, and experimental. It became scientific. Thorndike and Hull and Skinner and Pavlov explained how, and Watson explained why.

There was new terminology. Stimulus and response. The S-R approach. Behaviorism. Classical (Pavlovian) conditioning. The law of effect. Reinforcement. Drives. Secondary reinforcement. Secondary drives. Operant or instrumental conditioning. Schedules of reinforcement. Applications to complex human behavior. Without being able to pinpoint the exact time and place, people began to notice that learning theories were evolving into *general behavior theories,* which made them personality theories too. Skinner is now being accepted as a personality theorist and his influence in other theories is strong and growing.

In the early years of learning research, the approach and the methods were prominent. The content and the concepts developed slowly

[10]Skinner uses this quote from Lana in Chapter 1 of *Science and Human Behavior,* Macmillan, 1953.

but surely. The whole thing was most easily applied to simple experiments on subhuman animals, the rat in particular. But it was not considered a psychology of the rat; the principles were generalized, in some cases to an extreme. Mice and humans. Slowly, the approach and the methods became more sophisticated and were applied to experiments on the college sophomore. (The college sophomore, as far as the researchers were concerned, behaved much like the rat, so a lot of the content and many of the concepts found solid ground on the human level. Some did not, of course, and new thinking had to be done.) But we were "into it" now, this new science and its new technology.

It has been argued that Hull's general behavior theory failed because it was too general in a science that was moving toward specialization; however, it was the generality of the later learning theories, both Hull's and Skinner's, that made them successful, especially in penetrating the area of personality, which by definition requires broadness. So perhaps it's inappropriate to speak of "success" and "failure." It might be better simply to view the process of scientific advance in any field as one of increasing knowledge about more and more detailed events. Learning theory began with simple ideas about how cats get out of boxes. It moved to more detailed analysis of motivation and reinforcement. Now it is concerned with increasingly minute aspects of the memory process: encoding, storage, and retrieval. The basic early discoveries, such as the law of effect, are more or less simply assumed; the less specialized theories are replaced by more specialized theories that incorporate the previous ideas.

A similar process has characterized personology. Freud stated the basic issues. Many of these basic issues were studied in more detail, and a more specialized theory was born. In many cases, concepts from learning theory have proven more specialized and more appropriate. They are therefore "appropriated" by the personologists, and learning as a field moves on to still more detailed inquiries. Personology adopts, uses, and expands concepts from other fields in psychology, which it must, because it is the most general field.

Skinner's theory still has much to offer and is certainly still being used; so is Hull's, for that matter, although in modified forms. But learning theory and research seem to have turned to other questions. In a recently published introductory text, the concepts of motivation and reinforcement are not even mentioned in the chapter on learning, and the concept of stimuli, never used with much precision before, is tackled with great vigor. In personality research, however, the concepts of Hull and Skinner are being applied and tested with humans in situations of obvious importance to the personality theorists. We're beginning to see how concepts and processes from learning theory can be used to promote our understanding of the human personality.

The basic message of this chapter is this: behavior is created and maintained by reinforcement. If you see action, ask how it was produced and why it is being exhibited. Think about stimuli that might be associated with a drive or a reinforcement or that might be used as a cue to effective behavior. What schedule of reinforcement is being used? If the behavior is undesirable, how can it be changed? If a desired behavior is *not* being exhibited, how can it be produced? There are answers here, and there are answers still to come.

Suggested Readings

If you want to follow up on learning-theory approaches to personality, here are some places to start. J. Dollard and N. Miller's *Personality and Psychotherapy* (McGraw-Hill, 1950) reflects the influence of Hull, while A. Bandura's *Principles of Behavior Modification* (Holt, Rinehart & Winston, 1969) leans more toward Skinner. A textbook by E. R. Hilgard and G. H. Bower, *Theories of Learning* (Prentice-Hall, 1975, 4th ed.) presents good summaries of the various theories from the standpoint of the learning-theory specialty area.

Well worth reading, too, are Skinner's three books: *Science and Human Behavior* (Macmillan, 1953), the novel *Walden Two* (Holt, Rinchart & Winston, 1959), and *Beyond Freedom and Dignity* (Bantam, 1972), all available in paperback. They're fun. Skinner has also written his autobiography, and, if you're intrigued by the man (or, as he would put it, by the personal conditions that impinged on him and made him the "locus" of this theory), you'll find it fascinating. R. W. Lundin has a personality text based on Skinner's approach, *Personality: A Behavioral Analysis* (Macmillan, 1974), that you might find useful. For discussions of more general issues in behaviorism, try "Teaching Machines" (*Science,* 1958, *128,* 969–977), "Pigeons in a Pelican" (*American Psychologist,* 1960, *15,* 28–37), and "The Design of Cultures" (*Daedalus,* 1961, *90,* 534–546), all by Skinner. If you want to teach animals, there are few better cookbooks than Skinner's "How to Teach Animals" in *Scientific American,* December, 1951.

And, if you're specifically interested in psychotherapy, try *Theory and Practice in Behavior Therapy* by Aubrey Yates (Wiley, 1975) or David Martin's *Learning-Based Client-Centered Therapy* (Brooks/Cole, 1972).

Notes and References

An authoritative textbook summary of the theories of Thorndike, Pavlov, Hull, and Skinner can be found in E. R. Hilgard and G. H. Bower's *Theories of Learning* (4th ed.) (Prentice-Hall,1975). E. G. Boring's *A History of Experimental Psychology* (2nd ed.) (Appleton-Century-Crofts, 1950) contains much historical information on behaviorism, especially on the early years; the biographical material on Descartes can also be found there. There is a series of books, now totaling five volumes, entitled *A History of Psychology in Autobiography.* Volume 3 contains the stories of Thorndike and Watson. Hull is in Volume 4, and Skinner can be found in Volume 5. Skinner's history of his own scientific method can be found in Volume 2 of the series *Psychology: A Study of a Science* (McGraw-Hill, 1959), edited by S. Koch.

The primary sources for each theorist are as follows:

For Thorndike:

Animal Intelligence. *Psychological Review Monograph Supplement,* Vol. 2, No. 8, 1898.

Animal Intelligence. Macmillan, 1911.

The Psychology of Learning. Teachers College, 1913.

The Fundamentals of Learning. Teachers College, 1932.

For Watson:

Psychology as the Behaviorist Views It. *Psychological Review,* 1913, *20,* 158–177.

Psychology from the Standpoint of a Behaviorist. Lippincott, 1919.

Conditioned emotional reactions. *Journal of Experimental Psychology,* 1920, *3,* 1–14 (with R. Rayner).

For Pavlov:

Conditioned Reflexes. Oxford University Press, 1927.

For Hull:

Principles of Behavior. Appleton-Century-Crofts, 1943.

Essentials of Behavior. Yale University Press, 1951.

A Behavior System. Yale University Press, 1952.

For Skinner:

The Behavior of Organisms. Appleton-Century-Crofts, 1938.

Science and Human Behavior. Macmillan, 1953.

Schedules of Reinforcement. Appleton-Century-Crofts, 1957 (with C. S. Ferster).

6

Interlude

Direction is the legacy of the past.

Charles Pauling

Let's take a step back for a moment and look at where we have been, where we are, and where we are going. We have met Sigmund Freud, dignified and diligent. We have seen Adler and Jung and Rank dissent from Freud and explored the reasons why. We have delved into the beginnings of the individual-differences approach and seen some of its effects. And we have looked at another field of psychology, learning theory, trying to discern its influence. These are the four great lines of thought that run through all of personology. We have seen the roots.

Psychotherapy is a supreme testing ground for personality theories. The prevailing view among psychologists has always been that, if a theory cannot explain the most extreme (deviant) forms of behavior, then it will have little power to explain behavior in general. True or not, this view has formed and molded the approach of the theorists. And so the four great lines of thought should be apparent in psychotherapy, and they are—very apparent indeed. You can choose a therapist whose approach is primarily psychoanalytic, or one who focuses on the humanistic aspects of your "dilemma," or one who espouses behavior therapy. These approaches are, respectively, the modern legacies of Freud, of the Freudian dissenters, and of the learning theorists. At times, each of them uses psychological tests, products of the individual-differences movement, as diagnostic instruments.

Of course, the above paragraph is obviously a vastly oversimplified and abstract description of what's really happening. Many therapists use all four approaches with little commitment to any single one—they do what they feel is required for each patient. Psychiatrists, who, unlike psychologists (Ph.D.s), have medical degrees (M.D.s), may prescribe drugs. Because theoretical approaches are continually being refined, a humanist may now have any one of a number of approaches, and so may an analyst, and so may a behavior therapist. And there are good and bad psychological tests. But, in general, we have encountered the first main lines of personality theory.

Let's look at a more graphic representation of where we are and how we got here. (See Figure 6-1, which is stolen from the fine mind of John W. Atkinson and adapted from a chart in Atkinson's *Introduction to Motivation,* p. 204.) The chart is a map of the field, but it is an old map. It shows the beginnings from the three implications of Darwin's theory of evolution: Humans are like animals (Freudian psychoanalysis, humans with unconscious instincts); animals are like humans (learning theory, animals with emotions and intellect); and individual differences exist among members of all species (for natural selection), leading to testing and factor analysis. The modified pre-Darwinian lines—humans as humans, animals as animals—are also included. "Humans as humans" is represented by humanism (an apt term) and, in this book, by Adler, Jung, and Rank. Animal as animal, which owes its development in part

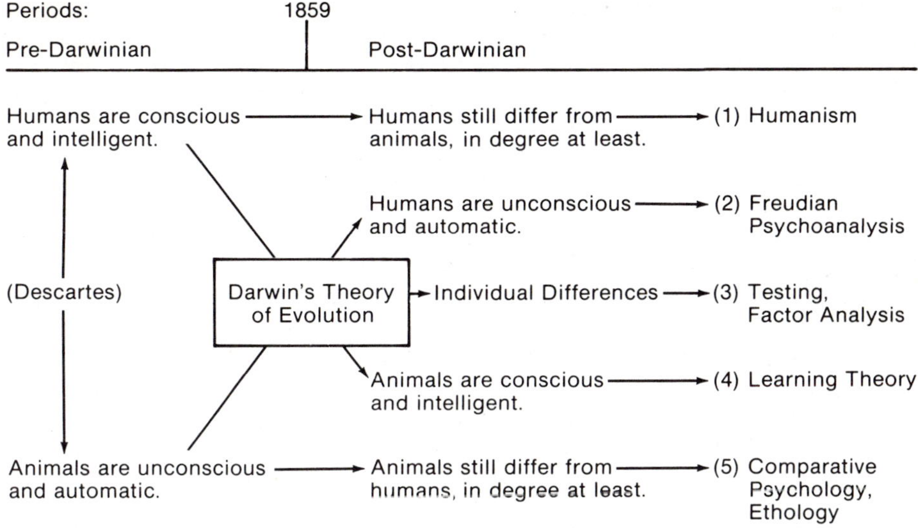

Figure 6-1. Major trends in personality theory. (Adapted from *Introduction to Motivation,* by J. W. Atkinson. Copyright 1964 by Litton Educational Publishing, Inc. Used by permission of Van Nostrand Reinhold Company.

to John B. Watson, led to comparative psychology and later to ethology, which are both strong areas of research and theory but are not direct lines in the history of personality theory.

It is probably best not to treat these lines in personality theory as separate and incompatible approaches. Each approach developed historically in a somewhat different context, and each represents an honest search for the meaning of human behavior. Humanism and psychoanalysis come out of psychotherapy, where broad issues are faced daily and even vague and general answers can be useful. Testing developed from the notion of individual differences, and its growth was (and is) largely a function of advance in statistical methods. Learning theory has remained a laboratory-based line, where broad issues and general answers clearly hinder progress rather than help it. The object of study is the same in all cases—the human animal—and the different approaches are saying different things about that object of study; in that sense, they are incompatible.

But there is incompatibility and there is incompatibility. As we've already seen, learning theory and psychoanalysis/humanism are difficult to relate to each other because the latter forces consideration of broad and general concepts and the former narrow and specific concepts. This was, is now, and probably always will be a major point of dispute.

There is also the problem of language systems. As each line develops, the theories develop individual concepts and ways of explaining relevant content. The relevant content may be the same, but the conceptual structures surrounding it may differ greatly from one theory to another. The id, ego, and superego versus habit strength and secondary motivation, for instance. Translations from one system into another can be made, but the old saw "It loses something in the translation" is true here as in literature. What is the ego in S-R terms? Perhaps that question can be answered, but how well? As of today, not very well. Not well enough to satisfy either the S-R people or the ego theorists, at least.

But this book is about a group of valiant people searching for ways to understand themselves and other people. They are serious scholars, and they are not fools. If they work primarily along one line, with one approach, they will not dismiss discoveries made by those who take other approaches. They will try to incorporate a new finding, take from it what they feel is valid, and move forward. Some use more than one approach at the same time, concerned more with usefulness than with loyalty. Many psychotherapists, for example, will use Skinnerian techniques on some problems, Freudian techniques on others, and Jungian techniques on still others. That's an ecumenical practitioner.

In the chapters to come, you are going to meet a group of such theorists. They are called *eclectic* theorists, meaning that they select what they consider best from the several approaches, from the various doctrines, from the many methods. A good eclectic must integrate all that he or she has gathered. (Bad eclecticism generally sounds like verbal garbage—no one but the theorist can (or wants to) make sense of it—and so it disappears quickly.) The theorists you will meet here will be the good eclectics. *Eclectic* is the word that psychology applies to such theorists; in some cases, they apply it to themselves as well. It describes what they do. They could be called "synthesizers" as well, in the sense of Hegel's thesis-antithesis-synthesis construct, a good description of how human knowledge advances. But we like the term *ecumenical.* Though it typically has a religious connotation, its real meaning is "worldwide." The spirit of ecumenicism is that there is one truth for the whole world, a singular truth, and not many different truths. In psychology, this means that there is one truth about human behavior. There are many differing approximations, but somewhere there is the one truth. Each theory may have parts of the truth, but none has all. Eclecticism is the process, but ecumenicism is the moving force.

The ecumenical theorists are themselves, however, of many different types. (Oh, would that science were a simpler process!) The next generation will have 8 or 16 or 32 approaches to integrate. Our chart (Figure 6-1) shows four lines. Atkinson went further, and his chart has arrows all over the page. It's progress, certainly—those that stand on the shoulders of giants can see farther even than the giants. But the complexity, as it becomes known, spawns a variety of interpretations: greater complexity, greater variety, more arguments, more splintering off. (It comes to mind that the system may someday break down and someone will state an uncertainty principle, glorifying ignorance and incorporating the enemy.) But the goal remains: understanding, knowledge.

It's a process that defies brief description here. You are about to see it in action, however, in the following chapters.

There will be examples of theories that could be called direct descendants of those we have already encountered. In general, psychoanalytic theories today clearly owe a large debt to Sigmund Freud. As a group, however, they are better labeled *ego psychologies,* a label that characterizes their increased theoretical concern for the ego processes (Freud concentrated on the id) and also indicates the influence of non-Freudian approaches. Included, too, of course, are some of the insights of Jung, Adler, and Rank, some of the discoveries of experimental psychology, including learning theory, and some of the methods of the mental-test movement. Similarly, there are direct descendants of the learning theories, now spiced with the insights of early humanism and psychoanalysis. A kind of cross-pollination process. Modern factor-analytic theories take what they can from the other theories, and personality tests have infiltrated all the other approaches. Outside fields—from philosophy to physiology—exert their own special influence as, for example, some theories take the form of computer models.

There will also be examples of theories that have no direct predecessors but are, rather, amalgams of two or more approaches, with sometimes surprising results. We will meet some sociological types whose approaches were affected by humanism, psychoanalysis, and learning theory but resemble none of these. We will meet one George Kelly, whose approach seems more like a theory of the scientist than a scientist's theory.

The ideas flow, blend, merge, separate. Synthesis, antithesis. And you, the reader, are a part of this process. As you read on, as you try to understand each set of ideas and find a place for them in what you already know and believe, you too will be creating theory. *Your* theory. You could do it—you may already have done it—with the material presented in these first five chapters. You will do it better as you add what is to come.

New theories, new faces. Although less biographical material is available for the more recent theorists and although "team efforts" have become more prevalent since the demise of armchair theorizing, the intellectual history remains dramatic, controversial, and exciting. The men and women involved, past and future, are by definition brilliant and creative. Great new ideas are perhaps more likely, even if they are less prominent because of their increasing number.

But take a nostalgic look back. Sigmund Freud. What a man! What a mind! Quiet, dignified, dedicated, yet a fighter. Polemic, hardnosed, visionary, as he had to be. In these respects, very much like B. F. Skinner. Understatements from Rank, overstatements from Adler and Watson, visions by Jung and Hull. The dedication and stubbornness of Thorndike and Pavlov and Cattell. All of them creative. The quirks of fate that turned out to be so important. Freud's discovery that patients don't always tell the truth. The dreams of Jung that did not fit the pattern. Wundt's tolerance of the brashness of J. M. Cattell. The decision of authorities to stop Thorndike's ESP experiments on children. Skinner's apparatus breaks down. Pavlov's dogs ruin his experiments on digestion by "anticipating." Failures made successes. It was an exciting time, the beginnings of knowledge. New ideas challenging old traditions. New ideas supporting old traditions. The beginning of psychology as a science, and the first scientific studies of human behavior.

One more thing. We have to get a sense of time. Our purpose in the preceding chapters was to proclaim the four major lines of personality theory and research. To do so, it was necessary to describe some theories that are currently evolving, currently productive, currently fighting for their place in the limelight. Take a look at still another map (Figure 6-2). It will give you some sense of time. The chart shows only the *approximate* period of time when *writings* were published that are *directly concerned* with our story of the search to understand the human personality. But it gives a good picture of the sequence of events. And it does do justice to the theorists (Cattell, Eysenck, and Skinner) who are very much alive and well at the time of this writing. Their ideas are very much alive, too, current and evolving yet.

It is interesting to note that the other theorists we will encounter in this book, with minor exceptions, are all in the post-1930 era. This fact is perhaps more significant in light of the number of pre-1930 personality theorists, of whom we can list only four: Freud, Adler, Jung, and Rank. Only four, and all analytic in approach. The other pre-1930 people in Figure 6-2 were not personality theorists; they developed the approaches that eventually became personality theories, but they themselves were not directly concerned. For 30 years, then, it was Freud and the Freudian dissenters—no other major voices. *They were personality theory.* The "individual-differences" line did not produce a real personality theory (by itself) until the mid 1940s. The learning-theory approach, its direct offspring, started production at about the same time. If one discounts Freud, personality theory and research is but 25 years old! Perhaps it can be said that personology is the youngest of the major specialties in psychology. Perhaps. But, then again, how can one possibly discount Freud?

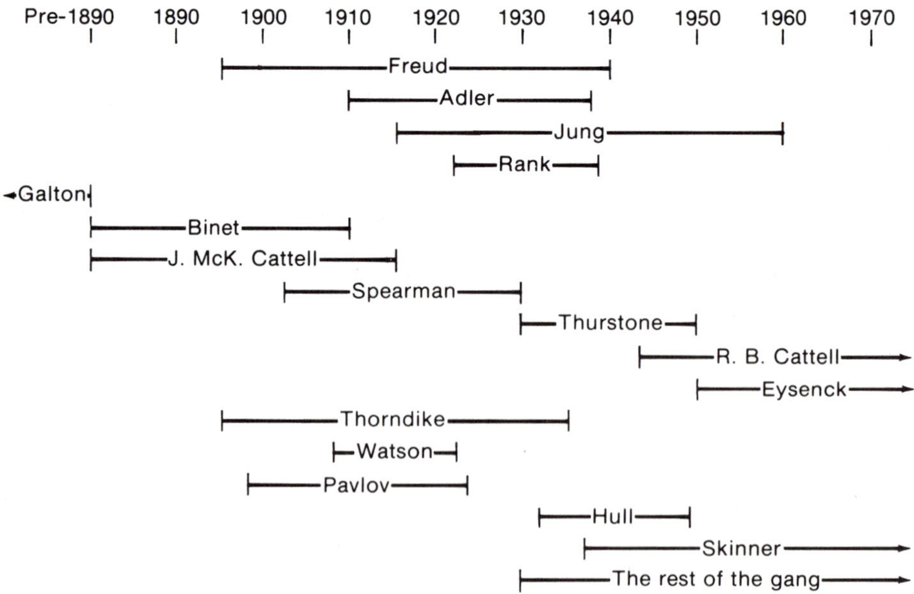

Figure 6-2. The period of active work by various theorists.

7

The Ecumenical Eclectics

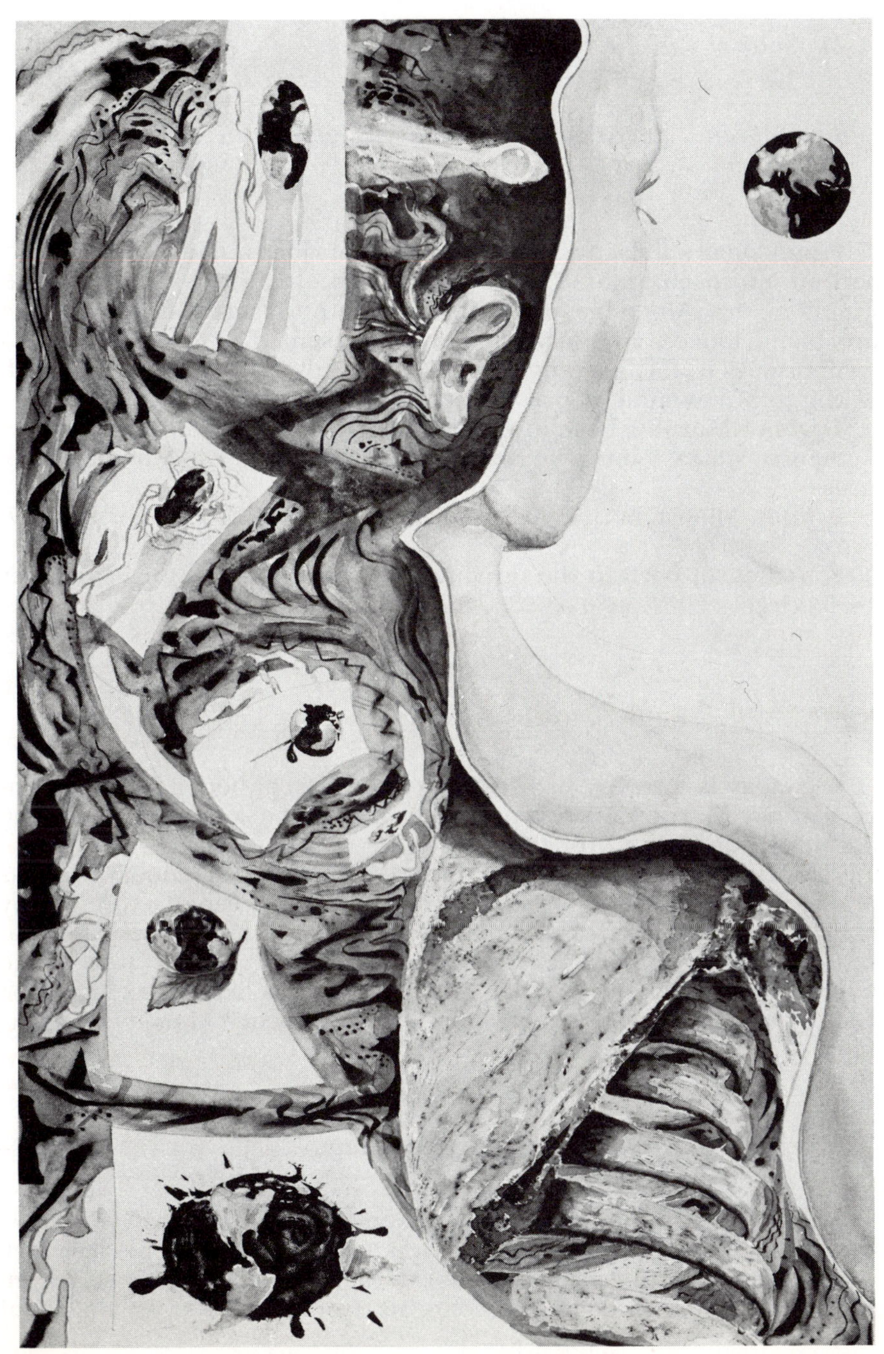

I believe it is better to be tentative, eclectic, and humble.
G. W. Allport

My book . . . is likely to be called "eclectic."
G. Murphy

I have been . . . a promoter, in a little way, of marriages of concepts. . . .
H. A. Murray

Ecumenical. Eclectic. A democracy of ideas and thus an all-American approach, right? Then add a dollop of German discipline and restraint to this American optimism and enthusiasm, and you have a hearty blend, indeed! Just such a blend is represented by the four theorists we will discuss in this chapter—four eclectics, all different yet all related, ushering in a new kind of psychology.

Gardner Murphy, born in Chillicothe, Ohio, on July 8, 1895. Cancer.

Henry Murray, born in New York, New York, on May 13, 1893. Taurus.

Gordon Allport, born in Montezuma, Indiana, on November 11, 1897. Scorpio.

Kurt Lewin, born in the province of Posen, Prussia, on September 9, 1890. Virgo.

Gardner Murphy the Crab

Astrology is a theory of personality of sorts, although hardly scientific. Gardner Murphy was born a Crab—that is, he was born under the sun sign of Cancer, and for that reason we suspect that he might share some character features with Ringo Starr. Perhaps it is the moon-madness characteristic of Cancers, the delightful lunacy that Ringo expresses by profession and that Murphy displayed in his enduring interest in parapsychology, that somewhat taboo collection of unusual topics like extrasensory perception (ESP). Cancers (being crablike) also tend to be collectors, and what better description of an eclectic? Murphy was certainly that.

Murphy's Biosocial Approach: A Preview

In 1947, Murphy published a book entitled *Personality: A Biosocial Approach to Origins and Structure.* It was mammoth, in scope, in effort, and in sheer length (over 1000 pages). It was eclectic, of course, an integrated collection of data and concepts from almost every realm of science and from some unscientific realms as well. It was Murphy's magnum opus. It contained a few terms that were new to personology: *canalization,* for example, describes the attachment of a drive or motive to an object satisfying that drive; the drive and the object have a canal or channel between them; and, when the drive is energized, the energy flows to the object naturally and directly like water down the canal to its natural goal. Murphy's theory was a *field theory,* meaning something like biosocial, the interaction of the person (bio) with the environment (social). Behavior occurs because of the field and not because of either the person or the environment alone. Perception is the means by which the two components relate. Reality is picked up by the senses and carried to the brain, and there something happens: cognition, individual thinking, autistic processes, the amalgam of the outside coming in and the inside coming up. Ultimately there is action. For Murphy, perception was the key.

It was 1931 when this key was given to Murphy. He was in the Grand Canyon at the time, with his wife and best-loved colleague, Lois B., who had just collaborated with Gardner on a prize-winning textbook, *Experimental Social Psychology.* She was a highly respected child and clinical psychologist, "constantly seeing personality issues of which I was astonishingly unaware," said Murphy. What happened to Gardner and Lois in the Grand Canyon is not recorded except for the fact that it was there that Murphy realized that "it was the inner world of the person that was most real to me, and that personality study would be my primary concern."[1] A couple of months later he was writing his first personality text, *Approaches to Personality,* with Friedrich Jensen. It appeared on the market in October 1932. Jensen, a European, covered Freud, Jung, and Adler. Murphy covered behaviorism, Gestalt approaches, and mental elements, which shows how much the United States had to offer at the time. Behaviorism was Watson, a predominantly North American influence. Mental elements referred to ideas about sensations, associations, and consciousness much like the material of the introspectionists that Watson attacked. *Gestalt* is a German word that means configuration, and it refers to a "movement" in Europe that objected to mental chemistry—single elements of sensation combined in associations leading to conscious compounds. Gestalt psychologists felt that simple "associationism" missed the point of human perception and cognition, and that the important features were organization and configuration. The sum of the parts does *not* equal the whole. For example, XX XX XX and XXX XXX are both composed of six letters, but you see quite different things: three sets of two and two sets of three. The configuration and organization are the important aspects. This made sense, but it wasn't "American." About 1/6 of Murphy and Jensen's book, then, consisted of ideas that had their roots in North American psychology, until the last chapter, which was a summary called "Eclecticism and Genetic Method," Murphy's original contribution.

[1]Quoted in Boring and Lindzey's *A History of Psychology in Autobiography* (Vol. 5), Appleton-Century-Crofts, 1967, p. 263.

In Favor of Eclecticism

In many ways, this single chapter was a condensed version of the magnum opus that was still 15 years in the future. It began by stating that eclecticism was desirable and perhaps necessary because there were six approaches, each with advantages, each expressing part of the truth. The "genetic" method was essentially the study of the child—certainly Lois Murphy's influence was strong—and it was a brilliant choice of field to illustrate good eclecticism. The clinician dealing with a problem child had as a focus the *child,* not some specialized area such as learning, perception, or even personality. The clinician used whatever information might be helpful. One could almost say that the child psychologist was eclectic by default; there was no other choice. Birth order (Adler) was considered. Regression (Freud) was common. Learning difficulties were often best viewed in terms of Watson/Pavlov conditioning. Gestalt theories helped when trying to understand the overall picture. Whatever works. Who cares what "school of psychology" is supported if the end result is a happier, healthier child?

Personality and Perception

The most prophetic section of that last chapter of Murphy's 1932 book was the one dealing with perception. Here Murphy revealed his main concern. A child is faced with a situation, a set of stimuli. How does the child react? What are the effects? Is the answer primarily in the stimulus? No, because several studies have shown that different children respond differently to the same stimulus situation. Is the answer primarily in the personality? No, because it can easily be shown that the situation is very important, and that a child (a personality) will behave quite differently in different situations. Perception and response clearly involve some kind of *interaction* between the *outside* influences, which means the stimulus situation, and the *inside* influences,which include both personality and momentary conditions such as fatigue. The inner and the outer combine to determine how a person views the world. And personality, Murphy believed, *is* largely the way in which a person views the world.

The Perceptual Habit. The grand eclectic was now in a period of great productivity. In addition to the social-psychology textbook and the personality treatise, Murphy published a text on the history of psychology and another text for introductory classes. In all, four highly respected books on four different topics in a period of four years—1929 to 1933. His students at Columbia had called him "GM" for Gardner Murphy, but now they felt that Great Man was more appropriate.

Murphy and his students were pursuing the premise that perception was the key to personality. Their goal was to demonstrate the influence on perception of inner states, inner stimuli. To do this, they devised situations in which they manipulated inner influences while holding outer influences constant. When the influence of external stimuli was kept at a minimum, internal effects could be seen more easily. Subjects were shown ambiguous pictures, for example, and asked to guess what was there. Those who hadn't eaten for a time (internal state = hungry) were more likely to guess food. Other studies showed that people tended to perceive things in ways that had been rewarded in the past, even when that tendency led to "inaccurate" perceptions. Attitudes were shown to affect even associative memory—not only the perceptual process but also the recollection of what had been perceived. Many psychologists thought of these studies as evidence of the effect of personality variables on perception—as simple as that. But Murphy was pursuing bigger game: personality itself. Personality, he began saying, is largely a collection of perceptual habits, of ways of perceiving the world. How do these habits come about? In the same way behavioral habits come about: because of past satisfactions. Drives and attitudes and such lead to perceptions that in some way bring satisfaction, and the result is a perceptual habit.

Autism. The perceptual habit was the concept Murphy was looking for, something between the outer and the inner, and integration of the two. He called the whole process, from the first meeting of person and world to the developed structure or habit, *autism.* This was an extremely unfortunate term to choose because it put far too much stress on inner determinants and made people think of autistic children, terribly withdrawn, in their own world, totally inner, an implication he certainly did not intend. It was true enough that Murphy felt pressure to demonstrate the effects of needs—internal states—on perception, not to demonstrate how perception is influenced by reality. But in so doing, he seems to have been pushed a bit too far. His intent was clearly to find a bridge between the purely biological world of the body and the social world outside. If that is understood, then the organization of his next book (the magnum opus) becomes immediately clear. Part I of *A Biosocial Approach to Origins and Structure* is "organic foundation," and Part II is "learning"; Part III is called "the personal outlook" and is the bridge to the remaining three sections on self, wholeness, and the individual in the social world. *The psychology of the personal outlook:* that in a nutshell is Murphy's theory.

Murphy and ESP

Then there was the matter of Murphy and ESP. Murphy was probably the most important believer in ESP among psychologists until J. B. Rhine came along—but Rhine, unlike Murphy, isn't well known for anything *but* his ESP research. Murphy became interested in ESP as a Harvard graduate student, influenced by a teacher with the strange position of Fellow in Psychical Research. He was to remain interested in ESP throughout his career. Perhaps extrasensory perception stimulated his interest in and understanding of ordinary perception, or was it the other way around? In any case, Murphy was into it and researched it as he would any other problem. For example, it was shown that subjects who believe in ESP do better than chance in "guessing" pictures and those who disbelieve do worse than chance. Well-adjusted believers do better than poorly adjusted believers, and well-adjusted disbelievers do worse even than poorly adjusted disbelievers. The interpretation of such results runs something like this: well-adjusted people pick up the "signals"; the believers among them report what they perceive, so they do better than chance; the disbelievers don't report their perceptions because they are unwilling to believe them, so they do worse than chance.

Most psychologists are nonbelievers. They'll offer all kinds of fancy reasons for not believing: the statistics are faulty, only the rare, significant results are reported, and so on. But, as Donald Hebb once put it (Hebb was a president of the American Psychological Association—as was Murphy, by the way—and perhaps had more common sense than any other figure in the history of psychology), disbelief in ESP is not so much a matter of research evidence as it is a matter of how to integrate the idea into existing systems of thought. And Murphy agreed. ESP, true or false, simply doesn't make sense. There is no way one can understand it in terms of traditional beliefs about people and the world around them. It's magic, scientific or not. The term itself is magical: *extrasensory* perception. Extrasensory? Something beyond the senses? How is it transmitted, and how is it received? It makes no sense because it has no "sense" of its own. We have been deluded before, say the critics, by horses that could do mathematics, by spiritualists, by all sorts of occult phenomena. They have been shown to be deceptions, though not always intentional (it is unthinkable to accuse men like J. B. Rhine, who has done the bulk of the ESP research, and Gardner Murphy, of fraud). If ESP exists, say the critics, it too will turn out to have a simple explanation, in terms we can understand. It has been shown, for example, that the belief of the experimenter (not the subject) can affect results of an experiment in a number of subtle ways. If you believe that ESP exists, you would probably make errors in perceiving, recording, and tabulating data, and the errors would probably be in your (ESP's) favor, just as the grocer rarely seems to give you too *much* change. If your subject can see you during the experiment, you may unconsciously give visible signals about what the correct answer is. A left-eye twitch means there's a triangle on the card, a right-eye twitch means a circle, and so forth. Or perhaps the statistics are faulty. There are many ways to go wrong.

What is happening, you see, is that the nonbelievers are looking for the confounding variable or procedure that they believe is there, someplace. The basic point is that ESP is incredible. It is not plausible. So there must be something else to explain the positive results.

Many scientists who do research in ESP complain that the standards set for their experiments, in procedure and in statistical analysis, are much stricter than those set for other research topics. This is, in fact, true, but it is also highly appropriate: higher standards have always been and should be set for research on topics that do not fit traditional modes of thinking. But, even then, the burden lies on the pioneer, the prophet, the iconoclast. The believer in ESP simply must provide a system in which the phenomena can be understood or a way of integrating them into existing systems. So far that has not been done, and so far most psychologists remain skeptical. Murphy knew this and understood it and respected it. He sought a system in which ESP could be understood, but, by his own account, he failed. "I rather suspect," he said, "that we are dealing here with difficulties in the definition of time and space. . . ." Could well be. But the burden of resolving such difficulties lies with the proponents of ESP.

The issue of ESP has not been resolved. The opponents have not found (all) the confounding factors, if they exist, and the proponents have not found a way to make ESP intelligible, if that is possible. Perhaps the more relevant feature of Murphy's moon-madness excursion into the realm of taboo topics was the way in which he researched them: studies of the effect of personality variables on perception (even if that perception did happen to be occultish and extrasensory). Perception was still the key.

The Magnum Opus

By 1947, Murphy was ready to use that key to throw the doors of personality wide open. His new book, *Personality: A Biosocial Approach to Origins and Structure,* the outline of which we have already previewed, was really an extended treatment of the topics in the last chapter of his 1932 book. Much had happened in the meantime, of course. Hull and Skinner had joined Watson and Pavlov as powerful advocates of learning theory. Factor analytic approaches were beginning to show their promise in people like Eysenck, Cattell, and J. P. Guilford. Anna Freud, Sigmund's daughter, was leading new advances in psychoanalysis. Kurt Lewin, Henry Murray, and Gordon Allport had all published and had become important influences. It was a good time for the eclectic who had found a way to make his approach a system rather than simply a collection.

Organic Components of Personality. Murphy began his systematic approach with a discussion of the biological nature of humans. His goal, as a personality theorist, was not so much to give a brief description of what was known about human physiology as it was to show how biology was likely to affect one's personality. What he was trying to establish was a physiological basis for a system of *organic traits,* a class of biological components of personality. One person might have a more active hunger drive, for example, and a less active sex drive. The fat man who's not very interested in women. But that's too simple. Murphy took a view that was much broader than the traditional hunger/thirst/sex/pain-avoidance classification of basic biological motivations. Murphy saw life surging within the biological person, life active and continuously striving, each and every cell in the body a motivator. Striving for food and water, of course—the tissue needs—but striving too for activity and stimulation, almost as if each cell were trying to become the best of all possible cells. Adlerian cells, striving for superiority. Exploring and curious cells. Exploring and curious people.

For Murphy, motivation was best defined as that which lowers a threshold for behavior. What does it take to get a child to eat? If the child is stuffed with candy, it takes a lot. Very high threshold. But what about starving kids? What does it take to get them to eat? Not much. Very low threshold. As hunger increases, the threshold for eating goes down—it takes less "push" to get the hungry person to eat. When the threshold notion is used, drives can be much more broadly defined. Muscle tone is a drive. It reduces the threshold for a response involving these muscles. Intellectual stimulation might be biologically desirable after an orgy. An orgy on the weekend might be nice after final exams. (Except for the fat fellow who dislikes women; for him, a juicy steak.)

Organic traits allow drives to be people-specific. A particular drive may lower the threshold for behavior A for one person and behavior B for another. Anxiety may turn Jack into a compulsive house-cleaner; Jane may become a compulsive hot-fudge-sundae eater.

Biological and Social Interaction. There is much evidence for the kind of organic trait that Murphy describes. General levels of body activity, for example, and of body responsiveness to stimulation of various types turn up regularly and strongly in some of Cattell's factors. "Lethargic," "nervous," and similar traits seem to have strong biological components. It's an interesting topic of research that has not been studied as much as it should be. Are there sex differences, for example? Are women more "emotional" than men, in the biological sense? The increasing liberation of women has brought some of these questions to the fore, and the answers are sadly lacking. The few answers that we think we have are also hard to interpret, for reasons that would be apparent if one understood Murphy's theory and knew Cattell's data. *Nothing is not biosocial.* One can speak of biology and biological components or society and social components but only in the abstract. In real life, biology and society are in constant interaction, so that whatever results is a combination of the two. Is the female physically weaker than the male? Most people would guess so. But physical weakness, real or construed, in any individual tends to be reinforced by society at large and by the individual himself or herself. Social customs develop, and a cycle gets started. The man opens doors and bottle tops. The woman does not learn how to change a tire. But many of these customs have, in fact, little to do with ability. Biological and social components of traits can be distinguished from each other for purposes of exposition, but in reality there are no pure examples.

In the interaction between the individual and the social world, organic traits become *symbolic traits.* Traits full of symbolic meaning: femininity means weakness and sensitivity. Masculine sexual prowess becomes a symbol for power and achievement, which are themselves word-symbols for more basic motives. The social system is a symbolized means to an end—the satisfaction of organic needs. Symbols are like Pavlov's stimuli, lights and bells and words that come to be related to the basics, to the organic hungers (plural). Learning, the conditioned response, the response according to the conditions, connects new meanings to old stimuli. The ego looks at the conditions instead of the id looking at the needs, and the ego responds in new ways. The conditioned responses are the first overlay on the organic traits, the first move toward what we know as the human condition.

The Consummatory Response: Canalizations

When considering learning, Murphy was puzzled by a certain type of response, the consummatory response. If one is hungry, for example, the consummatory response is eating. If you are hungry and beans are available, you will eat beans; if steak is available, you will eat steak. Eating bananas when you're hungry is rewarding, right? By the laws of learning, the response is stamped in; it becomes stronger or more probable. Suppose you wanted to eliminate the behavior of eating bananas when you were hungry; how would you do it? By extinction, of course. Eliminate the reinforcement that follows the response. All you have to do is make sure that eating does not satisfy hunger. But how does one extinguish a consummatory response? Except in highly unusual circumstances, it is not possible. For all practical purposes, one cannot remove the eating response *as reward* from the eating response *considered as reinforced behavior.* Eating is its own reward.

Murphy thought about this paradox of learning and suggested that consummatory responses are unique simply because they cannot ordinarily be extinguished. He called such responses *canalizations.* If you have a need and you satisfy that need, the response that directly allowed the satisfaction becomes canalized: it becomes a learned response impervious to extinction, and it becomes a preferred (more probable) means of satisfying that need when the need arises again in the future. There is a connection between the need and the way of satisfying it.

Consider the old saying that there's no accounting for taste. Canalization is such an accounting. It also accounts for much of the consistency in personality over the years: Jack always did love hot dogs. Jill always was a reader. New canalizations may come with the years, but the old ones are still there and may even help direct the formulation of new ones. The hamburger lover turns on to steak. The high school athlete turns to golf or bowling.

Personal preferences, however, are just one of the many aspects of behavior that canalization explained for Murphy. Others include the notions of identity, self-respect, and the like, all of which can be contained within the theoretical domain of selfhood. Murphy saw selfhood as deriving from a kind of basic body-canalization, a kind of preference for one's own body that develops because so many biological motives are satisfied by things we do with or to our body.

Perception as Interpretation

Biological dispositions. Learning by conditioning and canalization. They are basics that underlie the key concept, the *perceptual habit.* The perceptual habit is the naturally developing mediator between the inner world of body cells and ingrained past experience and the outer world of stimuli and social situations. The way one "sees" the world determines how one will react. Peter sees it as hostile and responds defensively; Laura sees it as loving and responds with love. This, of course, is not perception in the simple sense, simple without interpretation; it's complex, interpreted, integrated. An enemy makes a gesture that would ordinarily be considered helpful. Is it an attempt to reconcile, or is it a trick? A father discovers his daughter smoking pot. What does he see? An embryonic heroin addict, unable to function in the "real" world. It makes him sad and mad. The daughter sees her father as a war criminal because he invests in exploitative industries. Complex perceptions indeed. The typical North American family of four is composed of at least 16 "people": each individual perceiving herself or himself and each individual perceiving each of the other three. An unsung hero (the husband), a well-meaning slave (the wife), a dangerously naive saboteur (the son-in-law), and a heroin addict (the daughter). It's all in the family: Archie Bunker's.

Situationalism and Social Roles

We've looked at all the dispositions, habits and canalizations, and perceptual habits, but we have yet to examine in detail the other, outer, primarily social world. Murphy asserted that human behavior can be explained by the social demands of the situation, with little recourse to inner personality determinants, and he called this approach *situationalism.* Much of the explanatory power of situationalism comes from the concept of social role. This view is not unlike that of the world as a stage and the people all players on it. If you play Hamlet, you are one kind of a person; if you play General Patton, you are another. You in your roles as parent's child, college student, and life of the party produce different behaviors to the objective observer. Have you experienced the wonder (or possibly the dismay) of returning home during vacation, leaving your role as Big Wheel on campus, only to be treated as a child again by your parents? And found yourself in the midst, therefore, of a full-blown temper tantrum, born of frustration and incidentally proving their point? (The student-body president is having a temper tantrum! Incredible.) Social demands are indeed strong; social roles extort a heavy price. The price is paid by "proper" behavior. The prediction is proper behavior, given the situation and the social role. Everyone will respond in pretty much the same way; our personalities are not too important.

Take, for example, the social role of president of the United States. Many people feel that it doesn't make much difference who is president because the demands of the situation will be strong enough to wipe out the effects of personality differences. Sure, Lyndon Johnson had a different style, different from Nixon and Ford and Carter, but was their behavior all that different? Were the policy decisions different? Times change, of course, so the demands on Nixon were somewhat different from those on Kennedy, and the policy decisions were therefore different to some extent. But, given the role, the nature of the decisions that have to be made, the mood of the country, and such factors, couldn't you predict fairly well the behavior of a president? Many scholars believe so. The personality of the individual makes little or no difference. A situational-role interpretation.

Correlation of Personality and Social Role. Whether or not you believe this interpretation, there is a conceptual problem involved, and it is this: the social role and the personality are not distinct concepts, separate from each other. A social role and the personality of the person filling it are correlated; a role naturally recruits a certain type of person. Presidents, for example, must be over 35 by law, and few will be elected if they're over 65. Candidates are rich by the standards of the average citizen, and their past experience has usually been in law and politics. They tend to be White, middle- to upper-class, Protestant males. Their IQs are high, and their personalities are generally strong but not too abrasive. They enjoy power and are used to it. They are married and usually have children. One could go on and on depicting the similarities among presidents, similarities that are not necessarily unusual but certainly are not universal either. The total personality of any president is clearly more like that of another president than it is like that of a citizen chosen at random.

So what determines behavior? Is it the personality or the situation? The answer is both. It's really a question of how one looks at the issue. Look only at the situation, make your predictions from that, and see if anything is left for personality to explain. Well, not much is left. But turn the question around—look only at personality and ask what is left for the situation—and you get pretty much the same answer. Not much is left, because the role and the person overlap.

Murphy in Brief

On the whole, Murphy believed that the interaction of the inner world and the outer was the only basis for the prediction and control of individual behavior. It is perhaps natural that he focused on perception and perceptual habits as the key to this interaction, this field from which behavior emanates. Perception was the gateway of the outer to the inner *and* of the inner to the outer. What you see is not simply either the outer or the inner; you see the outer transformed by the inner, the social transformed by the bio, and vice versa. It was a truly biosocial theory.

Henry Murray the Bull

Henry Murray was born under the sign of Taurus the Bull, as was Sigmund Freud. Also Barbra Streisand, Willie Mays, and Kate Smith. Earth-loving, stubborn, with an excellent financial condition, supposedly. Murray's father was a very rich business executive who was married to the daughter of the president of Mutual Life Insurance Company. Murray was never what you would call strapped for funds.

Some Personal Background

This fact was one determinant of Murray's career direction, for it was his independent income that allowed him to accept a very meager financial offer from Harvard to help in inaugurating the new psychological clinic, under Morton Prince, a clinic Murray later headed and from which he issued his ecumenical reports. He had many acrimonious fights with the then-president of Harvard, James B. Conant, who wanted to fire Murray because Murray had embraced that weird European philosophy, psychoanalysis. But Murray was stubborn. And rich. What did he care? And he felt no pressure to work along acceptable lines in acceptable ways, a feeling often fueled in young professors by a thinly veneered economic motive and a desire to gain job security. That's tenure, and, in most cases, the young professor is under 35 when it is granted. Murray was 55 when he finally got it (and he didn't need it).

Murray's money (or, anyhow, his father's money) enabled him to maneuver into a position in which his insights could be of great benefit to psychology. There is, however, considerable doubt as to whether or not his insights were of great benefit to Henry Murray. It's a sad thing, really, when a person is stripped of excuses. He cannot say he did it for the money; he had no great need of income from his work. He had no need for status; he grew up with it, in both the societal and the scholarly sense. Murray had nothing left but to be right, to create a new system of truth. The core of his soul was involved in what he said and did, bare and without excuses. And that is a tremendous burden.

Murray bore that burden well, though perhaps not by his own standards. Most of his writings begin with an apology, running something like this: I had in mind something better. I tried, but I was not successful, so I must give you what I have. I know it is not enough, and I am sorry. Most readers were delighted with the "imperfect" product. They were stimulated by new insights. They pronounced the product great and left the man to deal with his own self-torture. Murray always qualified his remarks, speaking of "some things to consider" or, as he put it in the title of one of his most influential articles, "Preparations of the scaffold of a comprehensive system." He tried many things, but perhaps the most eloquent testimony comes from his autobiography.

> After being vouchsafed an extremely happy and full-freighted life, with a few troughs and many peak experiences, [I] was confounded in 1962, on the one hand, by the sudden death of [my] superlatively good and loyal wife, and, on the other, by the fading of the mental energies on which [I] had been counting to deal with one or two at least of the ten-half-finished books that are calling for completion . . . [2] And were never finished.

[2]Quoted in Boring and Lindzey's *A History of Psychology in Autobiography* (Vol. 5), p. 307.

At the Harvard Psychological Clinic

But, in the beginning, the possibilities must have seemed as boundless as Murray's youthful enthusiasm. He had taken over the psychological clinic at Harvard and had with him an impressive collection of scholars and researchers: poets, physicists, sociologists, anthropologists, criminologists, physicians, and psychologists of every breed and species. Who but a questioner, someone not dogmatic, an eclectic in the supreme sense, could have headed such a group? As Gardner Murphy once said, in a clinic in which people with problems are the focus, not theories with problems, one is at least *free* to be eclectic, and, because much of the work is done "by staff," very often the director *must* be eclectic. And that describes Murray.

Explorations in Personality. Murray's most influential work was published in 1938 under the tentative, qualified, questioning title, *Explorations in Personality.* The authors were the "workers at the Harvard Psychological Clinic" headed, of course, by Murray (who wrote most of the book) but including some 27 others, many destined to become great psychologists in their own right. The book was dedicated to no less than five people, including both Freud and Jung. It was intended to be a collection of articles integrated into a whole by means of procedure—not writing procedure but the experimental procedure that created the data and the concepts: "to have all experimenters study the same series of individuals" and to "collaborate in accomplishing a common purpose: the formulation of the personality of every subject."[3] Together, the philosophical eclectics, who were also the methodological eclectics, set foot (or is it "feet"?) into that "virgin forest of peculiar problems": personality theory and research. Murray had the advantage of being permanent tenant of the clinic and resident status symbol, of course, so he exerted much influence, more than the others. But, more than the other theories we've discussed, this theory so far was a group effort. We call it Murray's theory out of convenience, just as *Explorations in Personality* is commonly referenced as authored by Murray *et al.* Who wants to list 28 authors?

Time Structure: A New Concept

Proceeding and Serial. One of the major differences between Murray's work and that of most other theorists has to do with the time structure of what he looked at. He did not try to explain the single response because its meaning is part of an integrated series of responses, an event, a *proceeding.* To interpret the integrated series leads you further, he believed. He would go further yet, in fact, explaining proceedings not as isolated units but as integrated series. A "study" proceeding, for example, will occur many times in the life of a student, and each occurrence is part of a greater proceeding. We could call that greater proceeding

[3]The goals of Murray's 1938 book are elaborated in that work on p. viii.

a *serial.* A serial is a collection of proceedings unified by their direction: they all have the same goal or purpose. I study many times to get a degree, or to earn more money, or to advance the quality of human life.

Now the question changes. What accounts for these serials? Do you see the difference in approach? Murray preferred to work from the top down, unlike others who worked from the bottom up. Explain the serial and the explanation of a single response is easy. If the purpose of my studying is to get a degree, and someone asks me why I turned the page of my textbook, I look up with disbelief. To get to the next page, of course. You want to know how I learned to read from left to right, how I developed the eye/hand coordination necessary to turn a page, and what makes me expect a continuation of meaningful communication on the back of the page I have just finished. I'd say you're another weird psychologist. Who cares about those questions? *I* understand why I turned the page. Although, if you'd asked, I would have admitted that I'm not exactly sure why I'm working my head off for a college degree. But, you see, *Murray* asked. He was that kind of person. It was a different level of explanation.

Thema. If proceedings and serials are the organized sequences of events to be explained, the next question is how to explain them. What concepts are useful? Murray proposed a kind of nonanswer, a question-in-disguise to "answer" a question he did not feel ready to answer. *Thema.* A thema is a dynamic structure of an event, said Murray. Now, that's as pure an example of gobbledygook as one is likely to find outside of politics—but it sounds nice. It sounds logical. Its power and usefulness however, turn out to lie in the image rather than in the definition. A theme! Every proceeding has a theme. Human behavior is like a playlet. It has a plot, and plotting is for a purpose. The purpose of an action is its defining characteristic. So how do we explore the purpose of a person? Murray certainly didn't ask easy questions.

Critique of Behaviorism

Murray was not a psychologist by training. He was a bona fide medical doctor, an M.D. trained as a surgeon. He also earned a Ph.D. but in biochemistry, not psychology. When he became attached to the Harvard Psychological Clinic, he had yet to take his first psychology course. What he knew of psychology came from writers like Herman Melville, author of *Moby Dick.* Perhaps we can be thankful. Murray was naive enough to think that human behavior had a purpose. Because of his position and his personality (and we shouldn't forget his independent wealth), he was more or less impervious to the Watsonian onslaught that toppled more than a few good American psychologists who had been playing around with "nonbehavioral" ideas. Murray could persist.

He had another advantage as well. As a biochemist, he knew Watson was talking nonsense. He said this of himself:

> Watson's proposal to limit the science of psychology to concepts that pointed only to perceptibles struck the former biochemist [there's Murray!]—all of whose critical concepts had referred to imperceptibles—as

> a naive, juvenile perversity, even though it succeeded in rescuing psychology from the meanderings of the traditional forms of introspection.[4]

Murray had sensed the purpose even of Watson's behavior. Murray kept on with his quest. Nobody could disturb his status as a scientist—he had been a chemist!—so that, while methodological considerations were dictating the topics of study in other psychological labs, he preferred to study the important topics, trying to use the best *possible* methods but not giving up the topic for lack of an acceptable experimental procedure. He was beyond that. So when Murray said he wanted to study the purposive behavior of people, he meant it.

Derivation of Behavior

From what does that purpose derive? Think about it in a naive way and you may come up with something resembling Murray's answer. Purpose derives from the needs of the individual actor and the pressures of the situation. That's Murray's theory in a nutshell. It was his belief that, if one could identify what the person wanted to do (his or her needs) and also what the situation wanted the person to do, so to speak, one would know purpose and hence action. Or perhaps we should say purposes—plural—for the needs of the person and the demands of the situation might be at cross-purposes. *Needs,* then, and *press,* Murray's new label for situational pressures; the key concepts. (Press, said Murray, with a kind eye toward writers, was to be the same word in both singular and plural form.) But what have we here? Another of Murray's questions-in-disguise? What are needs? What are press? How do we identify them?

Needs are the easier to identify, or so it was thought. If purpose is defined by the need, then the need can be defined by the purpose. A bit circular, but it will do for a start. How do you yourself identify a need in a friend? Don't you look at the series of behaviors the friend has presented (the proceeding) and ask what's the purpose? If Ahab is trying to lance a great white whale, what is his need? To lance poor Moby Dick? That's too specific (or is it?). He is hungry and needs food. He needs the money from the sale of blubber. He needs the glory. He needs revenge. Which of the above? We can leave it to others to sort through Captain Ahab's motives, and concern ourselves instead with the general procedure—to identify a need, look for the goal, the event that would satisfy the need, the event that would mark the end of the sequence, the proceeding, or even the serial. If the need is hunger, food will suffice. If the need is for attention, applause, applause. But the unified trend of a person's behavior toward a goal is not an easy thing to see clearly; there is always more evidence to be had, more proceedings and events that may surprise you—"no moment or epoch is typical of the whole."

Viscerogenic Needs. To identify a need, then, one should look at a sequence of behavior from beginning state (B.S.) to end state (E.S.). The unified trends of human behavior are away from B.S. (except possibly

[4]From Boring and Lindzey (Eds.), *A History of Psychology in Autobiography* (Vol. 5), p. 292.

in the case of some college professors) and toward E.S. Need is a hypothetical construct used to identify the *direction* of the actions in between. That energy is present is a basic assumption. But the direction needs to be explored. How? By observing proceedings from beginning to end. If you observe enough people enough times, you should be able to come up with a list of needs by sorting sequences into categories. Murray did so, and of course he was influenced by traditional views as well as by behavior. He came up with two types of needs: *viscerogenic,* basic and presumably physiological, and *psychogenic,* secondary in some unknown manner, perhaps developing from the primary or viscerogenic needs but nevertheless clear and present in the behavior trends of adult human beings. He listed a dozen viscerogenic needs in all: the needs for air, water, food, sex, lactation, urination, and defecation; the needs to avoid harm, noxious stimuli, extreme heat, and extreme cold; and finally the need for sensory stimulation. The thirteenth, mentioned but not listed, was the need for passivity (rest and sleep). Altogether, nothing unusual in Murray's viscerogenic collection.

Psychogenic Needs. Psychogenic needs were so named because they had no clear origin in periodic bodily functions as the viscerogenic needs did. Most psychogenic needs are fairly well defined by their names (See Table 7-1). There are a total of 29 psychogenic needs listed in Table 7-1, giving a combined total of 42 viscerogenic and psychogenic needs. Murray was a prolific list maker. But what do we have when we have Murray's list?

Reading through *Explorations in Personality* with list in hand doesn't seem to help. The list is changed here and there in the book itself (not to mention Murray's later works), as new ones are introduced (such as the need for understanding) and old ones disappear or change in meaning. Qualifications are rampant. Needs are sometimes latent (inhibited), sometimes manifest (exhibited), or both. Very often one finds the statement that a certain need "is not truly a separate need"; the need for counteraction in defense of self-respect, for example, is supposedly the need for achievement or aggression "acting in the service of" the need for inviolacy. It's all very confusing. Many psychologists responded to the confusion in typical fashion: they ignored it. They simply took one of Murray's lists and used it as a definitive classification of human needs. This is certainly an understandable response (the need for order?), but it was a serious distortion of Murray's aim and in all probability a serious mistake for personology. Murray was asking questions, and his questions were mistaken as answers.

The TAT. Naturally, this mis-communication generated some problems between Murray and his colleagues. Gardner Lindzey, for example, a student of Murray's who later achieved his own greatness, kept trying to use acceptable validation procedures on one of Murray's creations, the *Thematic Apperception Test,* commonly referred to as the TAT. The TAT consists of a number of pictures with relatively ambiguous content,

Table 7-1. The first list of psychogenic needs in Murray's 1938 book.

I. Five needs relating chiefly to inanimate objects
- *Acquisition*—to acquire property
- *Retention*—to retain it
- *Conservance*—to preserve, as in repair
- *Construction*—to build things
- *Order*—to organize and arrange

II. Three or four needs having to do with ambition and prestige
- *Superiority*—to be superior
- The need for superiority includes the needs for
  - *Achievement*—to strive and overcome; and
  - *Recognition*—to excite praise
- And possibly the need for
  - *Exhibition*—to attract attention
- (But recognition and exhibitionist needs are hard to distinguish in practice)

III. Four or five needs involving defense or prestige
- *Inviolacy*—to preserve self-respect
- The need for inviolacy includes the needs for
  - *Infavoidance*—to avoid failure and shame
  - *Defendance*—to defend one's self-respect as in offering reasons or excuses
  - *Counteraction*—to overcome by striving harder
- And possibly the need for
  - *Seclusion*—to be alone, physically or psychologically
  - (But seclusion needs may be the opposite of exhibition, or is it recognition?, needs)

IV. Five needs relating to power
- *Dominance*—to influence or control
- *Autonomy*—to resist influence
- *Deference*—to admire and serve a leader
- *Similance*—to agree
- *Contrarience*—to disagree

V. A brace of aggression needs
- *Aggression*—to cause injury or hurt
- *Abasement*—to surrender; to be hurt (in extreme form, the ever popular Sadist and Masochist)

VI. A quartet of affection needs
- *Affiliation*—to form friendships
- *Rejection*—to reject, as in snub or ignore
- *Nurturance*—to nourish or help
- *Succorance*—to seek help

VII. Two brainy needs
- *Cognizance*—to explore and inquire
- *Exposition*—to transmit information

VIII. Miscellaneous
- *Play*—to amuse oneself
- *Blamavoidance*—to avoid blame by inhibiting antisocial impulses

such as a young man kneeling at the feet of an older woman. It is a projective test, now one of the two most frequently used (Rorschach's inkblots being the other). The subject is instructed to tell a story about the picture: what led up to this scene, what are the people thinking and feeling, what will happen, and so on. The basic premise, as in all projective tests, is that, since the stimulus offers few clues to the answer, the response will reflect the personality of the respondent. People will divulge their own needs in their answers, perhaps even needs of which they are not aware.

But that was a presupposition that needed to be supported by data. Lindzey set out to gather the necessary supporting data, only to be horrified to learn that Murray wanted to change the pictures, to create the son of TAT, then the grandson of TAT. Murray kept moving forward; he had some new ideas; it took all of Lindzey's considerable might to restrain him. It was hard on Lindzey. It was hard on Murray. "My temperament," Murray confessed later, "was more suited to the making of coarse maps of newly explored areas than to the refinement of relatively precise maps of familiar ground."[5]

The Applied Murray: World War II

In 1937, after the big book *(Explorations)* had been written but not yet published (they were having trouble with the consultant to Oxford University Press, who steadfastly argued for rejection of the manuscript!), Murray and his wife and daughter traveled in Europe. Hitler was in full swing by then, and Murray was sad and filled with foreboding. He spent three weeks with Jung and a memorable evening with Sigmund and Anna Freud. But Hitler's fruit was ripening fast, and soon Freud was in England, and then Freud was dead, and Henry Murray was working for the U.S. government, assessing men for their fitness to kill. From 1943 to 1948, Murray became the practical applied psychologist, taken away from his theoretical pursuits. The war affected him greatly, and much post-war energy on his part was directed toward total abolition of all war. A very good cause. But, as a result, his theory of personality did not advance much after the 1938 volume. Who knows what would have happened had there been no World War II?

The Concept of Press

World War II was what one might call a powerful press, a strong environmental demand. Press, as we've seen, is the concept Murray developed to explain the influence of the environment on the person. Just as he had chosen to focus on the intended *effect* of personal behavior rather than on the behavior itself, he similarly chose to focus on the potential *effect* of the environment on the person rather than on the objective description. I may drop a cyanide pellet into water or pull the trigger of a gun—both behaviors are intended to kill, and in Murray's

[5]From *Psychology: A Study of a Science,* Vol. III, 1959, p. 12.

view that intended effect is the important aspect. Environmental stimuli (including the responses of other people) also have "intended" effects—they "push" in one way or another, and the task here is to specify what they push toward.

Perhaps the best way to begin is to look at an example in which the environment is another person with intentions of influence (it is hard to think of a rock with intentions). Suppose a parent is trying to get a teenage child to conform. The parent may threaten or promise or may "use psychology" or any one of a number of behaviors equivalent in their intended effect: to obtain conformity to standards deemed desirable by the agent of influence. There is press for conformity. This does not mean, of course, that conformity will result, as any parent or child will tell you. It means simply that the situation to which the person, the personality, must respond is one in which conformity is being pressured. Pressed.

Alpha and Beta Press. The same approach can be used for inanimate objects or social situations. When the national anthem is played before a football game, the relevant problem facing each person is that he or she must decide how to respond to a call for patriotic behavior. A lowly rock, sans intention, effects its press too: if it is above your head and falling rapidly, it calls for decisive action. If it is seen. And here is another distinction, an important one for which Murray coined another term. *Alpha press* is the potential effect of a situation that is *objectively* determined; the plummeting rock has the objectively potential effect of making a sizable dent in the top of your head, one that would probably hurt, one that calls for harm avoidance. *Beta press* is the potential effect subjectively determined; that is, it represents the situation as perceived by the person involved. If you see the rock, alpha and beta press will be more or less identical, but, if you don't, they are quite different. Both alpha and beta press are important, alpha because, in the long run, reality determines subjective perception and beta because, in here-and-now situations, the demand you perceive is the "environment" that will determine your response. If our enemy tries to make a sincere attempt at apology and reconciliation (alpha press) but we perceive it as a devious move to have us relax our defenses (beta press), beta and not alpha will determine the response.

Interaction of Needs and Press. Murray's press were never listed simply and completely as the needs were. It has always been difficult to integrate environment into personality theories. From the point of view of the theorist, there is one person but many environments. And the environment in reality is not so important as the environment in subjective (beta) form. The effective environment is, therefore, really an internally perceived aspect of the person. The environment is a cognition. For the most part, therefore, press were defined similarly to needs. It was, in fact, as if a press were a "need" of a person or object other than the one being studied. If we study Kate, her needs, then the press around her are analogous to the "needs" of the people and objects with whom she interacts. If I have a need for affiliation and exhibit it to Kate in a friendly gesture, that gesture calls out for a response from Kate in the same mold. For me it is a need for affiliation, but for Kate it is a press of affiliation. If I am protective, the press for Kate is nurturance and the need called for in her is succorance. If I am dominant, I want her to be submissive. Note that some pairs are similar (affiliation/affiliation) and some are different but complementary (dominance/deference).

The press scheme looked nice, but it was unwieldy. Take the case of a rock. A rock can be a press in several ways. As Murray defined it, "the *press* of an object is what it can do *to the subject* or *for the subject*—the power that it has to affect the well-being of the subject one way or another."[6] A rock is a little limited in its innate powers, but still it can do to or for you in a number of ways. It can certainly frighten or injure you by falling on you. You can use it (it is *for* you) to scrape gum off your boot or as something to throw at the pigs. It may have value; perhaps it is a diamond; you can sell it or give it. You may see it as a happily unemotional object suitable for venting your aggressions. You kick it. It may injure your toe in return, but you can be fairly sure that it will not rise up and actively smite you. Amazing what a rock can do to or for you. But you come across a rock. How does one describe the press? Is there a way?

Murray's answer to these questions was to coin a new term—his typical response to the press of confusion! He coined a bunch of new terms, all with the function of putting press into various categories. A rock is an *immobile* press, meaning that it ordinarily requires the person to initiate the action. Of course, if the rock is in the air traveling rapidly toward your head, then it is a *mobile* press, meaning that the rock has initiated the activities. Press were also classified as *positive* or *negative* (the threatening rock is negative; the diamond in the rough is positive). Mobile press were sub-classified as either *autonomous,* when the press have their own power, or *docile*, when they are more or less regulated by the person; mothers are autonomous, servants are docile. Lots of new theoretical constructs. But the new coinages did not help much with the basic problem. When you respond, to what are you responding? It remained difficult to specify in advance the press of a situation the person was about to enter. Murray tried but did not succeed in getting the environment out of the person. Press could only be specified with any degree of rationality after the fact. After the response.

Still, the concept of press was useful, for it allowed Murray to achieve an important goal. The complete theoretical description of an event in terms of its dynamic or motivational components. The *thema*. In simplest form, a thema is composed of a need and a press. Murray gives the example of a proceeding in which one person approaches another, is snubbed or ignored, and snubs and ignores in return. The thema of this proceeding is "press : rejection" followed by "need : rejection." You were snubbed (rejected), and you reacted with your own behavior, rejection, fueled by your need to reject. Another person might react aggressively; need : aggression. The idea, you see, is to try to specify the needs in advance (at least the needs) so that the response can be predicted.

[6]The definition of *press* is from Murray's 1938 book, p. 121.

Unity-Thema

Every proceeding has a thema to "explain" it. Some of these thema seem to repeat themselves regularly throughout the life of an individual. Murray called these *unity-thema,* and in his view they represented a major aspect of the consistency of personality. In practice, the concept of unity-thema means that people are not simply reactive; they do not simply respond to press that occur. Rather, people often actively seek the press to which they want to respond. If you, for example, have a strong need to help and give comfort (nurturance), you will place yourself in situations in which that need can be satisfied; you might become a priest, a parent, a teacher, or a nurse. Unity-thema can also represent childhood fixations in the Freudian sense. You may respond typically to the press of succorance (someone needs help) with anxiety and behavior stemming from your need for autonomy—reenacting your early struggles with a mother who sought to make you dependent by continually acting the invalid. Unity-thema are recurring themes in the personality's life history.

For various reasons, among them the difficulties encountered with the concept of press, Murray began to think increasingly of thema in terms of the interaction of two people, each with his or her own needs. In other words, press for one person became the needs of another and vice versa. Since the conceptualization of needs and their assessment was more rigorously developed, this notion of a *dyadic system* (dyad = pair) worked better. The press could be better specified in advance. If one person had a need to tell a joke and the other was in the mood to be amused, the resulting behavior when the two came together could be predicted fairly accurately.

Lives in Progress

Still, the general emphasis in Murray's theory, in practice, was on *post*-diction, which means something like "predicting the past." It's a respectable scientific enterprise, though certainly not as fraught with danger as *pre*diction. It's "second-guessing" in a sense—what the quarterback should have done, or, more appropriately, why what he did do didn't succeed. In other words, after intensive study of one individual and his or her background, needs, and so on, Murray and the staff got together and tried to make sense of that total individual life. The result was a collection of some of the most complete and most interesting case histories ever published in psychology. And they did make sense. A good example of such work is in a book published in 1952 entitled *Lives in Progress,* by R. W. White, who took over as director of the Harvard Clinic after Murray.

Three case histories are presented in the book. Data, in Murray's view. In 1938 he had said "Case histories are the proof of the pudding. That is to say, a personological theory can be tested best by utilizing it in the writing of biographies, and its worth judged positively by its general success in ordering the facts . . . and negatively by what it leaves uninterpreted."[7] If one accepts that premise, Murray's approach worked well. One cannot read the case histories without coming away with the feeling of knowing the individuals intimately.

But, alas, it is not so easy as that. In 1966, White produced a second edition of his exciting and informative book, and it was a shocker. It shocked those of us who had read the first edition, and one suspects that it shocked White as well. And Murray. In the 14 years between the first and second editions, two of the subjects had been contacted and interviewed at length to see what had happened in their lives since the original study. One of the two, a man called Joseph Kidd, was living a life that one could have predicted only with mystical powers. And we had known him so intimately—his problems, his needs, and the directions and trends in his life. Perhaps we knew too much. In any case, he had made an incredible about-face in lifestyle, and all the predictions of what he would and would not do were wrong. How could this happen? White struggled valiantly, pointing out the similarities between the past and the now-present, but it was of no use; it was like pointing to similarities between a cockroach and a man. It was not to be denied. It was a stunning reversal.

If case histories are the proof of the pudding. . . .

What did it all mean?

Gordon Allport the Scorpion

Gordon Allport, in common with Billy Graham and Adolph Hitler, was born under the sign of Scorpio. An interesting group, isn't it? But not so strange as it might appear at first glance. What do you need in order to be a successful evangelist or a successful dictator? First of all, an overriding confidence, a kind of inner sense of power, a determination to stick to your guns (or your Bible) in the face of any and all opposition. That's Allport, too. In his own quiet, gentle way, he was unyielding. He knew what was important in the study of the person, and that was what he would study. Come criticism, come scorn, come anything. Tentative and humble, maybe—but underneath the velvet glove, the strong-willed certainty of Scorpio.

Trait Theory

Allport was a trait theorist supreme, sure that traits were the best unit of study for the personologist. Traits came in two categories, common and unique. A *common trait* is a theoretical concept, the trait we all know and love. Like ego strength. An attribute. Something each of us has to some degree. It is called common because we all have it. A *unique trait* is one that only one person has. Allport insisted for years and years that unique traits were the more important of the two. Common traits, he asserted, were merely semi-useful abstractions, adequate for the descrip-

[7]From Murray's 1938 book, p. 606.

tion of groups but limited when the individual is discussed. The individual is unique. You may call that person "aggressive" but that unique aggressiveness is not like the aggressiveness of anyone else. Each person is unique.

The concept of the unique trait never made headway in personology. Some people may have assumed that Allport the Scorpio was too secretive to let people know what he really meant. None of his critics, of course, denied the claim of uniqueness for the individual, but they saw that uniqueness in the particular configuration of common traits, not in the traits themselves. If there were a trait that was completely unique, they argued, there would be no way of describing it and using it anyway; there would be no word for it in our language. Allport may have been trying to say that the common-trait approach, largely a result of the individual-differences and testing movement, did not pay sufficient attention to the *relationships* among a person's traits, the patterning, the configurations. Ironic. His assertions were effectively challenged by his own arguments. And so he both won and lost.

Traits and Stimuli and Responses

Though he was not really an advocate of the trait approach as it was typically practiced, Allport did more than anyone else to define the concept. The way psychologists today think of traits is largely his doing. Traits are bigger than habits, like nail-biting, and smaller than types, like extravert or introvert. A good working definition might be: systems in the personality that tend to make certain things more or less equivalent. For example, a certain person has a trait called "Communistphobia." This trait renders more or less equal a whole collection of stimuli: Russians, college professors, liberals in general, the late Martin Luther King, and most Jews. They all call for the same kind of response, defensive hostility. But the specific response to such stimuli need not always be the same; the trait also renders equivalent a whole collection of specific responses—writing hostile letters, voting against liberal schemes and candidates, maybe even throwing a few rocks and bottles in the heat of a demonstration. This definition has the added advantage of directing us toward the practical assessment of a trait: by noting the stimuli among which the person does not discriminate, as well as the different responses treated as the same thing. Isn't this the way we describe someone in everyday life? If you feel that there are many situations in which it is appropriate to express your self-pity, and you do so, you may well be called a self-pitying person. You have the trait.

Some Personal History

Gordon W. Allport was born in 1897 in the Midwest, the son of a doctor, in a pious, hardworking, Protestant-ethic home environment. He was the baby of a family with four sons, one of whom was Floyd Allport, destined to become one of the greatest social psychologists in the United States. Allport had what we think of as a typical Midwestern childhood: warm, loving, and disciplined. Like Murray, he seemed to have experienced none of the hardships and emotional turmoil that produced the great men of European psychoanalysis. Life was simpler in the United States. Although both Murray and Allport became advocates of psychoanalysis, in part, neither had had the kind of childhood experiences that allowed them to swallow, whole-hog, Freud's emphasis on the first few years of life. This inability was to lead to some interesting theoretical formulations, as we shall see.

Allport at Harvard. In 1915, Gordon followed his brother Floyd to Harvard. It was a jolt. Where Allport came from, people tended to value decency, hard work, and basic honesty and fairness. If you were intelligent, that was nice, but if you weren't that was fine too. Are you decent and human? That was the important thing. For a person with Allport's background to go to the coast, either coast, was a step into a new world, one in which a high premium was placed on intellect and culture. For better or for worse, it was certainly a jolt. A new experience.

Allport experienced the jolt and quickly adopted some new values, in particular a new sense of high intellectual standards. He won a prize for his academic efforts (his hard-work habits did pay off), a copy of *Marius, the Epicurean.* Allport hadn't the slightest idea of who Marius was, of course, but he had won it. He was on his way. And on his way into social service, too. All through college he supervised a boys' club in Boston; he worked for family-service organizations, served for a bit as a volunteer probation officer, and registered homes for war workers (World War I was then raging). He worked for a humane society and assisted foreign students. All this and academic prizes, too. But the social-service experiences no less than the intellectual pursuits influenced his world view: where is the common-trait approach more abused than in welfare work? Numbers, tables, bureaucracy. Is there a difference among welfare recipients? Allport discovered that there were real human beings out there. Unique.

After graduation, Allport did not go on directly to graduate school. He taught abroad for a year at Robert College in Constantinople (English and sociology) and decided that he liked teaching. Then a cable arrived offering him a fellowship for graduate study at Harvard; he accepted eagerly and set off on the journey back to Cambridge.

Allport Meets Freud. It was 1920. "With a callow forwardness characteristic of age twenty-two," Allport wrote to Sigmund Freud and suggested a meeting of "mutual" benefit. The kindly Freud accepted the "opportunity," and they met in Freud's inner office. The young Allport had nothing to say; he wanted only to touch Freud, get his autograph, and maybe tear a souvenir from his coat. But, of course, the situation and the manners of the time would not permit it, so the two sat stiffly and stared at each other. Finally, in desperation, Allport remarked about a perfect case of dirt-phobic behavior he had witnessed on the tramcar he had taken to get to Freud's office. Warming to his theme, Allport related the story of this 4-year-old boy who refused to sit down because the seats were so dirty; everything was dirty. The little boy's mother, Allport said, by way of Freudian explanation, was "well starched" and dominant. Perhaps Freud could use this interesting "case history."

Freud was silent for a moment. Then he spoke, kindly. "And was that little boy you?"

Can you imagine Allport's feelings? He was, in his own words, "flabbergasted." He nervously changed the subject and blabbered on until, to the relief of both, the meeting came to an end. Allport walked out "traumatized," though he protected himself by calling it "amused." The encounter with Freud started a "deep train of thought." What had happened? How could Freud have been so wrong? Was he so accustomed to neurotic defenses that he could not perceive the rather simple motivation of a curious young psychology student? Allport decided that the depth psychology of Freud and the analysts, whatever its merits, could at times miss the forest for the trees. It did not give enough emphasis to the simple surface motives.[8]

Functional Autonomy

Allport's later work was designed, in large part, to prove the point. In his 1937 opus, *Personality: A Psychological Interpretation,* he wrote: "To understand the dynamics of the normal mature personality a new and somewhat radical principle of growth must be introduced...." The new and "somewhat" radical principle was given the name *functional autonomy of motives.* It was an interesting concept; it was an attempt to give substance to the so-called superficial motives in life.

Take a man entering a sporting-goods shop. He asks for fish hooks, pays, and leaves. Why did he do that? What was his motivation? We might guess that he did it because he wanted to go fishing. We could be wrong, though; maybe he wanted to "fish" his ring out of a drain. Either way, the explanation is relatively simple. But a good depth psychologist, interested in underlying motives, buried in the subconscious mind, would go further. Why does he want to go fishing? He likes trout. Why does he like trout? They look like his mother. The depth psychologist nods happily. But, asks Allport, even if the explanation is true, of what value is it? Perhaps, if this man were losing his job and his health and his wife because he fished every day, yes, then it might be useful to know. But for the fishing-equipment salesman and for us, in the normal situation, that he wants to go fishing is explanation enough. It is *motive* enough. To want to go fishing is a motive. It may have developed from childhood experiences (it certainly developed from something; few newborn babies express such a desire)—but it is probably now functionally autonomous. It is for all practical purposes now independent of the more basic motives it once served. Maybe he went fishing as a child with his mother, leaving the father behind to listen to the baseball game, thereby satisfying some devious Oedipal drive. But now both parents are dead. The original motivation, at least in literal form, is no longer capable of satisfaction. The drive to land a trout has separated itself from the original force. It is functionally autonomous.

[8]From Boring and Lindzey's *A History of Psychology in Autobiography* (Vol. 5), p. 7.

Note that Allport is picking up a theme of Adler's and Rank's, that the present state of affairs can explain enough in most cases and that lengthy investigation of related childhood experiences is unnecessary. But Allport said it better. His concept had a ring to it—"functional autonomy," a beautiful phrase. It was a controversial concept, as we shall see, and it was to have a tremendous impact on American psychology.

Secondary Gain. It does not do, of course, just to say that motives somehow become functionally autonomous. There must be an explanation of why and how it happens. Part of the answer is shared with all personality theories, psychoanalytic in particular—it has to do with what a Freudian might call "secondary gain." Take a young woman who has just married and is quite frightened at the prospect of sexual intercourse. She thinks it is dirty and painful, and she is anxious. On the wedding night, she becomes paralyzed—a hysterical paralysis—and her legs won't move. Her fear of sex produced the hysterical symptom, but, once she has become an invalid, she discovers that being an invalid has certain *other* advantages. She does not have to work. She is waited on and cared for; she gets attention and love. In some ways, it is quite a nice situation. So, even if her fear of sex should abate or be helped through psychotherapy, she might well remain paralyzed. Not for the original reason, but for the new reason, for the secondary gain. The motivating force has become functionally autonomous. In our fishing example, the man may have fished so that he could be with his mother, but, once he started fishing, he may have discovered other good reasons. These "other good reasons" might be primary reinforcements for primary motives (eating and hunger) or secondary reinforcements for secondary drives (good catch equals status, related to satisfaction of hunger, thirst, and sexual needs, and avoidance of pain).

Personality Organization

The Proprium. But secondary gain is not, for Allport, the only answer, the fundamental why and how. The real answer lies in the *organization* of personality. An analogy can be made with a business organization. Suppose there is a need in society for a certain commodity, such as food. A business organization develops to serve that need. It buys from the farmer and sells to the consumer. Once the organization has developed, new needs develop. Self-preservation of that particular organization, for example. Or, on the more positive side, its growth. Charitable organizations designed to fight tuberculosis and polio did not "go out of business" when these diseases (largely because of organized efforts) became less threatening; they expanded and took on new problems ranging from air pollution to birth defects. The food business wants to expand too; it wants to "diversify." The organization comes into being and with it come a need for preservation and a desire for growth and expansion.

The individual personality can be viewed as a similar organization. Most theories have a concept labeled "ego" or "self" to describe this organization. The individual organization has an original purpose—primarily the satisfaction of hunger, thirst, shelter, and sexual needs—the basic needs, at least at the beginning. But, once formed, the organization itself develops needs such as self-preservation and growth. *These are not bodily needs,* and they are not basic. Someone might even let his or her body be destroyed in order to preserve "personal integrity."

Seven Parts of the Proprium. Allport called this personal organization the *proprium.* The corresponding adjective is "propriate," which is related to the more common word "appropriate," meaning "to belong to in some unique sense." In his 1961 revision of his 1937 theory, Allport listed seven aspects of parts of the proprium: (1) the sense of one's body and bodily sensations as being "mine" in some unusual sense. This sense of a bodily self develops early, but it is not innate. A young child is often surprised to learn that others do not (and cannot) "feel" the pain the child is feeling; (2) the sense of continuity through time, a kind of self-identity, the "knowledge" that the "me" of yesterday and the "me" of today are the same; (3) self-esteem. A liking for the "me." And a desire to do things by "myself" (and take all the credit for success). Allport asserts that these three facets of the proprium develop early, in the first three years of life, but are ever-changing throughout life. The basic organizational essentials are already present, sufficient to elicit defensive reaction to a threat to the organization and desires for "personal growth."

Later, roughly between the ages of 4 and 6, (4) the sense of self-extension and (5) the sense of self-image develop. Here the individual acquires knowledge that the body does not define the limits of the proprium and knowledge that other people are evaluating the goodness or badness of the proprium or propriate acts. Amazing discoveries from the point of view of the child. That "my" parents and "my" toys and "my" creations are also part of "me," an extension of "my-self." That there is a "good me" and a "bad me" as defined by others—parents, other relatives, peers and siblings, other people in society. Even as adults, people may act on these principles, perhaps buying an ugly painting because it is in vogue, because they know that what they do, what they buy, reflects their "taste" (the quality of their propriate activities) and will be judged good or bad by others.

Two additional aspects of the proprium develop later. The first involves the discovery that the world is fairly orderly and that rational problem solving not only is effective but is esteemed by others. The self becomes a (6) rational coper; the organization presents itself as one that attempts (at least) to cope with reality in an intelligent manner. And finally (7) propriate striving develops, in which the organization tries to attain goals, especially long-range goals, that "fit in" with the organization as a whole: occupational goals, for example. I will go to college, for I am a potential contributor to the world of science. Or I will study music or art. Or I will drop out, for I need time to think. It's propriate striving (unique to me) because it's no longer a general prescription. I will major in psychology, but I don't think everyone should; it's right for *me* but not for everyone.

Proprium as Determinant of Learning

As the proprium develops, it becomes a major determinant itself of later development. Allport admits, in his own unique way, that "quasi-mechanical principles" (his term for the basic laws of learning and motivation) can account for the "emergence" of the proprium. Basic animal motives lead to simple reinforcement and learning. But . . . "once established, the proprium becomes the principal source of subsequent learning."[9] Take that, you Skinnerians and Hullians!

The principle of functional autonomy in its most prominent expression is directly related to the activities of the proprium. In other words, basic motives are related to basic needs at the beginning, and secondary motives may well arise from association with basic motives. But, as the integrated organization of processes we call personality develops, these motives—whatever their original source—take on a new role, serving a *new* master: the personality itself. If the original source loses potency, the new support can sustain and even amplify the motive's workings. Look around at your friends and fellow students: isn't their sexual behavior related to their personalities? Aren't their study habits, their choice among premium beers, and the kinds of pain they are or are not willing to endure also related to personality? And isn't this what is meant by the autonomy of motives? That the motive is separated from its initial source (satisfying basic hunger, sex, and pain-avoidance needs) and is integrated into an organization of motives directed toward personal growth or preservation?

Personal Growth. The implications are not as obvious, perhaps, as the rationale. Take a simple example. Success is a reward, a reinforcement, for many responses. If you do something and are successful at it, chances are that you will do it again, right? Consider certain games. Suppose you are an excellent tennis player. Suppose you play one match and win 6-0, 6-0. Success. You would want to play against the same person again, right? Definitely wrong. That opponent is too easy. Allport suggests that, in tasks that vary in probability of success, there is a tendency to *not* repeat a successful experience; the tendency, rather, is to try something a little bit harder—to move up, to grow. Most of us prefer to *compete* with those who are approximately *equal* to us in skill, whatever the game. And, if our "equal" starts losing to us regularly, we start looking for bigger game. A 100% reinforcement schedule on the tennis court is not desirable, and that's a contradiction of "quasi-mechanical principles" of learning. Rather, it demonstrates a principle of personal *growth.*

The sense of personal growth relates to the proprium, obviously. Growth is whatever increases the sense of value in that organization, the proprium. To be a better tennis player is important if you like tennis, but the principle has a much broader scope. It applies to all sorts of activities. Occupational choice, for example: most people aspire to a *little more* than their parents have attained. Social behavior: we tend to choose

[9]From Allport's *Personality,* Holt, 1937, p. 191.

companions who (sometimes, occasionally) will push us, stimulate us, and challenge us at least a little.

Principles of Propriate Striving. Let's return to our original question of how the functionally autonomous motives develop. The answer we proposed was "by incorporation into the proprium." Now let's amplify that answer. In 1961, Allport proposed three aspects of propriate striving, in the form of three general principles. The first of these principles is called *propriate learning;* it refers to the "unusual" learning processes described above. Once personality develops, the propriate motives guide future learning. A student who is "involved" (or, better yet, "ego-involved") in a course will learn more than one who is not. Teachers know this; it is almost a truism. What it means in Allport's terms is that the organization of personality (the proprium) tends to work for and retain that which is congruent with the organization and tends to reject that which is not. It's a principle of *consistency.* It describes the desire to protect a developed organization.

The second principle is *mastery and competence* and refers to the desire to strengthen the personality, to make it better, to allow growth. Whatever enhances and increases the personality will be retained. The third principle is organization of *the energy level.* It states that motives function in part to "consume" energy and that, if present motives do not suffice, new ones will develop. If you work hard all your life for economic security and attain it, you then have energy available that is no longer necessary for the "hard work." You will not stagnate but will seek "higher" activities—such as art or social reform.

Proprium and Lifestyle. The organization (the proprium) is all important. If threatened, it will be defended. Vigorously. As individuals, we will try to enhance it. And we will try to use its powers and potentials to their utmost. If this sounds idealistic, it is because this discussion has focused on the more positive sides of the process. However, the same principles have a less positive side. For example, one of the reasons it is difficult to "cure" a person with a problem, even if the person wants to be cured, is that these behaviors are not isolated events but are integrated parts of a whole lifestyle. Alcoholics may recognize what alcohol is doing to them, but they cannot give up their friends, especially the friends they see only in bars. They are caught between the desire to improve their proprium by eliminating the dangerous drug and the fear that the proprium will be damaged by losing the desirable features (the camaraderie) of the existing lifestyle.

Allport's Legacy

Gordon Allport was a prominent psychologist and an original thinker. He was roundly criticized for many of his notions. The concept of "unique trait," for example, was never accepted, and his plaintive calls for the study of the individual as a completely unique entity either went unheeded or resulted in some of the most atrocious research ever seen in technical journals. But, at the same time, the concept of "trait" as a general theoretical construct became the *type* of construct to beat, in all personality theories, and Allport deserves much of the credit. Other psychologists perhaps could not understand Allportian uniqueness, but his shrill and erudite epistles on the topic got everyone thinking about unique *patterns* of traits in personality.

The Motive Here and Now. Similarly, many people were startled by Allport into paying attention to the individual with whom they were dealing; they were a little less likely to subject people to tests or theories that might not "fit" them. And (Heaven forbid!) they might even ask a person what he or she thought. The concept of functional autonomy produced much confusion, but it also generated considerable research, much of which probably does not recognize its debt to Allport. If nothing else, "functional autonomy" opened the doors to the study of the effects of *today's* motives and needs. Allport did convince us that it was not always necessary to dig up the childhood roots of every single impulse or drive and that it was very often enough simply to identify that motive here and now. Allport "greased the slide" for Murray and his psychogenic needs, to mention just one beneficiary.

A Criticism. If there is a really telling criticism of Allport's theory, it is the old familiar prediction problem. His theory did not do a very good job of predicting behavior. And that is the goal of a personality theory, isn't it? (Sometimes one wonders.) Allport once said that behavior did not interest him much because it was so often determined by the social situation. His goal, he said elsewhere, was to know how to write the life history of an individual. He was more interested in understanding than in prediction, if such a distinction can be made in any meaningful sense. Allport thought it could, although most psychologists today think otherwise. But who knows? Allport, the eclectic, exhumed insights and conclusions of a number of thinkers of the past whose influence had died with them. Perhaps Allport will be similarly reincarnated if the winds of change continue to blow in favor of humanism and against behaviorism. Or if they blow both together to create a new blend of understandings.

Kurt Lewin the Virgin

Kurt Lewin was born under the sun sign Virgo, the virgin, and thus has a basic communion with Lyndon B. Johnson, Peter Sellers, and Sophia Loren. Fussy and dogmatic, given to hair-splitting arguments, analytical and precise. Virgos are thus described, and, in Lewin's case, the description does fit! Lewin the model-builder, Lewin the mathematician, Lewin the coiner of exact definitions and careful explanations.

But also Lewin the brilliant, Lewin the creative, Lewin the truly original thinker. Kurt Lewin's students and colleagues viewed him with the kind of awe-ful reverence that is inspired by only a truly extraordinary mind. (Freud was another of these.) These students and colleagues, through their writings and research, define much of Lewin's impact on psychology; his own writings are not well organized. His theory must be reconstructed from a set of papers on various issues, for it was never delineated in rigorous fashion in a major book. Lewin was too busy polishing this detail or that, poking into some new application and getting it right, to go back and put it all together once and for all. Virgos are like that.

Basic Concepts

Dynamic. Lewin's interests were broad, ranging from memory to group dynamics, for he never felt constrained by the artificial boundaries of his specialty. In fact, "Lewin's specialty" is a self-contradictory phrase: he was a general psychologist if there ever was one, and the only concepts that earned his unvarying loyalty were *dynamics* and *fields.* And these concepts, in his view, had universal relevance.

Dynamic means active; the concept of dynamics is an energy concept. Lewin at various times referred to the dynamic base of action as the will, as psychological force (comparable to physical force), as tension, and as need. In this discussion we'll use the term *tension* in most descriptions; tension, more than the other terms, gives the flavor of what Lewin was trying to express. An individual's behavior results largely from what he or she *intends.* One is "in tension" in regard to a particular thought. action, or object, and the ensuing events in some fashion reflect that intention.

Tension and Intention. Tensions, however, do not exist in isolation; they always occur in a field of interrelated events and objects. Tensions come and go as the field changes. I am in tension as I walk down a Manhattan street alone late at night and a man approaches; he is huge and ugly, with scars on his face, brass knuckles on his hands, and a knife in his belt. He turns, crosses the street, and disappears from sight, and the tension eases. Somewhat. To say that a theorist has a field theory is to say that the theorist wants to consider, somehow, the person and the person's perceived environment at the same time. The person can not exist as that person apart from an environment, and indeed the environment does not exist apart from a perceiving person.

Memory. Early in his career, Lewin became interested in the relationship between intention and memory. Memory isn't a strictly mechanical thing, Lewin argued; it's bound up with the intent—the tension, the needs—of the rememberer. From his early work (and from other sources, too, for Lewin was always an eclectic) came the realization that intention influences a host of other behaviors. What you want, what you need, the many things you want or need and can't have, and the resulting conflict. Could conflict be the basic concept, the key to all the rest?

Conflict

Lewin spent a great deal of time analyzing the various types of conflict that could arise in a field. There are really two types of tensions. One, which we can call approach, is pushing toward something; the other, called avoidance, is pushing away from something. Lewin used these terms to describe various common conflicts.

Choosing between Desirable Alternatives. Approach/approach conflict occurs when the force toward one thing leads you away from something else that is also desirable. Suppose you are invited to a fine party by good friends on the same night that you have tickets to a fabulous concert by your favorite performer. You are "moved" toward both; there is a certain anguish over missing either. But compared to other conflicts, this one is not bad. If only all conflicts were so good, choosing between two very desirable alternatives.

Choosing between Undesirable Alternatives. Avoidance/avoidance conflicts are much less pleasant. Let's say that it's 1969 and you're a pacifist. You have to go into the army or you have to go to jail. Neither alternative is particularly desirable. An avoidance/avoidance conflict, moreover, is not easily resolved, for avoidance tensions increase as either choice comes closer. You decide to go into the army, but, as the day approaches, your aversion grows stronger and stronger. You may decide you cannot do it. Then, as the day of being arrested comes closer and closer, your aversion to this event increases. What to do? Lewin suggested that two negative forces working at odds with each other promote a tendency to "leave the field." If you take a marble, for example, and push it to the left with one pencil and to the right with another pencil, most likely the marble will slip and roll off your desk. People experiencing avoidance/avoidance conflict may simply remove themselves from the situation. The young pacifist, asked to choose between war and jail, may go to Canada.

Approach/Avoidance. An approach/avoidance situation is one in which a single event has both positive and negative aspects. Living in a dormitory or apartment building has certain advantages over living in a house; you meet a lot of nice people and don't have a lot of responsibility for upkeep. But there are disadvantages as well; you have less privacy and less storage space. Most situations in real life are like this; they are good in some respects and bad in others. Going to jail for your principles, for example, is not altogether bad; jail is no fun, but you may derive pleasure from an increase in self-esteem. In approach/avoidance conflict, you are not as likely to leave the field (the tension to approach pulls you to stay), but it is still not an easy conflict with which to deal. Lewin suggested that, as the goal comes closer, the tension to avoid increases at a faster rate than does the tension to approach. Typically one approaches, then backtracks, and generally vacillates at the point where the tension to approach equals the tension to avoid.

Doubled, Tripled, or Quadrupled Conflict. Although most situations in real life may involve approach/avoidance conflict, events in the life of an individual rarely occur one by one. Instead, the typical conflict a person faces may well best be described as a double or triple or quadruple approach/avoidance conflict. In the double approach/avoidance conflict, the individual is torn between two events, each having positive and negative aspects. The decision to marry, for example, may involve choosing between freedom and loneliness, on the one hand, and companionship and obligation, on the other.

These concepts are fairly simple. Tension pushes a person in two or more different directions at the same time. The approach/avoidance concept has wide applicability to a variety of issues. And Lewin was not hesitant to apply it widely. Let's turn to the overall model of personality that he constructed and see how approach/avoidance fits in. Be warned, though, that it may take a while. Virgos build very complicated models.

A Personality Model

Lewin began by stating the obvious. He said that the world contains two kinds of things, people and not-people. If we intend to understand and define the nature of personality, we must take both into account. The *whole* thing. But we must also differentiate between the two. If you draw a circle, it divides the space on the paper into two parts, one part inside and the other part outside. Inside the circle is the person. Outside is the not-person. Simpleminded? Maybe, but it's basic to Lewin's theory. The person is separate from the rest of the world but is also a part of and surrounded by the rest of the world. You can't have one without the other, but they are always two different and distinct things.

The Life Space. Everything in the outside world, however, is not directly relevant to you. A pump-house operator on the Alaska pipeline decides to wear a red shirt this morning. You don't know about this decision, and it is not at all likely to affect your life in the slightest. Draw a second circle, enclosing but not touching the first. This second, larger circle is the *life space*. It's that part of the whole environment that can affect you, that you are capable of knowing about or being touched by. It's the world as you understand it, which may be quite different from objective reality. It is like Murray's beta press. But objective reality certainly influences your life space, shapes it, intrudes upon it. The pump-house operator's red shirt attracts the attention of a fellow worker, who fails to watch an important gauge at a critical moment. The pressure goes up, and the pump house explodes. Stories of the incident appear in the papers. You read the stories and think about the ways in which small incidents can have unforeseen consequences. A new "fact" has entered your life space.

Regions. The life space, then, contains facts. Not facts in the ordinary sense of the word but facts that are constructed on the basis of experience. Lewin used the word *region*, to fit in with the analogy of moving (psychologically) from one place (fact, idea) to another. Each region contains one fact, and two regions are connected when their facts can influence each other. But what does that mean? Well, it makes more sense if you understand that there are regions inside the person, too. The *events* of life are interactions between regions, inside and outside the person.

But let's stay outside, in the life space, just for a moment more. Regions are separate from one another. They have boundaries. Go back to your two circles and draw some lines in the outside one (leave the inside one, the person, alone for the time being). Carve the outside one into chunks. Now the life space is divided into some regions. These regions are different, but in what ways? Your first answer is probably that they differ in size and shape. But that answer is irrelevant. Irrelevant? How can it be irrelevant? What kind of theory is this, anyhow? Well, says Lewin, it's a topological theory. And what does that mean? Topology is a branch of mathematics that deals with the *relationships* among spaces. To a topologist, a donut and a coffee cup are exactly the same thing: a shape with a hole through the middle. It's the relationship between the thing and its surroundings that counts, not the fact that it is neat and symmetrical or has a big lump on one side with a hollow place in it.

Relationships among Regions. So the size and shape of the regions are irrelevant. What counts is their relationship to one another. Now what about their relationship is important? Well, some are close to each other and some are farther away. That's Lewin's *nearness/remoteness* dimension. The more remote two regions are from each other, the less influence either is likely to have on the other.

The kind of boundary between regions is important, too. A region may have a thick, hard boundary; it may be relatively *firm*. Or the boundary may be quite *weak*. Logically enough, the firmer the boundary, the less likely a region is to be affected by something outside.

And, finally, the region itself has a quality—we can call it a texture—of *fluidity* or *rigidity*. It is easily molded and changeable or stubbornly resistant to change.

The Person in the Life Space. So much for the life space. Let's leave it now and turn to that inside circle. It, too, can be carved up into regions. Put a whole lot of regions in it, but make sure that some of the regions are clearly on the outer edge and some are clearly inside. The outer regions are the *perceptual/motor* cells, and the inner ones are the *inner/personal* cells. In order for a fact in the life space to affect an inner/personal cell (or vice versa), it must work through one or more perceptual/motor cells. Something in your life space, outside of your self, affects you only if you see it, hear it, or run into it. And you can affect that outside-you space by touching, talking, making contact. The cells that make up the perceptual/motor region are two-way streets, but they are the only streets. All of the inside-the-person cells, both perceptual/motor and inner/personal, have boundaries too, and qualities of nearness/remoteness and firmness/weakness and fluidity/rigidity.

Locomotions. Now, sit back and look at the circles you've drawn. That's a ridiculous picture of a person. And, indeed, Lewin would find it so, too. That diagram is a slice in time of the whole picture, one frame of the movie. The regions in the person and in the life space flow and change. At a given moment there may be only one region within the person. If I am hungry, that may be all I am thinking about right now. My life space has only one region: this ham sandwich . . . this piece of a ham sandwich . . . this crust of a ham sandwich . . . hmm, I wonder whose voice that is behind me? And now there are more regions in my life space and probably more inside me as well. It all flows. Lewin talks about the flowing in terms of *locomotions*, of movements from region to region. When I stop concentrating on the ham sandwich and turn to look at the people behind me, I have performed a locomotion. I can perform internal locomotions as well, as I turn my thoughts from one fact to another. Locomotion is a dynamic construct, in contrast to the structural constructs like life space and region and boundary.

Valence. The other dynamic constructs that depict the nature of tensions and locomotions (internal and external; thought and behavior) are *need, valence,* and *vector*. Valence is the most interesting of the three. It is a value construct, and it refers to a region. Valence of a region is the value of that region for the particular individual under consideration. The incentive value of an activity is another reasonably synonymous term for valence. Valence provides a sort of force field, like a magnetic field. It can be positive, attracting, or it can be negative, repelling. Valence, positive or negative, can also vary from weak to very strong.

Vector and Psychological Distance. Valence makes everything "go" in the Lewinian theory. The attraction or repulsion of a region produces a *vector,* a force, a push or a pull. That force directly determines thought and behavior. A vector is represented mathematically by an arrow and has three characteristics: direction, intensity, and point of application. In Lewin's diagrams, the direction of a vector is indicated by the direction in which the arrow is pointing; its intensity is indicated by the length of the arrow; and its point of application is generally on the person in the life space. Now, one can ask why Lewin needed the vector construct, if vectors are completely determined by valences. If you use the magnet analogy, the answer becomes clear. A magnet may be strong or weak, and it may attract or repel, but its power is also a function of distance. A piece of iron close to a magnet is attracted with more force than one farther away. Lewin, neatly tying together the structural and the dynamic characteristics of his model, used the term *psychological distance* as the additional factor in the determination of force. Vector is a function of (1) the valence of the region and (2) the psychological distance of the person from the region. And here, finally, we get back to the approach/avoidance conflict. As the person moves closer to the region with both negative and positive aspects, the tensions increase. The tension to avoid increases faster than the tension to approach, in most cases. Dynamic conflict: the essence of the human situation.

Need. There is another question. What determines valence? Well, think about your own life space for a second, as the "regions" come and go. What determines what you find attractive and aversive? One of the prime determinants is need. If you are hungry, a steak has a high value. If you have just finished a big meal, a piece of meat might have no value or even a negative value. But need is not the only factor, is it? Lewin also mentioned, with intentional vagueness, "the perceived nature of the object or activity." In other words, objects and activities have their own negative and positive incentive value, and, when these objects and activities become represented in the life space as regions, valence and vectors are set up. Social approval from someone with high status might have high valence. Some theorists, of course, postulate a need, learned or unlearned, whenever there is valence involved, but Lewin thought in terms of the field, and such distinctions did not seem necessary.

Consider a very simple case, that of a hungry man. The amount of force pushing him toward the refrigerator is partly a function of his need, his hunger, and, if there is anything edible in the refrigerator, the force will increase as the hunger increases. But the force is also dependent on what is in the refrigerator—or what he remembers as in the refrigerator. The force might be greater if there is a steak sandwich than if there is only an old, decaying apple. The need and the perceived nature of the goal object combine to produce valence and, through valence, the force or vector.

In Conclusion

Here we will stop.

This is, of course, only a superficial glance at Lewin's field theory. We could fill page after page with cross-hatched diagrams, showing the conflicts and tensions and resolutions that ebb and flow as a person thinks and acts within the life space. In this discussion, we have barely scratched the surface. But it is enough to give the flavor of what Lewin was about. He was building a general-purpose model, a model that could be applied to any human activity, a model that would be equally sensitive to internal and to external events. And, to a remarkable degree, he succeeded.

Back to the Eclectic Beginnings

Murphy, Murray, Allport, and Lewin had many "debates" among themselves in their day, but, in hindsight, we group them together. All were thoughtful, impressed by literary scholarship, eclectic. Each was a generalist and reflected in his theory a concern for the whole person. They respected Freud but did not always accept his dogma. They had a kind of optimism, a feeling for the greatness of human-ness. They were scientists, but they often decried the sterile behaviorism of the era. They studied, thought, proposed, criticized, defended, rethought, puzzled, and accepted both support and attack. In the end, they left as a legacy a curious combination of concepts, approaches, and techniques that borrowed from Freud, humanism, the individual-differences approach, and behaviorism, with a bit of the Protestant ethic mixed in, to produce a general trend of "original eclecticism" that still pervades North American personology.

A Brief Review

In the end, Murphy, Murray, Allport, and Lewin will be remembered for their unique contributions: Murphy for his work on autism and his concept of canalized response; Murray for his list of needs and the development of the TAT; Allport for the concepts of trait, the proprium, and functional autonomy and the advocacy of uniqueness and individuality; and Lewin for field theory and its practical applications in group dynamics and social psychology in general. If you want to be remembered as a scientist, you'll probably have to attach your name to a unique contribution, preferably a law or theory or a technique or instrument, as Rorschach did with inkblots, or Skinner with his box, or Freud with his theory of psychoanalysis. This state of affairs is unfortunate in some respects, for, by focusing on only the unique contributions, we often overlook small but significant changes in emphasis in existing theories. We may slight the importance of the organization of the theorist's thought. And we sometimes miss the true impact of his or her work. For eclectics such as Murphy, Murray, Allport, and Lewin, these effects are especially pronounced.

An Important Change in Emphasis

Murray's "Less Basic" Needs. All personality theories are concerned with the "springs of action"—the drives, the needs, the motives. Prior to the work of the four theorists discussed in this chapter, the emphasis in personology has been on the very basic biological drives such as hunger and sex. Now that emphasis changed radically. Allport claimed that in most situations the so-called superficial motive could be used to understand behavior; it is unnecessary to explore the roots of the manifest motive. The simplest way to find out why you act as you do is to ask you—in most cases, you will tell us the important factors. Functional autonomy was the concept used to break the link between basic drives and the developed motives. Murray listed some of these "less basic" needs: the need for achievement, the need for dominance, the need for autonomy, and so forth.

It is difficult to describe fairly the tremendous impact of this shift in emphasis from the basic and biological to the manifest and human sources of behavior. Subsequent research focused on the human motives; researchers no longer felt the necessity of relating these motives to biological or childhood sources. Personality theory turned away from biology, and the Freudian emphasis on early-childhood experiences—already weakened by Adler, Jung, and Rank—received another blow.

Allport's Traits. Coordinated with this shift toward human motives was the emphasis on general response dispositions—traits, in Allport's lexicon. Traits may or may not have strong motivational connotations;

aggressiveness is one trait with such a connotation, and there is not much difference between the trait and, say, what Murray called the *need* for aggression. In formulating these general dispositions, Murray and Allport gave scientific credence to a long-held popular belief that such dispositions do exist. The energetic search for traits and human needs began in earnest; Murray's TAT and Cattell's factor-analytic approach both came to the fore.

Murphy's Perception. Murphy's emphasis on perception as the key link between the internal and external worlds of the individual added another dimension to the changes in personality theory and research. Murphy saw clearly that perception is directed and strongly influenced by needs and that needs are strongly influenced by percepts. Some purists objected to his loose use of the term *perception*, claiming Murphy was really speaking of cognition. Perhaps they were right, for the trend toward *cognitive* theories was given a big boost by Murphy's writings.

Lewin and Murphy: Interaction. The interaction between person and environment—the need for both—the essential unity of the whole thing. Here is where Lewin and Murphy came together at center stage. Murphy's biosocial emphasis and Lewin's life space. The emphasis was different, to be sure: Murphy the physiologist, Lewin the mathematician. Murphy wrestling with what really happens, physically, as one interacts with one's environment; Lewin struggling to build a schematic model that would represent the psychological reality.

Needs, traits, perception, interaction. These are the primary thrusts of Murray, Allport, Murphy, and Lewin. In Freudian terms, the ego was being examined in more detail than the id, and the positive impulses were given greater consideration. Although the four heroes of this chapter were often critical of psychoanalysis, the "counter-reformation" in psychoanalysis closely paralleled (and was undoubtedly influenced by) their changing emphases—the ego in psychoanalysis has been strongly reaffirmed. Individual differences among people in perception, in needs, and especially in traits was a concern of the three Americans and also of those who were developing assessment devices. Perhaps the only line of development in personality theory that was not strongly influenced by these three was learning theory, and Lewin's work was to have its impact there, much later, and continues to make itself felt.

When the learning/personality theorist emerged, it looked for a while as if a rapprochement would be possible. But the seeds of conflict that were always there have become firmly rooted. Today the eclectic amalgam that is in part the legacy of Murphy, Murray, Allport, and Lewin—part humanism, part psychoanalysis, and part individual differences—faces the challenge of the new behaviorists. This is the major division today.

But we are not yet ready to describe these battle lines. We have still to examine the emerging learning theories, the new developments in humanism, psychoanalysis, and individual differences, and some new inputs—from biology, anthropology, sociology, and from other fields in psychology.

Chapter Summary

The optimistic eclecticism of Gardner Murphy, Henry Murray, Gordon Allport, and Kurt Lewin has been discussed in this chapter. The theories are *eclectic* in that they borrow heavily from other approaches, and they are *optimistic* in that they focus on more positive trends in personality as compared, for example, to early Freudian theory.

Murphy's theory was primarily directed toward the understanding of how the inner world (the personality) and the outer world (reality) interact to produce behavior. Armed with the belief that personality is largely the way one perceives the world, Murphy built his system around the *perceptual habit*. Much of his research was designed to investigate the creation and function of these habits. For example, rewards for certain perceptions make those perceptions more likely in the future; and active needs can be shown to influence percepts. The concept of *autism* was introduced to mark the fact that, since no two personalities are exactly alike, no two people will perceive reality in quite the same way. These differences in perception are the key to personality and probably to behavior. To predict behavior, one must know both the person and the environment. Murphy conceives of this person/environment as a field and calls his theory a *field theory*. His theory is also called *biosocial;* two words, "biological" (personal) and "social" (environment) are combined into one, just as Murphy thinks they should be. They are not separate and distinct factors.

Murray asked questions. What is to be explained? His answers were always tentative and subject to revision. The *proceeding,* an event with a beginning and an end, or the *serial,* an integrated set of proceedings occurring over time, is what will be explained. How is one to understand the proceeding or the serial? Well, in the beginning is the *need,* and in the end is (hopefully) the satisfaction of that need. The *press* of the environment may support or divert the behavior from its goal of satisfaction. Together, the need and the press define the theme of the proceeding.

Allport once said that, together, the concept of *functional autonomy* and the theory of *traits* are sufficient to explain most human behaviors. Or one might say that the concept of functional autonomy makes the theory of traits by itself sufficient, since traits are dispositions to behavior and, if understanding their development is not important, as functional autonomy suggests it is not, the traits can be seen as the immediate causes of action. But the potential Allportian must be wary of the use of trait concepts. In Allport's view, most information about single traits in isolation is not very useful; it is the pattern and integration of traits in the proprium that is informative. It is probably this distinction that led Allport to champion the unique trait and to derogate the common trait—"aggressiveness" in one person's *proprium* is not the same as the "aggressiveness" of anyone else. Still, Allport's conception of the trait as a psychological structure that renders equivalent a number of stimuli and responses has influenced psychologists' thinking about traits in all approaches, including the individual-differences approach, which tends to focus on the "noted" common trait.

Lewin was the model builder. (At least, for our purposes here, that's what he was. He was many other things, too.) Concerned, like Allport, with the person here and now. What are you doing? How do you move from this region (fact, feeling, idea) to that? What constrains and what facilitates the back-and-forth-and-together flow between you and your life space? Lewin loved terminology, just as Murray did: *vector, locomotion, region, boundary*. His theory was cumbersome, and it did little to predict behavior. But it offered a perspective, a framework, a new point of view from which to examine the transactions that constitute human existence.

Murphy, Murray, Allport, and Lewin all influenced the direction of personology as a field, especially in their thoughtful analyses of the proper units of study. Traits, regions, cognitive habits—all structural concepts—turned personology away from dynamic conceptions of personality and toward attempts to clarify and assess personality structures. Even the dynamic aspects of Lewin's theory could not overcome that trend. It was reinforced by the natural activities of personologists interested in testing. All four of this chapter's theorists were determined to include the whole person in their conceptualizations, to emphasize the positive potential of human striving, and to promote a tentative, yet energetic, eclecticism. Choose concepts wisely, on the basis of merit, and do not disparage the insights of others. That is the pragmatic influence.

The four horsemen have ridden off. Their hoofbeats still echo in our ears.

Suggested Readings

The basis of three of the theories presented in this chapter are reviewed well and in more detail in three important books: Murphy's *Personality* (Harper & Row, 1947), Murray's *Explorations in Personality* (Oxford, 1938, with 27 co-authors), and Allport's *Pattern and Growth in Personality* (Holt, Rinehart & Winston, 1961). The first two are available in paperback editions and the third is soon to be.

Probably the best summary of Lewin's field theory is in the second edition of Hall and Lindzey's *Theories of Personality* (Wiley, 1970). This book also provides more information on Allport and Murray, but you'll have to scrape up a first edition for what they have to say about Murphy—they dropped him in 1970. Information about all four can be had in Geiwitz's little paperback, *Non-Freudian Personality Theories* (Brooks/Cole, 1969).

Notes and References

The primary substantive references used in the discussion of Gardner Murphy were three books, the 1932 book (Coward-McCann) *Approaches to Personality*, by Murphy and F. Jensen; Murphy's 1947 book (Harper & Row) *Personality*; and Murphy's 1958 book (Basic Books) *Human Potentialities*. The first two are probably more important. The last chapter of the 1932 book is an interesting forecast of the entire 1947 opus, but, alone, the 1947 work is the best. The 1947 book was reprinted in 1966 with a new introduction, and that introduction is informative.

Examples of Murphy's research can be found in the *Journal of Psychology*, 1942, *13*, pp. 283–293, and 1949, *28*, pp. 457–475; and in the *Journal of Experimental Psychology*, 1943, *32*, 335–343.

Henry Murray's basic stuff is in *Explorations in Personality* (Oxford, 1938), but he was always a tentative kind of scholar. Other valuable references include his work in three edited volumes: *Personality on Nature, Society, and Culture* (Knopf, 1948), *Toward a General Theory of Action* (Harvard Press, 1951), and *Psychology: A Study of a Science* (Volume III, McGraw-Hill, 1959). See also his article in *Dialectica*, 1951, *5*, pp. 266–292, and the case histories in R. W. White's *Lives in Progress* (2nd ed., Holt, Rinehart & Winston, 1966—but, if you have the time, read the Kidd history in the first edition first).

Allport has two primary books, *Personality* (Holt, 1937) and *Pattern and Growth in Personality* (Holt, Rinehart & Winston, 1961). Three good collections of his articles are available, entitled *The Nature of Personality* (Addison-Wesley, 1950), *Personality and Social Encounter* (Beacon, 1960), and *The Person in Psychology* (Beacon, 1968). More specifically, you might read *Psychological Review*, 1946, *53*, pp. 335–347 for Allport's views on the differences between quasi-mechanical and propriate learning, the principles of. For his views on traits, you'll find useful articles in *American Psychologist*, 1966, *21*, pp. 1–10, and in the book *Assessment of Human Motives* (Holt, Rinehart & Winston, 1958).

Apart from the Hall and Lindzey chapter on Lewin, the major sources for his work are his own *A Dynamic Theory of Personality* (McGraw-Hill, 1935), J. W. Atkinson's *An Introduction to Motivation* (Van Nostrand Reinhold, 1964), and M. Deutsch's "Field Theory in Social Psychology," in the Lindzey and Aronson *Handbook of Social Psychology* (Addison-Wesley, 1968). Boring's *History of Experimental Psychology* (2nd ed.), Appleton-Century-Crofts, 1950, has a short treatment of Lewin, chiefly of interest for biographical details.

8

The Humanistic, Holistic, Organismic Revolution

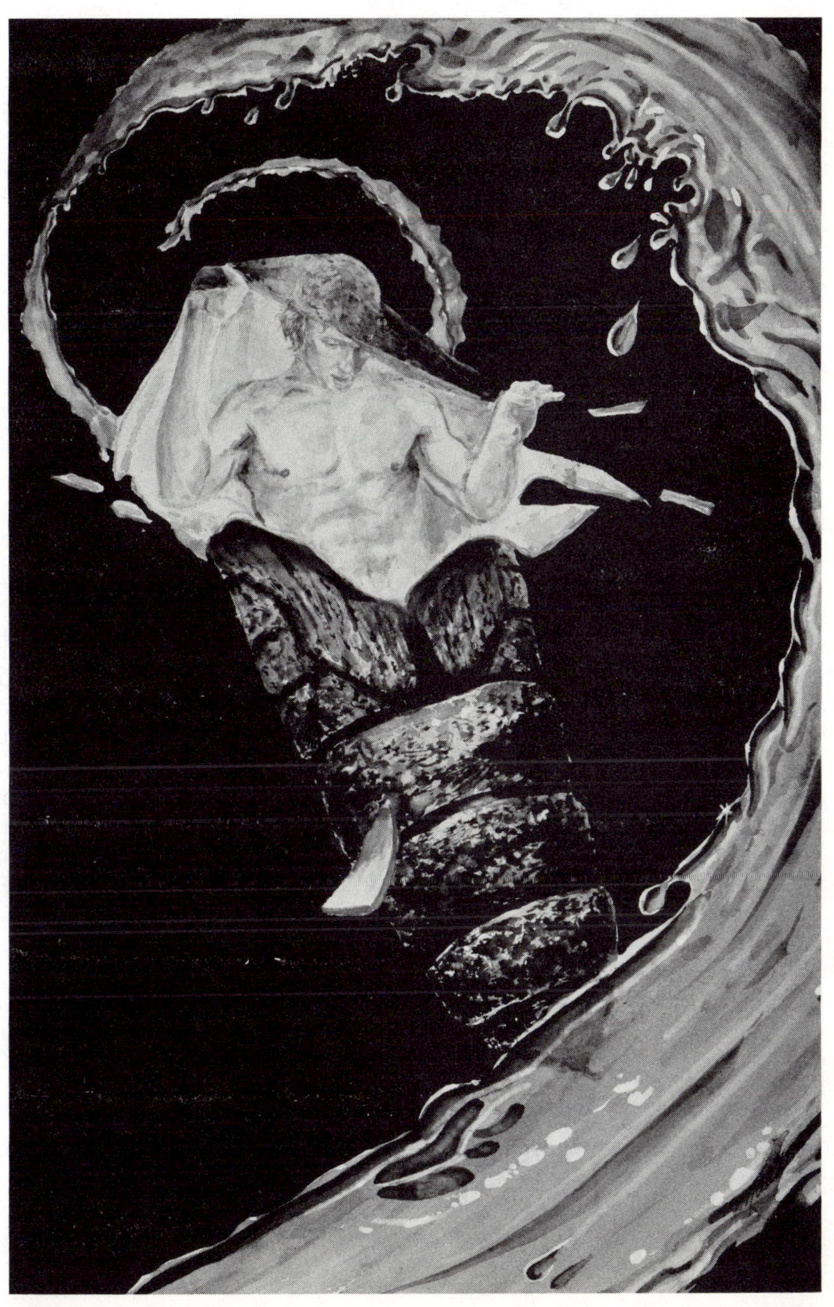

"(While you and i have lips and voices which
are for kissing and to sing with
who cares if some oneeyed son of a bitch
invents an instrument to measure Spring with?"

e. e. cummings[1]

What is it that is distinctively human about the human condition? What do we lose in our attempts to be "scientific," to analyze, analyze, analyze, to invent an instrument to measure Spring with—when the object of our study lives, breathes, thinks, loves, and hates, existing in and through time in the fullness of personhood?

Many psychologists feel that these questions, full of faith and values, have no place in personology but are the province of poets and philosophers. Others, being poets and philosophers as well, believe that personality theories that do not grapple with these issues are sterile and lifeless and wrong. Thus, we have theories in personality that are a little poetic, a little philosophical. In this chapter you will encounter some of the more prominent examples.

The Organismic Premise: Kurt Goldstein

Organismic, as used in psychology, means holistic; it refers to the whole, which must be distinguished from the sum of the parts. It means that a single act cannot be viewed in isolation from the total organism, mind and body. Just as the activity of any single individual on a football team makes little sense when considered out of the context of the team play, behavior, too, must be viewed in the context of organismic activity.

Jung, Adler, and Rank started the humanistic movement in personology, and they all used the organismic premise to varying degrees. Allport, Murray, and Murphy were eclectic, holistic, and, to some extent, humanistic. But the theorist who is now associated most strongly with the organismic premise is one Kurt Goldstein, a brilliant neurologist and psychologist who, in 1914, turned his academic knowledge to practical use as a director of a military hospital for brain-injured soldiers during "the war that would end all wars."

A brain injury, especially in a young man, has remarkable effects; one might even go so far as to say that the behavior of brain-injured youths is proof that action must be interpreted in context, for that is certainly the case for these unfortunate victims of military adventures. Some of the effects can be traced directly to the injury, of course—the soldier is blind or paralyzed or has difficulty interpreting or producing speech. But this is hardly an adequate description of behavioral changes

[1]The lines from "voices to voices, lip to lip" ONE XXXIX are reprinted from *is 5*, poems by E. E. Cummings, with the permission of Liveright Publishing Corporation. Copyright 1926 by Horace Liveright. Copyright renewed 1954 by E. E. Cummings.

following the trauma; other effects can be regularly observed. For example, brain-injured patients are typically neat and orderly, often to an extreme, and this behavior pattern can be observed in a whole range of patients with widely varying neurological destruction. Orderliness is not a direct effect of the injury; it is a secondary symptom.

It was quite obvious to Goldstein and his staff that secondary symptoms reflected an attempt to adjust to a new life marked by reduced mental or sensory capacities. The commonly exhibited neatness, for example, did not represent compliance with the hospital routine so much as a deliberate attempt to avoid surprises. Brain-injured patients have lost some of their ability to cope with novel situations, so they adjust by avoiding the unexpected and by ordering their lives and their environments as best they can. Everything is in its place. If it is not, it may be lost completely—lost to memory, irretrievable.

One of Goldstein's patients tied a string to his bedpost; without it, he could not identify his own bed. He went to work or dinner by following other patients; he could not remember the paths he had traveled so many times in the past. He could not distinguish fact from fiction and became very upset when someone would tell a "story." If someone read "It was raining," he would complain "It is not!" He became agitated when facing a mirror, for there was nobody behind it, as he expected there to be. Is it any wonder that he had a desire for a neat and orderly life? To him, the slightest deviation from routine was a potential nightmare.

Secondary symptoms, in other words, represent the striving of the total organism to adapt, given the direct effects of brain injury. Those we have mentioned, neatness and orderliness, could be classified as *defensive:* that is, they are used to avoid situations that might present problems. Just as a heart-attack victim avoids strenuous exercise, the brain-injured patient avoids tasks that might overstrain his or her mental capacities. Goldstein noted that tests showed many of these soldiers to be more disabled than they actually were, because they refused even to try tasks that they could, in fact, do.

Other changes in behavior could be classified as *compensatory*. If you are blinded, chances are that you will try to develop other senses. Goldstein observed that soldiers who had lost completely a psychological or physical function (like vision) adjusted more quickly to the loss and generally fared much better than those who experienced only a partial loss of that function. The partially deprived patients kept trying to regain the old ability, whereas the completely deprived patients quickly established their goal as compensation and had much greater success. The partially blind, in other words, strove to be able to see the way they had before, which was usually impossible, and did not develop their other senses as quickly as the totally blind did.

Goldstein noted a third category of secondary symptoms, and it was this discovery that secured his place in the history of personality theory. This category consisted of the *growth* behaviors, attempts not to defend against trauma nor to be as before, but to grow and become better than before, even with the deficit of brain injury. Repeatedly Goldstein observed the same sequence: first defense, then compensation, and finally the striving for growth and improvement. Goldstein saw the motive force underlying growth behaviors as *self-actualization*, the striving to be the best one can possibly be.

In brain-injured patients, of course, the best one can be is somewhat limited, and the results of self-actualization in these cases are much like those of an idiot savant. (An idiot savant is a person, usually mentally retarded, who becomes unusually proficient in one or two very circumscribed abilities, such as playing the piano.) Goldstein noted one such case, a boy who learned to perform exceptional feats of computation and amazing reproductions of musical tunes he had heard.[2] This mentally deficient boy had focused all his life energies on these two potentials, counting and mechanical musical reproduction. He actualized what little potential he had. He grew in the few directions open to him.

Self-actualization in normal people, as we shall see, proceeds in many directions and toward many goals, and the exceptional behaviors are more varied and integrated. But, before leaving our discussion of the brain-injured soldiers, we should point out another distinction Goldstein made, one that is perhaps as often associated with his name as are the organismic premise and the concept of self-actualization. Goldstein had a sizable number of patients whose injuries were in the front of the brain. These soldiers could not make *abstractions* from concrete experiences. This ability is such a common one that you may find it difficult to understand what it means to lose it. The person who is unable to handle abstractions cannot, for example, tell a story from a report of facts or see a mirror as a reflection of reality, as we have seen. Such a person cannot set a clock or follow a plan or instructions. Goldstein told some patients to cross out all the e's on a printed page; they began correctly, but soon they were crossing out all letters. They could not solve simple analogies if the terms were abstract. No doubt every reader of this book can give the correct answer to the following question: "Shoe is to foot as glove is to what?" People with injuries to the frontal lobe of the brain cannot answer it at all; the question, to them, makes no sense.[3]

Discovering that certain kinds of brain injuries led to an inability to abstract higher-level meaning from concrete experience was important; today tests for this ability are used in order to distinguish between brain-damaged and physically normal (but neurotic or psychotic) patients. But, in the history of personology, Goldstein is best remembered for his organismic, holistic approach, and not as a diagnostician. All the secondary symptoms we have discussed—defensive, compensatory, and growth-oriented—make little sense as isolated behaviors. But, as attempts of the total organism to adjust to the loss of some normal capacity, they are quite reasonable.

And self-actualization! Jung had spoken of it before, and Goldstein showed us what it meant in terms of actual behaviors. As concept, self-actualization was waiting for a hero, someone to apply it to all psycho-

[2]See Scheerer, Rothman, and Goldstein's account of a boy with unusual computational and musical abilities, "A Case of 'Idiot Savant': An Experimental Study of Personality Organization," in *Psychological Monographs*, 1945, *58*(4).

[3]See Goldstein and Scheerer's article "Tests of Abstract and Concrete Thinking," in A. Weider (Ed.), *Contributions toward Medical Psychology*, Ronald Press, 1953.

logical endeavors, to the normal as well as to the abnormal. Abraham Maslow was to be that hero.

The Hierarchy of Needs: Abraham Maslow

Abraham Maslow is usually labeled a humanistic personality theorist. He taught for several years at Brandeis University, where his faculty colleagues included Kurt Goldstein. Maslow focused his attention on human motivation—needs—and he is famous for (among other things) his views on the relationships of different needs to one another. Needs, said Maslow, arrange themselves in a hierarchical structure. The defining characteristic of the hierarchy is prepotency. Lower needs are *prepotent* over needs that are higher on the list; that is, lower needs must be satisfied before higher needs will make themselves felt.

Lowest on Maslow's hierarchical ladder are the physiological needs. These include hunger, thirst, sex, and other desires that lead to behaviors that are necessary for the survival either of the individual (like eating) or of the species (like copulation). If unsatisfied, these needs can become extremely compelling, totally dominating a person's thoughts and actions. A starving person has no interest in philosophy.

Second in the hierarchy are the safety needs. These include the needs for security, stability, order and law, and freedom from fear. The physiological needs are prepotent over the safety needs, but, in turn, the safety needs are prepotent over the categories of needs still higher on the list.

The belongingness and love needs, the needs for friends, lovers, and children, are next on the list. When these needs are not satisfied, one feels lonely and rejected, cut off from society and from oneself. In North American society today, belongingness and love needs are prominently apparent, and many new cultural institutions—singles' bars, encounter groups, and the like—represent attempts to gratify these basic human desires. We might speculate on why such institutions are appearing now rather than at an earlier time in history. Has our society finally reached a point where the lower needs are satisfied more or less automatically for most of us, so that we are more aware of our hunger for love and belongingness? Or, perhaps, does modern Western culture fail to meet these needs as well as previous social arrangements have done? Or is it that both things are happening, that, by some strange quirk of cultural evolution, we are most able to be aware of our relationship needs at the very time when society is least able to meet them? But these are questions for sociologists and philosophers; let us turn back to the need hierarchy as Maslow conceived it.

If the love and belongingness needs are satisfied, esteem needs emerge. We need to respect ourselves, and we need the respect of others: recognition, status, fame. And, finally, at the top of the heap of needs, self-actualization becomes a driving force. Maslow defines the need for self-actualization as the desire "to become everything that one is capable of becoming." "What a man *can* be, he *must* be."[4] But, of course, the

[4]From *Motivation and Personality* (2nd ed.), 1970, p. 46.

need for self-actualization becomes motive only when the lower needs are at least reasonably satisfied. What do you do when you have everything? You self-actualize. You pursue the great values: justice, honesty, creativity, a sense of purpose. If this fails, if you can't meet these highest needs, you present the picture of the rich and thoroughly bored socialite who wonders why, after trying so many things, and having so many opportunities there is nothing at the end of the rainbow. In the words of the popular song of the '70s, you ask "Is that all there is?" You know that you want—need—something. Something you don't have.

Maslow called all of the needs, from the physiological drives to the self-actualizing tendencies, *instinctoid.* By this he meant that the needs are innate and cannot be denied. He did not mean that all needs will be prominent. Intrinsic to the notion of prepotency, as we have seen, is the fact that higher needs will not direct behavior in people who are starving or who are striving for security. But, in someone for whom the lower needs have been gratified, higher needs will inevitably emerge; there is no escape. One does not *learn* to desire to be the best one can. The need emerges. It is instinctoid. It is part of being human.

The self-actualizing person is at the other end of the spectrum from the neurotic. One can be normal and healthy, but one can also be more. Maslow said that Freud gave us the sick half of psychology and that it was now time to develop the healthy half. To do this, he studied, rather informally, the lives of people who, by various standards, would be considered "abnormally" healthy. These included both people who were living and people who were dead, among them such historical figures as Abraham Lincoln and Albert Einstein. The living subjects were interviewed, and the dead subjects were examined from biographies and other writings. From these imperfect studies, Maslow constructed a list of the characteristics that are most prominent in successful, healthy, and happy people. The list is given in Table 8-1. The list sounds about like what we all wish we were and in that sense is not surprising. What is surprising is that these characteristics do show up—regularly and grouped together—in certain outstanding individuals.

Metaneeds and B-Values

The self-actualizing person is directed by growth needs (G-needs) rather than by deficiency needs (D-needs). In other words, the behavior of the self-actualizer is designed to enhance life and living, to make it something more, rather than simply to make up for some loss or lack. A starving person needs food to alleviate a bodily deficiency; this is a D-need. If you are reasonably well fed, you "need" food in a different way; you may become a gourmet, an expert on the sensual values of food, or you might create a mealtime adventure where you and your friends can experience the pleasures of interpersonal fellowship. These are responses to G-needs. They not only still the craving or heal the hurt, but they also leave the organism better, more whole, more fully functioning than it was before.

Table 8-1. Characteristics of self-actualizing types.

Characteristic	*Comment*
Self-actualizing people 1. perceive reality accurately, 2. even in regard to themselves and 3. are not afraid of it.	Self-actualizing people detect absurdities and dishonesty quickly, even their own; they do not live in a dream world.
4. They are spontaneous and natural.	They are unorthodox, especially in their thoughts. They do not act rebelliously simply because they disagree with the opinions of others. They do not act for effect unless the principle involved is highly valued. They have ideals, in other words, but they also understand reality.
5. They focus on problems, not on themselves.	They are not focused on their own personal problems to the exclusion of the problems of society; they think in terms of contributions they can make.
6. They like privacy and detachment; 7. they can be called autonomous.	They are relatively independent of both the physical and the social environment; they enjoy but do not *need* friends.
8. They have a continued freshness of appreciation.	Life does not become old and stale for them.
9. They have peak experiences.	They have out-of-the-world-of-the-ordinary (mystical) experiences.
10. They have a feeling of comradeship and unity with all people and 11. profound interpersonal relations.	They are realistic reformers, attempting to improve the lot of all people, and their personal friendships and love relationships are also intense.
12. They have a democratic character structure and 13. discriminate between means and ends.	They are not prejudiced, and they have a strong sense of ethics.
14. They are creative.	They see new relationships and new solutions and are willing to risk trying those solutions and relationships out.
15. They have a philosophical sense of humor.	They laugh at absurdities, not at other people's failings.
16. They resist enculturation.	They are not overly influenced by society.

The characteristics in this table are described in Chapter 11 of *Motivation and Personality* (2nd ed.), 1970, by Abraham Maslow.

The G-needs are also called *metaneeds,* a term that has a sense of prepotency even though the need to self-actualize is the least potent in the hierarchy. Maslow hypothesized that these highest of needs, once experienced, can become extremely potent. If you have experienced a profound sense of what justice really means, you might give up your life in its pursuit. The quest for self-actualization may take precedence over hunger or belonging or respect—but only after you have experienced the "high" of living at the level of self-actualization.

In the course of self-actualizing, there are setbacks and disappointments, to be sure, but one also has peak experiences, mystical experiences of the totality and unity of the universe. Probably all people have some peak experiences; self-actualizers have more. Examples include religious peaking, those marvelous moments of feeling at one with God and the universe and understanding in some gut-level, nonverbal way what existence is all about. An intense sexual/love experience, when you seem to contact the very soul of another person, is another example. Maslow noted that some drug experiences may fall into this category and that the psychedelic drugs may increase the probability of a peak experience. (Of course, they may also increase the probability of a "valley" experience or create false "peaks," a kind of plastic high that blinds us to our real potential.)

Growing implies growing *toward* something; metaneeds have goals, and peak experiences include at least partial attainment of some of these goals. Maslow referred to the goals, the ends, the consequences of this psychological growth as B-values (values of "Being"). Primarily derived from descriptions of peak experiences, the B-values include truth, honesty, beauty, justice, order, and playfulness. Playfulness? Yes, indeed! B-values are not grim and serious. They are joyful, creative, and exciting. Life is not a desperate flight from imminent disaster; life is growing and being. And not least of all, life (as it should be lived) is fun!

Maslow believed that the B-values reflect universal and instinctoid human desires. In many respects, the trend of his thought was similar to that of Jung, who mentioned many of the same values as projections from the collective unconscious, the universal human reservoir of timeless needs.

Kurt Goldstein started theorists thinking about self-actualization and the organismic premise. Abraham Maslow furthered this line, gave it impetus, and forced other psychologists to consider it. In particular, the concept of the hierarchy of needs and the notion that lower needs are prepotent over higher needs but higher needs may become overriding in their own right represented important steps forward. Also, Maslow pointed to the necessity of exploring the great goals of humankind, the B-values. Half researcher, half philosopher, Maslow began to describe the exact nature of the need hierarchy and the B-values. He was not completely successful; perhaps nobody could be completely successful. But the value of his work lies in its acknowledgment of the existence of human striving that transcends ordinary animal needs. While other psychologists were making calm, competent statements about "this is how people are," Maslow shouted and whispered and exulted "This is how people shall be!"

Andras Angyal

Here was a truly innovative theorist, so innovative, in fact, that few psychologists have read his books or even heard of him. His big year was 1941, the date of publication of his major work, *Foundations for a Science of Personality*. That was more than a dozen years before Maslow wrote his major book, *Motivation and Personality*, but our discussion of the development of holistic, humanistic theories flows more intelligibly if we include Angyal now rather than earlier. Also, given that a number of contemporary psychologists are now discovering Angyal for the first time and given that his theory dovetails with many developments in learning theory, perception, and physiology, it may well be that the period of major impact of this theory will follow that of Maslow's. We shall see.

Andras Angyal, we should mention, was at Brandeis University when Kurt Goldstein and Abraham Maslow were there, and many people would rank these colleagues as the top three in the Organismic League standings (ordering in dispute). There is no dispute about the intellectual climate at Brandeis during those years. What an exciting, heady place to have been! There was undoubtedly much cross-fertilization of ideas, and the similarity among the three theorists should come as no great surprise.

Angyal set out to produce a dynamic definition of personality. Now, most personality theorists claim to see the human personality as "dynamic," but many only pay lip service to the concept. Personality theories are filled with structural concepts like needs and traits. Angyal claimed that to hold a dynamic view was to see personality as an active, ongoing *process*. One should not speak of motives and habits; instead one should describe the patterns of the process, the flow and direction of life as displayed in its currents and eddies.

So here is Angyal's "motivational" base: *All living things tend toward autonomy*. Autonomy means being self-governed. The trend toward autonomy is *away from* heteronomy (which means being governed by the many outside forces). The heteronomous outside forces are those described by physical laws, such as gravity or inertia. Inanimate objects are governed totally by these laws and forces, but living things have their own life forces that can oppose (or support) the heteronomous forces. A rock cannot fall up, but a flower can, up against the force of gravity, seeking the sun.

Autonomy is close to a definition of life. Take two cats, one dead and one alive, and drop them out of a window. They will hit the ground at about the same time, for both are subject to the laws of gravity. But the live cat will land on its feet! Its autonomous efforts change the predictions that can be made on the basis of physical laws alone.

Anything that happens in the life of a living organism is partly a function of autonomous forces and partly a function of heteronomous forces. The trend through life is to increase autonomy. Imagine, for example, that you are learning to ski. The first time you go down the slope, your behavior is pretty much a function of physical laws describing the movement of an inanimate object pushed off the top of a hill. With learning, however, you begin to look less and less like a rolling rock and more like a skier. You are in control now, instead of "Monster Ridge."

An event in the life of an organism can be described in terms of a ratio between autonomous effects and heteronomous effects. This ratio varies as a function of many factors. The human animal, for example, is more autonomous than a plant; a plant dies in a cold spell, but the human puts on a warm coat and survives. Goldstein's brain-injured patients were more subject to heteronomous forces, because of their reduced capacities, than were average people. Learning increases the relative contribution of self-governing or autonomous forces. So the ratio of autonomy to heteronomy varies across species, across situations, and across individuals of one species in the same situation. Nevertheless, the trend through life in all cases is to increase autonomy. Though a brain-injured soldier may never achieve the autonomy of a normal person, he still strives to do his best.

It is important to recognize that this biological trend does not mean that the organism is *aware* of what it is striving for. A plant has no awareness of seeking the sun, and even people, who are aware of much, do not always consider the biological significance of their actions. How often do you, for example, think about preserving the species when you are making love?

The trend toward autonomy is one pattern of the life process. A second trend, according to Angyal, is a trend toward *homonomy*, a tendency to increase harmony and joint action with other individuals in a group. Homonomy is not contradictory to autonomy; in fact, it can be seen as a distinct means of increasing autonomy. Many animals band together to gather food or to protect their group members from predators. A lone wolf cannot bring down a deer, but a pack can. A lone citizen cannot defeat city hall, but an organization might.

A number of distinctly human behaviors are determined by the trend toward homonomy: any description of an order that includes but supersedes the individual, for example. A family business. A mutual-defense pact among nations. An ethical world order. The priesthood of all believers. Social cohesion has clear evolutionary advantages, and the abstract, philosophical significance of this can lead, in the abstracting animal, to notions of a grander scheme of things.

Life in the Biosphere

Biosphere? Does that sound like an echo of Murphy, with his famous dictum, "Nothing is not biosocial"? It should, for Murphy and the others who emphasized the essential interaction between person and environment paved the way for the even more dynamic theory of Angyal.

Given Angyal's two "motivational" trends, then, how should we describe the human personality? Obviously, growth is explained in terms of these trends. And mental illness is growth diverted for physical or environmental reasons into societally unacceptable channels. But this statement is too general; we must get down to specifics.

Angyal claimed that personality theorists use the terms *person* and *environment* inaccurately. The person and the environment cannot be considered separately; they must be considered together, as a *biosphere*. In the biosphere there are events or happenings. Some of these events are primarily autonomous and others are primarily heteronomous. Generally we refer to autonomous happenings as "person" events and to heteronomous happenings as "environment" events. Consider, for example, a person driven by environmental events (heteronomous forces) to act silly, to drive recklessly, or to commit murder. We say "He was forced to do it" or "She was not herself." We recognize (perhaps dimly) that a heteronomous event cannot reasonably be ascribed to a single (autonomous) source. Yet it is all too easy to ignore or forget this awareness. Over and over, we find ourselves trying to understand human behavior as if the behaver were the main—or sole—factor to be considered. "He wrecked his car because he was angry." "She abandoned her family because she loved someone else." "He acts that way because he never resolved his Oedipal conflicts." Angyal keeps pulling us back, reminding us that this sort of explanation is, at best, only half an explanation. Both autonomous and heteronomous forces influence behavior; neither can be left out.

The process of personality, with an emphasis on "person," is a trend toward becoming self-governing and effective. For the beginning skier, arriving at the bottom of the hill in one piece is at first both a mystery and a joy. Later, after practice, the ability to ski becomes part of one's personality. *I* am skiing down the slope. This is not just a collection of environmental events; it is more *person*al. It is *I*. Autonomy overcomes heteronomy but never completely, never all the way.

The Science of Personality

The biosphere is neutral with regard to the person and the environment: neither element is more important than the other, and either may be the primary force behind a given event. However, the events in the biosphere can be viewed from the perspective of the person or from that of the environment. Consider the list in Table 8-2. Consider it in terms of a cougar and a deer, and you're the cougar. You are very hungry, and you spot a deer. Read line 2 in Table 8-2. You have a *drive* to eat (the deer). The deer has *valence* or value in relationship to your drive; it could satisfy the drive quite nicely. In the neutral biosphere, there is *tension* between the cougar (person) and the deer (environment).

Table 8-2. Different perspectives on motivation.

	From the Perspective of the Person	*From the Neutral Perspective of the Biosphere*	*From the Perspective of the Environment*
1. Potentials Personal Values ←	Attitudes	Readiness to tension	Relevance → Ethical Values
2. Actualized dynamic factors	Drive	Tension	Valence
3. Conscious (symbolized representations)	Craving	Interest	Demand quality

Adapted from *Foundations for a Science of Personality,* by A. Angyal. Copyright 1941, 1969 by The Commonwealth Fund. Used by permission of Harvard University Press.

Now imagine that you are a satiated cougar and again you come upon a deer. Read line 1. Since you are not hungry, you have no drive, just an *attitude* ("That would make a fine meal, *if* I were hungry"). An attitude, in Angyal's system, is a *readiness to tension*. The deer has *relevance*; it is not unimportant in your life, but right now everything's cool.

Cool consideration of one's attitudes leads to consideration of one's personal values in life, whereas cool consideration of life's relevancies leads to a set of (impersonal) ethical values. Does that make sense? It may not for a cougar, but it should for you, a human being. Aren't your personal values an integrated set of attitudes about vocations, interpersonal relationships, religion, and the like? Aren't your values simply a higher level of classification than a single attitude? And, when we speak of the impersonal, transpersonal, universal, ethical values, aren't we speaking of the goals, the relevancies, the things that one should seek in life?

Line 3 in Table 8-2 represents the conscious or, in Angyal's terms, the *symbolized* aspects of lines 1 and 2. People are symbolizing creatures; that is, we create ideas to represent aspects of our experience. Thus, a biospheric tension is symbolized as a *craving* from one's perspective of oneself and as a *demand quality* from one's awareness of the environment. In other words, when you are hungry, you are conscious of a craving for food, and food takes on a quality of "demanding" your attention.

Symbolization of experience is a notion of some importance in Angyal's theory. First, the science of personality is broader than the science of conscious thought (which is psychology proper, in Angyal's view). The science of personality includes conscious thought, of course, but it also includes what we define in the broad sense as biology, the study of *life*.

On the other hand, conscious thought is an important aspect of biological-personality theory, for ideas in awareness affect behavior to an extraordinary degree. An aspect of experience that has been symbolized has a much stronger effect on behavior than an equally significant (objectively considered) aspect of experience that has not been symbolized. Nonsymbolized experience forms the basis for the unconscious in Angyal's theory. The danger of slighting unconscious forces, described by Freud and Jung among others, becomes, for Angyal, the danger of relying *only* on symbolized information.

Some of this danger is due to the fact that symbolization only rarely reflects experience accurately. We have already suggested that people tend to symbolize autonomous forces as "self" or "person" and heteronomous forces as "environment" and "not-person" and that this rough approximation breaks down in some instances. Also, those forces represented as "self" may be too much in the foreground and may lead an individual to action that is not in his or her best interests in situations where the heteronomous forces of reality are powerful. Most people have a somewhat exaggerated view of their own abilities and do not respect environmental influences as much as they should. This view is due, at least in part, to the fact that they have symbolized—brought into conscious awareness—a greater proportion of "self" experiences than of the ever-changing aspects of "environment."

Symbols, being abstractions of sorts, are by definition economical. They are diagrams or caricatures of reality. They leave out some characteristics of the specific in order to represent the general: your flop-eared, shaggy cocker spaniel is a dog, just as my perk-eared short-hair is. Their individual differences are ignored. Economy in symbols has some advantages and some disadvantages. The advantages are primarily the savings in time and effort in thinking, making more "philosophical" thought possible. Children, for example, tend more than adults to think in literal visual images (pictures). Although such thinking is very "accurate," it is not optimally efficient. As adults we move toward thinking in linguistic terms (meanings).

The disadvantages of economy in thinking are the flip side of the coin. What is left out in a highly abstract symbol may, for a given situation, be quite important, and thus the symbol reflects only poorly what is happening. Misrepresentation, misunderstanding, danger.

Angyal noted that recurring anti-intellectual movements usually focus their attacks on what is left out in intellectual abstractions, including the finer detail of sensory experience, emotions, and so forth. In essence, anti-intellectuals conclude that the whole person must become more aware of immediate senses and emotions and that "mind" often inhibits, obstructs, and distorts the true nature of personal experience. This conclusion seems to be a truism, true by definition. Some abstraction is, of course, necessary (see advantages, above), and anti-intellectual movements perhaps function most effectively to counter strong tendencies to see life in mathematical terms.

Anti-intellectual movements in personology are typically humanistic and holistic. The de-emphasis of mind is really a plea for a more complete acceptance of all the forces that are operating in an individual, and few personality theorists would reject this call. Few, however, have explored the implications as thoroughly as Goldstein, Maslow, and Angyal have. And more than a few others have paid lip service to the organismic premise and the dangers of abstraction only to concentrate their research efforts on relatively trivial problems, simply because such problems lead to "sound" research with proper operational definitions. How can one do experiments on love? That which can be symbolized—operationalized—can be studied, true enough. But, as Angyal pointed out, it is hardly the totality of personality. Angyal was an intellectual anti-intellectual. He gave us symbols for understanding aspects of experience that had been mindless forces, the experiences of pre-language and beyond thought.

Your Basic Carl Rogers

Carl Rogers, our next hero, was born on January 8, 1902. He was raised in a Midwestern environment somewhat similar to Allport's, in which hard work, close family ties, and strong religious attitudes were highly valued. As a boy on the farm, Rogers studied dusty volumes on agricultural research; as a college student, he preferred the hard sciences, the physical sciences. But, like so many psychologists before and after him, his college years were years of development toward a more social view of himself and the world and a rejection of the fundamentalistic religious beliefs of his family. After college he went to Union Theological Seminary for two years, to find a "modern" religion. Clinical psychology—helping others in trouble—seemed a reasonable calling for a scientific humanist, so Rogers went "across the street" to Teachers College, Columbia University. He got his Ph.D. in 1931, the same year B. F. Skinner got his. It was apparently a very good year for Ph.D.s and, had they known the future, newspapers might have headlined these events. But of course how could they know? Besides, the football coach at Notre Dame, Knute Rockne, had just died in a plane crash.

Rogers started slowly. For 12 years he worked in a child-guidance clinic in Rochester, New York. But, as Gardner Murphy pointed out, a clinic is an eclectic place with little room for dogma, and Rogers became aware of viewpoints other than those of Freud or Thorndike. One of the radical viewpoints Rogers encountered was that of Otto Rank, one of the first humanistic psychologists. Rogers says this about Rank: ". . . his thinking . . . helped me to crystalize some of the therapeutic methods we were groping toward."[5]

Rank's thinking, as we have seen in Chapter 2, was based on the interpretation of resistance in therapy as an indication of a positive force directed toward self-improvement. The goal of therapy, said Rank, is to try to "sense" the direction of this positive force (will) and to empathize with its goals if not its direction; if the patient's will can be brought out of hiding, so to speak, and can act freely without fear, the patient will cure himself or herself by redirecting that will.

Such a method of therapy—nondirective and supportive—appealed greatly to the religious Rogers. The scientific Rogers, however, choked on the word *will,* so he gave it a new name to disguise its true identity. The *actualizing tendency*. In reference to oneself, *self-actualization,* a tendency, a disposition. All these words mean will.

But how to handle the actualizing tendency gone wrong? Many therapies would intervene—tell the person what's wrong and/or what to do instead. Both Rank and Rogers felt uneasy about interventions; they preferred to see good therapy as creating *conditions,* a situation that would allow certain *processes* in the patient to occur. And these processes result in personality and behavioral changes. The new behavior is an *outcome* of the therapeutic conditions experienced by the patient.[6]

The initial conditions (before therapy) consist of a state of *incongruence,* which means that there is some discrepancy between the way one perceives oneself (the *self*) and the way one experiences life. I might see myself as open, honest, and friendly but experience only hostility and rejection from other people. I can't understand these incongruencies. I get anxious or depressed or both, and I recognize in some vague sense a condition of threat. My integrity is being threatened, and it seems possible that the whole organization of my personality could break down. I try to avoid the threats and the anxiety by defensively distorting my expe-

[5]From *Psychology: A Study of a Science* (Vol. 3), 1959, 187.

[6]Much of the research reported in this section on Rogers is from *The Therapeutic Relationship and Its Impact,* 1967.

riences—by insisting that people do *not* reject me. In many cases, the defenses are only partially successful and I seek professional help.

Now you, the Rogerian therapist, enter the picture. Your job is to alter my conditions, to allow me to experience myself as I really am and may become. Three aspects of your therapist role are crucial. First, you must be *congruent* even as I, the patient, am not; you must not distort your experiences. Of what help can you be to me if you do not perceive accurately the nature of your relationship with me (the "client," as Rogers preferred to call the patient)? Second, you must have *empathy*, the ability to sense my thoughts and feelings. And third, you must feel *unconditional positive regard* for me; you must value me, your client, as a person of worth and power. A distinction is made between the person and the person's behaviors: the person is always to be valued even when the person's acts might be reprehensible. (This distinction has a strong religious flavor and, in fact, is a basic tenet of most religions.)

The therapist not only must be congruent and have unconditional positive regard and empathetic understanding but also should take pains to convey these things to the client. In fact, some of the research done by Rogers' students suggested strongly that the client's *perception* of therapeutic conditions was much more important in bringing about positive change than was the actual level of the conditions that the therapist was able to provide. If the client experiences good therapeutic conditions, this creates a new kind of situation, and a "process" occurs. Old defenses are no longer necessary, and innate tendencies to improve come out in the open. The client begins to openly discuss himself or herself and the experiences that have been experienced as incongruent. The outcome is a reorganization of the self—the "cure" in Rogers' system.

The outcome, of course, follows from the process, but note, too, how the process depends upon the conditions. Unconditional positive regard makes it possible to experience and talk about disturbing incongruencies by removing the necessity for defensive distortions. Congruence and empathy allow the therapist to help the client deal with distortions and eventually resolve them. Still, the therapist only helps; the client does the curing.

The ideal outcome can be phrased in the same terms used to describe the conditions the therapist provides: the client becomes more congruent, less defensive, and less anxious. Perceptions of self and of life experiences, therefore, are more accurate. One feels more (unconditional) positive regard toward oneself, even if it is now more accurately perceived as somewhat less "perfect" than before. Both the *ideal self* and the *real self* are perceived more realistically; or, if you're tired of all this jargon, the client is a more mature and better adjusted individual.

The Self

A humanistic theory of personality is one that focuses on the distinctly human abilities of the individual and, among these, on the abilities promoting a happy and productive existence. Thought and planning are examples. Almost all humanistic theories are organismic theories as well (although the converse is not true), for the organization of personality is a distinctly human fact. Subhuman animals cannot create in themselves a proprium like the one Allport (he, too, was a humanist) describes for humans. Perhaps animals have a sense of "self" in a way we cannot imagine, but only humans could inspire a therapist to say something like "The client's goal was to *become* his or her *self*."

Rogers noted this fact and was inspired to make statements like that. But he was very uneasy about terminology. "I began my work," he said once, "with the settled notion that the 'self' was a vague, ambiguous, scientifically meaningless term. . . ."[7] Unfortunately (or fortunately), Rogers was in a clinic, seeing live patients, and had little inclination to tell them what or what not to do or talk about. They used the term *self* consistently. It must have been very hard for Rogers to be empathic at the time: they thought the word meaningful, and he thought it meaningless.

Rogers concluded that, even though a self could not be seen or measured, at least *attitudes* toward this abstract entity could be measured. He predicted that attitudes toward self would become more positive with therapy, and research supported his prediction. He began to think that the self was, in fact, a *perception* of the *organization* of the thought and actions of the individual, somewhat like an attitude. In support of this assumption, he offered case histories of clients who seemed to alternate between one and another (or more) selves: "I am a great person; I am a poor soul totally without abilities; I am just an average guy." A common observation among clinicians. Rogers was happy. The term *self* now made sense, and attitudes toward self were meaningful. Perhaps they were even identical with the concept *self*.

Rogers then moved from the clinic to the university. It was quite a change. With patients you can say just about anything: "You're in love with your grandfather's lapel." The patient says "That's ridiculous!" The therapist says "Defensive, defensive . . . remember, you're a sick person." But, if a student in your class says "That's ridiculous!" you're in trouble. You can't tell students they're sick, even if they are, because the statements made in a university are judged by different criteria. Statements must be logical and clear, and they must have some research support. The change was good for Rogers. He had to sharpen his thinking. One year after Freud died, Rogers made his first public pronouncements about a new therapy. And, not coincidentally, a new theory of personality.

The primary concepts in the theory of personality are the *self* and the *actualizing tendency*. The self is a perception of organization or system. We speak of self because all our thoughts and actions seem to go together in some way. An unusual or unexpected behavior by you will elicit comments like "You aren't yourself." Self behaviors fit together and make sense; nonself behaviors don't make sense. Also included in this grand perception we call our self are feelings or awarenesses of *being* and *function* ("I am" and "I can do"). The organization that is perceived as self moves (behaves) in a direction dictated by the actualizing tendency, which is the motive force in the theory. Life is rosy . . .

[7]From *Psychology: A Study of a Science* (Vol. 3), 1959, p. 200.

. . . except for the need for *positive regard.* The fly in the oilment. Think of a child, a young girl. As she grows and becomes more aware, one of the things she becomes aware of is the tendency for other people to *judge* the quality of her actions (good/bad). Sometimes it seems that parents can look into her mind and see her thoughts. Even inner thoughts are judged. Thoughts and acts should be good. If they are good, the child is good; if she *acts* bad or *thinks* bad, she *is* bad. The value of thoughts and behaviors get translated into the value of the self. Nobody wants a bad self: she will try to do good.

This positive regard is *conditional.* The child is good if and only if she acts good. She is not worthy of regard if her behaviors are bad. Because of her perceptions of conditional regard—which are, in fact, not accurate—she becomes selective in thought and behavior so as to satisfy those who set up the conditions.

And therein lies conflict. A person's thoughts and behaviors are now motivated by two tendencies. One, self-actualization, approaches or avoids according to whether or not the resulting experience is seen as something that will enhance or strengthen the self. The second, based on the need for positive regard, approaches or avoids according to whether or not the resulting experience is seen as something that will meet with the approval of others. Needless to say, there will be times when one motive says "go" while the other says "stop." That's conflict. For example, learning a new skill often means embarrassment in the early, awkward stages, but, when the skill is mastered, it adds to the competence of the individual. The actualizing tendency says "Full steam ahead," but the person is afraid: "People will laugh when I sit down to play." It is within the conflict of these two basic needs that the trauma of individual history is enacted. Advance and relapse, adjustment and maladjustment—all can be traced to the working out of the individual's solution to this conflict.

To the extent that the need for positive regard dominates behavior, incongruence between the perceptions of self and experience will develop. I know that deep inside of me lies dormant a great pianist, but the real me can't play a note. Or is the real me dormant inside? It's all so confusing. I'll give up all this nonsense about becoming a great pianist. So I'm a little bit less than I could be. So what? Actually there's no great pianist inside me anyway; I'm sure of it now. I am as good as I can possibly be, right? Then why do I feel this nagging desire to play the piano? It's like the flu; it'll go away.

I think of other things. I want to love. I want to form an intimate union with another human being. But people will laugh at me. They don't want me. They don't like me. I must build a shell around myself. Oh, what a shell this will be! Cool, sophisticated, doing all the right things, saying all the right things, *thinking* right! No one will crack my shell. I will be invulnerable to laughter and scorn. I will be attractive. Then everyone will love me. People will never see my fears, my real goals in life, my doubts about myself—or is it my shell that is real? I've forgotten. No matter. Someone loves me now. I only wish I could love in return.

The person "for the sake of preserving the positive regard of others has now come to falsify some of the values he experiences and to perceive them only in terms based upon their value to others."[8] But incongruence has its cost. Vague anxieties, depression, constant effort to preserve the invulnerability of the shell, a constant threat that someone might poke a hole and see the monster inside. Or whatever's inside. I've forgotten . . . is there anything inside?

Here comes my therapist. I'll test her. I'll tell her she's a fraud. And I'll put my cigarette out on her new carpet. She doesn't like that. She's going to charge me for carpet repair. Now she'll tell me to leave. But no. She is still warm and friendly and wants to know why I'm testing her. I'll show her. I'll let her peek inside my shell; that would scare anyone off. She says the monster is beautiful. I tell her I want to play the piano in Carnegie Hall. She doesn't laugh. Says she wants to also. I tell her I want to love. She says everybody wants that. Is she putting me down? Am I an abnormal dwarf of a personality, that I can't love? I wonder why I can't. I'm just like James Bond and he can love. Or can he? I wonder. Maybe he's worse off than me. He doesn't have my doubts and fears. Maybe he's less human. Maybe I'm more human. Funny. Now I feel more human. I feel warm blood and honest emotions. I am not a monster inside. I am a butterfly. I am about to emerge. I'm happy. I cry. My therapist cries too.

Humanistic Research

A good theory leads to research. A good personality theory, however, may lead to less research than, say, a good theory of perception. The theoretical constructs in most personality theories are a bit abstract, sometimes almost mystical—for example, an actualizing tendency—and doing research requires finding a valid test or set of behaviors to indicate the presence and the degree of the construct. For example, how do you measure the self? Rogers got lucky. About the time he got his theory going, a man named Stephenson developed a procedure called the *Q-technique*.

The Q-technique presents to the person a collection of statements about himself or herself (his/her self). Examples are "I am calm and placid most of the time" and "I am very self-conscious about sex." The person is asked to put these statements in various categories. One category is to contain those statements that are "most characteristic of me," and another category is for the "least characteristic" statements. Others range between these extremes. The person is allowed to put only a certain number of statements into each category, a restriction that allows for fairly elaborate statistical treatment. The result is a fair description of how the person perceives himself or herself (his or her self). An enormous amount of research was generated using the Q-technique.

One of the advantages of this technique is that it can be applied to several selves. For example, you can be asked first to sort the statements for your "real self" and then to sort them again for your "ideal self." The difference between these two sortings gives a kind of measure of incongruence. Rogers' theory predicts decreasing incongruence as ther-

[8]From *Psychology: A Study of a Science* (Vol. 3), p. 226.

apy progresses, and the Q-sort measures support his contention. Generally.

But research has a funny way of raising questions where there were none before. It was long assumed, for example, that if one's attitudes toward oneself became more positive and accepting, one's attitudes toward others would improve also. For most people (the "normals"), a positive self-image does seem to be correlated with positive feelings toward others. But several studies of people in therapy failed to find this relationship. Perhaps some defensive individuals, as they improve and develop more realistic perceptions, see themselves as more positive and others as less superior. It's an unanswered question. But the old unquestioned assumption of a strong relationship between self-regard and regard for others is no longer unquestioned.

Another surprising finding of one large study was that therapists' views of therapy were more optimistic than those of the clients; in fact, the more optimistic the therapist, the more pessimistic the client. It is perhaps understandable that therapists tended to be optimistic. What is hard to swallow is this fact in relation to Rogers' dictum that a *good* therapist is accurately empathic—that the therapist does not misperceive the situation. Maybe accuracy is less important than Rogers thought. Maybe unconditional positive regard is more important.

What does all this mean? The primary result of therapy is a more positive perception of oneself. How can we resolve it all?

The research on Rogers' theory utilized not only the Q-technique but also rating scales and content analysis of tape-recorded therapy sessions. The above-mentioned studies used the other techniques, mostly rating scales. The Q-technique was used in a number of studies to show that the client was becoming more congruent, as indicated by an increasingly high relationship between the real and the ideal selves. A typical study would show that before treatment the correlation between sorting for real and ideal self was zero or close to it. After maybe three dozen therapy sessions, the correlation was around .30. "Normals" show correlations of around .50 or .60, but the "neurotics" were at least moving up on this scale of congruent perceptions. But . . .

Psychotics (severely disturbed) give us correlations of about .40. Psychotics are more congruent than neurotics both before and after therapy? How can that be? What do all these numbers mean? One thing is clear: if one wishes (consciously or unconsciously) to present oneself in a favorable light, the Q-technique can't really prevent it. Some patients rate their real self more positively than they rate their ideal self, and such data make no sense at all. The Q-technique and rating scales in general require a certain degree of honesty and are subject to defensive distortions. The relatively high correlation between real and ideal self for psychotics probably reflects this fact. The neurotic is probably a little more honest.

Rogers' theory of personality obviously borrowed insights from other theorists—from Rank, for example—and the concept of self-actualization was adapted from several who used it before Rogers. The contributions of Goldstein and Angyal and Maslow did not go unnoticed. At some points in his discussion of his theory, Rogers speaks of organism and self, with self being the "symbolized" aspects of the organism—similar to Angyal. The organism tries to actualize and so does the self, and these two actualizing tendencies can sometimes work at cross purposes—another description of incongruence and conflict. Therapy, which allows distortions and defenses to be examined without threat, allows the client to talk about (the phrase we used before) or symbolize (as Angyal would say) the conflicts that underlie overt problems. Once symbolized, the problem can be dealt with more effectively.

Personality and Groups

In 1964, Carl Rogers moved to the Western Behavioral Sciences Institute in La Jolla, California, where he and the rest of the staff focused their efforts on group processes. It was a natural move for Rogers—the move to group processes, that is. (La Jolla's not a bad decision either, actually.) All his life he had studied the nature of a two-person group process, one we call therapy, and his insights had been primarily concerned with what makes for a good, productive, improving relationship. Surely these insights could be applied to "ordinary" relationships as well. To be congruent, to have empathy, to communicate unconditional positive regard—what would happen if you did this with just anyone?

Remember the term *encounter group?* (We used it, and skipped over it, earlier in the chapter.) It is a group of people who have gotten together for the purpose of "truly encountering" each other. To meet another person without facades or defenses. To tell it like it is. To interact on a truly human level. To be congruent, to have empathy, to communicate unconditional positive regard. The members of such groups are typically normal, or reasonably so, with no great problems. Their goal is not so much to relieve symptoms as it is to grow, to become healthier, to self-actualize, to achieve joy. . . to become truly human.

Encounter groups have a rather strange history. One antecedent was the group therapy that became common around 1945. Group therapy (one psychologist or psychiatrist and several patients) was necessitated by the large numbers of traumatized soldiers returning home after World War II; there simply were not enough professionals to treat all these GIs. But what was born of necessity was nurtured as advantage, for group therapy turned out to be superior in some respects to individual therapy. The sharing of trauma lessened the pain, for example, as guilt-ridden soldiers found that they were not alone in feeling relief when they survived battles that took the lives of their best friends. More generally, it was discovered that groups offered an opportunity to practice interpersonal relations, those interactions the patients could not handle but would have to face sooner or later. If a particular behavior was going to be viewed as weird, or insulting, or cowardly, or childish, it was better to find out now, before returning to the "real" world. Now, while at least one skilled professional could point it out and suggest remedies. Even the comments of other patients were useful. They were neither as benevolent nor as duty-bound as the psychologist, and perhaps, therefore, they reflected more closely the possible reactions of society in general. And the clinician, too, saw advantages: by observing directly the interpersonal interactions of the patients in the group, he or she was in a better position to interpret the problems of each patient. In individual therapy, many of these interpersonal tendencies would not have been so apparent.

The sharing of specific problems in a group setting is the basis for collective therapy exemplified today by such groups as Alcoholics Anonymous. The interpersonal aspect of group interactions remains an important feature of group therapies with neurotics and psychotics. Encounter groups, though the participants are "normal," also utilize sharing and interpersonal interactions but for the purpose of growth toward self-actualization.

Group therapy developed along another line in the context of big business. As business came more and more to mean corporate enterprise, decisions were made more and more by groups (called committees) and less and less by the elders of a family holding. Psychologists were called upon to help make these group decision processes more efficient; that is, they were asked how best to solve problems in groups. The psychologists set up training camps, where executives were brought in from all parts of the country to form groups with arbitrarily designated problems to solve. The psychologists expected that they would have to teach the principles of effective problem solving and the groups would learn and grow. These "training" groups (T-groups for short) soon dashed the hopes of the most cynical theorist. The members learned quite a bit, but they did not always apply what they had learned.

Imagine a typical committee with an industrial problem to solve. Joe is the boss. Joe is a creep. He offends me. I could help him solve the company's problem, but I won't because I don't like him. To make this group effective, someone would have to convince Joe to stop calling me "boy." Joe, of course, is unaware that his words offend me; he even calls his wife "boy."

So T-groups evolved, naturally enough, into what were called sensitivity-training groups, or sensitivity groups for short. The idea was to bring out into the open all the offenses, real, imagined, or both, that each member perpetrated or received. In Rogerian terms, each participant was taught to be empathic and congruent. At this point, sensitivity groups were quite close to encounter groups in goals and aspirations.

With one leg in the morass of World War II and the other in the growing monopolies of big business, encounter groups can be said to be a product of the military/industrial complex. Nevertheless, at best they had silver linings, with sharing, interpersonal encounters, and increased awareness in the individual of his or her effects on others. There can be real growth, self-actualization, in such groups. And, even without growth, they afford their participants a certain kind of intimate human contact that seems to be rare in America today. But—we must add the caveat—encounter groups can be dangerous, especially those "led" by someone without the ability to spot imminent disaster. Some people, stripped of defenses or unexpectedly forced into situations beyond their capacities, will fall apart, and it's possible that nobody will be able to put the pieces together again. The powerful effect for good can become a powerful effect for not-good.

Chapter Summary

Some humanistic psychologists like to think of themselves as being involved in a revolution, a movement, a "third force" beyond psychoanalysis and behaviorism. Though Jung, Adler, and Rank should be classified as early humanistic personologists, there is no doubt that there is today a growing humanistic movement. Much of it is trendy—astrology, nudism, sexual "freedom," and other fads are becoming more and more popular. Humanistic trends in psychology both reflect and encourage similar trends in society. Many scientists observing the movement are dismayed by the anti-intellectual, antiresearch attitudes displayed by some humanists. Fads come and go, in science as elsewhere, but many psychologists distrust charlatans who offer therapy in orgy form, and they fear for the psychological well-being of people who get caught up in the movement. Those within the movement, of course, fear for the well-being of those without. At times the whole scene resembles a three-ring circus, complete with bright lights and dancing bears and parading elephants, Abraham Maslow on the trapeze, Carl Rogers, Master of Ceremonies.

Most impartial observers admit to being alternately excited and infuriated by these new developments. They see the better aspects of the movement as "attention calling," pointing to significant characteristics of human existence that have not been well handled by science. They hope that science can eventually incorporate many of these more abstract humanistic concepts, and they also hope that some of what they perceive as pseudo-humanistic excesses will be discarded. The anti-intellectual, antiresearch aspects can be seen in Angyal's terms. The lack of symbols for these significant characteristics of human existence at once (1) makes the intellect suspect; (2) makes research that uses operational definitions trivial; and (3) makes humanistic treatises read like poetry, lacking direct symbols, full of allusion and emotion.

The serious theorists presented in this chapter have done much to articulate (create symbols for) the concerns of the humanists, as have theorists such as Jung and Allport, humanists also. The organismic premise, for example, has received the attention of, most notably, Goldstein and Allport (see the discussion of the proprium in Chapter 6). They have shown rather conclusively that the whole person is more than the sum of his or her parts. More specifically, Goldstein showed that the behavior of brain-injured patients could not be explained in terms of their injury alone; in secondary symptoms we find evidence of defense needs, compensation needs, and positive-growth needs. The positive-growth needs led to the further articulation of the self-actualization concept. Rogers used that concept as the basis of both his theory of personality and his therapy.

Both Rogers and Maslow have added richness to the self-actualization concept. Rogers delineated the role of congruence, empathy, and unconditional positive regard. These features of the self-actualizer are strikingly similar to those depicted by Maslow. Maslow also described the B-values, the goals of the self-actualizer. So we now have a good picture of the source of the self-actualizing drive—the organization of personality—and a fair picture of the resulting behaviors. Angyal's trend toward autonomy is thoroughly compatible, as a "neutral" view of the process in terms of biospheric directions.

Rogers and Maslow have also begun the necessary explorations of the conditions conducive to growth and self-actualization. Rogers has pointed out that the attributes of the self-actualizer—empathy, congruence, and unconditional positive regard—are also conditions facilitating the release of instinctive actualizing tendencies. Maslow has stressed motivations in his hierarchy of needs. Self-actualizing behaviors will be exhibited when the lower needs are gratified. One can easily see how the therapeutic setting described by Rogers would satisfy many lower needs—esteem and safety, for example—and thus release the less potent, higher-order self-actualizing tendencies in his clients.

Not many personologists, not even our chapter's heroes, think of these beginnings as anything but a start. Much more research on these topics has to be done before the positive and the human aspects of personality can take their place next to the more thoroughly studied negative and animalistic features. The antiresearch attitudes of many humanistic psychologists certainly are an impediment in this regard; but the theorists of this chapter, especially Rogers, are pro-humanism *and* pro-research. These men are against sterile research, to be sure, but they certainly do not consider science and the intellect unimportant to a humanistic psychology. (Those theorists who do might consider the source of their attitudes in Angyal's terms.)

Suggested Readings

The reader interested in humanistic-personality theories can find many books on the topic, lots of them atrocious. There is probably more nonsense written about this area than about any other area in psychology, and there are only a few good, secondary, summary sources. (The bad books are rarely dull, however, and many are fascinating; they can be read for entertainment.)

Perhaps the most readable of the dependable writings is A. H. Maslow's *Motivation and Personality.* It is available in paperback, and the second edition is the one to get. Maslow's *Toward a Psychology of Being* (2nd ed.) is also adequate. If you are interested in Maslow's theory, however, you must read *Motivation and Personality* first, for his other works do not hang together well without that background.

Angyal's *Foundations for a Science of Personality* is high level, sincere, and exciting, if you enjoy observing a fine mind at work. A fair introduction to Goldstein's thought is his *Human Nature in the Light of Psychopathology.*

Carl Rogers' best theoretical statement is contained in *Psychology: A Study of a Science,* Volume 3, edited by S. Koch. A readable survey of his humanistic trends can be found in his *On Becoming a Person.*

Gordon Allport's short book *Becoming* is also highly recommended.

Notes and References

The following books are the primary references used for the theorists discussed in this chapter. We've marked the single most useful work for each theorist with an asterisk.

For Goldstein:

The organism. American Book Company, 1939.*

Human nature in the light of psychopathology. Harvard University Press, 1940.

After-effects of brain injuries in war. Grune and Stratton, 1942.

For Maslow:

Motivation and personality (2nd ed.). Harper & Row, 1970.*

Toward a psychology of being (2nd ed.). Van Nostrand, 1968.

The farther reaches of human nature. Viking, 1971.

A theory of metamotivation: The biological rooting of the value-life. *Journal of Humanistic Psychology,* 1967, *7,* 93–127.

For Angyal:

Foundations for a science of personality. Commonwealth Fund, 1941.*

A theoretical model for personality studies. *Journal of Personality,* 1951, *20,* 131–142.

For Rogers:

Counseling and psychotherapy. Houghton Mifflin, 1942.

Some observations on the organization of personality. *American Psychologist,* 1947, *2,* 358–368.

Client-centered therapy. Houghton Mifflin, 1951.

A theory of therapy, personality, and interpersonal relationships. In S. Koch (Ed.), *Psychology: A study of a science* (Vol. 3). McGraw-Hill, 1959.*

On becoming a person. Houghton Mifflin, 1961.

The therapeutic relationship and its impact. University of Wisconsin Press, 1967. (This work is edited by Rogers.)

Autobiography. In E. G. Boring and G. Lindzey (Eds.), *A history of psychology in autobiography* (Vol. 5). Appleton-Century-Crofts, 1967. (Goldstein's autobiography is also included in this volume.)

Psychotherapy and personality change. University of Chicago Press, 1954. (This work is edited by Rogers and R. F. Dymond.)

9

The Ego Ascendant

The ego had to wait his turn. When the community discovered he did not live alone, that he lived with the id and the superego, they were naturally interested in these, especially the id. The ego's reputation was not too good, but he was bound to recover, sooner or later.

Charles Pauling

By 1940, Freud was dead and a second World War had begun. Most of the best psychoanalysts were in Allied countries, driven from their homelands by the Nazis; many settled in the United States. English became, in large part, the language of psychoanalytic discussion, and that discussion now centered on the roles of the three main characters in the drama of the human psyche—id, ego, and superego. The ego was soon to take its rightful place center stage.

We are speaking metaphorically, of course, when we refer to id, ego, and superego as separate entities. There are no three distinct, quarreling creatures living inside us, no three characters jostling for supremacy. Rather, there are classes of psychological functions—impulses and primary processes, reality testing and logical action, and guilt and internalized moral standards. But the metaphors, the images, convey the sense of drama and conflict. Let's play along in order to capture this sense, to get a feel for the human condition.

For a long time personologists had been unable (or unwilling) to recognize the id. The id is an ugly, alien creature, and, though it lives in our psychic house, we prefer to ignore its presence and its influence. It inhabits the dungeon of our soul, and we do not care to open those doors. But Freud said that the id lives. It may be criminal, but it is not weak. It has inherited the family fortune, and other members of the family must come to it for their allowance. Though it can be outwitted or beaten back, it is nothing if not persistent. It may even burn down the house if given the chance.

The superego is a respectable member of the family. It counsels the ego in ways of righteousness. It warns that the ego will become ugly and alien, too, if it does not face up to morality. The fire and brimstone that fill the cellars of the psyche will be the eternal lot of those who follow the ways of the id.

Ego stands in the crossfire. Id says "We want," and Superego says "We must." Neither is realistic. If I do what Id suggests, thinks Ego, I will be hung. If I do what Superego suggests, I will be hungry. I can't decide; I am hung up.

In Freud's descriptions, the ego was often portrayed as weak and desperate, incapable of dealing with the surging, traumatic conflicts in the psychic house. It often had to resort to infantile ploys, like paralyzing the legs to thwart the id or compulsively repeating some trivial atonement to satisfy the superego. If this household sounds neurotic, it should; it describes the conflict going on in the patients from whom Freud took his theory. To define neurosis as a relatively strong id and/or superego and a weak ego—well, there are worse definitions.

As Freud turned his gaze from the abnormal to the normal—when he began seeing psychoanalysis as a general theory of personality—it was natural that his focus should shift to a consideration of the characteristics of a strong ego. His later works were the beginnings of an ego psychology. The ego was ascending.

Ego and the Dissenters

Adler, Jung, and Rank. Sounds like a law firm. Attorneys for the plaintiff, Ego. Adler argued that the plaintiff was being harassed, that its strivings for superiority were being discredited. It was not Id, he said, that wanted the mother; it was Ego, for the mother conveys status in the home. Rank saw the "will" of Ego as the dominant motive in life. Jung claimed not only that Ego was dominant but also that it used Id (or its equivalent, the unconscious) for its own purposes. A strong ego, said Jung, turned the id into a kind of librarian/clerk, spending its time shuffling through the wisdom of the age . . . or ages, if need be.

Chief Justice at the time was Sigmund Freud, and he ruled in favor of the defendant, Id. Adler, Jung, and Rank were disbarred for slandering Id, for giving it less credit than was due; after all, its existence was a great discovery. But the Chief Justice Freud did not rule *against* the importance of Ego.

Freud was old. He was dying of cancer, and he needed help firming up his ego theory. He got help from his daughter and nurse, Anna.

Anna Freud and Child Analysis

If your mother or father is famous, life is both a little easier and a little more difficult. If your father is dying of cancer and needs care and attention, life is hard. The child of Sigmund Freud might have become a bum, a philosopher, an author, or a business executive. But his daughter Anna became a psychoanalyst. No one then expected a woman to compete. A woman cared for children. So, in an interesting combination of the innovative and the traditional, Anna became a pioneer in the psychoanalysis of children.

There were a surprising number of female analysts, almost from the beginning. Among the most famous were Princess Marie Bonaparte, a French analyst who was a member of both Greek and Danish royalty; Melanie Klein, a British analyst whose fertile mind produced ideas that often placed her in opposition to the Freuds; and of course Anna Freud. Many of the female analysts took their "proper" role as child analysts. In this case, though the sexism of the era can't be denied, the outcome was benevolent, both for the children who were saved and for the theory of psychoanalysis in general. The ego is never so clear as when it is growing up.

Child analysis was for many years considered impossible; the focus instead was on education of the children. Though Freud's theory was based on the outcome of psychosexual conflicts in early childhood, free association—the prime psychoanalytic technique—was not much use with children. However, one could be aware of the conflicts the child was going through and help the child fight and win. The great world wars provided an opportunity for expansion, for more learning, by leaving a sizable population of children with no parents and no homes. Camp schools, largely supported by American relief funds, were set up for these children, and some were staffed by educators familiar with and sympathetic to psychoanalytic theory.

Education enlightened by knowledge of personality development soon became "guidance," and soon after that trained analysts were helping children solve their problems. Child analysis was now a fact.

The Ego Growing Up

Psychoanalysis of children must proceed in a somewhat different manner than the analysis of adults. Adults can use conscious memories as prime data, but children have few memories of value. The analysis of adults uses free association to uncover the meaning of various ideas and memories, but children do not free associate well; this is perhaps a verbal ability that develops with age.

On the other hand, children, like adults, do dream, and their dreams can be interpreted. In addition, the dreams of children tend to be more direct and less distorted and devious, with the manifest content reflecting more closely the true intent (the wish fulfillment). And children like to analyze dreams; they have not yet learned to think of their dreams as bizarre and unreal fantasies. Like their analysts, they consider dreams to be important and meaningful. Children also daydream more, and their daydreams can be interpreted.

The transference of feelings of love and/or hate for other significant people, usually parents, to the analyst occurs in both adults and children. But there was and is much debate over the meaning and usefulness of transference. Anna Freud believed that children, unlike adults, did not give up their neurotic loves and hates for others and replace them with neurotic loves and hates for the analyst. Other theorists, however, claimed that unusual attitudes—based on previous relationships—did occur and could be interpreted. Anna Freud agreed but added the warning that one cannot do much with a negative (hostile) transference with a child. It's not useful or workable, as it may be with an adult. A hostile child will simply refuse analysis. Only positive attachments produce progress.

So child analysis both resembles and differs from adult analysis. Perhaps the main difference is that, whereas the adult must call up the memory of conflicts, the child is in the midst of them. The ego is growing up before your eyes.

Anna's Analysis of Defenses

Anna Freud's chief contribution to psychoanalytic theory was a more precise description of defense mechanisms, those processes by which the ego fights its battles against the insurgent id and the developing superego. Her vivid description parallels ours:

> Peaceful relations between the neighboring powers are at an end. . . . [The id makes] hostile incursions into the ego, in the hope of overthrowing it by a surprise attack. The ego on its side becomes suspicious; it proceeds to counter-attack and to invade the territory of the id. Its purpose is to put the instincts out of action by means of appropriate defensive measures, designed to secure its own boundaries.[1]

The task of psychoanalysis with children and adults is to provide insight into unconscious conflicts and the underlying, unconscious mechanisms. Analysis of the id is easier with adults, with their fine associative abilities; in children, one has to interpret distorted behaviors that somehow represent a hostile id impulse battered and jacketed by a defensive ego. These behaviors reflect the unconscious impulse, the ego's unconscious defensive operations, and the conflict between id and ego. Through analysis of the child's defenses, the behaviors may begin to be understood. Analysis of defenses developed primarily in the context of child psychoanalysis, and the ego became a focus of study. Defenses are the weapons of the ego.

The Ego's Arsenal

The superego is righteous; it draws power from its faith in a moral order and is supported by the community. The id is strong; it controls the energy of the system, the furnaces in the cellar that drive all the machinery up above. Pity the poor ego; what can it do to protect itself against a moral crusade on one side and a libertine revolt on the other? It has no power except what it can steal from the id. The ego can argue "Look, guys, if we don't do what I say, we'll die." But the id and the superego seldom care. The id says *now* and the superego says *never.*

The ego is cunning, though, and therein lies its real power. The id is an idiot, and the superego can't think beyond its oughts and ought-nots. The ego uses a kind of intellectual judo, using the id's own strength to defeat it, and has even been known to pit the id against the superego. While they're fighting, the ego can get on with business. A strong ego wins by outsmarting its opponents.

The mechanisms of defense are really nothing more than a bag of intellectual tricks commonly used by the ego. One of the most common ego tricks is "the gambit of the professional spy." A professional spy is

[1]From A. Freud's *The Ego and the Mechanisms of Defence,* International Universities Press, 1946, 7–8.

trained to be prepared if caught doing something untoward—with one hand in the cookie jar, so to speak. Unlike most of us, who would invent elaborate explanations for the presence of our hand in the jar ("I was just scratching the back of my knuckle"), the spy might simply deny that there was a hand in the jar. The eyewitness says "But I saw you." The spy replies, calmly, "Sir, you are mistaken." A preposterous lie is sometimes more effective than a mere distortion, and the more preposterous the better: "There is no cookie jar. And anyway I was in Rome at the time in question." Planned carefully, a preposterous lie will leave eyewitnesses doubting their own senses.

Repression and Denial

The ego uses the preposterous lie frequently. In *repression,* unacceptable or painful ideas and impulses are actively excluded from consciousness. "I do not have sexual feelings toward my mother, and I never did." So preposterous is this lie that it was believed for centuries, until Sigmund Freud managed to trap the ego living in his own body and make it confess. Even then, kindred egos in other people fought acceptance of Freud's ideas about himself as actively as they fought acceptance of the idea in their own psyche. Egos are very clannish in matters of general importance.

Denial is a similar ploy, although it is more specific and does not usually gain the support of other egos. A traumatic event occurs, such as the loss through death or desertion of a loved one. "My mother is not dead." Egos with live mothers see this tactic as dangerous—it might blow their cover—so they work actively to soothe the distraught one, while setting it straight, claiming that *they* are committed to truth. A rather ridiculous claim, don't you think? But the ego is cunning.

Projection and Introjection

Once the ego has discovered that there are two worlds, "me" in here and "others" out there, it uses this division in an attempt to claim all good qualities as "mine" (*introjection*) and to disclaim all bad qualities as "not mine; in fact, yours" (*projection*). Introjection is a rather benevolent defense mechanism and can form the basis for normal personality development. "I am the equal of my parents," says the child; the child is wrong but heading in the right direction. Projection is a kind of verbal game played by reversing the subject and object of a sentence: "I hate you" becomes "You hate me." The superego rather likes these games (in fact, many believe that the superego is born introjecting the moral standards of parents), so the ego enlists a powerful ally in its fight against the monstrous id.

Introjection and projection are somehow related to love. Certainly "eliminating" bad qualities and "introducing" goodness makes one more lovable, and all people love at least themselves. (Oh? Always? Everyone? Oh, all right, maybe that was a rash statement. But don't derail this train just yet; *most* people love themselves.) Love of another person often takes a similar form; we say "love is blind" because we typically ignore the bad in our lover and exaggerate the good. Some psychologists have been known to *define* love in these terms, which is akin to saying that two egos conspire in their projections and introjections, support each other, and become lovable, at least until the honeymoon is over and reality sets in.

Reaction Formation

Reaction formation is an ego tactic that treats an id demand as its opposite. Hate becomes love and love becomes hate. It is another preposterous lie. The id, determined to murder the woman who has been so unkind (its mother), looks out the window of the unconscious and sees the ego-controlled body acting with great solicitousness and obvious (overly obvious) affection toward the mother. The ego speaks and tells the world it loves its mother very, very much. The world is pleased, and superego gives the ego a gold star, and the id retires in disgust to plan a new attack. But this strains its miniscule brain, and it goes to sleep.

Isolation and Intellectualization

Isolation and *intellectualization* are among the most sophisticated weapons in the ego's arsenal (and the most commonly used by college students and educated adults). It's really a sly trick, to split the idea and the emotion. "I am a scientist; I am expected to be dispassionate." So I can say "Yes, yes, I did once want to possess my mother sexually. Freud's theory makes sense." And, as I speak, I feel nothing, no emotion whatsoever, except perhaps a strange sense of abstraction, coolness, the unusual feeling of no emotion. The stupid id thinks it has gained a victory; its idea has reached consciousness. But it's a sterile idea, devoid of force, and the id puzzles over the fact that no action follows the idea. The superego is wary. The idea should not have been allowed public expression, but the superego is mollified by the lack of action. The ego is in absolute triumph. It has beaten both id and superego, satisfying both and satisfying neither.

Sublimation

The sublime defense mechanism, appropriately called *sublimation*, involves a careful channeling of id desires into socially approved activities that will earn the approval of the superego. A magnificent obsession, so to speak, and another outstanding ploy by the ego. It is so cunning. The angry id wants to cut somebody, so the ego becomes a doctor, a surgeon. The ego cuts and the superego is pleased. The id is a little bewildered, as usual, because this cutting is not as much fun as it had imagined. The superego is too happy about it.

If the id wants to rape, perhaps the ego will become a literary critic. If the id wants to smear feces, a great painter may be born. And so on. The ego is toying with the id; the ego is in control.

Are all doctors murderers, all critics rapists, all artists anal? The ego is much too cunning for that. One can rape in a variety of ways, and benevolent rapists can be found in every profession. One can choose a vocation, a "calling," for an infinite variety of reasons. And it will not do either to think of all human activities as born of perversions, unless you want to consider all human love and striving as a perversion. The ego can be rather a nice creature, if given half a chance. Its family—the id and the superego—can force it into evil at times, but the ego is content to live and let live. Peace and maximum joy are its goals.

Puberty: The Adolescent Ego

We have been looking at the functioning of a relatively strong ego. If the id or superego is stronger or the ego is weaker, for genetic or environmental reasons, the picture is quite different. Then we have the neurotic picture, a weak ego driven first one way and then another, doing stupid things demanded by the id, and being robbed of pleasure by the superego. An ego with no time to plan, no chance to be cunning; a desperate ego, employing desperate defenses that it cannot give up if they prove even minimally effective. The neurotic ego is an addict. It knows that its palliatives lead nowhere, but it cannot give them up. It lives in fear. It fights, but it lacks cunning. Its fight is that of a cornered animal.

All of us experience neurotic episodes when the forces of id, superego, and the external world conspire to attack all at once. Even the strongest of egos must struggle at times, and it is a sorry sight. A moral dilemma, a traumatic event: we have to "come to grips." One of the universal periods of extreme danger is puberty, at which time the id suddenly finds ten new furnaces at its disposal along with a new supply of fuel. It stokes them mightily, trying to overcome the pointy-head liberalism of the ego. It is as if an old enemy were suddenly given a new weapon. Like a nation that has just secured its boundaries when suddenly the tribes to the North obtain guns from the traders and the tribes to the South get horses. The nation in the middle must adapt, somehow, or it will surely die. And so must the ego adapt during puberty.

Puberty is a period marking the beginning of sexual maturity, which is nice, but all kinds of events occur—traumas, really—for which the developing ego is ill-prepared. Sexual desires come flooding in from the furnaces of the id; in males, hair grows on the face and genitals, and the voice starts cracking, seeking its lower register; in females, breasts develop, and menstruation makes its appearance, sometimes rather startlingly. If this weren't enough, everyone watches with horror or amusement as pimples grow on the most public of body parts, the face. Adults make unfunny remarks, which they seem to think are hilarious. The ego faces its greatest test.

In what Anna Freud has called "the storms of instinct and affect,"[2] the ego must fight desperately. The adolescent ego, if it is strong, is fairly cunning, but, in the face of an all-out id attack, it must act too quickly. It intellectualizes to an extreme—this is the period of paramount idealism—trying to break that damned link between idea and affect. "What is the meaning of life? Quickly! Quickly!" With no time to plan wisely, it tries to divert the surging instincts into a cause. Any cause will do. It denies as best it can; it enlists the aid of the superego; it becomes a moralist. Sex is dirty, adults are hypocrites, and one must be pure, in thought and deed. The ego will not hear of compromise.

At times, we can witness the ego in a full retreat, known in psychoanalysis as regression. Unable to hold its position at a higher level of maturity, the ego retreats to earlier positions, to establish a new line of defense. It becomes more infantile in the process. It hopes that this line of defense will hold.

Such a regression marks the id's finest hour. It advances and the ego retreats. The id breaks through the ego's defense line and overruns the territory. Anybody watching the whole person sees strange and contradictory behaviors: outright selfishness one day, moralizing the next. They are witnessing a great battle. Who will win? Will the ego take sides with the id and become a psychopath? Or will the ego ally with the superego and live life as an inhibited, guilty moralist? Or commit suicide? (Suicide is the *ultimate* defense mechanism!) Or will the ego, in its cunning, manage somehow to play off the id against the superego? Will it play spy and counterspy successively? Will it survive as an independent force? This is a human drama unlike any other, and the outcome is watched nervously by parents, who make jokes only because this battle, which they too have experienced, is much too serious to take seriously.

Ego and Adaptation

The ego, if it survives long enough to become an adult, has many scars, and late at night it may limp ever so slightly. Veteran of many battles, victorious in most but at tremendous cost, it faces more battles ahead. Ultimately, of course, it will lose the war, for it will die when its fleshy envelope disintegrates. Is it all worth it?

Heinz Hartmann said it this way: Animals whose behavior is primarily instinctive cannot adapt to new or changing environments. They are, in a sense, pure id creatures, with only a modicum of ego. The human, who has an ego that must dominate the id in order to survive, is therefore much more flexible and adaptable. And therein lies the fruit of victory: *freedom.*

In other words, the ego is intelligent and capable of learning. The human baby is born without all the behavior patterns necessary for

[2]From *The Ego and the Mechanisms of Defence,* International Universities Press, 1946, 173.

survival and must therefore spend several years dependent on the support and protection of adults. Perceptual, motor, and intellectual abilities develop slowly, and, by the time the ego graduates into more or less full capability, its skills are a unique, polished amalgam of innate capacities and experiential learning. That the ego is threatened by the id is really just another way of saying that, as humans, we must learn to direct and control our instinctive drives (there are few innate controls over those drives), and this fact promotes flexibility in adapting to the environment. The id, for all its storm and bombast, is the rigid one; the ego provides flexibility and adaptation.

Structuralized Delay

One of the most significant of human abilities—specifically of ego abilities, specifically related to intelligence—is the capacity to *delay gratification.* An adult who is unable to delay gratification of his or her desires or needs is generally ineffective and constantly in trouble with the law, the community, or both. David Rapaport, one of the most systematic and scholarly of post-Freudian Freudians, is generally credited with the development of this concept after Freud. He proposed that, with the growth of the ego, a drive no longer has to result in direct action. Instead, in a process called *structuralized delay,* drives may result in planful action and in experimental action through thought. An appropriate and socially acceptable object is anticipated and located. Plans are made that are intended to put the organism into a situation in which it can safely obtain the object. In other words, typical mature, adult behavior.

The Ego in Control

The ego is centrally involved in the entire process. It is the ego that designs and executes the various control mechanisms, including defense mechanisms, that result in delay; the term *structuralized* delay is meant to imply that id impulses are efficiently handled by a strong ego, that there are more or less automatic institutions (structures) for keeping the id in its place. The id phones the control room with a demand, and its call is automatically put on "hold." The ego does the thinking and the planning. If the drive itself is unacceptable or if the object that would satisfy the drive is unavailable, the ego may decide to change some aspect of the drive. It says to the id "Sorry. Smearing feces is not an acceptable activity right now. How about a nice messy daydream instead?" The id grumbles, but not too loudly. The daydream is wild, wild. The ego lets the id plan it and pretend it will really happen tomorrow.

Erik Erikson

In 1927, Babe Herman Ruth hit 60 home runs, breaking his old record, and the Yankees won the pennant. Charles Augustus Lindbergh flew by himself to Paris and became an international hero at the ripe old age of 25. And, that same year, Erik Homburger Erikson, also 25, took a train from Karlsruhe, Germany, to Vienna, Austria, nearing the end of his youthful wanderings. He did not become a hero until much later.

Erikson was a hippie in his youth, even though hippies were not yet invented. He might have been called a bum were it not for the rise of Fascism in Germany and Italy; he was lost in the sea of traveling youths, members of Fascist organizations that encouraged independence and adventures, although he himself was no Fascist. He was a bum. Or an artist, if you prefer. He went on long walks, for a couple of months at a time. He traveled to Florence, on an artist's pilgrimage. He wandered to Munich, where he had an exhibition of his woodcuts. After high school, he had stuck out a year of art school before dropping out. Now he was an artist/wanderer.

Erikson Meets Freud

In 1927, all this changed. Peter Blos, a high school classmate of Erikson's and a fellow hippie, had been a writer and a bum. While bumming in Vienna, he was engaged as a private tutor for the children of an upper-class lady from New York (a Tiffany, no less) who had come to Vienna to see the mysterious Dr. Sigmund Freud. Two years of this work was fine, but then Blos was ready to wander again. He was so highly regarded, however, that, in an effort to retain him, his employer offered him his own school, with a real building, 20 kids, and a free hand. Blos could not refuse this chance to give public expression to his young ideals; he accepted the offer. Now he had to create a faculty for the new school. One more free spirit, at least, was required, and his thoughts returned to his old friend Erik Erikson. Blos could teach science and German; Erik could teach art and history. Erik was summoned, and he came. And, in due time, Erik met Sigmund and Anna Freud.

Anna Freud by this time was well into child psychoanalysis. Anna Freud was the mother of child psychoanalysis. She was the first; Erik Erikson was about to become one of the seconds.

Erikson's first decision was to be psychoanalyzed, by Anna Freud. His second was to study the theory of psychoanalysis. By 1933, the year Hitler came to power, Erikson was "graduated" as a fully accredited psychoanalyst in his own right. (The only formal degree he would ever obtain was his high school diploma.) The economic depression, the rise of Hitler, and marriage to a Canadian-American all conspired to convince him that he should travel again—to the United States. He was the first child analyst in Boston, Massachusetts.

Now sit back and imagine, if you can, the situation. Here is a 31-year-old hippie with no formal degrees beyond high school. He has no credentials or formal qualifications. Nevertheless, he is *given* a position on the faculty of the Harvard Medical School. Have times changed so quickly? He is given a staff position in the most prestigious of Boston hospitals. He opens his own office. He is Boston's only child analyst.

Erikson met Henry Murray (see Chapter 6) and became associated with the Harvard Psychological Clinic; that at least makes sense, for Murray was a little freaky himself, and cared little about formal credentials. He knew a good mind when he saw it. Erikson enrolled as a Ph.D. candidate at Harvard (even though he had no bachelor's degree), but, after a couple of months, he dropped out. Offered a plush position at the Yale Institute of Human Relations, he took it. Two years later he was on the Pine Ridge Reservation in South Dakota studying how Sioux children were raised.

An itinerant scholar. A psychologist-at-large. Getting Erik Erikson to stay in one place was like stopping a hummingbird. After working on the Sioux reservation, he went to the west coast—to San Francisco, where he practiced child analysis, and Berkeley, where he hooked up with the Institute of Child Welfare, now the Institute of Human Development. He stayed in the vicinity for about ten years.

In 1950, two of the most important books in the history of personology were published. One was *Personality and Psychotherapy,* by John Dollard and Neal Miller, an "integration" of psychoanalysis and learning theory (see Chapter 10). The other was *Childhood and Society,* by Erik Erikson. It was his major work. The book could have been titled "Ego Grows Up."

The Psychosocial Stages

Sigmund Freud had described the psychosexual stages, which were really descriptions of accommodations between the id and the ego as the id turned its desires from the mouth (the oral stage) to the anus (the anal stage) and then to the penis (the phallic stage). The ego, however, must make accommodations with reality as well—with the surrounding culture—and thus the new emphasis on the ego meant that someone had to describe the psycho*social* stages. Erikson did it. (As an aside, the ego must also resolve conflicts with the Superego, and we await publication of some theorist's brilliant description of the "psychospiritual" stages—or is that what humanistic psychology is all about?)

Erikson called his psychosocial stages "ages," and there were eight in all. The Eriksonian ages were somewhat correlated with Freud's psychosexual stages, especially in the early years of life. Let's take a look at them from the point of view of the ego.

Receiving and Accepting. As Heinz Hartmann had pointed out, at the beginning of life there is a lump, a mass of potentials and instincts. Out of it all develop both the id and the ego. Some of the perceptual, motor, and intellectual abilities that exist in relatively undeveloped form at birth are to be the ego's for life, so it is not fair to say that only the id is present at the moment of birth. The ego opens its eyes and sees only a breast. Its life consists of sucking. Freud called this the oral stage. Erikson also called it the oral stage but viewed it as a psychosocial age, a time of receiving and accepting. A basic approach to the environment is learned. The ego learns the basic meaning of the verb "to get."

We are speaking of the very first year of life, so when we say "basic," we mean "primitive-basic." Something akin to saying that a kid selling lemonade on a hot day is learning "big business." Very primitive. But the ego learns, in this very basic sense, that sometimes it gets and sometimes it doesn't get. It is completely dependent and doesn't even have many muscles to control; its only possible crusade is a massive, undirected movement called an infantile temper tantrum. If it gets—most of the time—it decides that the world is *basically* trustworthy. If it is frequently deprived in times of need, it decides that the world is basically untrustworthy.

Taking. As teeth develop and biting becomes an ego skill, it learns a more active modality—to take. Teething can be a rather painful process, not only for the infant but also for the mother. And the ego learns that "to take" does not always mean "to get"; it tries to explain this to the id, but such distinctions are beyond the id's intellectual capacity. The ego is still weak (whereas the id is strong) and dependent. The ego must trust its mother. Thus, the first and most basic learning task of the ego, according to Erikson, is to gain some primitive sense of trust *and* mistrust. Some have misinterpreted Erikson's remarks to mean that the ego becomes *either* trusting *or* untrusting at this stage, but that is wrong. The ego must learn both, for a completely trusting ego will not fare well in this world. A readiness for danger and an anticipation of discomfort are necessary for survival.

A favorable prognosis for the ego can be made if it survives this period with a ratio of trust and mistrust in favor of trust. Such a ratio is the basis for *hope.*

Holding and Letting Go. In the second and third years of life, the ego gains control over the anal sphincters, and it finds its parents quite interested in that ability. They want the ego to ignore the childish demands of the id, to retain feces and urine when the id wants to expel them, and to expel them only at the proper time and place. The ego learns what "holding on" and "letting go" mean, although it does not always act on what it has learned. It has not yet learned to regard the id as ugly and as an enemy, and it is not yet sure that its mother is a more desirable ally. It learns the meaning of *autonomy*—to be distinct from id *and* parents—and of *shame and doubt.* Acting on its own (the beginnings of autonomy) exposes the ego to shame and doubts about its individuality. With a favorable ratio of trust to mistrust, however, reinforced in this stage by encouragement of its autonomous strivings with a minimum of ridicule, the ego comes through with a second favorable ratio: autonomy outweighs shame and doubt. Again, however, it must also sense the importance of shame and doubt. An ego with no doubts about the correctness of its actions . . . well, we all know some adult egos like that. A favorable ratio of autonomy to shame and doubt provides the basis for *will power.*

Making. At the end of the third year or thereabouts, the genital area becomes the most important body zone in psychosexual development; Freud called this the phallic stage. The ego is more muscular now.

It can get around and "into things" by walking and running. It can make things happen; it learns the meaning of "to make" and "to be on the make." There is a difference at this age between the learning tasks of the male ego and those of the female ego, a difference that some (like Freud) relate to the differences in genital structures but that is *at least* also related to differences in the way most cultures treat males and females. The male ego is expected to be more intrusive, more active, more on the make. The female ego, on the other hand, is supposed to make things happen in a more subtle fashion; according to Erikson, it is expected to learn the meaning of "to snare."

The "favorable ratio" at this age is that of *initiative* to *guilt*, and it is the basis of *purpose*. The ego has learned to be mostly trusting, and it is fairly autonomous. Now it has to learn to initiate actions leading to a goal. Still young and relatively incompetent, however, the ego often initiates actions that are not acceptable to society, and it must learn to feel guilty for these. The superego, who may have been first introduced by shame and doubt, now moves into the psychic house for good, and the ego must learn to deal with this new power. The superego is there on instructions from the parents and society to keep the ego's initiative "within bounds."

Acting. Next, the ego enters the latency stage, a period of relative peace and quiet before the instinct storms of puberty. It is expected to get its house in order—that is, to organize its relations with the id and superego so as to be able to act effectively in the world. In every culture, the ego is now exposed to the technology it is expected to master as an adult; in our society, it is sent to school. It is expected to be *industrious*, productive, useful. It learns what "superior" and "inferior" mean. It learns *competence*.

Seeking Identity. Then the id rises up in full adult strength and strikes some mighty blows. Puberty, the hurricane season, has arrived. The ego retreats: the superego is aghast. The ego says "What is going on here? I thought I had it all together, and now everything's disintegrating. Am I in control or not?" A dispassionate observer may note that the person is now capable of an adult role—procreation. But, inside, it's a time to search for ego *identity*, a time of turmoil. The id breaks through the defenses, and a delinquent act is committed. A gun at its back, the ego steals a car. The superego roars in righteous rage. The ego cannot think for two weeks, because it feels so much guilt. The ego intellectualizes for all it's worth. It has to stabilize this boat in the storm. It must find the proper direction. Who is it? How strong is it? Can it prevail, or is this the end?

Eventually, the tempests of puberty subside, but there is still some *role confusion*. The thief, the priest, the doctor, the lawyer, the Indian chief. Which of these is me?

The Identity Crisis. Erikson was responsible for labeling the *identity crisis*. The decisions of youth during this age are doubly difficult. Not only has the id gained strange new powers, but, in the midst of the battle, society calls on the young person to choose the directions that will largely determine the course of his or her life for the next 60 years or so. It's hardly fair. Imagine a soldier on the front lines, grappling with an enemy soldier, each with a knife poised above the heart of the other; in a second, it will be death for one and victory for the other. Into this scene enters a man in a business suit with an umbrella and a briefcase. He says to the soldier "Pardon me, my good man, but what do you plan to do after the war? Have you considered plastics?"

The favorable ratio in this period is, as you might have predicted, ego identity over role confusion; the lesson is *fidelity.* Fidelity, at the time of puberty, is not so much virtue as it is desperation: the ego is under attack and seeks support in community—in friends and in groups. The ego secures its boundaries by becoming a member of an "in group," whether that be a school clique, a nation, or a street-corner gang. The adolescent ego is almost neurotically loyal to its group—one for all and all for one—though it can be terribly cruel to members of "out groups."

Utopian Love. If it survives what in some respects is the most threatening of stages, the ego is now a young adult. Its next task is to solve the dilemma of *intimacy* versus *isolation* and to learn the virtue of *love.* This means true, genital love in the Freudian sense: beyond conquest, beyond instinct. As Erikson describes the utopian ideal, love includes:

1. mutuality of orgasm
2. with a loved partner
3. of the other sex
4. with whom one is able and willing to share a mutual trust
5. and with whom one is able and willing to regulate the cycles of
   a. work
   b. procreation
   c. and recreation
6. so as to secure to the offspring, too, all the stages of a satisfactory development.[3]

This listing can be misinterpreted as (1) glorifying the orgasm and (2) depicting homosexuality as sickness. But Erikson views procreation as a survival need of a species, and hence male/female pairs are desirable. "Mutuality of orgasm," similarly, means love—not altogether physical—that is considerate, free, uninhibited, intimate, and trusting.

Creating and Re-Creating. In full adulthood, that calmer period before the id is severely crippled in menopause (male or female), the issue facing the ego is *generativity* versus *stagnation,* and the virtues are *production* and *care.* Here we see Erikson's great stress on procreation, for generativity means to him primarily the bearing and education of offspring. In the ideal case, the children—the new generation—are taught what the parents know and are given some clues to unsolved problems, so that the child may *exceed* the parent. That is the meaning of life. But

[3]From Erikson's *Childhood and Society* (2nd ed.), Norton, 1950, 266.

we may easily expand the concept of generativity to society in general: the wholesome ego is one that has faced the terrible problems of its species and has tried to do something about them. It is better that one had lived than not. But, again, the ego knows what stagnation means and sometimes even desires it, for it is a base of re-creation.

Finally, the ego reaches its "golden years." It has fought the great battles, and it has prevailed. Its old enemy, the id, is dying, and the ego knows that, when the id dies, it too will expire. It has a strange fondness now for this ugly creature that has lived in the cellar of its house all these years. An old enemy is more revered than a new friend; there are not so many games to play. Even the superego comes down once in awhile to—heaven forbid!—have a few laughs with the id and ego. They toast the good old days, and they tell of old victories. The id tells of its great moments of pleasure, the superego of the moments of spiritual euphoria; the ego describes its tricks, and they all laugh and have a last glass of wine. Its taste is sweet.

There is only a hint of despair, a faint distrust of death. It doesn't last. "I had a job to do," says the ego. "I did it. I have fulfilled my destiny." It looks at its offspring. The ego sees part of itself in the new id, part of itself in the new ego, and part of itself in the new superego. Death is not so hard when life continues.

A Note on the Superego

It is fair, if not exact, to say that the early Freudians (and especially Freud) viewed the id as primary and the ego and superego as developing out of the id. Later psychoanalytic thinkers, as we have seen, have ascribed a more autonomous line of development to the ego. It seems quite likely that a similar fate will befall the righteous superego; it is reasonable to expect some new Freud or Erikson to fully develop a theory of psycho-spiritual stages. (In fact, a man named Lawrence Kohlberg has come close to doing so already.) But, to stay more within the psychoanalytic fold, let us briefly consider the work of the British psychoanalyst Melanie Klein.

Melanie Klein

Like Anna Freud, Melanie Klein was one of the earliest child analysts. Camps led by these two analytic giants were constantly feuding over methods and theory, primarily because Klein worked with younger children than the Freudians thought desirable. A pioneer in the use of play as a source of data on inner dynamics (a substitute for free association), Klein made rather direct interpretations of infantile dynamics, interpretations that the defense-minded followers of A. Freud considered dangerous to the integrity of the young ego.

Anna Freud, largely through the efforts of her student Erik Erikson, became the dominant force in child analysis in North America. Melanie

Klein held England, but she was not too well known in the United States. However, politics aside, what is of interest to us here are Klein's views on the early development of the superego.

A Carl Jung might believe in innate moral predispositions that eventually become organized as part of the superego. But other analysts universally employ the mechanism of introjection to explain how the morality of society gets inside the child. Freudians see the primary period of superego birth as between the ages of 3 and 5 years, when the Oedipus conflict leads to castration anxiety and hence to introjection of parental standards, a kind of "If you can't beat 'em, join 'em" strategy. Freudians do recognize the obvious fact, however, that this relatively late consolidation of impulses and control mechanisms that we call the superego has antecedents in early life.

The Persecutory Position. Klein saw the basis of introjection and projection in the taking in of food and the expulsion of feces, the earliest biological events of human survival. As the infant begins to distinguish itself from its environment, it quite naturally distinguishes good and bad. Good is a breast full of warm milk. Bad is an empty or absent breast and erupting teeth. Bad is frustration and aggression. Badness, in some primitive sense, is expelled and projected onto the mother: she is frustrating, she is a bad mother, she is trying to cause me pain. Klein called this the *persecutory* or *paranoid position.* The infant is about 3 months old.

The Depressive Position. But there is also a good mother, with full breasts; she is here, and the milk is good, and sucking is such pleasure. The infant would like to keep the good mother and destroy the bad. Then, perhaps only dimly, it begins to realize that the good and the bad mothers are the same! Oh, were life more simple! The bad mother cannot be destroyed without destroying the good mother as well. Depression. This second attitude Klein called the *depressive position.* The infant is still in the first year or so of life.

Unable to cope with the possible loss of the good mother if the bad mother should be destroyed, the infant introjects both. There is now a good "me" and a bad "me"—and the basis, at least, for the superego is formed, if not the superego itself.

Another Kleinian analyst by the beautiful name of Money-Kyrle has suggested that Klein's two "positions" describe two extremes in the adult superego. There are some people who operate morally under the fear of punishment, derived from the paranoid position, and some who operate under the fear of injuring something lovable, derived from the depressive position. The former tend to be authoritarian, the latter humanistic.

There is a certain ring of truth to these descriptions (though they do seem a bit pessimistic), and some psychologists have gotten very excited about the implications. But, as yet, the psychology of the superego is not as fully explained as that of the id and the ego. Moral development is becoming a hot topic in developmental psychology, so maybe the righteous superego will soon be able to solve its identity crisis.

The Neo-Freudians

Partly because orthodox psychoanalysts disliked their theories and partly because they were creative theorists in their own right, Karen Horney, Erich Fromm, and Harry Stack Sullivan are not usually considered Freudians. Neo-Freudians, maybe, but Freudians? No. They smacked too much of Adler. They emphasized interpersonal, social aspects of human psychology too much and dismissed the biological bases of Freudian psychoanalysis too easily. Still, they wrote later than Adler, their views were more in line with the ascendancy of the ego in orthodox psychoanalysis, and thus their writings were more influential. We might consider them together as prime discussants of the role of ego in a social context.

Karen Horney

Karen Horney didn't think too much of the ego, or of the id and superego for that matter. She preferred to think in terms of a whole person moving toward self-realization. In so doing, she naturally focused on what Freudians, at least, would call the ego in the social context. She believed that, when a basic need, *security,* was frustrated, a basic motive, "basic" *anxiety,* resulted. One's basic goal in life is to feel safe and secure, and the social environment is hardly one in which such feelings are easily maintained. The basic evil is a lack of warmth and affection from the social environment—that is, in the early years, from the parents. But everyone, to some extent at some time and place, feels isolated and helpless and experiences basic anxiety. In an effort to relieve this anxiety, the person resorts to "safety devices," which, in Horney's theory, approximate defense mechanisms.

The Ten Neurotic Needs. The safety devices Horney describes could be called *neurotic needs,* and she postulates ten of these. These in turn fall into attitude categories; there are three of these. Consider neurotic needs. Such needs are unrealistic solutions to the problem of security and are marked by their insatiability. They are bottomless pits; they can't be filled; there is never enough. (1) The neurotic need for affection or love: "If they love me, they will not hurt me." People driven by this need will do almost anything to please. The first, inevitable sign of displeasure or rejection drives them up the wall, and the game is over. (2) The parasitic need. A common safety device in dependent people. "I will become her man, and then I will never fear insecurity; I will be her slave." (3) The need not to try. Or to try softer. A restrictive need based on the assumption "Nothing ventured, nothing gained . . . or *lost.*" (4) The need for power. "If I am the stronger, you cannot harm me." (5) The need to exploit. "I came, I saw, I conquered, but I put no part of *me* on the line."

Neurotic needs number 6, 7, and 8 are concerned with prestige, personal recognition, and personal achievement. They have to do with fame and/or fortune. Who can harm a famous person, one whom others hold in high esteem, or one who has made a remarkable achievement?

Neurotic needs 9 and 10 have to do with independence and perfection. "I need nobody" and (even if I did) "Who is qualified to criticize an expert?"

The Three Neurotic Attitudes. In later works, Horney set aside this taxonomy of needs in order to describe human behavior in terms of more basic, more abstract attitudes. One can orient (1) toward people, as in love, (2) away from people, as in independence, or (3) against people, as in power or exploitation. All of the neurotic needs can be subsumed under one or more of the neurotic attitudes. Horney's three attitudes or stances are strikingly similar to those discovered by animal psychologists. Schneirla, for example, once said that two concepts can be used for the descriptions of all animal species: approach and withdrawal. Horney merely goes one step further and distinguishes between two types of approach, affectionate and aggressive.

Now, all humans move toward, move against, and move away from at various times. In some respects it is a measure of the truth of Horney's position that many people can identify themselves in one or another of her proposed categories. Not only do most of us use these attitudes to protect ourselves, but also we tend to use one more frequently than another. This does not mean, however, that we are neurotic. All people must love, aggress, and withdraw at times. Those who love when the situation calls for hostility, those who withdraw when the situation calls for love—those could be called neurotic. It is the inappropriate response that is adhered to rigidly that denotes the neurotic.

Consider, for example, the so-called "unliberated" woman. According to Horney, she has a neurotic need for affection and an "unnatural" need for someone to run her life for her. She has a romantic view of love and desires only to find "Mr. Right." These needs might well keep her from realizing her true potential, but they are fostered and reinforced by society (or at least a part of it), so much so that often a woman *without* these needs is considered abnormal. What Horney is saying, in effect, is that a certain segment of society expects women to be neurotic and that, if they are not, they are apt to be labeled "neurotic."

Needless to say, Horney doesn't think much of Freud's concept of penis envy. Instead, she reasons, the dominant role of the male in Western societies requires women, if they are to establish a reasonably secure position in life, to become subservient to men. They are allowed to manipulate men in subtle, "feminine" ways, but they are not allowed to challenge their basic authority. Men, on the other hand, are required to play the dominant role, and, if they choose not to exploit their wives, they face being called weak, hen-pecked, or worse. Thus, for societal reasons, men and women have for centuries played out their roles of ingenious slave and benevolently ignorant master. Those unfortunate persons who have not chosen to play these roles have had to face uncomfortable social sanctions.

Horney is not exceptionally well respected by orthodox Freudians. The main reason for this lack of respect is her cavalier disregard for some of the basic tenets of Freudian psychoanalysis—in particular, the biological bases for the human psychology, for basic concepts like the unconscious, and for the structural concepts of ego, id, and superego. There can be little question that Horney offers only a superficial analysis of many important Freudian concepts. On the other hand, it is also true that she concentrated her efforts on understanding some of the relationships between the ego and society, a topic given far too little attention by many Freudians.

Erich Fromm

Erich Fromm, like Karen Horney, was born in Germany, trained in psychoanalysis at the Berlin Psychoanalytic Institute, and forced into exile in the United States in the early 1930s. Like Horney, Fromm based his views of the human personality on the isolation of individuals from the world. Horney stressed the feeling of helplessness that leads to basic anxiety and, often, neurotic needs. Fromm stressed the feeling of loneliness.

The Ego in a Historical Perspective

A devoted Marxist, Fromm made his most significant contribution in his description of the relationship of economic institutions to the human personality. The ego is examined in historical perspective. In most primitive people, the ego had only a dim awareness of its existence as a separate being; it was in a very real sense at one with its fellow egos and with the rest of the world. The person, the environment, the clan, the supernatural world of the spirit—all were part of a functional and indivisible whole. This fact protected the primitive from loneliness, but it also inhibited flexibility and productivity.

As economic conditions changed, so did the problems of the ego. In the feudal society of the Middle Ages, the ego had lost its sense of oneness with the physical environment, but its identification of itself in terms of a social caste or class was still pronounced. "I am a serf." "I am [a] noble." There were obligations associated with one's class, and to fail to meet a God-decreed responsibility was unthinkable.

The Industrial Revolution broke the remaining ties of the individual ego to others. A merchant class was created, and it turned out not to be a class at all—at least, not in the traditional sense of the word. One could move up or down on the social ladder, and where one went depended on personal initiative and ability. Religion, in its social function, scampered to catch up; the Reformation broke the ties of individuals to their classes and made each person fully responsible, and alone, before an awe-inspiring God. The wealthy, rather than the poor, became God's children, and the Protestant ethic became a driving force for achievement and productivity.

In today's technological society, the ties that bind are still being broken. It is becoming increasingly *uncommon* for a person to keep the same job or spouse for life or to live in the same place for life. People are becoming increasingly free, increasingly "individual" . . . and increasingly lonely. Of all human emotions, according to Fromm, loneliness is the most difficult to tolerate over long periods. The ego plots its escape from loneliness; it struggles to escape from freedom.

Escape from Freedom

One of Fromm's best known books is entitled *Escape from Freedom,* and it depicts the desire of German people to regain a sense of relatedness in subjugation to the authoritarian Nazi regime. But one can escape from freedom in many ways in any society: compulsive patriotism is evident in all cultures, religious zealots are common enough, and the fans (fanatics) of any team have a remarkable sense of group identity. A person may choose to escape by choosing an authoritarian spouse or an authoritarian work situation. Freud once said that religion, one of the escape possibilities, was a mass neurosis; Fromm said that neurosis, rather, was an individual religion. So neurosis is an escape, too, as Adler had imagined when he accused neurotics of a lack of responsibility.

Fromm saw humans as faced with several existential discrepancies: one's reach exceeds one's grasp, one lives with the certain knowledge of death, and one can be free and lonely or controlled and frustrated. These humanistic dialectics must be dealt with by all human societies, and some handle them better than others. Fromm was not hesitant to label a whole nation as "sick" if its institutions failed to provide for expression of these basic human needs in a productive fashion. He even described a "humanistic communitarian socialism," a social system he felt would solve most of our existential problems, and he saw Marx as the progenitor of such ideals. (It seems safe to say, however, that Fromm would not glorify authoritarian Communism.)

Fromm's Character Types

The manner in which someone escapes from freedom has a profound influence on his or her (neurotic) personality. Fromm used the term *character type* to describe the extreme adaptations of the ego to its antagonistic needs. There is first of all the *receptive character.* For this type, all good comes from an external source. To obtain this good, one must be submissive and masochistic. One achieves relatedness and rootedness by selling oneself into what is essentially slavery. The *exploitative character* takes rather than receives. This character type is essentially sadistic in interaction with others—a true Nazi or robber baron—and relates with hate, the opposite side of the coin from compulsive love (as in the receptive character). In other words, this type escapes from the necessity to relate humanly by denying the value of relationship. In the political arena, the exploiter is often supported by the receptive character, for the exploiter can provide the kind of inhuman authority that receptives so dearly desire.

Hoarding characters are miserly sorts, working, saving, and collecting. They are neat and orderly and often politically conservative. They are the stodgy business executives. They possess spouses and families and houses in much the same way as they hoard other goods, and their religion is the best in town. Here is the Protestant ethic in caricature.

The *marketing character* is a product of more recent American economic changes. This character literally sells himself or herself to the boss, potential spouses, and friends. Dress is important—it is the "packaging." Fits of loneliness intrude (society is becoming a lonelier place), but how can a can of Campbell's Soup feel lonely for long? So many love this commodity/person; soon someone will pick it off the shelf, and it will be had. Fromm saw a lot of these characters in his adopted homeland, the U.S.A.

Like a stage theory, a type theory must include the ideal. In Fromm's case, this ideal is the *productive character.* Only the productive character is capable of what Marx called "free conscious activity." This type can love and hate without compulsion and will balance the emotions of loneliness and frustration to make a creative life. The productive character is a self-actualizer, is in fact self-actualized; an ideal sort, seldom if ever observable in pure form.

With technological advances occurring so rapidly, one might expect that Fromm would discover new character types, born of new economic conditions. Something like the *modular character* described by Alvin Toffler in his book *Future Shock.* The product of modern society faces projects rather than jobs and must increasingly develop skills that will allow one to be "plugged in," to fill a role in a new project initiated by a large technological corporation. Such a character is highly mobile and hates to "play games"; there is so little time.

Fromm, however, turned in a more philosophical direction and described two characters labeled *necrophilous*—lovers of death—and *biophilous*—lovers of life. The biophilous character is optimistic, hopeful, and humanistic; the necrophilous character is frustrated and pessimistic. Fromm shocked the political community in 1968 by stating that the supporters of Eugene McCarthy were more biophilous, whereas the Robert Kennedy supporters were more necrophilous. That's the trouble with types. They can be used so easily to classify people according to one's own biases.

Harry Stack Sullivan

Harry Stack Sullivan was born in the United States and was influenced by the trends in social psychology that were developing there. He is often quoted as saying that personality is an illusion and that it can be observed only in an interpersonal (that is, social) context. Are those two claims contradictory? Well, that's the way Sullivan talked and wrote. Reading Sullivan's works often gives the reader the feeling, as one writer described it, of being "on the precarious summit of a brilliant display of fireworks." Sullivan coined a new term for every old idea and for some new ideas too, and he alone seemed fully adequate to the task of understanding and manipulating this wealth of new symbols.

After several rereadings of Sullivan's writings and transcribed lectures, most psychologists have discarded some of Sullivan's terminology, keeping old familiar names when they will do just as well as the new ones. For example, there is not a significant difference between Sullivan's *selective inattention* and Freud's *preconscious;* both have to do with ideas of which we could be conscious if we were willing to focus our attention on them. In Sullivan's terms, *dissociated* ideas are *unconscious.* But why add new words unnecessarily?

Also, the statement that personality is an illusion is quite intriguing. But the product does not quite live up to the promise. The product is one of those run-of-the-mill field theories (like Murphy's) that sees behavior as a joint function of the social environment and the person. The person, however, remains a "locus" of significant action and a "dynamic center" for various important processes. In short, Sullivan does little more than stress the effects of interpersonal interaction on personality.

If it sounds like we're belittling Sullivan, it's true, but only in the sense of asserting (without empirical evidence) that Sullivan was not God. On the topics to which his theory was particularly well suited, he was . . . well, maybe not God, but "gangbusters" at least. Fireworks. A pyrotechnic display. He had a peculiar gift for empathy—feeling what another must be feeling—and he used this gift in dramatic interactions with schizophrenics. He used the term *empathy* as a major construct, and he used it to explain in great detail the interaction between a person's cognitive goings-on and the events in the social environment. Thus he brought social psychology into psychiatry.

Sullivan's Three Modes of Thinking

According to Sullivan, modes of thinking fall into three broad categories. The first is called *prototaxic.* In this mode the person experiences discrete and unrelated events in the "stream of consciousness." There are no "logical" connections among these states; that is, there is little or no sense of causality, and the logical concepts of time and space—which in the adult account for many of the perceived relationships among events—have not yet developed to any great extent. Primary processes; the most primitive of primary processes.

The sense of causality is the major difference between prototaxic and *parataxic* thinking, the next mode. But this sense of causality is still very primitive in parataxic thinking, and events closely associated in time and/or space are likely to be seen as related, even if there is no true connection. In therapy, one often sees this kind of thought in such experiences as extreme guilt following a death wish come true. Stated simply, a child, angry at a parent or sibling, wishes secretly that the offending person would die. Then the person does die, for reasons totally unrelated to the child's wish. But the events—"I wish him dead" and the actual death—are so close in time that the child (or sometimes an adult) feels that somehow his or her thoughts have *caused* the death. And the burden of guilt can be overwhelming.

Parataxic thinking is generally quite autistic and personal in quality. Few conclusions are tested against "reality" or the opinions of others (consensual truth). "If an earthquake strikes when I am urinating, then, by golly, it's true. My urine causes earthquakes!" It is another characteristic of this mode, in a more interpersonal vein, that the individual creates images (personifications) of himself or herself, of other people, and of events, images that are totally unrealistic and often inconsistent. "I am good/bad, powerful/powerless, and the world is against me for all and for none of the above reasons."

The third mode of thinking Sullivan calls *syntaxic*. It is an adult manner of describing event relationships in logical, linguistic terms; it checks assumptions and conclusions against what others think, and it is very reality-oriented. It is much like Freud's secondary-process thinking with its reality orientation. Syntaxic thinking is the kind we do . . . most of the time.

Empathy

So we have three modes of thought. Now let us look at the concept of *empathy*. Whatever empathy is, Sullivan had a lot of it. Perhaps that is why he didn't define it carefully but simply assumed that others were, as he was, full of it. It was a kind of "emotional communication" or "intuition" of the feeling states of others. Children demonstrate empathy, said Sullivan, as early as six months after birth. At this age, empathy can be defined as a more or less direct reflection of the mood of the mother; if she is anxious, the child is anxious, and, if she is at ease, so is the child.

Need Tensions versus Anxiety Tensions

Next we can add the distinction between *need tensions* and *anxiety tensions*. Need tensions are created by biological needs, and they are *satisfied* by appropriate input. Food satisfies hunger. Anxiety tensions, however, develop from threats to *security* and are interpersonal and cultural in nature. Originally anxiety is experienced by means of empathy and has little "meaning"; that is, the emotion is thought of prototaxically or parataxically. "Something's wrong" is the verbal equivalent, but the nonverbal feeling is something children know they should avoid, and security becomes something to approach and desire. Security needs, in Sullivan's view, are more important than biological needs. This is another way of saying that interpersonal relationships are more a part of personality than are biological, innate drives.

Human Development according to Sullivan

Now we are ready to trace the development of this human personality. The first stage is *infancy*, extending from birth to the development of speech. Thinking in this stage is prototaxic, gradually changing to parataxic. At first the infant is aware of only a series of seemingly unrelated experiences. But the infant has empathy (after 6 months), and some of these experiences involve the feeling of anxiety or of security and comfort. Such feelings come from the attending adult—in most cases, the mother. If *she* is anxious, the infant becomes anxious through empathy. They share the feeling of ease and security in the same way. With the development of parataxic thinking, the feeling of anxiety tension becomes something to be avoided, although the infant does not, of course, know why this is so.

Personifications, personalized images of people, begin to appear. There is the "good mother" who is comfortable and satisfying. There is the "bad mother" who is anxious and frustrating. These personifications, in empathy, are reflected also as the "good me" and the "bad me," the beginnings of what Freudians would call the Superego. Eventually these distinct personifications become more complex, and the good/bad mother is just Mom, and the good/bad me is just myself. (Do you recognize echoes of Klein here?) But the "just myself" is the self (an organized pattern of activities) whose goal is to be secure (avoid anxiety tensions) and to praise good work and forbid bad. Born of empathy with the mother, the self grows in power (the ability to obtain comfort and avoid anxiety) and is destined to grow in complexity. The self, after all, is the sum of "reflected appraisals," and it is only fate and genetics that dictate the fact that the earliest appraisals are those of the mother. Others are to come.

The next stage, childhood, brings three basic lessons. First, the child learns language and thus acquires the basis of syntaxic thinking. The child also learns that there are people "out there" other than mother and that few of these others have a devoted interest in his or her well-being. Sullivan calls this the *malevolent transformation,* the decision that the world is essentially hostile. Even in the best of cases, a little paranoia is necessary for survival. More and more people appraise "my self," and my self changes as a result. The third lesson is *sublimation:* we learn to channel impulses into socially acceptable activities. This is good because it avoids aggravation.

In the next stage, the juvenile stage, the person moves farther afield, outside the family: I have friends, and more appraisals of my self are obtained. I am learning to love and to be intimate, although, in this stage and the next, preadolescence, intimate friends are of the same sex. I have a need for a "chum."

In early adolescence, which includes puberty, one becomes lustful. As Sullivan sees it, the issue at stake here involves the difference between sex and love. The adolescent loves friends of the same sex but is physically attracted to members of the opposite sex. Therefore (1) sexual inclinations can be directed toward the people one loves (this is Sullivan's view of homosexuality), (2) the division between sex and intimacy can be retained and opposite-sex people treated forevermore as objects, or (3) the intimate inclinations can be turned toward the people who are sexually desired. The third option is generally considered optimal.

There are a couple more stages—late adolescence and maturity—but they are not too important in Sullivan's theory. They have to do with becoming and being an adult, and the discussions are of training in our culture.

The Ego in a Social Context

Horney, Fromm, and Sullivan were contemporaries, classmates of sorts, friends, and colleagues, and thus it should come as no great surprise to find that their theories are similar in many respects. Though they themselves did not use the term *ego,* it is clear that the topics they chose to discuss would be ego topics to a Freudian. All chose to focus on the ego's sense of security in a changing social environment and also on some of the debilitating things the Ego might do in the face of threats to its security.

Along with Adler and Erikson, these three theorists turned our attention from the inner struggles among id, ego, and superego—in a more or less unchanging culture—and brought, essentially, a fourth misty figure to life in the psychic house. This figure does not live in the house, but it comes to visit. It is the bookkeeper, the creditor. It is reality; it is culture. It is the one with whom ego must balance accounts. It says to ego "You have incurred a debt. It must be paid back on time, or you will be imprisoned." The Ego must struggle to comply and at the same time satisfy its siblings, id and superego.

Some creditors are good and relatively human; some are devastating. The latter correspond to cultures that demand more than the ego can reasonably give and thus drive it to despair and delinquency. They are sick cultures. All of the theorists discussed in this chapter grew impatient at times with various cultures and damned them for their improprieties—Germany for its authoritarianism, the United States for its restrictive business ethic—and some, like Fromm, proposed alternatives that would allow more freedom, security, and creativity. It is perhaps significant that, in theories such as these, there is not so much a utopian developmental stage (for example, the genital stage) as there is a utopian environment. We are told that the ego adapts and that what it adapts to will determine its quality. We seek once again to return to the Garden of Eden.

Chapter Summary

The ego grows up. That has been the theme of this chapter. Not only did the ego become a major theoretical construct, but also the study of society and interpersonal relations became a topic of study for psychoanalytically oriented psychologists.

The ego grows up. We can also say that one of the prominent causes—and prominent effects—of an emphasis on the ego has been the study of the child, in whom the ego is in the process of growing.

The five major theorists discussed in this chapter were Anna Freud, Erik Erikson, Karen Horney, Erich Fromm, and Harry Stack Sullivan. Their theories have much in common, both in approach and in content. Freud, using her father's theory but extending it, and Sullivan were concerned with the nature of thinking. The stream-of-consciousness thinking that Sullivan called prototaxic and the primitive causality of the parataxic mode together correspond roughly to primary-process thinking in Freudian theory, and the logical, symbolic secondary-process mode corresponds to Sullivan's syntaxic thinking. What Sullivan has done, in effect, is to distinguish between two types of primary-process thought.

The study of defense mechanisms (Freud), safety devices (Horney), or escape mechanisms (Fromm) is a prominent concern in these theories. The threats to ego integrity from the id were described by Freud, and the threats from society are a prime concern of Erikson and the others. Threats from society seem to elicit discussions of anxiety, as distinct from the pressures of id impulses; Sullivan, for example, expressly distinguishes need tensions (physiological) from anxiety tensions (interpersonal). Horney talks of basic anxiety born of isolation and helplessness. Fromm, too, stresses isolation, and, for him, loneliness is a concept not too different from anxiety.

In response to anxiety, various defense mechanisms are employed. Those discussed by Freud can be understood most clearly in terms of struggles of the ego with the id or with the superego for control of the psyche. The safety devices of Horney and the escape routes of Fromm involve societal factors more directly. Since theoretical constructs are a way to label empirical events, it is natural to find similarities in these conceptual formulations. Horney speaks of the neurotic need to exploit and Fromm of the exploitative character or orientation; Fromm's receptive character is driven by a neurotic need for affection, and the hoarding character is marked by needs for prestige, admiration, and achievement.

Because the ego is a growing entity, because it is not fixed, all of these theories make some statement about developmental levels or stages. Even defense mechanisms have a developmental tint, for some (like repression and projection) are more primitive than others (like intellectualization).

The eight ages of the human being, as seen by Erikson, are well summarized in Table 9-1. The ages are listed on the left, and the basic conflicts to be resolved during each age are listed on the right. There may be some differences in the timing of the various ages among cultures; and the years listed represent the time of *very significant* learning, not the only time of learning. For example, in the first age one must learn about basic trust and mistrust, but learning about trust continues for a lifetime. In the fifth age is the identity crisis, but decisions about identity occur to some extent in all preceding ages as well.

The Freudian psychosexual stages are also reflected in Erikson's chart. The first four ages reflect social happenings in the oral, anal, phallic, and latency stages, and the last four ages portray in more detail the learning tasks that occur during and after puberty that, with luck, will lead to the utopian genital stage.

Table 9-1. Erikson's eight stages of human development.

1. oral/sensory	birth–1 year	Trust versus mistrust
2. muscular/anal	1–3 years	Autonomy versus doubt, shame
3. locomotor/genital	3–5 years	Initiative versus guilt
4. latency	6–11 years	Industry versus inferiority
5. adolescence	12–18 years	Identity versus role confusion
6. young adulthood	19–35 years	Intimacy versus isolation
7. adulthood	35–50 years	Generativity versus stagnation
8. maturity	50+ years	Ego integrity versus despair

There is an eerie universality to these stages, both the psychosexual and the psychosocial. On the one hand, there have been comments from animal psychologists like Konrad Lorenz, who speaks of the psychosexual stages: "What irks me about [the theory] . . . is that it can be applied, with very little or no change, to animals which do not have, never have had, and never will have either a penis or a vagina."[4] On the other hand, Fromm's character orientations can be related to the history of political and economic development. The exploitative character—the robber baron—was a popular orientation in ages past, and it fit well with the receptive character of most serfs. The hoarding character was a prominent figure during the Industrial Revolution, and the marketing character comes a little later. Thus Fromm's character orientations can be seen as stages in the evolution of culture.

The biological and cultural support for the psychological stages of the ego—what does all this mean? Are humans progressing toward the utopian (genital) stage or the utopian (productive) character? Or is there simply change, change leading to . . . what?

Suggested Readings

Anna Freud's books are always delightful and informative. *The Ego and the Mechanisms of Defence* (International Universities Press, 1946) is a classic introduction to her thought. Erik Erikson's classic is *Childhood and Society* (2nd Edition, Norton, 1950). His more recent *Identity: Youth and Crisis* (Norton, 1968) is less theoretical. Robert Coles has written an excellent intellectual biography of Erikson (*Erik H. Erikson: The Growth of His Work,* Little, Brown, 1970).

Horney's *Neurotic Personality of Our Times* (Norton, 1937) and *New Ways in Psychoanalysis* (Norton, 1939) are good introductions to her later work. Similarly, Fromm's *Escape from Freedom* (Rinehart, 1941) is a good beginning. Sullivan fans should start with *The Interpersonal Theory of Psychiatry* (Norton, 1953).

And, finally, Part 3 of Ruth Munroe's *Schools of Psychoanalytic Thought* (Holt, 1955) is an excellent source for integration and comparison of the work of Horney, Fromm, and Sullivan.

[4]Quoted in Erikson's *Childhood and Society* (2nd ed.), Norton, 1950, 92.

Notes and References

The primary references for the work of Anna Freud are, in order of estimate of value:

The Ego and the Mechanisms of Defence. International Universities Press (IUP), 1946.

Normality and Pathology in Childhood. IUP, 1965.

The Psycho-analytical Treatment of Children. Imago, 1946. (This book contains three papers originally published in 1926, 1927, and 1945.)

Difficulties in the Path of Psychoanalysis. IUP, 1969.

The series of volumes entitled *The Psychoanalytic Study of the Child* (IUP) contains many papers by Freud, and those that do not bear her name bear her imprint. Many of these references and others are contained in *The Writings of Anna Freud,* a multi-volume set; publication by IUP began in 1966 and continues through the present. IUP also published much of the important work of Heinz Hartmann, including *Ego Psychology and the Problem of Adaptation* (first published in 1939, in English translation in 1958); see also the papers by Hartmann, Kris, and Loewenstein in *The Psychoanalytic Study of the Child,* including "Comments on the Formation of Psychic Structure," in Volume 2, published in 1946. David Rapaport's systematic organization of psychoanalytic theory, together with his news on delay of gratification, can be found in S. Koch (Ed.), *Psychology: A Study of a Science* (Vol. 3).

Erik Erikson's main works are *Childhood and Society* (2nd Ed., Norton, 1950) and *Identity: Youth and Crisis* (Norton, 1968). A psychobiography of Martin Luther provides a good look at Erikson's ideas in application (*Young Man Luther.* Norton, 1958). Also worth reading is Robert Coles' biography of Erikson (see Suggested Readings).

Four of Horney's chief works, all published by Norton, are *Neurotic Personality of Our Times* (1937), *New Ways in Psychoanalysis* (1939), *Our Inner Conflicts* (1945), and *Neurosis and Human Growth* (1950).

For Fromm, we would suggest *Escape from Freedom* (1941), *Man for Himself* (1947), and *The Sane Society* (1955), all published by Rinehart. *The Revolution of Hope* (Harper & Row, 1968) is a more recent variation on the theme, and *Marx's Concept of Man* (Ungar, 1961) gives Fromm's Marxian view of Marx's views.

Sullivan didn't write much, but luckily he talked a lot. His lectures have been put into book form, and the two most theoretically interesting are *The Interpersonal Theory of Psychiatry* (1953) and *The Fusion of Psychiatry and Social Science* (1964), both by Norton.

Secondary sources of value are the Coles biography, referenced above, for Erikson. For Fromm, Horney, and Sullivan, C. Hall and G. Lindzey's *Theories of Personality* (2nd Ed., Wiley, 1970), J. A. C. Brown's *Freud and the Post-Freudians* (Penguin, 1964), and R. L. Munroe's *Schools of Psychoanalytic Thought* (Holt, 1955) provide summaries. Brown's book also has bits on Anna Freud and Melanie Klein, but don't expect much.

10

Follow the Leader: Modeling and Imitation

Better . . . to accept the inevitability of imitation and then to imitate good things. The ancients had this right. Greatness without models? Inconceivable.

Saul Bellow, Mr. Sammler's Planet

The Wild Boy of Avignon, so they say, was raised by wolves (or wild dogs) and knew nothing of human society until he was well into his teens. What a find for psychology! Who wouldn't give an arm and a leg to work with such a child? You'd have a chance to see what sorts of behaviors and characteristics were innately human and which were learned from others. Unfortunately, there is some pretty good evidence that none of us will ever have such a chance, because Wild Boys (and Girls) really exist only in the imagination of their wishful creators. People simply don't seem to be able to survive without some contact with other human beings. And this need for contact goes beyond simple physical caretaking—it isn't enough to keep the baby dry and let it suck a bottle when it's hungry. Children reared like this, with their physical needs taken care of but without holding or cuddling or talking to or playing with, get sick. They lose weight. They literally dwindle away. Eventually, if their situation doesn't improve, they die.

People need people. We spend our entire lives in the actual or symbolic presence of others. For everything we do, someone is watching or might be watching, or we imagine what it would be like to have someone watch. We exist in an other-saturated environment.

Social-Learning Theory

Personality then—at least, that part of it that *is* acquired and not genetically determined—must be acquired in a social context. In the context of interactions with other people. Of watching and being watched. The learning theorists are right (as far as they go): we do acquire many of our behaviors through learning, and that learning is governed by some fairly simple rules. But the rules have to take into account how we learn from others, because that's what we do most often and most efficiently.

Enter the Social-Learning Theorist. Plugging a gap here, straightening out a relationship there, and generally tidying things up. Suddenly, learning theory doesn't look so abstract and formal and forbidding. The rats have come out of their cages, and—look!—they aren't rats any more! They're people!

It's hard to say where the recognition of the importance of social processes really begins in the history of psychology. In some sense, it's always been there. The ancient Greek philosopher-types to whom psychology traces its ancestry were certainly aware of and concerned about human interactions. And surely nobody could accuse Papa Freud of ignoring or glossing over the importance of things we learn from and about others. Perhaps it would be more accurate to say that the social-learning theorists *re*-discovered social processes, after those processes had been lost in the behaviorist jungle that sprang up in the United States in the early 1900s and spread rapidly across the psychological landscape. Watson, Skinner, Hull: the very names conjure up images of creatures pressing bars, getting shocked, running around in mazes. Stimulus, response, reinforcement. Identify a behavior, count it, graph it—there's a picture of learning, stripped of all the confusing nonessentials.

But is it, really? If you take all the potatoes and onions and carrots out of a stew, have you got a stew anymore? If you take all the human interactions out of learning, have you really got human learning anymore? Can a "personality" grow and exist all by itself? Be understood all by itself? Or must it be seen growing with, interacting with, bouncing off of other personalities?

Miller and Dollard Make Their Entrances

In 1941, Neal Miller and John Dollard published a book entitled *Social Learning and Imitation.* It wasn't an enormous and authoritative text, and it didn't say much that was really new. But it did pull a lot of ideas together, and it did set the stage for a lot of thinking about how people learn from each other. In that sense, it makes a convenient starting point for us to look at how a *social*-learning theory of personality has come into being.

Copying and Matched Dependent Behavior

Miller and Dollard started with a relatively simple observation: people act like other people. In fact, they act so much alike that it's hard to account for the similarities of their behavior in terms of simple stimulus-response-reward sequences. It seems much more reasonable to assume that two people act the same because one is copying—imitating—the other or because both of them are imitating some third person. Using the standard variables of learning theory—drive, cue, response, and reward—Miller and Dollard went on to identify three sorts of "matched" behavior: that is, two or more people doing the same thing. The first of these is the least interesting from a social-learning standpoint; it is the case in which two people just happen to do the same thing in the same situation because each has (independently) been rewarded for doing so in the past. In other words, it is a nonsocial learning situation, one in which the "old" behaviorism is perfectly adequate to analyze and explain the behavior.

Observer and Model. Next, though, Miller and Dollard talk about "matched dependent behavior." Here person O (for Observer) observes that person M (for Model) does something and is rewarded for it. O doesn't know why M does it or under what circumstances; but O does note the sequence of "M does it" followed by "M gets a goodie." So, being a logical sort of person, O decides to try the same thing. And a goodie is forthcoming for O, too. Gradually, as this sort of thing happens again and again, O learns that "doing what M does" is a goodie-producing strategy, and the imitating behavior has been learned.

Miller and Dollard's example of matched dependent behavior is one of two brothers, age 5 and 2, playing at home. The front door opens, and the older boy recognizes this as a sign that Daddy is home from work. He knows that Daddy is often good for a piece of candy, so he runs to him—and is promptly rewarded with candy. Younger brother notices all of this and makes a connection: big brother runs, big brother gets candy. So the next night, when big brother runs to daddy, younger brother runs too—and also gets candy. But it doesn't work *whenever* younger brother runs; younger brother could run all day long, and still the candy would only be passed out when Daddy came home. So, quite naturally, what younger brother will eventually learn is that he will get candy if he runs *when big brother runs.* The stimulus for him to run is not the arrival of Daddy but, rather, big brother running. His behavior is *matched* to that of his big brother, and it is *dependent* on big brother's behavior.

Miller and Dollard contrast this "matched dependent" behavior with what they call "copying." In copying, the sequence may look quite the same: person M does something, person O sees the behavior, and person O does it too. But, in copying, there is a deliberate attempt to find out what M does *in a particular situation* in order to get a reward. The copier, then, can repeat the learned behavior when that situation occurs again, whether M is there or not. O's behavior, once learned, is not dependent on M to set it off; the cue for copied behavior is the same for both Model and Observer. If the little boy in our previous example had been copying his big brother, he himself would now respond to the sound of the front door opening and would run for his reward whenever Daddy came home.

The Cue. The essential difference, then, between matched dependent and copying behavior has to do with the *cue* that initiates the behavior. In matched dependent behavior, the behavior is *matched to* and *dependent on* what the Model does; the Observer must see the Model do it, every time. The Model's behavior is the cue for the Observer's behavior. In copying, however, the cue is the same for both Model and Observer; the cue is the external situation or happening that signals to both of them "now such-and-such a behavior is likely to be rewarded." Once having learned how to behave in that situation (from the Model), the Observer can continue to repeat the behavior appropriately even when the Model is gone.

Why Imitation?

Miller and Dollard didn't stop here, of course. They went on to discuss drives, stimulus discrimination, cues, reinforcements, and all of our old familiar learning-theory friends, in great detail, relating each of them to the two kinds of imitation. But, according to some critics, they stopped just short of the really important point: why does imitation occur in the first place? What is the mechanism that allows a person to learn to do what the other guy did? Once imitation, or copying, or whatever, has happened, it's relatively easy to analyze the reinforcement patterns that make that behavior likely to be repeated. But how does it get started? Too often, the explanation is circular: what is imitation? It's when somebody does what somebody else does. Why do people do what somebody else does? Because they get reinforced for doing it. But how do they start doing it in the first place? By imitating someone. . . .

O. Hobart Mowrer

One theorist who wasn't satisfied with that kind of circularity was O. Hobart Mowrer. (What does the "O" stand for? Does anybody know? This may be one of the great unsolved mysteries of psychology.) Mowrer was one of those frighteningly knowledgeable people who knew so much about so many fields of psychology that he could hardly even be considered a "generalist"; he was more a "multiple specialist." He is also one of the few psychologists since Freud who has had the courage to hold up his own life, especially its less comfortable and less flattering aspects, as a way of illustrating his beliefs about personality. Mowrer was not, for most of his life, a happy man. He describes his private life as "subjective, secretive, and tortured." He suffered from recurring depressions that lasted for months at a time and left him more or less incapacitated. Perhaps these miserable episodes explain (in part) how he came to be such a multifaceted psychologist. He was clearly fascinated by experimental psychology, by the challenge of devising a theory that would capture in numbers and symbols the intricacies of human behavior. But his own experience told him that numbers and symbols weren't enough—not the kinds of numbers and symbols being used by the learning theorists, at any rate. There were feelings, too, and feelings were too important to be ignored. Maybe they were the most important things of all! So he became a clinician, a personality theorist, as well as a learning theorist. It's not surprising to hear a clinician talking about such things as "hope" and "fear," and we are used to hearing about reinforcement schedules and generalization gradients from learning theorists. But here is a man who is *both* and who used both sets of concepts to attack the phenomenon of imitation.

Hopes and Fears: The Two-Factor Theory

Mowrer's starting point was the fact that traditional learning theory, with its emphasis on what can be seen and measured (and measured accurately and consistently), has left a very important something out of the picture of the learning organism. People don't just behave—they have feelings about their behavior. They have *hopes* and *fears* about situations—hopes that, if they respond in certain ways, pleasant things will happen, and fears that, if they respond in other ways, unpleasant things will happen. The situations in which we find ourselves as we move through life call forth these feelings of hope and fear because of our past experiences, our previous learnings. In other words, we learn to respond to some classes of situations with fear and to other classes with hope. This learning can be explained by the principles of simple classical conditioning, in the same way that Pavlov explained how his dogs learned to salivate on demand. (See Figure 10-1.)

Just as the sound of a bell, paired consistently with the smell of meat (which makes a dog salivate), will start by itself to cause the salivation response, so a given situation, paired consistently with a pleasant happening (which makes us feel good), will come to cause the feel-good response on its own. (Mowrer seems to use the words "hope" and "fear" as a kind of shorthand for "pleasant and positive feelings" and "unpleasant and negative feelings," and we shall do the same.) This conditioning of feelings is half of Mowrer's "two-factor theory" of learning; it explains how we learn a feeling-response, an emotional *sign,* that goes with a particular situation or set of stimuli. But learning the sign isn't the whole story. We also learn what to do about those feelings, how to use the situation to best advantage. We learn *what to do about* the way we feel in this circumstance or that. And this learning follows the rules of operant conditioning, à la Skinner and the rats. Both parts occur in any learning sequence: classical conditioning of feelings to situation and operant conditioning of external behavior.

All very well, you say. An interesting idea. But what does it have to do with imitation? Quite a lot, actually. Let's go back to those two brothers, waiting (though the little one doesn't know it) for Daddy to come home. Front door rattles. Big Bro runs. Little Bro runs too. Daddy gives everybody candy, and everybody feels good. The sign learning here is: brother running (situation)—feel good (hope). But let's take the sign learning a bit further. By a process of stimulus generalization, other situations similar to "brother running" will tend to create the same feelings of hope. What situation similar to "brother running" can Little Bro create? Why, some other small male type running, of course. When Little Bro runs toward that opening front door, he experiences the same sort of feeling of hope (in perhaps a milder version, but still pleasant) as he learned to feel when Big Brother did it. And—presto!—his behavior is rewarded by Daddy, and operant conditioning proceeds on its merry way.

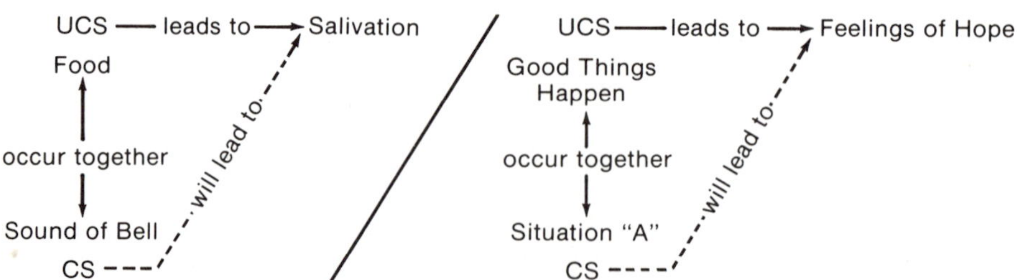

Figure 10-1. Mowrer's re-interpretation of the classical-conditioning model.

It's all very involved and elaborate, to be sure. And it's a shame to have to consider two processes instead of finding one simple, basic theme. But it does seem to make sense, and it does (finally) get some of the internal, not-operationally-measurable aspects of human behavior (the things personality theorists have known all along were important) into the picture. It also provides one possible explanation of the underlying mechanism that makes imitation work.

Albert Bandura

Miller and Dollard had published *Social Learning and Imitation* in 1941. The world was somewhat (to say the least) occupied with events of a larger scale at the time, and it took a while for the book to make a strong impact. Indeed, not until World War II was over did psychologists take a deep breath and plunge back into their basic, theoretical research with real enthusiasm. Mowrer wrote a paper for the *Harvard Educational Review* in 1947, a paper called "On the Dual Nature of Learning: A Reinterpretation of 'Conditioning' and 'Problem Solving.'" Hull's *Principles of Behavior* had come out in 1943, and he began publishing prolifically again in the early 1950s; Kenneth Spence, a colleague of Hull's, also returned to churning out reports around that time. In the midst of this heady, we-can-do-anything-if-we-set-our-minds-to-it atmosphere, a bright young student named Albert Bandura appeared on the steps of the State University of Iowa (where Spence was holding forth in the psychological laboratories). Bandura was interested in clinical, not experimental, psychology, but he couldn't escape the behaviorist climate of the day, which may have been more pronounced at Iowa State than anywhere else in the country. It seems, as we look back, to have been almost inevitable that he would try to apply learning theory to his clinical interests. The experimental model worked so well on rats and pigeons; why not apply it to psychotherapy?

Behavior Modification

Now this kind of approach was a pretty radical departure from what had been going on in psychology. Experimentalists tended to regard clinicians as a bunch of soft-headed intellectual lightweights, while clinicians viewed experimentalists as rigid, short-sighted mechanics who spent their time and energy on esoteric trivia rather than on the really important questions. But a new breed of psychologists, following Mowrer's example, were beginning to appear on the scene: a group who were bright (and unprejudiced) enough to see value in both sides of the psychological coin and optimistic (or foolish) enough to think that they could bridge the gap. Bandura was one of these—and one of the most successful. He became one of the chief architects of the growing technique that we now call "behavior modification."

But behavior mod wasn't quite enough. Like the other people we've met in this chapter, Bandura was concerned by the incompleteness of the traditional learning-theory model. The laboratory wasn't real life, and laboratory results on rats simply weren't sufficient to describe or explain human learning. If Skinner's rats, toiling away in their boxes, were to be maimed or bruised or killed for their mistakes (the way people would be if they depended on trial-and-error learning for such things as how to behave at a stop light or what to do on a hunting trup), we would see quite quickly that the trial-and-error model doesn't always work. Something was missing, and that something clearly had to do with the fact that people, unlike rats, can tell and show each other how to do things.

"The Right Circumstances"

Bandura, of course, had read the work of Miller and Dollard and Mowrer. So had a lot of other people. The difference was that Bandura took it seriously. Mowrer had said "Given the right circumstances, behavior can be facilitated, extinguished, or inhibited *without occurring*." It became Bandura's quest to explore that possibility: what were the "right circumstances"? How, exactly, did such facilitation and extinction and inhibition take place? Why, and when, and what did it all imply? Eventually, his contributions in this area were to become so extensive that it is impossible to discuss any aspect of social learning without using or being influenced by his ideas.

Let's look at those ideas.

According to the traditional learning model, what actually happens determines what is learned. In classical conditioning, a neutral stimulus gets associated with a non-neutral event: you may react negatively to the use of your full name, rather than your nickname, for instance, because, as a child, when you heard someone use your full formal name, you knew you were about to be punished. And in operant conditioning, what happens to you after you do something determines how likely you are to do it again. In both cases, it is what the learner experiences that is crucial for learning. How, then, can you learn from someone else—when you yourself don't experience anything except through the other person?

Except through the other person. That had to be the key. Vicarious experiencing. We've known about it intuitively for years. We know that you wince when a friend stubs a toe and that you smile when the friend opens a birthday present. But it had always been an awkward, left-over bit (more suitable for clinicians, perhaps, than for true theorists). Now the left-over bit can be the central block in the theory. The ugly duckling has suddenly turned into a swan!

Let's try it out and see how it works.

Rusty and Jenny are playing in their back yard, when a friendly dog, having escaped from the house next door, ambles up. Jenny, who is afraid of dogs, cries and runs inside. Rusty not only watches her reaction but also experiences it vicariously. He feels fear too in response to the dog-is-coming stimulus. It doesn't take many repetitions of this sequence to establish for him the same pattern of running and crying at the sight of a dog. Through classical conditioning, enhancement of behavior before that behavior actually occurs.

Another example. Jenny and Rusty again, and this time no dog. Rusty takes a bit of chalk and rubs it on the sidewalk, making a lovely white mark. Given that making a mark is reinforcing to him, he will probably do the same thing again. But Jenny is watching, and she vicariously experiences the same positive reinforcement. And, if more chalk is available, it's a pretty sure bet that she, in turn, will rub some on the sidewalk or on some other surface. "Rub chalk to make mark" has been learned, without the learner having to do it first "by accident" and experience the reward herself.

One important feature of both of these examples should be made clear at the outset: in neither of them did the imitating child repeat *exactly* the behavior of the model. Rusty probably cried at the dog in a different way than Jenny did, and he may have run to a different place for safety. Jenny didn't necessarily hold her chalk just as Rusty did, or rub it on the same surface, or make the same kind of mark. Observers—imitators—abstract from their model's behavior those features that are important and meaningful *to them,* and that's what is vicariously reinforced and learned. It is as if the observer makes a personalized template or pattern or blueprint of the observed behavior and later reconstructs the behavior in his or her own style, enlarging or expanding this or that aspect according to individual learning history. If the observer is very unfamiliar with the new behavior to be learned from the model or very unskillful at that sort of behavior, the first reproduction may bear only a slight resemblance to the original. Rusty may have drawn a well-executed portrait with his chalk, while Jenny produced a scribble. But, gradually, with repeated exposure to the model's behavior (and to the reactions of others and of the model to what has been done) and repeated opportunities to try for oneself and experience one's own consequences as well, the observer may reproduce the model's behavior with increasing accuracy. Or, more likely, may develop an interesting and complex blend of borrowed-from-model and developed-for-myself components that, taken together, become his or her own unique rendition of the modeled behavior.

But we're getting ahead of ourselves. Let's go back to Bandura, contemplating the how and why and when of imitating (or modeling, as he preferred to call it). One of the first things Bandura decided was that modeling wasn't just a single homogeneous blob of behavior but was, rather, a process that had a number of distinct parts or subprocesses. And that it made a lot of sense to begin by looking at these subprocesses one at a time, trying to find out when and why and how each of them occurred, before laying out rules for the whole thing.

Subprocesses of Modeling

Attention

The first subprocess in modeling is attending to the behavior to be modeled. I can't very well copy someone else's behavior if I didn't notice that behavior in the first place. This sounds so obvious as to be hardly worth mentioning, but it has some important implications. Having specified *attention* as a first part or necessary prerequisite to modeling, we can go on to ask about the kinds of things that affect attention. When is a person likely to attend to someone else's behavior, and when is one likely to ignore it? Or, to phrase the question a bit differently, what kinds of characteristics or situations of a model make the model's behavior likely to be attended to, and what characteristics or situations of the observer make that observer a better attender?

Discriminable Behavior. With regard to what sorts of behaviors are most likely to be attended to, an obvious answer is that we notice unusual or intense behaviors. A behavior that is different from what's going on around it, that is louder or bigger or brighter, is what catches our attention. Now, there's a fancy psychological term for such bigger or brighter or more different behaviors; we say that they are more *discriminable.* It's easy to tell them apart from the other things. The more discriminable a behavior is, the more likely we are to notice it and attend to it. (Up to a point, that is; a behavior may become so different that it is bizarre or socially unacceptable and therefore embarrassing to us, and we turn away and deliberately don't watch, to avoid discomfort. But that's an extreme situation that needn't trouble us here.) Note, though, that the level of discriminability of a behavior is not the same for every observer. To a nonskier, a group of people skiing down a hillside may all appear to be doing the same thing. To the untrained eye, no particular individual's behavior is discriminable from that of any other. But to a ski instructor, the fellow up there in the red warm-ups is skiing very badly and may have a serious accident any minute, whereas the woman in the blue jacket is obviously an expert. And the instructor might very well model either of these behaviors at some time in the future: red-warm-ups might be used in the instructor's next class as an example of what *not* to do (the behavior is modeled so as to be not-modeled by others, which is a rather peculiar example . . .) or blue-jacket's style on a christie might be deliberately imitated during the instructor's next trip down the hill. The point is that the more you know about some general area of behavior, the better you are able to discriminate (or the less you will be able to ignore) shades of difference within that area. Discriminability is a function of the observer as well as of the behavior being observed.

Arousal. Another important aspect of the observer is degree of alertness or arousal. The more alert and on your toes you are, the more likely you are to notice and attend to what is going on around you. Other things being equal, that is—you may be very "up" for some challenge, like a chess game or a difficult exam, and concentrate on it so hard that you're quite oblivious to everything else. But you will surely notice every motion, every gesture, of your chess opponent; such behavior will be highly discriminable to you in your alert state. A person's "arousal level" appears to be a physiologically based phenomenon, involving such things as adrenalin level and the like. People vary from day to day and from hour to hour in arousal level, from deep sleep, to drowsiness, to relaxation, to alertness, to hyperactivity. Along most of this range, the higher our arousal level, the more attentive we are to the behavior of others.

In summary, then, behavior that is highly discriminable and that occurs in the presence of aroused observers is most likely to be noticed and attended to and therefore is most likely to be modeled. Think about the implications of this statement. For example, why is it that kids seem to imitate "bad" peer behavior so much more often than they imitate "good" peer behavior? Well, which is more discriminable to other kids, throwing spitballs in class or working on your assignment? Which is more likely to create a state of heightened arousal in the observers, so they'll be even more likely to notice what you do next? You're right—and don't forget to duck, or you may get a spitball in the ear!

Retention

Attention is important in modeling, but it's not the whole show. It's necessary but not sufficient, as our egghead friends might say. You won't model a behavior that you didn't notice, but you also may not model lots of behaviors that you *do* notice. Another necessary part of the process is *retention.* To model a behavior, you've got to remember it after you notice it—at least long enough to do it yourself. So what sorts of things affect retention? Well, our old friend discriminability is surely one of the things. But our own behavior as observers is crucially important in determining how accurate this recollection is. Two observer behaviors, in particular, have a strong effect on how well we remember modeled behavior: *coding* and *rehearsal.*

Coding. Few if any of us can watch a model and then reproduce that model's behavior in every fine detail. We abstract certain things from the model's behavior, things that (for various reasons) are important or meaningful to us. These things are what we remember and can thus reproduce. Not only do we abstract aspects of the model's performance, but we also give them *labels* of some sort: Bill did this, then he did that, then he did the other thing. The labels are often verbal ones, but they may be visual. We may remember the crook of a tea drinker's finger or the tilt of an actor's head. But they are labels—ways of categorizing—and together they form a sort of coded representation of the behavior. To the extent that we abstract out the right things ("right" being, of course, subject to dispute according to who is doing the modeling and for what purpose and who is evaluating it), and code them accurately, we will have a better chance of modeling the behavior.

Rehearsal. *Coding* the model's behavior helps us to store it away until we need it. But sometimes we forget where we put that information, or, if we find it, we can't remember just what the code means or how to translate it back into behavior again. To keep that from happening, many observers engage in *rehearsal* of the observed behavior. Rehearsal may be overt or covert: we may openly practice the thing we are trying to learn from a model, or we may quietly adjust our posture or practice a muscle twitch when we think nobody's looking. Or we may rehearse *verbally:* "First he put the wood in the vise and tightened it up, and then he turned on the electric drill, and then he pressed the drill gently against the wood . . ."

Rehearsal helps us to remember what our coding means as well as to retrieve the code out of our memory when we need it. They are probably the two most important factors in determining whether the retention part of modeling will occur—and occur successfully.

Reproduction

Okay, I watched somebody do something, and I noticed what was done. I coded the behavior, and I rehearsed it, and I remember what it was. But I still may not choose to do it myself. Hence the next necessary step in modeling: *reproduction.* There's a big difference between learning what a model did and doing it oneself. In fact, learning why we do sometimes only one and sometimes both—why sometimes only acquisition and other times both acquisition and performance—may be the biggest problem of all in social-learning theory.

Part of the problem has been solved, and that part has to do with model consequences. Before Bandura got explicit about chopping modeling up into subprocesses, it was generally accepted that observers tended to learn from models who were rewarded for their behavior but not to learn from models who were not rewarded or who were punished. You let Zelda watch a model bashing away at a toy with a baseball bat, and then you either praise or punish the model for that behavior or ignore what was done. If Zelda saw the model praised for toy-bashing, she would be more likely, when left alone with toys and a bat, to bash a few toys herself than if she saw the model punished. So far, so good. We learn more from models who are rewarded for what they do. But it occurred to Bandura and his co-workers to ask all the children in such experiments if they remembered what the models did. And lo and behold! The kids *remembered* the behavior of the non-rewarded and the punished models just as well as they did that of the rewarded models. Apparently what happens to the model has little effect on retention but a great deal of effect on reproduction. We remember lots of things about people's behavior, but we reproduce those behaviors when we see that they have resulted in rewards for the model.

Reinforcement

Which leads us to the fourth part of the modeling process: *reinforcement.* And here's where it begins to get a little confusing. Because there are two sets of reinforcements: the ones that the model gets and the ones that the observer gets if and when the model's behavior is reproduced.

Vicarious Reinforcement. A reinforcement to a model has the same general sort of effect, though not as intense, as the same reinforcement would have had to the observer. That is, watching a model be positively reinforced for a behavior makes the observer more likely to reproduce that behavior, whereas watching a model be negatively reinforced makes the observer less likely to reproduce it. This is the notion of *vicarious reinforcement*—that an observer can share vicariously in the effect of rewarding or punishing a model's behavior. But before we go one step further, we have to elaborate on that last point. Watching a model get rewarded will act as a vicarious reward for the observer *so long as the "reward" would in fact be rewarding to him or her.* This seems to be the case in all operant-type social-learning situations. The consequences to the model are vicariously rewarding to me only if I would actually like to have that consequence myself. Watching a model speak up politely at the table and be rewarded by a second helping of sautéed snails would not be likely to enhance my own table manners, since I'm not rewarded by snails. In fact, it might have the opposite effect—I might vicariously experience the snail "reward" as a punishment and be *less* likely to speak politely as a result of watching the model.

At a conscious level, the mechanism at work seems to be that of watching what a model does and gets and then either reproducing that behavior or not, depending on whether we ourselves would like the same consequences. And, even when there appears to be only partial conscious awareness on the part of the observer, things seem to work pretty much the same way.

Vicarious Conditioning. It would be nice if this relationship held true for all kinds of social learning. But it doesn't. When we turn to the classical-conditioning situation—what is generally called "vicarious conditioning"—something else seems to be happening. Consider the following example. Laura is watching Bill being conditioned in a bell-and-shock experiment. Over and over, a bell is rung and Bill gets a shock. Just as we would expect, Bill soon comes to react to the sound of the bell alone in the same way he first reacted to the shock: muscle flexion, increased arousal, and so on. And, as we would also expect, Laura also comes to react emotionally to the bell. Vicarious conditioning has occurred; Laura's arousal level goes up when she hears the bell.

But now let's complicate things. Let's take a lot of Lauras and let them watch a lot of Bills. Some of them see Bill get a really hefty shock (one that they know would hurt *them*) and not seem to be bothered much by it. And some will see Bill get a very slight shock, one they know doesn't hurt much, but Bill appears to be really freaked out by it. Under which condition will we get the strongest vicarious conditioning in our Lauras? Unlike the operant situation, where the strength of the reinforcement has to do with how-would-I-as-observer-react, in vicarious conditioning it is the effect on the *model* that seems to be most important. Laura will condition faster, and stronger, when she sees Bill freaked out by a weak shock than when she sees Bill not bothered by a strong shock. Vicarious conditioning appears to involve feelings more than thinking; it taps into a more primitive process, one less under our conscious control. And, at that level, the whole cognitive trip of "would I respond that way myself" gets bypassed, and we pick up from the model a gut-level, empathic, emotional response.

Who Models Whom?

This emotional, noncognitive aspect of social learning is particularly interesting to students of personality. However one chooses to define personality, we must all agree that emotional reactions and reaction patterns are an important part of it. And, if Bandura and his colleagues are right, many of these patterns may be acquired through vicarious conditioning, through a vicarious experiencing of other people's reactions to stimuli. How many of our own feeling responses began this way? A fear of thunder storms, delight in the smell of baking bread, that faint tinge of sadness-loneliness that we sometimes experience at dusk. . . . Some of them may, to be sure, be the product of our own unique experiences: but surely many relate to feelings we thought—or, rather, felt—others were experiencing.

So far, it all seems pretty logical and straightforward. The problem comes when we take it out of the realm of theory and try to apply it to real-life situations. Here are Joe Blow and Jane Doe, walking along the street. They have seen literally hundreds of people in a week's time and were exposed to many more in the form of symbolic models on TV, in movies, and in books and magazines and newspapers. Whom are they going to imitate? Who will be a good model for them? Which of them, Joe or Jane, will be more likely to imitate—what makes one person easily influenced by others and another person an individualist?

Let's take the last question first: who makes a good observational learner? Or, to put it another way, what kind of person is most susceptible to the influence of a model? There is very little evidence at present to suggest that some "kinds" of people imitate more easily, or more often, than other kinds. Whether or not I model someone's behavior seems to be much more related to who that someone is, and what the consequences of that person's behavior are, and what sort of state or mood I'm in, than to any long-term personality traits of mine. One possible exception to this rule has to do with a conglomerate of related characteristics including such things as need for approval and low self-confidence and fear of failure. To the extent that I have a long history of failure, so that I've built up few expectations that I can succeed on my own, it is only reasonable that I'll be more likely to follow the lead of someone else, someone who is likely to be smarter and more capable than I am. Of course, even this sort of "personality package" fluctuates tremendously from time to time in any individual. Some days I feel pretty good about myself; I feel that I can handle things just about as well as the next person. When I'm in that sort of mood, I'm less likely to imitate others. But when I wake up to a dull, grey day, and I feel depressed and stupid, and I wonder what in the world there could be about me that would ever be interesting or useful to anyone else—in that state, I'll imitate just about anyone who seems to have things together.

Choosing a Model

Well, not really just about anyone—we have to qualify that a little. I'll imitate anyone who seems competent and confident and is accomplishing something that I want to accomplish. The consequences of the behavior to the model, both immediate and implied, are certainly important considerations. Along with asking who is likely to model, we have to ask "model what?" and "from whom?" They all go together; one doesn't make much sense without the others.

Congruence of Goals and Values. I'm most likely to model behaviors that are congruent with my own goals and values. If I see someone using a new teaching method and being successful with it (being rewarded), I'm very likely to imitate that person. On the other hand, I may read of a perfect bank robbery, one that made the robbers very rich with no chance at all of getting caught. But, even though these models too were highly rewarded, I'm not likely to imitate them; their behavior is not congruent with my goals and values.

Status. Also, in the opinion of most people a bank robber is not a very high-status person. And we all tend to model those who, in some sense or other, have a higher status than we have. The high status may relate to a very specific and narrow range of activities—the tennis pro may have an obnoxious personality but still have high status on the tennis court—or it may be a general sort of status—"that's a better (richer, more powerful, smarter, better looking) person and therefore worthy of respect." And of imitation. It's no accident that all those people in the advertisements who tell you to use Soaksitup on your armpits or to brush your teeth with Gnash are pretty and well dressed and enjoy a fantastic sex life. Advertisers know all too well who makes the best model, and they are careful to have such good models praise their products. (The virtual absence of Black people in commercial advertising up until very recently illustrates the same principle: for many Whites, who constitute the larger consumer group, Blacks were considered to be of lower status. Since people are less likely to imitate a lower-status model, a White model could be expected to sell more soap than a Black model.)

If you see characteristics or qualities that you value in another person, that person will have status for you. And the more status that person has, the more likely you are to imitate his or her behavior.

Once we accept this simple relationship, a number of interesting implications begin to peek around the corners. Such as: when you see a model get rewarded, what happens to the model's status for you? It's likely to go up, usually—the model really was smart, or agile, or sexy, or whatever, in order to have gotten that reward. And, if the model is punished, his or her status may go down. But be careful. What *you* see as a reward or a punishment may be quite different from what someone else sees as a reward or punishment. The teenager who is caught robbing a filling station and sent to jail is thereby punished. In the eyes of the law and of the law-abiding community. But to a group of buddies, such a person may be a hero. Wow! B.J. made the big time! A real "punishment," in their eyes, might have been to have sent B.J. home in the custody of parents. That would have been humiliating; it would have been treating B.J. like a child.

Models can reward and punish themselves, too. And these self-reinforcements can affect a model's status. How would you expect that relationship to work? Just stop reading, right there, and try to figure it out, before going any further. . . .

Okay, so when you see me reward myself for what I have done, does it make you more or less likely to imitate me? It depends, doesn't it, on who I am, and what you thought of me in the first place, and on what I rewarded myself for. There seems to be a kind of "rich-get-richer-and-poor-get-poorer" principle working in the case of model self-reward. If you don't think much of me to start with and you see me reward myself, you're likely to react with "What a nerd!" and think even less of me. And, if you see me punish myself (if, for instance, I struggle for some time over an exam, read it over to myself, and then wad it up and throw it on the floor), you think "Yep, what a nerd." But, if I start out with your respect, things are quite different. When I reward myself, you nod and say "There's someone who has it together, all right." Or if I struggle over the exam and then wad it up and throw it away, you respect me even more for having such high standards.

Now, after all this discussion, where are we? Are we any closer to being able to predict whom Joe Blow and Jane Doe are going to imitate? We think so. They are going to imitate those people whom they respect—who have qualities that Joe and Jane value. They are most likely to imitate them when they (the models) are doing things that fit in with Joe and Jane's own goals and when they are doing those things successfully. And Joe and Jane will be most likely to imitate when they feel least able to succeed on their own, when they've just experienced a string of failures, or when they're feeling depressed or in need of a pat on the back.

This is not to say, let us add very quickly, that only clods and failures imitate others. Very bright and very successful people are often skillful learners-from-imitation. They choose their models carefully and tend to be quite situation-specific in those choices: they imitate the follow-through of the golf pro or the accounting system of the fellow from H. & R. Block, but they don't start to "talk Southron" just because a Georgian was elected President or buy a particular kind of popcorn popper because some football star said to buy it.

So. Bright people, good learners, use models, and dull, insecure people use models. But bright people tend to use them constructively and selectively, whereas insecure conformers tend to imitate over a broader spectrum of behaviors and are therefore more likely to imitate the wrong things (or the right things in the wrong place or at the wrong time).

And Stir Gently

The story of social-learning theory is not really the story of one person's or a few people's ideas. Oh, it has its heroes, to be sure, and Albert Bandura is the super-hero. But mostly it's the story of following out the implications of ideas that have been around for quite a while, of individual bits and pieces stirred together to make a whole greater than the sum of its parts. So at this point we shall leave the sorting out of "who discovered what," and try to look at the whole thing and what it means for personality theorists as simply a body of ideas.

We've been talking about who models whom, or about what kinds of people model what kinds of people, as if these "kinds" of people really existed—as if people really had stable traits that could be appraised and evaluated by other people. This is perfectly consistent with many of the personality theories that we've looked at in this book. Certainly the whole "trait" approach to personality is founded on the assumption that such patterns are relatively stable and can be used to describe people—or at least could be if we could just find accurate ways to measure them. But there are others (there always are, aren't there?) who claim that trait stability is an illusion. That a person's behavior is simply not predictable without reference to what is happening to him or her right now. That, aside from some few characteristics having to do with innate mental ability (and even that may be suspect), what we call personality traits just aren't consistent at all. Traits are only stable in the sense that we *believe* they are: we believe that Mary is excitable or that John is shy, and we interpret their behavior in light of our belief. We see, in ourselves and others, what we expect to see. Variability can always be interpreted as caused by some external circumstance or as some "special" kind of unusual thing. If John is so shy, why was he running around at the party barking like a dog, with a lamp shade on his head? Well, he was with a group of people he knew really well, so he wasn't afraid of what they would think of him. But he's *really* very shy. Or, most of the people at the party were strangers, and that made him very nervous (because he's so shy, of course), and that's how John acts when he gets nervous. It's all because of his shyness, you know. Once you have decided that you, or someone else, "owns" a particular trait, then just about any behavior can be interpreted in light of that trait, so as to be consistent with it.

Interaction and Modeling

All of this means that it may not be so much the "traits" of the model and the observer that affect the amount of imitation but, rather, the beliefs that each of them has about what they and others are like. I assign certain characteristics to myself and to my acquaintances, on the basis of my (limited) experiences. And then I use or fail to use those acquaintances as models according to what characteristics I have assigned to them and to myself.

It's all very circular, isn't it? But that's really the way it has to be. When we talk about a relationship between two people, we have to go beyond how A feels about B and how B feels about A. The quality of a relationship is much more than just the sum of those two things. Each of them affects the other—what I think of you affects what you think of me. What you think I think of you affects how you will respond to me. The relationship between us is the sum and the product and the overall growing and flowing and being between us. Each of us will learn from the other, and the amount and kinds of learning will be a part of the relationship for us both.

We have only just begun to think about some of the subtle aspects of relationships and how they may affect social learning. For instance, what about the strength of the emotional bond between model and observer? We know that liking and respecting another makes that other a more likely model. What about loving someone? Being jealous of someone? When a model whom I dislike is rewarded, that's not rewarding to me; it makes me angry and uncomfortable to see that person get what I'd like to have. What happens to modeling theory under those circumstances—when the model is rewarded, for clearly competent behavior, but the observer experiences the whole thing as a negative reinforcement?

Model/Observer Similarity

We do know that there is a constant relationship between modeling and similarity (or perceived similarity) between model and observer. Up to a point, modeling is more likely if I, the observer, see you, the model, as similar to me. Not too similar, because, if we are just the same, then you are no better than I and why should I do as you do? But not too different, either. If your status is so much higher than my own, if you are so enormously different, then there's no use in my even trying to do what you do—either I won't be able to do it or I won't get the same rewards even if I do.

Similarity, though, isn't stable either. In fact, the very act of imitation affects how similar I feel toward my model. After I imitate someone, assuming that the imitation was successful, I like that someone better and feel more similar in other ways as well—I just see myself as more *like* the model. Which usually means that I am even more likely to imitate that model again in the future.

But the fact that imitation is occurring does not affect just the observer—the imitator. Imitation is an interactive process, at least in the real-world, you-and-me, two-person modeling situation. My observer behavior changes, both in terms of what I have learned from you and in terms of my attitudes toward you. But you, too, are involved. You are likely to know that you are being imitated, and this has an effect on your behavior and attitudes. In particular, you will tend to respond more positively to me if you know I am modeling your behavior. The saying "Imitation is the sincerest form of flattery" is very true; when we are imitated, we feel flattered. And it's hard not to respond positively to someone who says to us "I think so much of you (or of what you are able to do) that I want to imitate it myself."

This changing of the model's attitude toward the observer can have some fairly far-reaching effects. Consider the school situation, for instance. Some kids are good imitators; they learn well from demonstrated, now-do-this-the-way-I-do kinds of teacher behavior. Others may like and admire their teachers and copy the teacher's dress, speech, and hair style. The teacher is aware of this imitation and tends to be drawn (other things being equal) to those students who provide the positive feedback of modeling. And which student, then, is likely to get more attention, more "strokes," to sense more genuine pleasure on the part of the teacher in just being around that student? Why, the one who is the most successful imitator, of course. Which leads the student to imitate still more. The interaction is mutually rewarding by its very nature, and so it tends to perpetuate itself.

Reciprocal Imitation

Another interesting aspect of the interactive nature of imitation is the phenomenon known as *reciprocal imitation.* It has been shown that, in a wide variety of circumstances, when A imitates B and B is aware of the imitation, B has a tendency to imitate A. It's hard to say how much of the reciprocal imitation pattern is actually caused or triggered by the initial modeling and how much is simply a function of the generally positive relationship that exists between model and observer. But it does happen: when an observer has imitated a model, there is an increased likelihood that the model will in turn imitate the observer.

The implications here, too, are far reaching. Perhaps reciprocal imitation can help to explain the ways in which family members shape one another's behavior. Parents do a great deal of imitation of small children, especially in early speech behavior, and sustained reciprocal imitation patterns are common. An infant gurgles out something that sounds vaguely like a word; parent repeats it more closely in the form of the word; infant imitates parent; parent again says the child's word but pronounces it "better," and so on. Siblings, too, engage in a tremendous amount of modeling of one another. Theorists have expended a lot of effort to understand the modeling process itself; we might do well to look equally closely at the reciprocation of that modeling and how both the initial imitation and the reciprocation fit into the overall learning-from-each-other pattern in a given family group.

It is when we look at the combination of attitude change and reciprocal imitation, though, that we find the strongest sort of mutual growth and development. Between any two "pair-bonded" individuals (parent/child, sibling/sibling, teacher/student), there is a kind of need reciprocity, in which each member meets certain needs of the other. This is true at a biological level, as in the mother/infant pair where the child needs nourishment and the mother needs to suckle. And it's true at a psychological level: infant's need for cuddling meshes with mother's need to cuddle. So too with modeling: my need to be a model (to be respected and admired, to share my skills) fits with your need to learn (to acquire new knowledge, but also to respect, admire, love). As we each find the other meeting our needs, the bonding grows stronger. And the modeling process opens the way for new mutual need-meeting to occur—as I turn around and model *your* behavior, for instance, or as I encourage your imitation by rewarding it and thus meet other needs of yours, and by so doing meet my own need to be nurturant. . . . The cycle goes on and on, expanding infinitely.

Unfortunately, it can also work in the other direction. If a child fails to imitate his or her parents or a student his or her teachers, those parents' or teachers' needs will not be met. The parents or teachers will be unlikely to model reciprocally, and (perhaps more important) their attitudes toward the child or student will be less positive. They will become less nurturant, less supportive—poorer models. Which will make the child even *less* likely to imitate them. And so on, into an increasingly unpleasant forced interaction in which nobody feels satisfied and each is frustrated, puzzled, or hurt by the seemingly inexplicable behavior of the other.

Aggression and Modeling

One of the most thoroughly researched of all human behaviors is aggression. Psychologists, and philosophers before them, have never seemed to tire of speculating about what makes a person behave aggressively toward another. Closely related to aggression is competition and its opposite, cooperation. Cooperation, competition, aggression—do they form a continuum, with one shading gradually into another? Or is there some more complex, three-way relationship among them? Whatever the connection may be, it is difficult to discuss any one without at some point referring to the others. And it is extraordinarily difficult to discuss human behavior, and the human personality, without dealing with all three.

In view of the frequency of aggressive behaviors, and of the fascination that such behavior holds for us psychologists, it's not at all surprising that social-learning theorists too have studied it. In fact, aggression was one of the earliest of behaviors to be studied in terms of modeling. Bandura and his co-workers spent many, many hours exposing children to the sight of other children and adults behaving aggressively. Indeed, the image of someone flailing away at an inflated plastic, sand-bottomed Bobo doll has almost become the symbol of social-learning research!

Put in the simplest terms, Bandura and his students posed the question: "Does watching another person behave in an aggressive way cause the observer to increase his or her own aggressive behavior?" They let children of various ages watch adults or other children (or films or videotapes of the models) hit, kick, scream at, stomp on, and otherwise abuse toys and furniture in a playroom. Later, the young observers were left to their own devices in a similar playroom. And, sure enough, kids who saw the model behave aggressively tended to do a lot more hollering and hitting and destructive carrying-on than kids who spent the first part of the experiment coloring with crayons or watching slide pictures of Bambi. Apparently people—children, anyhow—can pick up aggressive behaviors just by watching somebody else behave that way.

Learning, Inhibition, and Disinhibition

Of course, that simple description doesn't really cover everything that's going on in the social-learning situation. It doesn't get at who makes the best (most effective) model for whom. Nor does it deal with the differences that occur in learning depending on whether the model is rewarded for behaving so violently. Even more important, it doesn't address the question of learning a new behavior versus *disinhibiting* an old one. Let's take a bit of a closer look at that question.

Say 5-year-old Sam watches an adult hitting a Bobo doll. Later on, left alone with the Bobo doll, Sam takes some healthy swipes at it himself. Can we really say that Sam has learned new behaviors from the adult and is now practicing them? That Sam didn't know how to hit things before and that now he does because the model showed him? It seems much more likely that Sam knew very well how to hit the Bobo doll (or his best friend, or his mother, or his little sister) before he ever came to the social-learning laboratory. But he also knew that such hitting was not to be done—at least not without good cause, or unless you could be sure of not getting caught. Hitting people had received strong and immediate negative reinforcement in the past, and Sam had also seen a great deal of actual and symbolic modeling of alternative ways of solving problems. The hitting behavior was not new; it had been in the behavior repertoire at one time but was now *inhibited.* The model's activities didn't teach Sam anything new but simply removed the inhibition. The model demonstrated that it's now all right to do the forbidden thing. Not only is that grown-up person doing it and not being punished, but also these people in the white coats are letting me watch! It's almost as if they're telling me to go ahead and do it too.

Much of the social learning of aggression, both in the laboratory and in the real world, is of this disinhibitory sort. We don't learn *how* to bash or kick something; rather, we learn that it's *all right* to bash and kick. We seem to learn that it's all right to *be aggressive,* to act on that impulse, at some very general level. The model may bash and kick, but eye poking and hair pulling may be the observer's response.

Consider a series of experiments done by Richard Walters and his associates in 1962. They asked college students to serve as "experimenters" in a "learning experiment." The students were to condition a "subject" by giving electric shocks, and they could choose how often the shock would be administered. Some of the students watched a highly aggressive film before serving as "experimenter," and some didn't. And—you guessed it—those who saw the aggressive film gave many more shocks to their "subjects" than those who didn't. In spite of the fact that the film had nothing at all to do with giving electric shocks. Whether you give the credit to disinhibition, or arousal, or what-have-you, the simple fact remains: exposing people to the sight of aggressive behavior resulted in increased aggression on the part of the observers.

Re-Inhibition of Aggression

But does it work the other way? Can we re-inhibit (create more inhibition of) aggression by letting our observer watch a model be punished for such behavior? If disinhibition comes about because the observer sees that the behavior is "all right," why not punish the model and thus tell the observer that the behavior is not all right but is all wrong? It ought to work that way, and it would be nice if it did. But it doesn't. To be sure, if we let Sam watch us punish the model for hitting the Bobo doll and then watch what Sam does, his behavior will be exemplary; no hitting, no kicking, none of the things that the model got punished for. As long as we are watching. But if we go away and leave the observer alone—whammo! Bobo had better look out, because he's going to get it. Punishing the model for aggression seems not to convey "aggression is not good" but, rather, "aggression is okay but don't let so-and-so see you doing it."

Learning Cooperation

Aggression, it seems, is peculiarly suited to being learned in a social situation. If we think back to those characteristics that make for good social learning, we can see why: aggressive behavior tends to be intense and thus easily discriminable; it tends to create arousal on the part of both participants and observers. Small wonder that, with the opportunity to imitate either an aggressive or a cooperative person, an observer more often chooses the aggressor.

What about cooperation then? Do those of us who believe in cooperation, behave cooperatively, and hope that others may follow our lead have any chance at all?

Most of the research on modeling, competition, and cooperation has been done in decidedly artificial laboratory situations. Participating in a silly psychology experiment is only a tiny, tiny fraction of someone's total experience. Likewise watching someone else in an experiment. So it really wouldn't be reasonable to expect such an experience to have a tremendous impact on one's overall tendency toward competition or cooperation—on one's personality. But—and it's a very big but—people watch models behaving cooperatively or competitively in all sorts of other situations. And, if we learn to cooperate or compete in a laboratory experiment partly through watching a model (which seems to be the case), then why not assume that we learn cooperation or competition in other situations through watching other models? After all, where did that "set" or style that people bring to the psychological laboratory or any other life situation come from in the first place? Partly from simple S-R learning, to be sure, but also partly through seeing and hearing about other people cooperating and competing, successfully and unsuccessfully.

If it were just a matter of providing models of successful cooperators and of unsuccessful competitors and aggressors, we could feel pretty comfortable about bringing up a whole generation of cooperative people. Unfortunately, we don't often get to start with our observers, our potential imitators, at the very beginning. People—kids—see lots of models who aren't intending to be models but are just living their lives as best they can: parents, teachers, peers, the ubiquitous TV. And many of these models are competing. We live in a competitive society. Many of them are aggressive. Our society (especially as portrayed on television) is pretty aggressive. It's very likely that most kids see successful competitive and aggressive models (and notice them; remember what we learned about attention as one of the subprocesses of modeling) more often than they see successful cooperative models. The dice seem somewhat loaded against cooperation.

When we consider a person who already tends toward a competitive orientation and think about what might be accomplished by showing that person a cooperative model, the loading of the dice becomes even more apparent. It works like this: people who are competitive tend to think that everyone else is competitive, too. Everybody is the same; they're all trying to get ahead; they're all looking out for number one. Cooperators, on the other hand, know jolly well that there are competitors in the world. They know that there are at least two sorts of people: those who prefer to cooperate and those who would rather compete.

In a situation where everyone is more or less like everyone else, any observable differences in behavior must be due to differences in the environment. Competitors, believing that everyone else is also a competitor, don't recognize cooperation when they see it; the cooperating person is either stupid or has been forced by circumstances to behave that way. Cooperators, knowing that other cooperators as well as competitors do exist, can observe both kinds of behavior and make some sort of judgment about which works best. Competitors tend not to be able to do that, because they don't recognize noncompetitors. For them, the other kind of model simply doesn't exist.

Amazing, isn't it, that in spite of all this people do learn to cooperate?

And frightening, when we think of all the models of competition and aggression that people, and especially kids, get exposed to every day.

TV as a Model

Bandura's work first came into prominence when he took a stand against television violence, maintaining that violent behavior shown on TV can and does affect the way people act in their everyday lives. The many studies carried out over the last 15 or so years leave little doubt that Bandura was right. People do imitate, often in very subtle ways, the behavior of television characters. Moreover, we have discussed in these last few paragraphs a number of reasons why TV modeling is likely to be selective. And the selection is pretty negative. We (and our children) will be most influenced by the most intense behaviors, and we are much more likely to notice and imitate competitive and aggressive behaviors than cooperative behaviors.

It seems highly unlikely that television violence will go away. Crime and conflict are more "newsworthy" than peaceful resolutions of problems; destroying cars and people appears to sell more products than putting them back together again. How, then, shall we provide countermodels? How can we expose people to other, more constructive forms of behavior and do so in such a way that the observers will notice and be attracted to those constructive forms? There doesn't seem to be any answer to that question, not yet. But we had better try to find one, if we want our society to survive. Individual competition and aggression, after all, are closely related to group competition and aggression. A child in a fistfight is not all that different from a nation at war. The older generation discovered and popularized a technology that makes models of fighting and war more available and immediate than they have ever been before. The new generation faces the challenge of somehow de-fusing those models—before they de-fuse us all.

Words and More Words: Language

That the use of language is a fundamental characteristic of human nature is a truism. The uniqueness of humans in using language has been pointed out by psychologists down through the ages (though it is currently being challenged by research on chimpanzees and on porpoises). Humans may not, in fact, be the only species capable of communicating among themselves through language. But it is indisputably true that humans would be something other than human if they did *not* have language. Our ability to communicate with one another about ideas is the basis of all of our social life. Which means society, which means culture, which means *peopleness.* Other animals do communicate: they growl in warning at a violation of territorial rights, or they signal readiness to mate by visual and verbal displays. But, so far as we know, nonhuman communication patterns deal with concrete, here-and-now phenomena. Wolves may fight over boundaries, but they don't negotiate them through discussions involving hypothetical future governments. Birds cooperate in nest building, but they don't quibble over where the nest should be situated or how large it should be. Only people are able to talk about what was, what will be, or what might have been. Only people can create conceptual worlds, parallel to but different from reality, and then share those worlds with one another.

Symbolic Modeling

This ability to create and describe something different from what is now is what makes social learning something more than just another special instance of learning that must be accounted for. With language, social learning takes on a pervasiveness and a richness that overshadows just about every other kind of learning that one can engage in. Symbolic modeling—the imitation of behaviors not directly observed—comes about largely through language. And language is everywhere. Consider your own recent experience: for how many hours out of the last 24 were you awake? Probably around 16, right? Now, during how much of that time were you not being exposed to language? Talking with friends, sitting in class, watching TV, reading a book—doesn't leave much out, does it? Oh, you spent several hours listening to classical music? Okay, maybe—just maybe—that was a language-free experience. But maybe not. What were you thinking about while you listened? Whatever thoughts you remember, and a large portion of those you don't, were structured in terms of language. And were probably influenced by language behaviors of other people. And are, in turn, capable of influencing you. The language environment with which each of us is surrounded is partly of our own making: we produce internal verbal symbols that can and often do serve as models for our behavior.

Are you convinced that language is important? That it's especially important in the context of social learning?

Imitation, Reinforcement, Shaping

Then let's go right to the beginning: where does it come from? We aren't going to get into the fascinating question of how language originated among homo sapiens. In the first place, it's not terribly relevant to our main concern, and, in the second place, nobody knows. There have been lots of theories, bearing such interesting names as the "yum-yum" theory and the "ding-dong" theory, about how our human talkativeness got started, but, since there seems to be no way to prove or disprove any of them, they remain simply speculations.

We can and do know something about how an individual child, born into a verbal human environment, learns to talk. But we know less than we used to think we knew. It seemed so obvious, a few years ago, that the key was imitation. Could you imagine a child (or anyone else) learning to speak unless there were speakers to imitate? It simply couldn't happen. That's why "Norwegians learn Norwegian; the Greeks are taught their Greek." We imitate the language, the speech patterns, even the accents and inflections of the people we grow up with. More recent work in linguistic analysis has shown, though, that things are much less simple than had been thought. A great deal of our ability to process symbols, the so-called "deep structure" of language, is wired in, genetically transmitted, common to all humans no matter what language they speak. Imitation accounts for vocabulary and little more.

But, even when we restrict ourselves to the modeling of vocabulary, the process is a fascinating one. Again, it's not a one-way kind of imitation. Indeed, the imitative process may well begin with parent imitating child. We referred to this process earlier in the chapter; let's think about it again. Picture a tranquil domestic scene. Baby Charlie is sitting in his playpen, waving a toy about and drooling down his chin, while Mother stirs a pudding on the stove. Is Mother likely to lean over and, out of the blue, say "Come on, Charlie, say 'ma-ma' "? No, it happens just the other way. Charlie babbles on and accidentally produces something that Mother (fondly, and by using just a *little* imagination) hears as "ma-ma." Then she leans over and says, " 'Ma-ma'—that's right—'ma-ma.' Say it again, Charlie—'ma-ma.' " Charlie, thus encouraged, may parrot back the sounds, and Mother again repeats them, and so it goes.

Reciprocal imitation, reinforcement, shaping—these are the processes that characterize the earliest speech-like behaviors among infants.

Gradually the child comes to realize that the sounds he or she is producing have utility. They achieved something. They *mean* something. The genetic, wired-in capability interacts with the social-learning process to create that incredibly complex phenomenon, verbal communication. There is probably no great moment of insight, no "Aha, this thing that I do with my breath and my throat is a signal or symbol for that person." Rather, there is a gradual awareness that when I make this sound it is somehow the same as when someone else makes the same kind of sound.

Egocentric Speech

The "someone else" notion brings us into head-on collision with another early speech phenomenon, that of *egocentrism.* Actually, egocentrism is not limited to speech behavior; it is a fundamental quality of childhood thought. But it is perhaps easiest to observe in speech. The young child's notion of "someone else" is primitive at best. At first, for the infant, the whole world is an extension of "me." The infant has not learned to discriminate between what is part of the self and what is not. Gradually, the child comes to learn that certain parts of his or her environment are self and are (more or less) under personal control. That object at the end of the long thing that hooks on to a roundish thing somewhere below my eyes is not just a hand; it is *my* hand. I can make it move when I want to, and I hurt when it bangs into the bars of the crib. Those bars, in contrast, aren't under my control; they aren't part of me. At this point, the world is simply divided into "me" and "not-me." Then finer discriminations begin to be made: things that move and things that don't; things that are good (warm, food-giving) and things that aren't; and so on. Still later comes a vague awareness that "people" are a very special class of things-in-the-world. For one thing, "people" talk—they not only make noises, but they also respond to noises from me and other people.

Awareness of "people" as a special category and of "people" as "other creatures like myself" are two different stages. And it is when the child has realized that these other-creatures-like-me do exist, and can be interacted with, that we see evidence of what is called egocentrism. For the just-like-me creatures *are,* to the child, just like itself. There is no awareness that others have their own separate existence, live their own separate lives, have their own ways of seeing and reacting to the world. As far as the child is concerned, others share the same thoughts, perceptions, and feelings. They must, because the child has not yet realized that there is any other way to think or perceive or feel. His or her only experience is of self, and so the self must be projected onto everyone else. And the child's speech reflects this projection. In trying to communicate with others, the child assumes that they know where he or she is coming from, that they share his or her own immediate experiencing. Indeed, the word *communicate* is probably misleading in this context; for why communicate with someone who already knows what you know and feels as you feel? It would be just like talking to yourself.

And that, essentially, is what egocentric speech is: the child talks to himself or herself, even when he or she appears to talk to others. Egocentric speech may be a way of gaining rewards and of manipulating the environment, but it isn't a sharing of ideas. It isn't what you and I know as communication.

Toward Communication

But, in a strange sort of paradox, it is probably through such egocentric speech that the child begins to grow out of egocentrism. It may be, of course, that one is genetically programmed to emerge from this stage at a certain point in one's development. We shall never know if children would do so in the absence of communication, because the child who grows up in such a communicationless environment (if he or she survives at all) is so multiply deprived that it would be impossible to isolate the effects of speech deprivation from everything else that goes with it. We do know that the experience of being misunderstood must teach the child that such a thing is *possible.* And, if I can be misunderstood, then the one who misunderstands me must not share (entirely) my perceptual and cognitive world. That person must be different. The just-like-me is not, after all, exactly like me. I have to "say it again," louder, more clearly, maybe in different words, to make someone else understand. And thus, haltingly and painfully, communication begins.

What we see, in this growing communication pattern, is an interaction of stimulus-response learning, imitation, and biological capability. As in every other aspect of human learning and growth, learning to talk involves trying something and, if it works, being more likely to try it again in the future. And it also involves trying it the way we saw or heard someone else doing it. We graft imitable patterns onto our innate speech capacities. Not just in the early and fumbling attempts of the infant but throughout life—"try it out" and "watch a more skilled performer" are inextricably blended. The school-age child picks up the vocabulary of his or her peers; the college student learns terminology and phrasing and speech/silence rhythms from the college environment; the adult learns the jargon and the logic of the social and work milieu.

Perhaps this ongoing process is most clearly seen in the acquisition of accents of inflections or dialects. It is not only the small child just learning to talk who picks up the soft drawl of Alabama or the clipped speech of New England. Anyone, of any age, exposed to a particular dialect, will find his or her own speech modified. We learn to talk as those around us talk. To some extent, specific external rewards may be involved in this process; we may modify our inflections in order to be more easily understood (and thereby rewarded). But this kind of reward is surely only a small part of what is going on. The greater part is imitation, conscious or unconscious. I borrow your pronunciation of a word because I like the way it sounds when you say it. I learn to say "in hospital" instead of "in the hospital" because "in hospital" has a British ring to it and I like to sound British. Or I find myself slipping into a particular regionalism because—because why? "Because everyone else says it that way" is really no answer, unless we accept the idea that there is a "natural" tendency to do as others do. And, in considering language behavior, it's often hard to find any other explanation than that.

Language and Thought

The learning of language and the role of imitation in the acquisition of speech would be no more than an interesting example of the interaction of modeling and innate characteristics were it not for the role that language plays in shaping all sorts of other behavior. When we think, we think in words. Linguists have argued for years (and are still at it) about whether the genetically wired-in patterns of thought, common to all humans, cause language to develop as it does or whether the language structure that we use is the "cause" of the way we think. Whichever comes first, it is clear that language and thought do bear a reciprocal relationship to each other. To an important extent, the words we use and the ways we string those words together determine how we are able to see and understand and think about things. We not only imitate other people's behavior directly; there is also an indirect connection because the way they (we) use words (which we acquire from each other) influences our very thoughts and perceptions.

Let's take a closer look at that idea. It's an important one. As infants begin to sort out and make sense of their world, they learn to categorize. Every single thing in their environment can't be unique and kept track of separately; things have to be put into groups. There are foods, and things to play with, and "no-no's," and people, and so on. Some of the groups overlap, and most of them can be further divided into subgroups, but that's all right; we can deal with that sort of complexity later. The important point is that we do generalize, and we do put labels on things that reflect our generalizations. And the labels in turn affect the ways in which we deal with those things from there on out. Once Beth decides that the vase on the coffee table is a "no-no," she will treat it differently than she did when it was a pretty thing to play with. When she is somewhat older, her categorization of a particular teacher as a reactionary or a communist or a bore or an egghead will affect her dealings with that teacher.

The labels we put on things do affect our behavior. And where do those labels come from? Often (theorists disagree on the extent of social influence here, but its importance can't be denied) from other people, through modeling. Beth the child is not likely to label the vase on the coffee table as a "no-no" without some parental intervention. Beth the student has acquired the reactionary/communist/bore/egghead vocabulary through direct or symbolic modeling and has probably learned from other students the accepted way of applying those labels to her teachers. Over and over, we borrow labels from others and stick them onto parts of our own personal world. And then the labels tell us how to see and use the things we've attached them to.

Listening as Communication

Speech, as we have seen, may occur with or without communication. The egocentric speech of the child does not communicate much to a listener, nor does the child intend it to. Even as adults, we often use other people as echo chambers rather than as part of a communication channel; we tell them something mainly in order to hear how it sounds to us. True communication, in which you and I share an idea that only one of us had before, is an even more fertile field for imitation. It is in true communication that *internal* behaviors can be acquired through modeling. By listening to what you say or reading what you have written, I can take on your ideas, your beliefs, your attitudes, your labels.

Listening. Like every other aspect of communication, it is both a vehicle for learning and a thing to be learned in and of itself. The unskilled listener (or reader) is likely to misperceive, to hear things wrong, to misunderstand, and thus to lose the chance to model the idea that is really being presented (or may model something that *wasn't* said or intended, which is perhaps more serious). Moreover, this unskilled listener will gradually get fewer and fewer opportunities to model verbally presented ideas (at least in a "live" conversation), because he or she has not learned how to encourage someone else to talk. Good listening, as well as good talking, involves sending messages: by facial expressions, gestures, and subvocals (ummm? wow! uh-huh . . .), the listener lets the talker know that communication *is* taking place. If you doubt this, try an experiment. The next time you find yourself in conversation with someone, deliberately suppress all your listening responses. Put on a wooden face, keep your hands in your lap, don't make a sound. It will take only a few seconds to kill the conversation—dead.

We learn to listen through a variety of processes, not the least of which is imitation. We watch other people listen—to others and to us. We pick up their behaviors. We learn to nod, to smile, to say uh-huh. Some listener patterns are fairly stable and universally accepted; others are "fads" that come and go, spreading with remarkable rapidity from person to person and then gradually dying out. An example of this kind of fad is the use of the word "wow" as a listening response. "Wow" probably got its start among the drug culture and was picked up by a whole generation of teens and young adults; for a while it was an extremely common way for a listener to convey "I'm right with you, I hear what you're saying, and I'm very interested in it and in you." The "wows" seem to be dying out now, to be replaced by—who knows? But whatever it is, we can be sure that it will spread through imitation.

In the speaking-and-listening sequences that we call communication, very few truly new ideas are passed from one person to another. Feelings may be shared and reinforcements handed back and forth, but beyond that what occurs is less one person acquiring a new idea or meaning from another than it is one person shuffling through old ideas and rearranging them to accommodate the message of another. As Mowrer points out, when we communicate with someone, we both must know what the words mean. If I talk to you about a "mugwick," we will do very little communicating unless you already have some idea of what a mugwick is. If you have never heard of a mugwick, I may explain that it has four legs, is about the size of a bread box, and is rather shaggy and reddish brown. That message will not communicate anything to you unless you know the meaning of "shaggy" and "bread box" and "legs." If you understand those words, then your meanings will be shifted around and rearranged; and you are almost sure to add your own personal embroidery to what you have been told. Think about that "mugwick." What sort of creature do you picture? What if I now add that a mugwick has a large stinger at the end of its tail? Does your mental picture change somewhat? But nothing that you were told in that original description was incompatible with the fact of a stinger. We rearrange our own meanings as a function of the things we learn from others, but we add to and elaborate the new arrangements. And often it's hard to tell where the original communication leaves off and the elaboration begins. We learn from others, to be sure, but in a very real way we construct that learning ourselves. This sort of construction is perhaps more apparent and easier to illustrate by example in language-mediated imitation, but it is no less true of situations where we model behaviors more directly.

Back to Symbolic Modeling

What *is* unique about language-mediated modeling is that it allows one person to model another's symbolic, rather than actual, behavior. I can *tell* you how to write a term paper or change a baby's diaper or build a bomb, without *showing* you how. You can imitate "me" without my ever having actually done the thing you are imitating. Now the "do as I say, not as I do" technique has not been notably successful in rearing children. But our ability to set up idealized models of human conduct, models that we can emulate some of the time, or in less than perfect ways, has certainly been a major factor in the ability of our species to develop cultures. It has allowed us to bootstrap ourselves up from savagery and anarchy into a society that has laws (however imperfect) and schools (however inefficient). It has allowed us to create symbols of behavior to which we can aspire, behavior that is "better" in some way or another than that which we are capable of actually carrying out.

Of course, the reverse is true as well. Language allows us to symbolize undesirable behaviors, too—behaviors that we might, at some level, like to indulge in but manage to restrain ourselves from. Our talking about them serves as a symbolic release, but it also provides models of those behaviors for others. And so we arrive, via another route, back at the problem of violence and aggression and competition.

Communication and Empathy

Speech, and the symbolic modeling in speech of destructive behavior, may be one way in which that behavior is spread. But speech and symbolic modeling may also be the antidote to the spread of violence. Humans, in communicating with each other through language, arouse in themselves the response they call for in others. The flow goes both ways, and it's hard (and not particularly useful, anyhow) to figure out which direction comes first. It suffices to say that, as we communicate, we share feelings about the subject of the communication. This phenomenon is called empathy, "feeling-with." As I share a thought, an idea, with you, I feel with you your response to that thought; and you feel with me my response to it and to you. Empathy makes it difficult to behave destructively toward another person. I don't want to cause you pain if I must share that pain. To the extent, then, that we can teach people to be sensitive to their empathic responses, we can begin to replace destructive with constructive responses, competition with cooperation, aggression with more conciliatory forms of interaction. And this teaching will—must—involve modeling.

Language is learned partially through social imitation and is the vehicle for social imitation. It is both effect and cause of behavior. It reflects personality, and it acts upon personality. In language, as in no other aspect of behavior, we find a great coming-together of symptom and substance, of that which was and that which may come to be. It is the very stuff from which personality is inferred and upon which it is built.

And Back to Personality

It isn't really hard, as we have seen, to demonstrate that one's behavior, habits, speech, and even ideas are affected to a very great degree by social-learning processes. There are some people who would argue that, having demonstrated this, we have by definition demonstrated the relationship between social learning and personality, that personality *is* the accumulation of a person's behavior, habits, speech, and ideas. For many of us, though, that isn't quite right. We have a sense that personality must be different from, or more than, or underlying the collection of things we say and do and think about. My personality must be more basic than that; it is my essence, my be-ness.

It's at this point that we're likely to get uneasy with the connection between personality and social learning. Am I to assume—to admit—that this basic, essential be-ness that defines me to myself was somehow acquired through copying other people? That could be a real put-down, pretty destructive to my need for uniqueness and my sense of self-worth.

Notice that I said "could be." It's true that we do acquire much of our individual be-ness through various forms of imitation. But we do it selectively, creatively, and the fact that social learning has an important role in the process of personality development detracts not at all from the uniqueness of each personality.

Values, Perception, and Self-Awareness

In the final section of this chapter on social learning, we're going to develop three topics: values, perception, and self-awareness. Each of these topics is particularly important in a consideration of personality.

Values represent a constant stratum that affects our reaction to the world around us and shapes or reflects (depending on where you want to start) our personality. Perceptual processes, in an even more basic sense, stand at the gateway to self; through them we let the world in, and they shape our very thoughts. Finally, self-awareness is our own sense of our be-ness. It is my best guess, at any moment in time, as to what my own personality is like. As such, it is worth exploring.

Values. The values we hold are the things we believe in, not only with our head, but with our gut. They are, when the nonessentials are cleared away, the things that give meaning to our lives. In this sense they provide a foundation to our personality; they give us some kind of consistency and continuity in time. They provide a link between past and future and allow us to define ourselves in terms of what is and will continue to be important to us.

So where do our values come from? (You know what's coming; you don't even have to guess. . . .) If we concede that a value involves more than a learned-from-personal-experience response to a stimulus pattern, then there's really only one explanation that makes any sense: we acquire our values vicariously, from other people. This idea is nothing new, nor is it the exclusive property of social-learning theorists. Freud talked about the introjection of parental values as a part of the formation of the superego. He didn't discuss the mechanism by means of which this introjection comes about (he really couldn't, in terms that would be compatible with today's psychology, because he didn't have access to all we know about learning), but it seems clear that he must have had some kind of social learning, some kind of imitative process, in mind.

As we interact with others or watch others interact among themselves (not just "live" but in books and on television), we learn what they think is worth having or worth doing. And we observe the consequences, to them, of behaving according to those values. We borrow, and try on, this or that value to see how it fits us. People who are brought up in a value-homogeneous environment, where everyone is pretty much in agreement about what is important and how life should be lived, usually take on those values wholesale, with very little questioning. They are frequently surprised and confused when, later in life, they run across people in situations that challenge those unquestioned values, and they may throw out their childhood beliefs altogether and exchange them for a new and different set. And feel angry and shortchanged because they were so "misled" or isolated as children. In contrast, people who are exposed to a variety of values early in life may develop some real skill and comfort in the process of analyzing value systems, looking for consistency, tailoring this or that belief so that it fits with what they have already made a part of themselves.

Values are acquired not only from parents and from other significant adults in one's childhood. The society we live in presents its values through a multitude of channels, with varying degrees of subtlety. In schools, in the news media, in reading (everything from comic books to Shakespeare), we are presented with behavioral consequences that we experience vicariously. It was no accident that the Motion Picture Association of

America for years insisted that, no matter what happened at the beginning or in the middle of a film, the "good guys" had to win in the end. Or that feminists are very concerned with the kinds of values vis-à-vis male and female roles that are presented in school textbooks. These are examples of media from which we acquire our value systems, often without conscious awareness that we are doing so. The factors determining which values we select from a whole array of possibilities are the same as those governing our choice of whom to imitate in other sorts of behaviors: relative status, perceived consequences of the behavior, our own state of confidence or comfort, and so on. The rules are the same, but acquiring values has more profound and long-lasting consequences than do most of the instances in which we imitate a simple behavior that we have seen in someone else.

Perception. Another thing that we learn from others is how to see what goes on around us. Now this doesn't mean that we have to be taught to tell one shape from another or to distinguish between red and green. Psychologists used to think that the newborn infant couldn't, in fact, do these things and had to learn how during its first few months of life. William James, the father of North American psychology, talked about the "blooming, buzzing confusion" that made up the infant's perceptual field. We know better than that now; in fact, babies are able to sort out various kinds of perceptions at a quite remarkably early age. There is evidence, for instance, that babies less than a month old can tell the difference between a straight-ahead view of a human face and a profile view of a face and may even prefer to look at a smiling rather than a frowning face!

But our culture—the people around us—does teach us what to notice and what not to notice. What is worth paying attention to and what isn't. We've already commented on the enormously important role that language plays in all this: simply by giving something a name we have implied that it is worth differentiating from all the other similar somethings in the world. But even beyond the influence of language itself, we learn vicariously how to see the world. Jan learned from her father, for instance, how to see and experience snow. He was a rural mail carrier, and, from his comments about the weather, she learned to notice whether the snowfall would make for difficult driving and blocked roads. She began to be able to enjoy and appreciate snow only when it fell lightly on Saturday evening, so that the county roads could be clear by Monday morning. The feeling of guilt that she learned to experience whenever she enjoyed playing in deep snow lasted well into her adulthood and is still present as a vague and faint uneasiness during the winter season.

It is when we turn to the effects of social learning on people-perception, though, that the implications of social learning for personality really begin to multiply. Think about it. We learn, vicariously, from other people an enormous number of things that have profound effects upon our personality. What we learn, and when, and from whom, is determined in part by our perception of the models available to us. But these perceptions themselves are governed by the ways we have learned to look at people. Consider 6-year-old Andy, for example, who has been reared in a family of racial bigots and who now discovers himself in a first-grade class with a Black teacher. If he is to use that teacher as a social model, he will pay a price of great conflict; he has been taught to perceive Black people as "beneath" him and not worthy of imitating. To a less intense degree, perhaps, we all respond to the characteristics of potential models in ways that we have learned (in part) from other models. Thus, the influence of a model doesn't stop with what that model teaches me; it extends to affect the things I might be able to learn from other models.

Learned ways of looking at people are especially important because we are so often unaware of what we are doing as we sort out perceptual cues. The kinds of generalizations about people that we pick up as children are seldom expressed explicitly. Marsha, for example, doesn't like fat people or New Yorkers. But her parents probably didn't tell her "all fat people are lazy and incompetent" or "you should never trust anyone with a New York accent." Rather, she overheard various sorts of comments about specific people and constructed her own generalizations, which may or may not have reflected the actual beliefs and perceptions of her parents. And not only did she construct them herself, with varying degrees of accuracy, but she very likely did so unconsciously. The negative reaction to fat people or New Yorkers would not be explicitly applied to a person: he's fat, so he must be stupid; or she's from New York, so I can't trust her. Instead, Marsha responds to the person without ever really considering why or what it is that she is responding to. Neither the fat nor the New York person is likely to serve as a model; they are automatically canceled out as potential models (or at least relegated to the ranks of less desirable models) by a perceptual-selection process that is completed before she has a chance to consider whether or not it is valid.

Self-Awareness. To any individual, the most intrusive and intense aspect of personality is one's own sense of self—the ongoing sense of unity and awareness that allows one to be and to feel the same person, in spite of changes in mood and circumstance, from one day to the next. Again, though, we must ask where this sense of self comes from. How do we learn who we are? Or who we think we are?

George Meade, a sociologist who has had a strong influence on many psychologists' understanding of the nature of the self (we'll be formally introduced to him in Chapter 11), has suggested that one's concept of self—one's sense of who he or she is—comes from a perception of what others think of him or her. This "looking-glass self," in which I find myself reflected in others' views of me, has two stages. In the first stage, I am aware of the attitudes and beliefs about me held by specific individuals, and I organize these attitudes into some coherent structure that I know as my "self." In the second stage, I further organize and generalize those beliefs and attitudes as if they belonged to some generalized other, some sort of construct of "this is how I appear to other people." Putting this into social-learning terms, we take on (imitate) not only other people's reactions to things and people but also those other people's reactions to us. If I believe that others respect, say, my ability to write books, I "imitate" that respect and incorporate into my self-image the notion of "respect-worthy writer." Or if I think people make fun of me because of my lack of will power, my self-image may be that of a lazy or wishy-washy person.

The things I reward myself for, too, depend on social comparison. I reward myself for (feel good about) things that I think others would reward in themselves or in me. I can feel proud of having jogged a mile if I remind myself how proud that fellow across the hall would be if *he* could have done the same thing. Much of our pleasure in or shame about what we do comes from imagining how some significant person would react to our having done it. And much of the guilt and pain that people feel about themselves comes from mistaken assumptions of this same sort: "What would they think if they only knew what I was *really* like!"

And again, like the ripples in a pond, the implications of modeling the assumed reactions of others go on and on. What I think you think about me becomes a part of what I think about myself; and this in turn helps to shape my further assumptions of what you think about me. My sense of self is an elaborate construction, built from bits and pieces of other people's reactions to me (filtered through my own perceptions) and cemented together by a myriad of social learnings acquired over the years.

Chapter Summary

This chapter has been much more "idea oriented" than "people oriented." At the beginning, we met a few learning theorists who started people thinking about the social aspects of learning: Miller and Dollard, with their different kinds of imitation, and Mowrer, who found a way to let feelings and emotions into the learning equations. But as soon as Albert Bandura walked onto the stage, with a whole cast of supporting characters (whose names didn't get on the program), the ideas took over.

As well they might.

What a can of worms we open when we take people out of the rat cages and away from the buzzers and shocks and let them interact with and learn from other people! What a host of new variables to contend with. Things get so complicated, so downright *messy.*

It's considerate of Bandura to chop the problem up for us, to help us to look at one part at a time. There's *attention* and what makes one person attend to what someone else is doing. *Rehearsal:* the effects of rehearsing and the ways in which we rehearse what we've seen. And *reproduction,* when and why someone is likely to reproduce a behavior noticed in someone else. And finally *reinforcement,* vicarious and direct, positive and negative. Put them all together, they spell ARRR; if you added Ghosts and Hobgoblins (which some traditional learning theorists very clearly accuse the social-learning people of doing), you'd have ARRRGH (which is the general reaction of many of those traditional learning theorists to social-learning theory).

We also talked about the kinds of *people who serve as models* and the kinds of *people who imitate* them. Who is likely to imitate whom.

And why. And when. Things like status and self-confidence and the difference between what "really" happens and what the observer thinks is happening. And how he or she feels about it.

And all those fascinating, never-ending complicated interactions between the observer and the model, in which each learns from and adjusts to and changes his or her feelings about the other.

The compelling thing about social-learning theory is that it has so many direct, immediate implications for all kinds of behavior. For short, one-shot interactions between two people and for the great social events like war and peace. The child who learns to crunch a Bobo doll grows up to be an executive who crunches competitors. Students in a laboratory may parallel the strategies of the Joint Chiefs of Staff in a high-level Pentagon meeting. The question of "shall I cooperate or shall I compete?" is asked at every level of social interaction, and the answer derives in large part from the social learnings of those who must answer it.

The factor that most complicates the whole social-learning picture is, of course, *language.* If all we had to worry about was whether A exhibited the same behaviors that A observed in B, social learning would be relatively simple. And relatively uninteresting. But let language in, and now we've got *symbolic modeling.* I do what you say. Or what I think you say. And what I think you say is determined by the way I use *my* language, which in turn is determined by what I've heard other people do with words. Behavior begets speech, and speech begets behavior, and it's the same kind of chicken/egg problem all over again.

And don't forget *listening,* which is also a kind of communication.

Communication. You might say that's what social learning is all about. How we communicate our learnings to each other. How I learn by communicating with you. What the fact of my having learned from you communicates to you about me and about yourself. Because we can communicate ideas, we can learn in different ways and learn different kinds of things, than do creatures that don't share abstractions with one another. We can learn more, we can learn faster and more efficiently—and we can learn wrong.

The kinds of learning that personality theorists are most interested in, though, don't have as much to do with "right" and "wrong" as they do with "same" and "different." Personality theorists try very hard to be value free, especially when they are talking about values. Who is to say whether the things I believe to be good really are good? Whether my idea of "right" and "wrong" is any "righter" than yours? What we can do, and what social-learning theory helps us to do, is trace back where those ideas came from. From whom did I acquire my good/bad's, my right/wrong's? Why did I get them from this person and not from that one? How have I adjusted and elaborated them through my life, and who has served as a model for that adjusting and elaboration?

Values, perception, and *sense of self* are the three topics we touched on last in this chapter. Each of them is a touchstone of personality, basic to the kind of person each of us is, the kind of person others believe us to be. And each of them affects, and is affected by, the ways in which we see and learn from others.

It never ends, does it? Every single thing I do or say or think is festooned about with social-learning implications for me and for the people around me. It's complicated, it's frustrating, it's messy.

It's also exciting and fascinating.

Ain't psychology grand?

Suggested Readings

The basic book here is Bandura's *Psychological Modeling* (Atherton, 1971). It will give you a good overview of the social-learning approach and introduce a number of research areas to which the theory has been applied. Miller and Dollard's *Social Learning and Imitation* (Yale University Press, 1941) is a classic and will be useful if you want to really dig into how the whole movement got started. Some parts of the book are fairly technical, but there are lots of detailed descriptions of experiments and many anecdotal examples. Mowrer's book, *Learning Theory and Behavior* (Wiley, 1960), presents his two-factor theory in great detail, relating his views to traditional learning theory at every step; it too can be tough going, but it explains Mowrer's views as only Mowrer himself could.

For a general introduction to social-learning theories, try Walter Mischel's *Introduction to Personality* (Holt, Rinehart, & Winston, 2nd ed., 1976). Or A. R. Sherman's *Behavior Modification: Theory and Practice* (Brooks/Cole, 1973). And for a really condensed presentation (with all of the advantages and drawbacks of condensation), General Learning Corporation has put out a 46-page "module," written by Bandura and entitled simply *Social Learning Theory* (General Learning Press, 1971). It's excellent—but take it slowly.

Finally, and almost parenthetically, Bandura has recently written a seminal paper in which he relates social-learning theory directly to self-concept. This paper, "Self-efficacy: Toward a Unifying Theory of Behavioral Change" *(Psychological Review,* 1977, *84,* 191–215), bridges the theoretical gap between social learning and cognition, and we call it to your attention again in that context. Under either heading, it looks like an exciting breakthrough. And it reads well, too.

Notes and References

The discussion of Miller and Dollard's work was taken both from their *Social Learning and Imitation* (Yale University Press, 1941) and from their *Personality and Psychotherapy* (McGraw-Hill, 1950). Mowrer's theory comes from his *Learning Theory and Behavior* and *Learning Theory and the Symbolic Processes,* both published by Wiley. The great bulk of what is covered in the rest of the chapter can be found in the Bandura work cited earlier: *Psychological Modeling* (Atherton, 1971) and *Social Learning Theory* (General Learning Press, 1971). We have also drawn from Bandura and Walters' *Social Learning and Personality Development* (Holt, Rinehart & Winston, 1963).

A number of the comments about language and imitation were based on C. B. Cazden's *Child Language and Education* (Holt, Rinehart & Winston, 1972). Piaget's *The Thought and Language of the Child* (Kegan Paul, 1926) and Flavell's *The Developmental Psychology of Jean Piaget* (Van Nostrand Reinhold, 1963) provide information on the egocentric speech of childhood; the role of listening in the communication process is expanded in A. T. Dittman's article "Developmental Factors in Conversational Behavior" (*Journal of Communication,* 1972, *22,* 404–423).

11

Role Theory: Through the Looking Glass

"I quite agree with you," said the Duchess; "and the moral of that is—'Be what you would seem to be'—or, if you'd like it put more simply—'Never imagine yourself not to be otherwise than what it might appear to others that what you were or might have been was not otherwise than what you had been would have appeared to them to be otherwise.' "

This interesting bit of advice was not particularly helpful to poor Alice, as she tried to make her way through Looking-Glass Land. In fact, its primary effect was probably to give her a dreadful headache. Psychologists trying to understand role theory sometimes feel a bit the same way. We are so used to focusing on the person, on individual characteristics, and on differences among people, that we feel turned quite upside down by the sociologists' point of view. The essential nature of the individual doesn't *matter*? We must consider the nature of the interactions among people but not worry about what those people *are* underneath? Because there really *isn't* any "underneath"? Because the interaction is the personality? Come on, that's just as much double-talk as anything that Lewis Carroll ever dreamed up! But is it? Perhaps it's worth a headache or two, just to understand what the role theorists are trying to tell us. Let's give it a whirl. . . .

The Concept of Role

Over and over again, as we have considered the nature of personality from the point of view of a variety of theorists, we have found ourselves asking "Why did those people do what they did?" Traditionally, personality theorists are concerned with the reasons underlying observable behavior. We look for some sort of continuity, some thread of sameness, that will allow us to say that *this* kind of person behaves in *these* sorts of ways, which are different from the ways in which *that* sort of person behaves. Personality theorists look under the skin, look past the apparent bewilderment of different behaviors, to find a basic unifying principle that will help us to understand and predict why people act as they do and how they are likely to act in the future.

In this chapter, we shall look at another way to approach the need for order and predictability. Instead of asking "Why did that person do what he or she did?" we can ask "What conditions led that person to do whatever it was?" Rather than try to peer into people, we can look *around* them, at the external forces that push and pull them to behave in various ways. This is the sociological—or, more precisely, the social-behaviorist—approach to personality. We have seen its beginnings in the field theories of people like Murphy and Lewin, and we have stumbled onto it again in the work of the social-learning theorists. It is time, now, to see where the approach will take us once we let go and give it its head.

It would be difficult to argue with the assertion that all human behavior takes place in the context of other humans. We do what we do in direct interaction, or in imagined interaction, with others. Even the hermit, who lives in splendid (or less than splendid) isolation, is notable because of that isolation from others, not because of any particular solitary behavior. To the social theorist, this fact of interaction is of primary importance. We behave differently, social theorists point out, depending on our interaction partner. Our speech, our posture, our facial expression, and even the feelings and thoughts we have are quite different when we talk with a respected teacher, or a dormitory buddy, or a vaguely aggravating little brother. The whole conglomerate of behaviors that a person displays in a given social situation has been termed a *role* (we shall say more about this definition in a moment), and the concept of role appears to be the central notion, the pivot point, on which all of social bchaviorism depends.

Role versus Traditional Personality Theory

It's important to recognize, at the outset, that a role approach does not necessarily conflict with the more traditional personality theories. Some role theorists claim to be quite comfortable with psychological concepts. Of course, as might be expected (social scientists being the contentious lot they are), others are not comfortable with them, and some go so far as to say that all of the personality theorists' work should be thrown out, because once we have thoroughly accounted for the effects of role there will be no "personality" left to study.

You, of course, will have to make your own decision about that, just as you must choose for yourself which of the other approaches to personality you find useful. I suspect that "useful" is the key word here: it's quite probable that *no* theory is "right" or "wrong." Rather, some are more useful to some people for some purposes than are others. At any rate, we should keep firmly in mind throughout this chapter that the essential and basic difference between social behaviorism—or role theory or whatever we choose to call it—and the psychological approaches to personality lies in where our attention is directed. Role theory emphasizes the ongoing social process, the interaction, the social situation. It looks *outside* the individual. It concerns itself with the constraints placed on one's behavior by the kind of interaction, and the history of interactions, in which one finds oneself. By looking inward, as psychologists are wont to do (says the social theorist), we obscure the most important variables of all: the gesture, the tone of voice, the place of the interaction, the expectations of the other parties involved, and so on. It is the dynamic ongoing situation, the composite of many social and physical factors, that molds and directs (some theorists say constitutes) personality.

Status, Roles, and Norms

Now, if you have dutifully read and assimilated the previous pages of this book, you will have received some pretty consistent training in the psychological point of view. That's going to present a few problems in terms of this chapter, because you're going to have to turn yourself around—you'll need to look at things from a different perspective, ignoring some kinds of data that were crucially important in other approaches and noticing other kinds that have been unimportant before. Also, there is some new terminology to deal with: sociologists have their jargon, too. We have already introduced the notion of role; let's talk about it a bit more now, in the context of two other important concepts, *status* and *norms*.

Each member of this sociological trio, role, status, and norm, has been defined and redefined many times. Which definition one chooses to use is not as important as is the consistency with which one uses it. So we shall select, arbitrarily, one set of definitions (selection being based primarily on the authors' personal preferences!) and use them throughout this chapter. A *status* is a collection of social rights and duties. The status of "doctor," for instance, includes the duty to protect the health of one's patients, the right to be treated with respect by nurses and orderlies in a hospital, the duty to be knowledgeable about the meanings of certain symptoms, the right to violate traffic regulations in some emergency situations, and so on. A status may have a positive value in our society (as with "lawyer" or "wealthy philanthropist") or a negative value (as with "felon" or "drug addict"), or it may be neutral or valued differently by different people or groups ("housewife," "teen-ager," "union representative"). Notice that a person may occupy many statuses; nobody has only one status. The President of the United States has the status of President, but he also occupies the status of husband, father, church member, property owner, and many more. So it is with all of us; the number of statuses varies, but we are all owners of several.

A *role* is the dynamic aspect of a status. A role comprises those behaviors that one engages in within a given status. We *occupy* a status; we *live* a role. As we shall see, roles may be defined with greater or lesser specificity: we may talk about the role of a "teacher" or of a "teacher interacting with the parent of a student." But it is impossible to separate role from status or status from role. One is the framework; the other is the activity within the framework.

Norms are descriptions of behaviors that are generally acceptable for given roles and statuses. They have to do with meeting the obligations and exercising the rights of one's status. Each status has its own set of norms, some very general (a norm for the status "U.S. citizen" is to have some knowledge of how the United States is governed) and some very specific (norms for the status "Roman Catholic" include detailed expectations for standing, sitting, kneeling, and genuflecting during church services). Norms may also be prescriptive—that is, indicating what is to be done—or proscriptive—indicating what is *not* to be done. Someone occupying the status of "student" is expected to go to classes, at least occasionally (a prescriptive norm), and to refrain from spitting on the floor or singing aloud during those classes (a proscriptive norm).

An Example: Personal Space

Many of the norms for various roles and statuses are so taken for granted that it's hard for us to notice them. They seem to be natural, given; it is only when we visit another social group or another culture that we realize with some surprise that different behaviors are now expected. This apparent naturalness presents another problem for the psychologist-turned-role-theorist, for we are in constant danger of overlooking or simply accepting without question some situational element that is, in fact, critical to the interaction being studied. A beautiful illustration can be found in Edward Hall's work with personal space. According to Hall, each of us has our own personal "bubble," an area of space around us that may only be entered by invitation. When someone encroaches upon our "bubble," we become very uncomfortable: we back away, look down at the floor, or use some strategy to make the other person move off. But different people appear to have different-sized "bubbles." What is encroachment to me may be a comfortable distance to you. And different roles/statuses have different size bubbles, too: the dentist or the opthalmologist may come very close to me without particular discomfort to either of us, but the undertaker had better keep farther away! The point here is that the physical distance between two interacting parties may be an important factor in understanding the nature of the interaction. The eyes-down, uncomfortable expression of one of the parties may have nothing to do with "shame" or "transference" or any other internal, psychological cause; it may simply be the result of a (deliberate or unwitting) invasion of the personal bubble by the other party. It takes a great deal of alertness, as well as a lot of practice, to become aware of the aspects of our interactions that most people simply take for granted, and we shall have to keep working at it.

Role Theory and Socialization

A final word of caution about the role-theory approach. Role theorists talk a great deal about socialization, the process through which people learn their roles and how to switch from one role to another. And much of this talk appears to imply that, whatever age you may be, your socialization has occurred in the past. You are the finished product, so to speak, of the socialization that occurred throughout your childhood. Nothing could be further from the truth. Socalization doesn't happen just to children; as adults we are each continually undergoing resocialization. Social learning and role taking are continuous, ongoing processes. The changes may be sudden and dramatic, as when someone is "converted" to a fundamentalist religious sect. They may be less abrupt but still marked, as when you are promoted to a new status in your job (or are fired or retired). Or they may be quite gradual and unnoticed, as happens in the slow flowering of a friendship. But we all do change, and we all are being resocialized, from birth until death.

Unlike many of the theories we have looked at thus far, role theory has no single best-known exponent. It is not Freudian or Jungian; it doesn't even have the "big two" or "big three" founding fathers as is the case with factor-analytic theory or social-learning theory. Instead, it rests on a long history of contributions from a whole series of theorists. Some of these theorist are well known and some not so well known; most are sociologists but many have been trained in other areas as well. To understand the approach, we shall have to go back to the ideas of some of the early thinkers, back to a point in time where role theory as such had not been thought of. We shall meet Charles Horton Cooley, the gentle small-town sage, and George Mead, the articulate urbanite. Talcott Parsons will have his chance to relate role theory to the Freudian school. We'll look at how the role approach can be useful in dealing with abnormal behaviors as we take a short detour through the writings of Emile Durkheim, Robert Merton, and J. L. Moreno. Finally, we'll see how the whole thing ties together in terms of two more modern approaches: from the point of view of the practicing social worker, Helen Perlman will talk about roles and personality; and Orville Brim will be the spokesperson for the research-oriented theoretician. It's a long trip—have you got your hat and your notebook?—we're on our way.

Charles Horton Cooley: The Looking-Glass Self

> *"Well, it's no use talking about waking him," said Tweedledum, "when you're only one of the things in his dream. You know very well you're not real."*

Tweedledum had a grain of truth in that statement, but he didn't get it quite right. (What can you expect of Tweedledum, anyhow?) We're about to explore a line of thought that will bring us to the conclusion that we *do* exist only insofar as we are seen by others—that our selves do depend upon the dreams that others have of us. But that doesn't mean that we are not real—contrariwise! Our very reality, as selves, grows out of the perceptions others have of us. To explain this idea further, let me introduce to you Dr. Charles Horton Cooley. Pull up your chair in front of the fireplace, put some soft classical music on the stereo, pour a glass of sherry. Are you comfortable? This is the setting in which it is easiest to imagine Cooley holding forth on his favorite topic: the looking-glass self.

Cooley was a gentleman scholar, and he wrote like one: calm, ordered, leisurely. Never a very gregarious person, he learned early in childhood to amuse himself with his own thoughts. Born in 1864, he was a painfully shy child with the added handicap of a speech defect and partial deafness. It must have seemed to him that he had been preparing for a retreat to an ivory tower all his life, and that is exactly what he did. He spent nearly all his life in or near the small town of Ann Arbor, the home of the University of Michigan, turning down offers to work in more urban and dynamic centers because he preferred the kind of life-style he had developed there. One's life, Cooley believed, should be lived—created—as a work of art is created. One does not profit from doing things that are out of harmony with one's nature. So Cooley lived, gentle and retiring until his death in 1929, writing and working with students and avoiding the stridency and bustle that even then characterized many parts of academia.

The Shaping of the Self

As a kind of self-trained philosopher, Cooley must have spent a great deal of time in introspection: Who am I? How did I come to be as I am? And he very quickly became convinced of the importance of *other people's opinions* in shaping an individual. We can imagine the early experiences of this lonely boy, teased by his schoolmates because he "talked funny," retreating into an even lonelier round of existence. Or the young college student, embarrassed to the point of pain by social prominence, reading social rejection into a casual remark or gesture. Why am I this way? How can others stand so easily and confidently in the limelight? Would things be different if I had not been taught through childhood to be shy, to avoid being hurt by others?

For Cooley, it was not just one's beliefs about oneself, one's *self-image,* that were shaped by the opinions and reactions of others. Their influence was much stronger than that; they shaped the actual *self.* You tend to become, said Cooley, whatever you think the people around you believe you to be. I'm writing a final exam, and I become aware of two things simultaneously: I was staring in the general direction of someone else's paper, and the instructor is now staring at me. I know that I wasn't cheating, but I also know that the instructor thinks I was. And, because of what *I* think that *teacher* thinks, I begin to feel and act guilty. I turn red, shift in my seat, look down at my own paper. I have become, in my own thoughts and feelings and behavior, what I think the instructor perceives in me.

This is only one example, and a common one; others are to be found everywhere. How many "heroes" in wartime behave heroically simply because their comrades expect them to act that way or at least because they *think* that's what their comrades expect? How many "young punks" earn that derogatory name by living up to what they think society (as exemplified by high school teachers, police, probation officers, and storekeepers) believes them to be? To the extent that I think others believe me to be good (intelligent, industrious, kind), I am likely to become so. To the extent that I think others think me bad (stupid, lazy, arrogant), I am likely to oblige.

The Perceived Opinions of Others

The "looking-glass self," as Cooley has termed it, is a highly dynamic concept. It is always changing, because the people around us are always changing, and our ideas of how we are impressing them change too. It is not just the self concept, not just the ideas of others, not just the interactive behavior. It is the patterned whole that emerges from all of these.

Cooley's major contribution to personality theory, then, was to point out just how important the *perceived* opinions of others are in shaping one's own self. Notice the emphasis on "perceived." What Debrah really thinks about me is much less important, in the shaping of my self, than what I believe Debrah thinks. That classmate you've been admiring for months may think you witty and sophisticated. But if you are convinced that she sees you as foolish and awkward, then in her presence you will feel like (and, to some extent, become) a clumsy, all-thumbs clod.

Three Parts of the Looking Glass

Although the looking-glass self is indeed a dynamic whole, Cooley didn't content himself with simply describing it as such. He went on to dissect it, to point out that it has three principal parts or elements. First is how we imagine we look or seem to the other person. Second is our imagination of how the other person evaluates that appearance—whatever they see, do they think it good or bad? And third is some sort of self-feeling, some reaction to the imagined evaluation. An example may help us to sort out these three elements. Let's say that you have just finished making a speech, and you're now having a cup of coffee with good old Buzz, who was in your audience. You will be sensitive to how Buzz thinks you look and feel: does he see you as nervous and flustered or as calm and at ease? Along with that more or less objective perception, you will expect him to make some sort of judgment about you: "Marilu seems very nervous, and I guess she isn't much of a public speaker to let this thing get to her" or maybe "Marilu really cares about how this speech went; she's the sort of person who puts her whole self into whatever she does." And, finally, there will be your reaction to Buzz's reaction: pride that you are appraised as being conscientious and concerned or shame at being thought incompetent or oversensitive. These three *perceptions* or *reactions* comprise the looking-glass self. They account for both one's self-image and the self one shows to others.

George H. Mead

If Cooley introduced the idea of the looking-glass self—my self molded from and developed out of my ideas of others' perceptions of me—it was George H. Mead who expanded the idea into a theoretical system, a way of looking at the whole relationship between the individual and society. Mead, just one year younger than Cooley, was in person about as direct an opposite to Cooley as would be possible to find. A prodigious reader, he also delighted in the company of others. Most of his writing was done at the University of Chicago, where he circulated in many social and professional groups. In fact, he was so busy listening and talking and teaching that he published very little of his theory and consequently had little influence during his lifetime. Most of his writings were published after he died in 1931, rewritten by students from the volumes of notes he had made.

Unity of Self: The Generalized Other

Mead saw clearly that one of the flaws, or at least a missing element, in Cooley's notion of the looking-glass self was the fact that we find ourselves in company with many different individuals and groups, and these people have (we know and believe) widely differing perceptions and opinions of us. If my self is formed out of those perceptions and opinions, how is it that such a self is not fractionalized, split, inconsistent? When I consider myself, the essence of "me," my sense is one of consistency and unity. I am the same person that I was yesterday, and I expect to be the same tomorrow. How can this be, if I am really only the reflection of a host of other people's opinions and impressions? Mead believed that this problem is overcome in two stages. At first, one simply organizes the perceived impressions of the others with whom one comes in contact, and a rough consistency emerges out of that organization process. Then, in the second stage, one begins to think and react in terms of the whole society to which one belongs; the group of specific others is transformed into a *Generalized Other,* an abstract notion of how "they" believe me to be.

According to Mead, it is the creation of the Generalized Other that makes thinking and reasoning and communicating possible. If we did not develop such a concept and develop it in some sort of agreement with one another, we would not have a common basis for understanding the world. Words would mean different things depending on who said them and to whom they were said. It would not be possible to form the sorts of social expectations on which society is based—the "if I do that, they are likely to do this in response" kind of thinking that we do in every social interaction, usually without realizing it.

Gesture, Response, Completion: The Social Act

In order to explain how this Generalized Other concept comes into existence, Mead went back to the nature of a social act. Each social act, each segment of any interaction between two individuals, is really a triad of events. First is a *gesture,* made by one of the individuals. The gesture may be an actual physical movement, or a word, or a facial expression. It is anything that signals to the other individual that some interactive event is about to take place—has, in fact, begun to take place. The other person, in turn, makes a *response* to that gesture: a signal indicating that the message has been received and that he or she has some reaction to it. Finally, the social act is completed, but it is not the same as when it was initiated, for it has been changed by the two elements that preceded its *completion.* No person can be solely responsible for any social act, for such an act is always the product of two (or more) individuals.

For Example: A Handshake. Consider, for example, the familiar social interaction called a handshake. Now, it's obvious that you can't shake hands with someone by yourself; the very definition of a handshake states that two people must participate in it. But the handshake involves more than just the physical gripping of one hand by another. It begins with some gesture of intention by one of the people—often a very subtle shift of expression or posture—that says to the other "I want to shake hands." The other person responds—again, subtly and perhaps unconsciously—signaling a willingness to reciprocate. And the handshake takes place. The first two parts of this process may occur in a fraction of a second, but they are there, and they are important. The awkwardness and discomfort felt by a would-be handshaker who misses a negative response to an initial gesture and is stranded with hand extended into empty air bears witness to that. And yet, the hand-extended-and-rejected is also the completion of a social act, a perhaps even more significant one than the completed handshake.

Social Empathy. At this point you, the reader, may be beginning to get a little impatient. "All this stuff about handshaking may be very interesting," you say, "but what does it have to do with personality?" Okay. Here's the connection: in responding to the *response* of that other person, the initiator of the social act has to take the other's point of view. In order to correctly interpret the meaning of the response gesture, I have to see myself as the other sees me. I must develop social empathy. I must view myself as an object, an object to be responded to, just as that other person does, in order to know how to finish the interaction correctly. And it is this process of becoming an object to myself, accomplished over and over again through thousands and thousands of individual social acts, that eventually coalesces and crystalizes into my self—my personality—as reflected in the eyes of the Generalized Other.

Interaction and the Formation of Self

While the concept of the Generalized Other is an important contribution, no less important is the introduction of interaction or activity into the self-forming process. Cooley insisted that the self is a dynamic blend of perception of *idea,* perception of *evaluation,* and *personal response* to those perceptions. But he did not emphasize, as did Mead, that those perceptions occur in the context of an interaction, a social activity. It is the act that occurs between two people that determines the relationship and the perceptions and responses between them.

Without the *experience of another* (and such experience can occur only in real or imagined interaction), there can be no self. The self can be experienced only as over against another. A plant, or an earthworm, has no self, for it cannot contrast its own experience of being with that of another plant or earthworm. When two people engage in some joint activity, each is stimulated to feel the same response as is felt by the other. Feeling (being aware of) the response of the other is an essential part of the social act. Because it is so, we have a sense of self; we know ourselves to be unique because we are different from those others whose responses we are aware of. If all the world were blue, we could not be aware of "blue" as a color; it has meaning for us only as it can be contrasted with other colors. A fish probably doesn't feel wet, because everything is wet and therefore "wetness" is a meaningless concept. The sense of self is the same: "self" only becomes meaningful when I become aware that there are other selves. And this awareness comes, slowly and sometimes painfully, out of participating in social interactions.

Trying Out Roles. We said, a moment ago, that each of the participants in a social act feels the response that is felt by the other. If you think about that statement for a minute, it may lead you in some interesting directions. When I initiate a social act, I must at some level recognize you as another self. Otherwise, I would not be initiating a social act but, rather, an interaction with some nonhuman object. To recognize you as a self implies that I know you will respond to me in the act I am initiating and that there are a variety of ways in which you may respond. But some of those possible responses are not what I want at all; I'd rather you didn't hit me, or spit in my face, or turn your back on me (all of which are possible). I must therefore signal to you something of my own intentions and perhaps something of my wishes for you as well. But how do I know how to do that? How do I know how you will respond to my initial gesture? How do I choose among my possible behaviors the one that is most likely to convey to you whatever I want to convey? There is only one possible answer: I do what I think would work for me *if I were you.* In other words, I take your role and try out my initial gesture to see how it works. I stimulate in myself the response I am calling out in you. If it works, I am likely to be successful in the activity I have initiated. If it doesn't, I learn that I was wrong—you didn't respond as I thought you would, as I, in fact, *did* when I role-played you.

Misinterpretation and Growth. Let's not stop there, though; let's take this idea a little further. If I am wrong, what happens? I mean for you to receive one kind of message, but you in fact receive something else. For you, what I meant is quite irrelevant—since you are unaware of it, it might as well not exist at all. Now we are at cross-purposes, because I think I have initiated one kind of social act and interpret your response in that context, whereas you think we are up to something quite different. The resulting interaction is likely to be different than either one of us expects; it is the dynamic product of those crossed expectations. From it, we both learn about the other and, through that, about ourselves. We gain new expertise in seeing ourselves as objects, through the eyes of another. Our selves acquire a new dimension. It is only through these crossed communications, these mistakes in interpretation, that the self can come into existence. If we were always right about the other, we could never change or grow, for there would never be any new information to feed that growth. Again, the contrast is important: dry with wet, blue with not-blue, self with other-self. That which is alien, not-me, is the only thing that allows me to be myself.

Self, Language, and Community

One of the reasons why it is hard for many psychologists to get into Mead's theory is that we are so inclined to think in terms of individuals or, at best, of collections of individuals. For Mead, the society—the community—comes first. The individual arises out of the community, rather than the other way around. A person is/has a personality because of being a part of a community; one takes over the institutions and attitudes of the community and molds oneself out of them. Language is basic to this process: it filters the ways in which one can apprehend ideas, and it serves as a channel through which the ideas of the community can be received. The very language one uses already incorporates a whole host of assumptions, assumptions that usually remain unquestioned unless one can get into a different language structure. To be "happy," for the English-speaking person, means to be content, to be bubbly, to be satisfied with things as they are, to have a certain zest for and enjoyment of life. For us, because of the way our language structures our ideas and perceptions, those qualities go together. The Spanish-speaker, in contrast, has two words for what we call "happy," one (*contento* or *contenta*) describing a kind of quiet, satisfied, at-peace-ness and the other *(alegre)* describing a bubbly, bouncy, active sort of happiness. For the Spanish-speaker, the two states are quite independent, and neither one implies the other.

Single-word examples of this sort are bound to be superficial, but they do illustrate the general idea. Now translate that example into the total communication flow between us and the people—groups, community—that surround us. We take the roles of others by means of language, and it is through this role-taking process that personality is formed.

Indeed, Mead would have community (and its language) basic to far more than the individual personality; he contends that *mind itself exists only in terms of a social environment.* Wow! That's heavy! Thought, as we understand it, can take place only in the context of social interaction. Only as people learned to communicate with others through developing common meanings for certain gestures (and an increasing number of these gestures became verbal symbols) did they learn to think. Thought depends upon words, and words depend upon commonality of meanings, and commonality of meanings implies social interaction. No talk, no think, no mind, no self.

But we wander off the track (that's not difficult to do, with Mead). As we pursue the idea of the nature of the self, of the personality, and how it develops, we find Mead saying that the self rests on even more than just interacting with others, even more than just learning to respond to one's self as others respond to it. In the same way that I take on the attitudes of others toward me, I also take on the attitudes of others toward the group, toward society and the common social activities we share. You can't have personality, Mead is saying, without an organized society of some sort, because the group attitudes about society, attitudes that arise through that society's functioning and interaction, are a fundamental part of personality. One begins an interaction with another individual, senses the other person's response to that beginning, and then participates in completing the (redefined) activity. And in the process one continues to re-form oneself. And the interactive process with society works the same way: one participates in social process, but the process and the nature of one's participation are always changing, always re-forming. One's self emerges from that changing, growing, interactive process. One is a complete self only to the degree that one does participate in this social process.

"I" versus "Me"

One of the most confusing points, in our study of Mead's work, is the way in which he appears to use certain terms interchangeably: *self, personality,* and *self-consciousness* all seem to be the same thing. Curiously, though, he does make one clear distinction—one that other personality theorists have shown little interest in. Mead takes great pains to differentiate between the "I" and the "me," assigning different qualities and different functions to each. "I" is different from "me"? Wait—this is supposed to be a book about personality, not grammar. No, says Mead, it's more than just grammar; it's a fundamental difference between two distinct concepts.

The "me," for Mead, is the self one is aware of. It is the essence of self-consciousness; it is the self as object, and it comes, as we have seen, from taking in organized sets of attitudes from others about oneself. The "I", in contrast, is the response of the organism to those organized attitudes. I am aware of who and what I am—that is my me—and my I is the part that does something about it, that *acts.* The I and the me are different "phases" of the self. Me is the framework, the structure, the continuity of the self. "I" is the dynamic aspect, the phase that takes action within that framework. The novelty of behavior, the possibility of change and growth and re-formation of both individual and society, come from the I.

There is a kind of future quality, a "forward-looking-ness" about the I. The me is a past-tense sort of thing; it is the accumulation of attitudes and beliefs and experiences, molded together, that make up what one believes oneself to be. The I gives a sense of freedom and initiative to move into the future. I may know who or what my me is, but I cannot know (for sure) what my I will do. Whatever action I may take, it is always slightly different from what I thought it would be; for the I to move into the future is a creative process, and creativity always involves some uncertainty. That creative, forward-moving process, the I of this moment in time, becomes part of the me of the next moment.

Neither the I nor the me, of course, could exist by itself. The whole self, the whole personality, is a give-and-take between the two. The I acts within the framework of the me, and the me is constructed out of the activity of the I and out of the ways in which the I perceives and deals with others' reactions to those activities.

Here, then, are some of Mead's basic ideas, ideas on which future role theorists will build: the I and the me, the interaction between self and others, the primary importance of society in the formation of the individual personality. Trying to collapse Mead's thoughts into a few pages is a little like trying to fit an elephant into a thimble; there are inevitably some major parts left over. But, for our purposes, these three do seem to be most essential. Mead was a thoroughgoing social scientist, with the accent on the *social.* For him, the society is prior to the individual, not the other way around; each individual has to be understood and explained in terms of the society in which he or she came to exist. Consciousness—mind—is located within social processes. We are able to think *because* we are a part of society. Through social role taking and symbol learning, people become human.

Mead and Cooley, together, built the foundation for a social approach to personality. Others have contributed greatly, as we shall see, to that approach, but all trace their origins back to the work of these two men. The looking-glass self, the personality constructed out of the perceived responses of others to one's own behavior, are the basic and fundamental concepts upon which all of the theory depends.

Talcott Parsons

> *"I must be Mabel after all, and I shall have to go and live in that poky little house, and have next to no toys to play with, and, oh, ever so many lessons to learn! No, I've made up my mind about it: if I'm Mabel, I'll stay down here! It'll be no use their putting their heads down and saying 'Come up again, dear.' I shall only look up and say, 'Who am I, then? Tell me that first, and then, if I like being that person, I'll come up: if not, I'll stay down here till I'm somebody else.' "*

It is truly amazing how Lewis Carroll seems to have anticipated so many of the developments in role theory as the sociologists were slowly and painfully putting it together. Alice wandered about down in the rabbit hole, cut off from all of her usual role relationships, and found that she didn't know who she really was. In her frightened musings, she quite naturally recreated the relationships she knew best: those with parental authority, the "they" who would (she hoped) soon coax her to "come up again." And she decided that she would only come up if "they" would allow her to be the person she had always been. If she had to be someone else (poor Mabel, for instance), she would stay where she was.

Role Theory Meets Psychoanalysis

The enormous influence of the parents in shaping the roles—the personality—of the child. The overwhelming importance of infancy and early childhood, when those parents (particularly the mother) are virtually the only other people in the world. Oh, hello there, Dr. Freud—yes, we *were* talking about you, in a sense. Well, at least we were about to do so. For here is where role theory and psychoanalysis finally come together.

The man known for pointing out this relationship is Talcott Parsons. Unfortunately, Parson's prose is even more turgid and impenetrable than that of the worst of Freud in its worst translation. Parsons is a shining inspiration to some sociologists and the despair of others. He had a great deal to say. But—oh, dear!—it took him *such* a long time to say it!

Parsons did most of his writing during the first part of the 1900s. He proclaimed himself a sociological maverick drawing more from European than from North American social science. Parsons seems to have had some difficulty in settling into a professional niche; he first planned to become a physician and later switched to economics, before shifting to sociology in 1931. He became the sociological apologist for Freud and devoted a great deal of his professional energy to the task of showing how Freud would surely have been a role theorist if he had just continued working long enough.

Society and Id/Ego/Superego

Freud, as Parsons pointed out, was quite clear about the importance of the sociocultural environment in shaping the superego. It is from important adults, particularly parents, that the child draws his or her superego, the whole hierarchy of do's and don'ts that make up the conscience and the ideal self. But Parsons went further, arguing that not only the superego but also the ego is founded on the social environment. Freud's theory, said Parsons, clearly implies that the ego grows out of an internalization of self/other relationships.

Object-Cathexes. The relationship between personality, as such, and the famous Freudian triad of id/ego/superego has always been a bit blurry. Some theorists seem to assume that personality (or at least all of the interesting or relevant or work-with-able aspects of personality) must reside in the ego, while others see personality as a broader entity that cuts across all three elements of Freud's triad. Parsons fell closer to this latter position. He believed that the main content of personality comes from social systems and the overall culture within which an individual develops and that this general personality is individualized, is made unique, through one's interactions with one's own organism and through the uniqueness of the specific experiences one has. It is as if the blueprint of what I will become is laid down socially and culturally, but the particular decorations and furnishings are up to me. The id enters into the process insofar as I (and every other person) must deal with my own biological givens, my own particular set of needs and drives (or, to use Freud's terminology, libido). But the rest of my personality, unique as well as general, is socially derived. It is unpredictable, since no one can know what experiences I will have. It is probably not specifiable, since no one can specify all the factors that impinge upon me as I experience a relationship or how those factors shall be weighted in determining the meaning to me of that relationship. But the personality is, said Parsons, acquired socially. As an infant, almost from the moment of birth, I begin to develop "object-cathexes": positive and negative attachments to the various entities that I perceive in my environment. It has been conceded by most (all?) personality theorists that these attachments influence the development of personality. Not enough, said Parsons. Object-cathexes don't just influence the development of the ego, the way climate influences the growth of a plant; they are "constitutive" of the ego. The ego is actually formed out of these relationships; they are the basic stuff from which it is made.

In a baby's earliest experiences, gratification comes through social interactions. To eat, the baby must suck and the mother must feed. It is the experience of hunger *satisfied in the context of this interaction* that is gratifying, not just hunger satisfied all by itself. (Harlow's experiments with baby monkeys, in which they were allowed to feed from either wire-frame or cuddly terry-cloth "mothers" and invariably chose the cuddly interaction, gives some experimental support to this notion.) In order to make the interaction work—that is, to gain the most possible gratification from it—the child must learn to infer the intentions of the mother. The child must learn to anticipate what the mother will do, in order to make the appropriate reciprocal actions. This learning what another person intends to do in a social interaction, said Parsons, is the beginning of ego. Ego is that which organizes one's behavior in accordance with external reality and especially with social reality.

Identification. Parsons also did a bit of redefining (he would call it clarification) of the Freudian notion of identification. Most of us think of identification in terms of learning to be like someone else or to think of ourselves as similar to someone else. If I "identify" with my mother, I see the similarities between us and learn to enact her roles. Not quite, said Parsons. Identification with someone doesn't so much mean thinking and feeling "I am like you" as it means being able to make inferences about your feelings and intentions in order to play a social role in interaction with you. The child who identifies with mother has not learned to imitate mother's behavior, but rather, to infer that behavior so as to successfully interact in the mother/child relationship.

Identification, then, does not mean taking on the identity of another. But the identified-with one still has a strong influence on the ego—the personality—of the identifier. When I infer another's intentions so as to make a good relationship for us both, I don't emerge from that relationship unchanged. I have been touched by the other person, whether I like it or not. Something has been added; my self has some new aspects that it didn't have before. The infant's self begins to form out of interactions with the mother, and, to a lesser degree, with other close family members. Gradually the whole nuclear family becomes a part of this process, and a new phase of identification emerges: that of member-of-family. The one-to-one interaction of child with mother or with other family members is still important, but there is something else besides. The family-member identification is much more complex than the child/mother identification, involving as it does a whole set of interrelationships. Parsons identifies three interdependent identifications that are part of the self/family relationship: identification with the family as a collectivity, identification in terms of sex, and identification by generation. The child who successfully negotiates these three aspects will emerge with a sense of self as part of group, with a sense of maleness or femaleness, and with an age orientation, a kind of simplified genealogical chart that allies the child with brothers and sisters and cousins, in contrast to parents; with aunts and uncles and grandparents; and (potentially) with nieces and nephews and eventually his or her own children.

All of these relationships, then, intertwined and interacting, are the raw materials of ego. And it doesn't stop there, for the child doesn't stop relating when she or he leaves the nuclear family. To be sure, the early in-family interactions are the most important, for they are first and basic. But all of one's interactions, all of the many roles into which one is thrust and in which one must learn to infer the intentions of others playing complementary roles, continue to shape the ego, to infuse it with new learnings, new ideas, new feelings. We learn to order our roles, to pick and choose which one we shall "be" depending on where we are and whom we are with. Thus the ego controls the roles, as the roles shape the ego. It is a cyclical process—perhaps the prototype of all interpersonal interactions?—a feedback loop of incredible complexity. Let one role get out of balance, one set of needs too great, or one interaction pattern out of control, and all the other roles are affected.

Thus Parsons on persons. There are behaving organisms, whose behavior can be observed. There are social systems, consisting of numbers of these behaving organisms, behaving relative to each other. There are cultural systems, overarching collective organizations that grow out of social systems and yet are the basis for those same social systems. And there is personality, which contains elements of all of these and which, over time, acts collectively to reshape them all. Organisms, society, culture, personality: each independent, yet each interpenetrating all of the others. And, running through it all, that same theme—the social role, the channel through which interaction takes place, the visible manifestation of personality, the stuff of which personality is made.

Durkheim and Merton

> *"Who cares for* you?*" said Alice (she had grown to her full size by this time). "You're nothing but a pack of cards!"*
>
> *At this the whole pack rose up into the air, and came flying down upon her; she gave a little scream, half of fright and half of anger, and tried to beat them off . . .*

The role theorists and social psychologists at whom we've been looking so far have concentrated, for the most part, on describing and explaining successful socialization, successful personality development. Parallel to this stream of work, there was another set of ideas unfolding in the sociological world: ideas about how roles could fail, about what happens to people when things don't work out properly, about how the individual may become detached from society and experience personality defect.

One of the first of these thinkers, and possibly the best known today, was Emile Durkheim. Coming from a long line of rabbinical scholars, Durkheim (like so many of his sociological contemporaries) was at first interested in a career in religion. His concern with religion lasted throughout his life, though as an adult he declared himself to be an agnostic. He was an intensely patriotic Frenchman, stoutly defending the old-fashioned virtues of tradition and obedience. World War I was a shattering experience for Durkheim; not only was his son killed in the war, but also his beloved France was trampled by enemy boots. It was more than he could bear. He died in 1917, exhausted by overwork and overwhelmed by grief.

Integration of Society into the Self

In spite of the personal tragedies of his life, Durkheim is credited with a number of insights that are still fresh and useful today. He, like the other sociologists of his time, was immersed in the problem of the relationship of the individual to society. For Durkheim, the problem was basically one of *size:* as society becomes larger and more complex, how does a person relate to it? Ishi, a member of a Stone-Age Indian tribe, could carry within himself the integrated whole of his civilization; he had internalized its rules, its values, its relationships. He was a microcosm of the society that had shaped him. But an individual today can't do this. Society is too big, too complex; one person can't be intimately related to the whole. Being a part of the huge sprawl of modern society leads one to feel oneself to be small and insignificant. Still, as a well-integrated person (a healthy personality, we might say, though Durkheim wouldn't have chosen those words), I do integrate in my self some *part* of society. I carry as a part of my self-concept the values and rules and relationships of that segment of society that I know best; I feel, and am, related.

One immediate effect of this relationship is that some firm boundaries are set on the kinds of needs I experience and the kinds of goals I set for myself. I cannot be happy or even continue to exist, says Durkheim, unless my needs are appropriately proportional to my means. To need—not just want, but need—the unattainable is not a condition that one can live in for very long. But people always *want* more than they have. What sets a limit on this process? How do we create the boundary between want and need, and how do we manage to set it at a place compatible with what we actually have a chance of getting? Durkheim, as we might expect, points to society as the limiting factor here. As one incorporates and internalizes society's values, one also incorporates and internalizes society's limits. Society acts as a "moral power superior to the individual" and determines the point "beyond which passions may not go." If you are well integrated into society, you may strive to acquire and achieve more and more, but you won't experience insatiable cravings for something you cannot possibly have.

Anomie

But societies change, and people move from one society to another. When a person moves into a new society or when a society changes faster than an individual member can keep up with, that member feels disconnected. The old rules and values and limits don't fit any more. Similarly, when society tells its members one thing but actually offers them something else (as, for example, in the case of the slum dweller who is told of the limitless opportunities open to all U.S. citizens but runs into a block whenever he or she tries to use those opportunities), the internalized limits of the individual are likely to be out of whack with the reality of what is available. The result: disconnectedness, rootlessness, a sense of nonidentity. Durkheim's word for this state is *anomie,* and Durkheim saw anomie at the root of most of society's ills, from suicide and crime to mental illness and drug addiction.

Durkheim's concept of anomie has come to have some new and interesting implications in light of social changes that have occurred since Durkheim's death. The early 1900s were a time of great upheaval in Western culture's notion of what freedom and individual liberty were all about. In the 19th century, church and state still had a firm grip on the individual. Tess of the d'Urbervilles, heroine of the Thomas Hardy novel, is a perfect example of this kind of cultural molding. Tess was told by her culture what she should believe, what values she should have. At the same time, she was not as entangled in the coils of bureaucracy as the modern individual is. The actual restraints on her behavior were likely to come through face-to-face interactions. She was expected to behave so as to please her family, her community, her lover. Because the controls on behavior were exercised at an individual level, this 19th-century person was important as an individual. The modern situation is in direct contrast to this. Formally, we of the 20th century are set free: increasingly, we are not bound by moral codes set up by church or state but are expected to "be ourselves," to live by some individually determined set of values. We are (theoretically) not ostracised if we are hedonists, homosexuals, hippies, or hermits. Live and let live is the motto of the day. And the price of this individual freedom is a lack of social rootedness and belongingness. If you are free to do what you want, you can't be terribly valuable to the society; if you were valuable or needed, society couldn't afford to allow you that kind of freedom. In setting ourselves free, we have cut ourselves adrift. And this surfeit of freedom, of individuality, has made association or solidarity terribly attractive—moderns seem to be desperately searching for something to belong to, to be a part of. It is as if we are suffering from a kind of collective, built-in anomie. We want to belong, to be valued, but as soon as that begins to happen we feel stifled by loss of freedom, and we rebel against the restrictions that real belonging always involves.

One consequence of this state of affairs is that the roles we enact begin to appear shallow and unreal. To truly internalize a role, to be shaped by it and to shape it to ourselves, involves commitment. It involves accepting the rules and values that govern that role interaction within a society. But this kind of commitment, this kind of acceptance, may feel like loss of freedom. To guard our freedom, then, we don't really commit ourselves to our roles; rather, we only "play" them, going through the motions but reserving the right to bail out if we feel like it. And the thing snowballs: if I'm in a role relationship with you, and I know you may bail out at any time, I'm not likely to commit myself to the relationship either. As soon as Alice (remember the quote at the beginning of this section?) denied her role relationship with the inhabitants of Wonderland, they all turned against her. And she, in fright and anger, had to defend herself, had to "beat them off." Fractured roles, disconnectedness, isolation.

Thus we can block ourselves from experiencing meaningful role relationships and, in so doing, block others as well. A large part of this blocking involves conflict about what we want to do, or ought to do, to reach our goals. Should we accept society's rules, or should we make our own rules? There is also a similar conflict about the goals themselves. Should we struggle to attain those things that society says we should want, or is it all right to reject those values? The degree to which we feel related to society and committed to role relationships within that society will determine how intensely we experience this kind of conflict.

Robert Merton's Paradigm

Robert Merton, a more recent sociologist who was strongly influenced by Durkheim, has suggested a paradigm for categorizing the ways in which role and value conflict can affect one's overall personality orientation (see Table 11-1).[1] He said that one may experience dissociation from socially accepted goals, from socially accepted means to goals, or from both. If one is comfortable with both the goals (ends) and the means to those goals, one tends to be a conformer. If one accepts the goals but not the means recommended by society, one is an innovator. One who conforms to socially acceptable means but does not accept (or feels blocked from attaining) the ends is a ritualist; the ritualist goes through the motions, and it is this activity rather than what it (supposedly) leads to that keeps one going. Dissociation from both ends and means brings retreatism: drug abuse, depression, isolation. The rebel may represent a variety of ends/means conflicts but is actively involved in trying to change things, trying to adjust the external world so that his or her "differentness" can be made to fit.

As Merton evolved these categories of disconnectedness or nonacceptance of social values, he became more and more convinced that society itself puts pressure on people—and on some people more than others—*not* to conform. Yes, you read it right—*not* to conform. Not everyone is equally suited to fit into the value system of a given society, and those least suited will often, in their reaction to the pressures they experience, become even less able to conform than they were before. I tried

[1]Merton's paradigm is taken from the chapter entitled "Social Structure and Anomie" in what is probably his best-known book, *Social Theory and Social Structure* (Free Press, 1957).

it; it didn't work; I'm *really* an outsider; the hell with it. Society makes the pressures, the pressures make behavior, behavior makes the society. Thus the great circle, and personality is intimately bound up in all of its parts.

Table 11-1. Merton's paradigm: the relationship between one's typical personality orientation and one's acceptance or rejection of socially defined goals and means.

Typical Orientation	*Society's Definition of:* *Means to Goals*	*Goals*
Conformity	Accept	Accept
Innovation	Reject	Accept
Ritualism	Accept	Reject
Isolation, Withdrawal	Reject	Reject
Rebellion	Accept or Reject	Accept or Reject

As we follow the development of the sociological study of the unhealthy individual, we see increasing attention being paid to the notion of "fit," of interaction, of the process of role relationship. The situational pressures that we experience certainly contribute to our psychological situation, as do our own individual needs and expectations. But it is the way these two fit together that is critical. And they fit together in the context of roles. What I want out of my interactions with others—and what others want out of those same interactions—determines for both of us our conflicts, our constraints, and our satisfactions. Both parties shape the roles that will be played; roles evolve out of mutual conflicts and constraints and pleasures. As I learn to shift from one role to another, I learn to maximize pleasure for both myself and those with whom I interact. If I can't do this sort of shifting, if I am limited to a small number of roles that I must use in every social situation, the likelihood of my finding a "fit" is reduced; I am more likely to experience conflict, blocking, pain. And my personality will be diminished, rather than enhanced, by such painful, nonfitting interactions.

Helen Harris Perlman

"I don't think they play at all fairly," Alice began . . . "and they all quarrel so dreadfully one can't hear oneself speak—and they don't seem to have any rules in particular: at least, if there are, nobody attends to them—and you've no idea how confusing it is all the things being alive . . ."

For many a "helping professional," especially at the end of a long day, that description of the world and the people in it may appear pretty accurate. People do seem to get themselves into the most incredible muddles, and they quarrel, and they don't follow the rules (if, indeed, there are any rules). And they don't stand still—they grow and change; they're alive.

The Social-Work Perspective

One of the major functions of a personality theory is to bring some order, some sense, into the confusion and chaos that seems, on the surface, to describe human behavior. For the social worker, focusing primarily on interactions among people rather than on a single person's recollections or problems or feelings, role theory would seem to be a perfect solution. And so it has proven to be, for many social workers. One person, in particular, has emerged to speak for role theory as it applies to social-work practice. That person is Helen Harris Perlman. Energetic and assertive, Perlman is described by her students as "the complete professional." In the classroom at the University of Chicago, she was all business, demanding a great deal of her students and no less of herself. But in her writing we find glimpses of a warm, caring, *people* person, a professional who was deeply concerned with how the client experienced the joys and the pain of relationships.

For Perlman, as for the role theorists, it is again the relationship that is the key to personality. We know ourselves through our behavior, and that behavior occurs in interaction with others. We know and feel our entire environment through the people who inhabit it. There is not a single sensory impression that is not festooned about with people-feelings—recollections, anticipations, delights, fears. The smell of newly-mown grass, the sight of lights going on in houses at dusk, the voice of a jay screaming at a neighborhood cat—all of these conjure up feelings that relate to people, to interactions, to the recollections and hopes and anxieties of our varied relationships. Notice, too, that it is not just the role relationships of the present that influence our reactions. We are affected by past relationships and by anticipated future relationships. The individual personality is an amalgam of all three: what we have been, what we are, and what we may become. And each of these is defined and experienced vis-à-vis some other(s).

A "Sense of Self"

To the extent, then, that we have experienced a variety of role relationships and can reasonably expect to continue to do so, we feel whole and human. Perlman speaks of being filled with a "sense of self" and insists that this sense of self grows out of a history of interaction and transaction with others, in which one's selfness is affirmed again and again. Through these processes we become "peopled within." Each role interaction gives us another small chunk of selfhood as we internalize both our own role and that of the other. This is the wellspring of personality, and it must continue to flow if the individual personality is to be maintained.

Perlman admitted that the childhood years are of primary importance in setting the stage for the kinds of role relationships that a person will engage in. She herself, though, was more interested in adulthood. Personality continues to grow and change throughout adulthood, particularly during certain "crisis" times and at the beginnings of new and critical role relationships. Entrance into adulthood is itself one of these critical periods. The mark of adulthood is the shift from an age-graded to a status-graded society. A child is positioned in its childhood society by age. One's peers are persons of one's age, school activities are largely determined by age, and the major events of life are largely age-related. As an adult, one is positioned by other sorts of status: occupation, marital status, income. And these positions are, to a large extent, acquired by the individual's own activity. You don't simply wait to be a doctor, or a parent, or a wealthy person, as you waited to be 6 or 12 or 16 years old; you make decisions and choices that help to determine whether and how quickly you attain this or that status. Enacting adult roles involves being given the right and the responsibility for making these choices, as well as accepting such rights and responsibilities.

Personality Change through Role Change

Changes in personality, as enacted in role relationships, occur throughout adulthood for three reasons, according to Perlman. People change in their roles because they want something that they don't now have. Or they change because they are afraid of losing something that they do have. Or they find that the environment has changed so that staying in the same kind of role is now dangerous or threatening. Many adult changes involve combinations of these three motivations. Consider the situation of a young person who is deciding whether or not to marry. Marriage usually involves significant role change: why should one decide to make such a change? Most obviously, one might want something one doesn't have, such as mutual commitment to and with another person, financial security, or whatever else one sees as going along with marriage. One might also fear the loss of something one now has: if I don't marry her, she will find someone else. Or the environment may have changed: when I was younger, everyone else was dating, but now all of my friends have settled down, and people are beginning to wonder what's wrong with me that I haven't found a marriage partner.

The "Vital Roles"

Entering a new role is often an uncertain, scary sort of thing. We don't know what will happen, what will be expected of us, whether we will be able to handle the new relationship. If roles were simply things we could try out, or "perform," discarding them at will and leaving ourselves unchanged underneath, new ones wouldn't be so threatening. But we don't simply play or perform roles—we *are* our roles, and we define ourselves through the roles we live. Some roles, in particular, are inextricably bound up with self-concept and personality. Perlman calls these the "vital roles" and maintains that they are necessary to one's total well-being. In a vital role there is investment of the self. As I draw a sense of self from my vital roles, so too do I become dependent upon them. Engaging in the relationships of vital roles always involves risk: only as I am able to become vulnerable in a role relationship am I able to enact it fully and grow in it. To the degree that a role—parent, teacher, marriage partner, wage earner—is truly a part of me, it is a vital role. And to the degree that it is a vital role, I am hurt or frightened or diminished when it is threatened.

Perlman went beyond simply asserting that roles are integrally part of the individual, however. She analyzed the ways in which one's roles affect one's inner self. First, she pointed out that one's socially recognized roles anchor one in the social system. They give one a sense of belonging and of purpose, a sense that is reinforced as other members of the society also recognize that role. Second, carrying a role gives order and regularity to life. It allows us to make more accurate predictions of how people will respond to us, of what demands they will make, and of what we may expect of them in return. Third, as we share a role relationship with another person, we can identify with that other. This may be a complementary relationship, as with husband and wife or parent and child, or it may be the relationship of shared roles: we are both parents of that child, or we are both employees of that firm. Out of such shared and complementary relationships come new insights, new feelings, new growth. Finally, when we enter a new role, we are particularly vulnerable to the influence of others. Because things are new and scary, we are looking for ways of coping, for someone to tell us or show us how we ought to look and act and feel. Our defenses become more permeable, making it possible for all sorts of new ideas and feelings to get in.

Work Role and Identity

One of the most important areas of role-relationship for adults is that of work. Adults—in this culture, at least—are expected to have jobs or professions. One's work role is a major part of one's identity. Perlman was very interested in the relationship between work and personality. Work, according to Perlman's definition, is an activity that has at least potential benefit for someone else, in contrast to play, which is engaged in simply for personal pleasure. This, of course, does not imply that work cannot yield personal pleasure for the worker, any more than it implies that play must not benefit anyone other than the player. It's a matter of priorities, of the main purpose of engaging in the activity. Work benefits someone else but may have personal pleasure as a by-product; play is for personal pleasure but may yield benefit to others as a by-product.

Personal Pleasure. In fact, not only *may* work yield personal pleasure as a by-product; for maximal fit between personality and work, there *should* be personal pleasure. Working competently can be rewarding in and of itself; the sense of "I am doing a hard and/or necessary job well" should simply feel good. If it doesn't, if the satisfaction of doing one's job well is wiped out by frustration with job conditions or general dislike of job activities, the job role will never be constructively integrated into the personality. Instead of feeling "I am a carpenter" or *being* a carpenter, the worker rebels against that job: "I shouldn't have to be a carpenter," "I'm not *really* a carpenter." The worker is denied that work-defined dimension of self.

Social Approval. Work, if it is to be gratifying, must offer the worker some chance for social approval. The approval may not be constant, or it may be denied in the present but potential for the future. But the potential, at least, must be there. "When they see what I've done, they'll like it" or "If they could understand what I'm doing, they would approve" can substitute quite effectively for tangible social recognition. But knowing (or believing) that what one is doing is really of no use to anyone —which is another way of saying that it has no potential for social approval—changes it from work to play. And play, masquerading as work, is hollow at the core. It may yield some temporary satisfaction in having conned society into paying for a sham, a kind of glee at having gotten something for nothing, but it cannot fill the gap left by a real work-role identity. As an adult with no such identity, you cannot be truly integrated in your society; you get, but you don't give. If we accept the contention of Perlman and her fellow sociologists that individual personality derives from social rootedness, it must follow that the personality that is so dis-integrated in society cannot be whole or fully functioning.

Time Structuring. Aside from this fundamental rootedness that work roles provide, work has some additional side benefits. For one thing, it regularizes and structures time. As we become an increasingly leisured society, with fewer and fewer of our hours devoted to work, the problem of how to manage leisure time becomes more apparent. Most (all?) people need some structuring of time. The lazy vacation, where one can just sit around and do whatever one wants whenever one wants begins to pall after a very few days. We begin to feel bored and itchy, and the days seem to stretch out forever, and (often to our surprise) we begin to want to get back to the old routine again. Work also provides an opportunity to experience a variety of role relationships both on and off the job. It's a social avenue, a forum for meeting and interacting with other people.

That work is in fact important, that it does provide all of these benefits, is nowhere more clearly demonstrated than in the plight of retired people. Consider Sam McGee, a retired business executive. Sam's work role is gone; he can no longer think about himself as a "merchant" or as "in sales," and somehow "ex-merchant" or "retired sales manager" doesn't quite fill the empty space. Time is empty and unstructured; Sam often doesn't know what to do with his hours. Social life is disrupted; the people with whom Sam interacted daily before his retirement are relating to other people now—and even when he does meet them from time to time, it isn't the same somehow. Retirement often hits men harder than it does women. Most women, even though they may have an out-of-the-home career from which they do retire, retain the work role of "homemaker" beyond the magical age of 65. On the other hand, the woman whose whole work role has been that of "mother/wife" can find herself "retired" relatively early in life, when all the children have suddenly turned into adults and husband has long since found other ways to pass the time. Here, again, we see the symptoms of the absence of a work role: faltering sense of identity, inability to use time comfortably, feelings of loss of social relatedness.

Our work roles, then, help to tell us who we are. They root us in society; they underlie our feeling that we have a right to be and to be as we are. They structure the ways in which we interact with others (as well as helping to determine whom we shall interact with) and how we use our time. They strongly influence our attitudes and values, our likes and dislikes. They don't just help to form our personality: to an important degree, they *are* our personality, fused with and inseparable from that elusive entity we call the self.

The Marriage Relationship

If work role is one foundation of personality, surely the roles of marriage partner and parent are another. The kinds of interactions and mutual relationships experienced in marriage and in parenting are unique; they do not (ordinarily) occur elsewhere. Let's look at each separately, for a moment.

Although the experiences of the marriage relationship are unique, no one comes into that relationship free from expectations of what it will be like. We are socialized—programmed—to expect certain things of marriage. These expectations exist, Perlman points out, at both conscious and unconscious levels. The young child, the adolescent, the bride- or groom-to-be, can each tell you what he or she thinks marriage is like, what sorts of things one gets out of being married. These are the conscious expectations. But at a deeper level, there is a whole host of unspoken and unknown expectations, growing out of the feelings and experiences of years spent in the company of married people. Both conscious and unconscious expectations affect the way one behaves as a marriage partner—the ways one reacts and interacts, the ease or willingness with which one grows and changes in the relationship, as well as the significance that the relationship and the role itself have for one's overall personality.

Differences in marriage expectations arise from a variety of sources. Most important, probably, are those childhood experiences of how mother and father get along that, being both early and nonverbal, have an inordinate influence on later perceptions. Many of these behaviors and behavior expectations are firmly rooted in socioeconomic class differences—even in our so-called "classless" society. Blue- and white-collar families, welfare and middle-income families, differ predictably on such issues as how conflict will be handled, who will do what jobs in the family, and how "all-fulfilling" the housewife role will be for the woman.

People *get* married and they hope to *stay* married, Perlman points out. But *being* married isn't a steady state; it is a process. Relationships are never static; roles don't hold still. No matter what one's expectations are about what it will be like to be a wife or a husband, the reality will be different, and it will continue to change as long as the marriage is based on a living relationship between the partners. The expectations of the partners will help to carry the marriage through rough spots if those expectations are complementary. But conflict in expectations, either between husband and wife or between conscious and unconsicous expectations within one or both partners, can be very damaging and painful. Conflict in expectation means conflict in role relationship: you don't do what I expect of you, and I don't do what you expect of me. Each of us is hurt, angry, disappointed, and often confused. Who was "right" and who was "wrong" gets to be more important (because being "right" means that my idea of my role and therefore of my*self* is right and being "wrong" is an attack on me personally) than what shall be done about it. The role relationship degenerates into a series of defensive battles, each a desperate struggle to keep intact some integral part of selfhood and each resulting in loss to both partners. The marriage deteriorates, the relationship dissolves, and with it goes that aspect of self that is defined by the marriage role.

The Parent Role

Parenthood is also a new and unique role for the young adult. Usually, but not always, it is coupled with the marriage role; one of the more difficult strains that can be placed on a marriage is the arrival of children too early, so that the marriage partners are forced to learn both marriage and parent roles simultaneously.

Just as with marriage, the parent role is a reciprocal one. One cannot play the role of wife unless there is a husband; one cannot be mother unless someone is child. The essential element of the reciprocal parent/child relationship is responsiveness: each member must respond in some way to the demands of the other. The response need not always be positive. Rebellion and resentment are familiar parent/child responses, on both sides of the relationship. But *some* response must occur; one can't be in a relationship with a statue or a rag doll. Perlman points out that the notion of "unconditional love" of a parent for a child is nonsense: love from parent is conditional on responsiveness from child. And, conversely, the child can love only a parent who is responsive to that child. The response may be punishment—even savage and unpredictable punishment—but there must be response. Without response there is no relationship, and without relationship there is no love, and no role.

The parent role, at least in the traditional family, is often more growth-producing (in the sense that it requires more new role behaviors) for the mother than the father. The woman who finds herself in the role of mother must, first of all, redefine her relationship to her own mother. Before, they were mother and child. Now they are two women who are both mothers. She must also accept and deal with a sense of responsibility for what her child is and does. She hopefully acquires a sense of competence, as she finds herself filling the role of "good parent." And later, as her child grows into and beyond adolescence, she must find a new sort of mother role, one that can let go and allow the child to become an adult in his or her own right.

All of these growth possibilities are there for the father, too, but in the traditional family the demands are not usually so intense nor the feedback so immediate for him. Still, for both parents, the role—or roles—and relationships of parenting are real, and the impact on personality is strong.

The social worker has a primary interest in helping clients to develop supportive and satisfying role relationships, as a means of living happy and productive lives. From this point of view, the importance of roles in shaping personality is self-evident; it is the basis of the social worker's professional expertise. But most social workers don't have time for theory; they are too busy responding to the needs of clients who are right then and there and not theoretical at all. The theory of social work is implicit rather than explicit; it can be inferred from how the social worker behaves but it is not likely to be spelled out verbally. Perlman is an exception to this rule—a most valuable exception, for she managed to blend the researcher/theorist's love of words and logic and "does-A-go-with-B-and-what-do-they-imply" with the social worker's concern and commitment to real people and their real problems.

Orville Brim

> *"Who are* you?*" said the Caterpillar.*
> *Alice replied, rather shyly, "I—I hardly know, Sir, just at present—at least I know who I* was *when I got up this morning, but I think I must have been changed several times since then."*

Our roles have a great influence on who we are. Conversely, who we are influences the ways in which we play our roles. Neither traditional personality theorists nor role theorists are likely to argue with either of those statements. But now it's time to look at a more radical point of view, one to which many role theorists, and most traditional personality theorists, would probably take exception: one's roles *are* one's personality, and one's personality *is* one's roles. Personality and roles are the same thing. Alice was one person when she got up that morning, but since then her roles have changed radically, and she is no longer that person. Her roles are different, so she is different. She has a different personality.

Heavy, isn't it? Makes your head hurt, just a little? But don't reject the idea, not just yet, anyhow. There's another sociologist, named Orville Brim, who makes a pretty good case for this point of view. Give him a chance; listen to what he has to say. Then decide for yourself.

Personality as the Role Repertoire

Brim's position with regard to personality is deceptively simple: "The learned repertoire of roles is the personality. There is nothing else." Personality theorists, Brim says, generally concern themselves with individual differences in such things as conformity or dominance or achievement needs. But this is just another way of saying variation in roles and in behaviors within different roles. Understanding what roles a person can and will and does accept, and how one's behavior changes as one moves from role to role, is the best way to describe and predict how one acts—how one *is*.

It sounds simple and straightforward. But the implications of such a view really rattle the bones of most of the theories we've looked at in earlier chapters. The whole trait approach, for example, is threatened. In order to talk about traits, we have to assume some kind of internal consistency within the individual. To say that Jack Jones differs from Henry Smith on the dimension of aggressiveness implies that Henry and Jack each have some fairly constant level of aggressiveness that can be compared. Brim challenges this assumption, pointing out that an individual's behavior varies enormously from situation to situation, from role to role. The question isn't (or shouldn't be) "How does Henry behave most of the time that is different from how Jack behaves most of the time?" but, rather, "What are the different ways that Henry behaves?" Instead of looking for consistencies in Jack or Henry's behavior, which will help us to define some unitary notion of "them," we should focus on the behaviors that vary as either Jack or Henry moves from situation to situation. These variable behaviors will help us to define the roles that Jack or Henry enact—and these roles *are* the personality.

Role versus Traits

An interesting example of how these two different points of view—roles and traits—lead to different kinds of personality research is found in a book about the relationship between behavior and personality edited by Krasner and Ullman.[2] They cite a 1954 study in which the characteristics of successful and unsuccessful psychotherapists were listed: the result was a description of two "types" of people, one that was likely to succeed as a therapist and one that was not. Since it would be very handy, for a number of reasons, to be able to predict whether a given person would be a good therapist, this study generated a considerable amount of interest. The only problem was that the predictions didn't work. Some people who fit the "unsuccessful" list turned out to be very good therapists indeed, and some who fit the "successful" list should have stuck to playing football or building automobiles. Ullman and Krasner (good role theorists that they are) pointed out that this is likely to happen when you try to generalize an individual trait or characteristic across a variety of situations. People who are successful in one setting (doing a certain kind of psychotherapy, with a certain kind of client) are not necessarily going to be successful in a different setting. Research that sets out to discover stable traits and to use these traits to define personality types is doomed to failure simply because behavior is *not* stable at all.

[2]*Behavior Influence and Personality* (New York: Holt, Rinehart & Winston, 1973).

Situational Pressures

Of course, to deny some underlying consistency about individuals is an unpleasant attack upon our sense of the way things ought to be—of the way we ourselves are. Intuitively, introspectively, we think of ourselves and others as "being" this way or that: "I'm really a very gentle person," "He always has to be the boss," "She acts that way because she's passive-aggressive." But this intuitive sense of self can be very misleading. If I am, indeed, the gentle person I say I am, why did I yell so loudly at my children this morning? Was that nasty letter I wrote to my insurance company consistent with "gentleness"? Oh, I answer, it may have looked inconsistent, but that's because you don't understand the situation. You see, I have this underlying trait of gentleness, but there are also situational pressures that may make it less likely that I will actually *act* gently. Nevertheless, in order to really understand me, you will have to look beyond my surface behavior and see how gentle I really am when I'm allowed to be. Brim describes this attitude as "a bit of legerdemain in which the theorist snatches identity from diversity by distracting one's attention from what one actually sees to something the theorist says is there, whether one can see it or not." It's a kind of psychological shell game, in which the theorist always wins: if you see my gentleness reflected in my behavior, then that's evidence that I am in fact gentle. If you don't see it, then you'll just have to work harder at finding a way to get past those superficial surface behaviors.

This, then, is what is wrong with a trait approach to personality: it simply doesn't work. Whole persons are too variable to be the units within which behavior can be expected to be consistent. We shall have to look to smaller units, units in which more consistency is apparent. The next smaller unit, says Brim, is the role. We can look for ways in which a particular trait may manifest itself within a particular role. I may be a gentle parent but a tyrannical boss. I may be dominant on the athletic field and submissive in a committee meeting. Descriptors like "dominant" or "aggressive" may be meaningfully applied to a person's typical behavior within a given role context, even though they can't describe that person in general.

Even more specific is the approach that takes into account not only the role but also the other people interacting in the role. I-as-committee-member may be relatively submissive when the chairperson of the committee is my boss but obnoxiously aggressive when the chairperson is a member of my secretarial pool. Many parents are kind and loving with one of their children and criminally abusive to another. Even within a given role, my behavior may change depending on whom the role relationship is shared with.

Probably the most specific unit of analysis is the role-plus-other-person-plus-episode unit. Here we take into account the fact that behavior varies from time to time even when a given person is in the same role with the same other. My "wife" behavior changes not as I move from husband to husband but as the situation changes from deciding who will take out the garbage to greeting each other after a day's work. I am a different "parent" to my daughter when we are discussing the state of her room (disaster area) and when we are examining a theme she has written for school.

There is no neat rule of thumb for determining which level of specificity is the "right" one for a particular bit of research. It will depend on the amount of variability you expect to find in a particular behavior and the amount of importance that you think the relationship partner, or the nature of the episode, will have. The thing to remember is that, in our zeal to find neat, simple predictors of behavior, we must not generalize too far—and end up with neat predictors that simply don't predict.

The Composite Self

It is apparent from all this discussion that the notion of a single "self," with its own unique set of characteristics, doesn't fit Brim's picture of how people operate. We don't have one self but many; each self that I have consists of a self-perception specific to some major role. I bring these selves together and integrate them in some way, and the composite image is that which I consider my self and within which I try to find consistency. The boundaries of my self shift, then, as I move from one "self" to another: the at-work self is assured and competent, the floor-scrubbing self is sullen and resentful, the cocktail-party self is giggly and vague. To the degree that I can move comfortably among my roles/selves and can sense some logical consistency in (or in spite of) the changes these roles/selves call up in me, I will feel like one person. But if I cannot manage the needed shifts, if I muddle my roles so that I use the wrong behaviors in them, I will feel confused and "split." Consistency in behavior, from this point of view, is not necessarily normal or healthy; it may even be a serious danger signal. Appropriate inconsistency is the healthy sign: comfortable variability in behavior as one moves from one role to another, as one changes from this self to that (equally valid) self.

Socialization

A person does not, of course, enter the world fully equipped with a set of selves that will last throughout his or her life. One's selves—one's roles—develop out of one's experiences of relationship. We call these experiences *socialization.* Infants are not socialized because they do not yet know what or who they are in their relationships. As infants begin to experience themselves vis-à-vis other people, they begin to become socialized: they begin to learn how to take on social roles, to interact predictably with others, and to be able to predict how those others will behave in interactions. And as this happens, the infant becomes a person, a personality.

Brim, like his fellow role theorists, insisted that socialization is an ongoing process throughout life but that childhood socialization experiences have the most significant consequences. New learnings occur more often during childhood, because the child hasn't yet acquired a repertoire of role behaviors to fall back on—young people are forced to learn new roles. Rewards and punishments for role behaviors have more intensity in childhood; the child is relatively helpless and vulnerable both to deliberate reinforcement and to the accidental or natural consequences of behavior. Brim also noted the evidence of learning theory, that primacy (the early items in a series of learning experiences are remembered better than average) and partial reinforcement (learning of a behavior is most permanent when that behavior is reinforced sometimes but not always) are characteristics of childhood learning and that both tend to strengthen the effects of such learnings.

It is important to emphasize that socialization emerges from interaction with other people; it is a "learn by doing" sort of phenomenon. The child learns what roles to play, what roles are fun to play (and this is essentially just another way of saying that the child learns what his or her *needs* are), and what sorts of things are expected in various roles. But the focus is always on the relationship, rather than on the expectations themselves. My 5-year-old son doesn't learn that he should be "polite" but, rather, that he should be "polite" to certain people or in certain relationships. He may learn to be helpless-child-with-mother and also to be playground-bully-with-peers. Norms and values are always learned initially in a role context. It is only at a later stage of development, in which one is intellectually able to deal with abstractions, that norms and values may be stated as generally desirable codes of behavior: that it is good to be honest or hardworking or loving. And even in adulthood, such values are more situational than we like to admit. Don Marquis, the famous columnist for the Chicago *Tribune,* had Archie the cockroach say "Honesty is the best policy, as long as it is kept strictly under control." We chuckle at Archie's words because they express openly what all of us are reluctant to admit: that the values we believe in are really situational and only work for us if we keep them under control—that is, tied to their appropriate role contexts.

Back to Roles, Values, and Norms

The significance of the socialization process, then, has to do not only with acquiring appropriate role behaviors and developing a commitment to social values and norms but also with bringing those two sets of learnings together. You, a well-socialized person, know which values and norms are acceptable in which situations. You have accepted the social "rightness" of applying one set of norms in this role relationship and another set in that one. One implication of this way of looking at socialization is that it brings us full circle back to the notion of the many selves/roles of each individual. It is the task of socialization not only to equip people with many selves but also to teach them when and how to shift from one self to another. Socialization teaches us diversity in our behaviors; it helps us to discriminate among situations that call for different role behaviors, and it helps us to develop sets of motivations that can be "switched on" according to the social situation.

Looking at instances of failure in socialization helps us to understand more clearly just what successful socialization entails. From the preceding paragraph, we can immediately infer one sort of failure: the inability to switch, to make the adjustment from one role to another. Socialization that is too rigid, that does not adequately deal with differences among relationships, does not lead to diversity in behavior. Rather, it leads to a restricted repertoire of behaviors and manifests itself in the person who always acts the same—always gruff or forever placating—no matter what the situation may be.

Role learning may also be too weak or too confused. If your whole socialization has failed in this way, you are likely to shift roles unpredictably *within* a situation, to change from whiner to bully or from cooperator to aggressor, leaving the other person in the interaction wondering what happened. These sorts of confusing shifts make it difficult for me to know what you will do or how you will respond to what I do, and it is therefore almost impossible to build a strong relationship with you. Since it is through relationship that further learning or relearning of appropriate role behavior can come, you are doubly penalized: you're handicapped by an inability to maintain an appropriate role consistently, and you're partially cut off from any chance to strengthen the very weakness that has cut you off in the first place.

Variables in Role Performance

Brim, being first and last a theorist, could only have written about roles in terms of a neat, no-loose-ends kind of package. Theorists are interested in wrapping things together, finding ways of accounting for uncomfortable knobs and bulges, summarizing with statements about A causing B leading to C. And Brim did it for role theory.

Differences in role performance among individuals, he said, are related to three intervening variables: differences in ability to perform, in knowledge of what's expected, and in motivation. Take a cross section of any two people at a given instant of time. At that frozen instant, they are likely to have been behaving differently, even if they were in very similar situations. Whatever differences we may see in their behaviors can be accounted for by these three fundamental factors: what they are *able* to do at that instant, what they *know* or *understand* about what's expected of them, and what they *want*.

Well, reducing the infinite variety of differences in behavior down to just three factors certainly seems to have gotten us somewhere—but not far enough. Where do those three differences come from? It's not enough to say that Jane and Sue act differently when they serve as heads of a committee because each is able to do some things better than others—*why* are their abilities different? The very nature of an intervening variable is that it does intervene; it comes between a set of causing conditions and a set of results. For Brim, the causing conditions are two-fold. One is the "social structural aspect of the person's environment, particularly during childhood." That is, the nature of the relationships one has participated in. Second is the culture, the over-arching set of beliefs and values within which those relationships occur. We might add one more item to the list: one's biological and physiological endowment. These three basic elements, social structure, culture, and biology, account for differences in ability, in knowledge, and in motivation. And differences in ability, knowledge, and motivation account for differences in the ways people enact their various roles.

And roles—the ways we enact them and move from one to another—are personality.

Chapter Summary

Alice, as she wandered about through Wonderland and on the other side of the Looking Glass, found herself in a constantly shifting and totally unpredictable series of role relationships. Things were never what they seemed: flowers talked, playing cards were people, cats turned into smiles and babies into pigs and croquet mallets into flamingos. No wonder the poor child was confused! She didn't know what the outside world was, or would be. And she didn't know who she was, or would be, either.

Cooley, in inventing the phrase *looking-glass self,* began a trend in psychosociological thought that has enormous implications for personality theorists today. The trend is not a direct offshoot of any one of our four major lines of psychological thought: it did not arise from psychoanalytical tradition, or from the early dissenters from that tradition, or form the individual-differences movement, or from learning theory. Yet it borrows from all of these; it brings together insights from each and blends them, in a new and often startling way, into a fresh and quite different approach to personality.

The looking-glass self of Cooley. The self that is defined by one's perception of others' evaluations. The self that is an amalgam of the mirror images (often distorted) of "me" that I discover in my interactions with others.

But more than just a structure, more even than a structure that is constantly being redefined and remodeled. Enter Mead, and enter *a distinction between "I" and "me."* The "me" is the structure, the thing that is built; the "I" is the builder, the doer, the creative force. "Me" is shaped by others, but not entirely, for "I" have a part in that shaping, too. "I" help to build "me," and, because of the dynamic, unpredictable, future-oriented "I," "me" need not be a helpless product of my environment.

Now add a dash of "legitimacy" by tying the whole thing back to the beginnings: relate it all to Freud's psychoanalytical theory. Parsons struggled valiantly to convince everyone that the whole role perspective was a natural outgrowth of Freud's work—that *Freud was really an embryonic role theorist.* It is doubtful that Parsons succeeded in this effort; his arguments are a bit too labyrinthine, too labored. But he did make the relationships clearer, showing how id and ego and superego can be seen in terms of developing roles and how roles emerge from those basic aspects of personality.

And when the roles don't work? When they don't fit, when they fall apart? When the self is left naked and formless in the social dance? Personality theories have traditionally been called upon to explain malfunctioning as well as health and growth. Durkheim and Merton have attended to that duty for us, detailing the consequences of role failure in terms of social rootlessness and mental illness. Disturbing ideas, these, because (to some extent) they describe us all: each of us has experienced role failure at some time or another, and each of us knows the pain of being out of phase with the others in our social environment. *Anomie.* Not-belonging. Withdrawal. Death.

It is the job of the social worker, in part, to help mend these kinds of broken relationships, *to help people enact their roles more fully,* more validly, more appropriately. The social worker's theory is likely to be a pragmatic one, more concerned with what works for real people in their concrete life situations than with defining abstract concepts. Perlman pulls it all together, makes it useful, applies it to you and to me and to all those folks out there who are trying to make it through tough times. She talks about how and why roles change and what happens to people when they find themselves in new (and often frightening) roles. She talks about the crisis points of life, when new roles are most likely to emerge. And she brings to the theory a kind of brisk, down-to-earth optimism, a sense of here's-what-may-happen-and-this-is-what-we-can-do-about-it.

But practice is practice, and theory is theory. While the two may (should) meet, it is not our primary job to deal with the "how-to" of building and mending roles. We are, at root, theorists, concerned with the implications of this concept or that for our understanding of the elusive thing called personality. Our last theorist brings us back to that point of view—carries role theory out to its logical extreme—and brings us face-to-face with it. Elusive, fiddlesticks! Personality is only elusive, says Brim, because we've been looking for something that doesn't exist at all. Focus on roles, on the ways in which behavior varies among and within roles, and you don't need anything more. *Our roles are personality,* and there's nothing elusive about role interactions. They're right out front, for everyone to see.

And so our search for a view of personality through the development of social roles has led us to a denial of the very thing we thought we were looking for.

Do you buy it? Is it useful for you?

Suggested Readings

It's really tempting to load a whole stack of books on you at this point: many of the sociological types write well and read easy, and you'd probably enjoy them. But we have to be realistic, right? So we'll try to pick out just a few for this section, and you can turn to the "Notes and References" if you find your curiosity is still strong when you've gone through this list.

George Herbert Mead's *Mind, Self, and Society* (Wiley, 1934) is a real classic and provides an excellent foundation for what follows. Mead isn't as much fun to read as Cooley (to our way of thinking) but he's more systematic, more comprehensive.

Parsons has good ideas, but his books and articles can make your head ache. We suggest you read Durkheim's *Division of Labor in Society*

(Free Press, 1933, 1960); it's not nearly as recent as Parson's stuff, but it's still relevant (and how!), and it forms the basis for a great deal of modern work on social problems.

Helen Perlman has written several books, all of which make good reading. Start with *Persona* (University of Chicago Press, 1968) and go from there as the spirit moves you. . . . Likewise, Brim has been somewhat prolific; most relevant to role theory is his chapter "Personality Development as Role Learning" in Iscoe and Stevens' *Personality Development in Children* (University of Texas Press, 1960).

And for sheer fun, don't miss Edward Hall's *The Hidden Dimension* (Doubleday, 1966)—but choose a time when you haven't much else pressing to do, because Hall is awfully hard to put down once you've started!

Notes and References

The specific references in the chapter come primarily from the books listed under "Suggested Readings," with the following additions:

Human Nature and the Social Order, by Charles Cooley (Glencoe, Ill.: Free Press, 1956, originally published in 1909).

"The Interpenetration of the Two Levels," an article by Talcott Parsons published in *Psychiatry,* 1958, *21,* 321–340.

William Glasser's *The Identity Society* (Harper & Row, 1972) contributed some of the ideas about the role of culture in determining roles. Similarly, a number of ideas found in Patrick Heine's *Personality in Social Theory* (Aldine, 1971) are interwoven through the chapter. Harlow's studies with the motherless monkeys are described in an article entitled "Love in Infant Monkeys" *(Scientific American,* 1959, *200,* 68–74). And you can find the full story of Ishi in Theodora Kroeber's *Ishi in Two Worlds* (University of California Press, 1961).

12

Mind and Thought

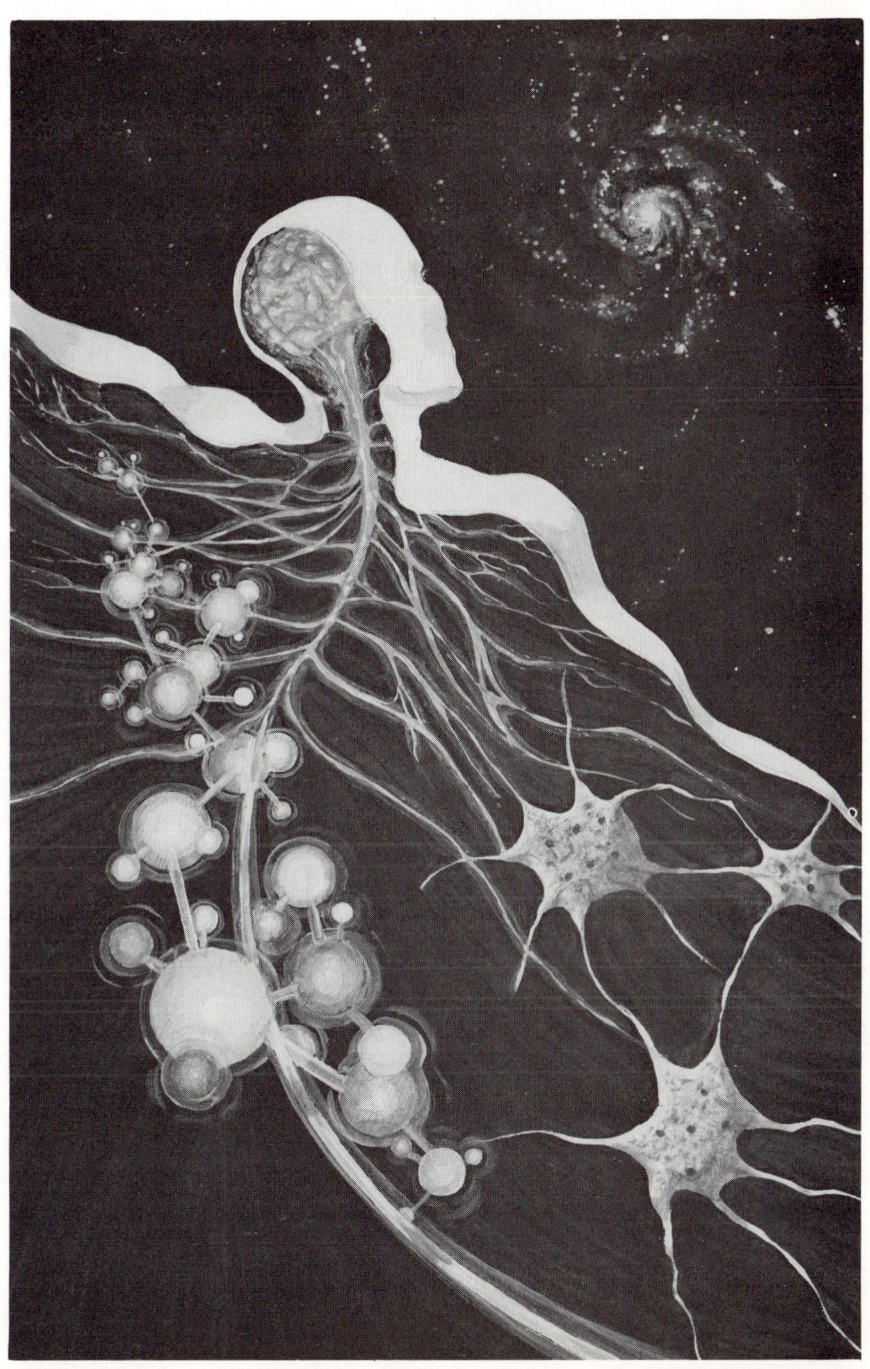

Both psychology and physics work immediately with experience, but they regard it in different ways; physics takes the "point of view" of experience "regarded as independent of the experiencing individual," psychology the "point of view" of experience "regarded as dependent upon the experiencing individual." These terms are Titchener's.

E. G. Boring in History of Experimental Psychology

Psychology was first defined as the study of the mind. It was distinguished from philosophy in that it was experimental—that is, scientific. It was distinguished from the physical sciences, as our opening quote indicates, by its point of view: experience "regarded as dependent upon the experiencing individual." It was cognitive psychology.

The word *cognitive* comes from *cognition,* meaning the process of knowing. And cognitive psychology is the study of higher-order mental processes like problem-solving and the states of knowledge that contribute to them. Perceiving and thinking. How and what we take in through our senses, and how and what we do with that sensory information once we have it inside.

Behaviorism versus Cognition

It was in the early part of the 20th century that the behaviorists, led by the invincible John B. Watson, attacked the assumptions, the definitions, the methods, and the accumulated knowledge of the cognitive psychologists. The attack was eminently successful, and the cognitive psychologists scurried for cover. Only personality psychologists remained cognitive and concerned with the workings of the mind. The others turned to the investigation of behavior. Psychology became the study of observable behavior. Nonobservables were taboo; cognition was left to philosophers, theologians, psychoanalysts, and other assorted kooks.

Today we are in the midst of a new revolution. The cognitive psychologists have recaptured key territories in the field of psychology—learning, memory, and perception—and the strict behaviorists are clearly on the defensive. Oddly enough, this counteroffensive by the cognitive psychologists in other fields is not being matched in the area of personality; there the on-the-run behaviorists are finding a home, and one could say that personality theory today is the only specialty in psychology that remains predominantly behavioral. Of course, if one said this, one would be immediately and rightfully accused of stretching the truth almost beyond recognition. But exaggerations describe trends better than do qualifications, and the trend is a truth, too. So, now, in our final chapters, we will examine this present and future truth. We will plot the trend through the history of personality theory; we will show how it represents a synthesis of many historical minitrends; we will extrapolate a little into the immediate future; and we will meet some fascinating characters. Not the least of which is, or was, Edward Bradford Titchener. He is first.

E.B. Titchener

E.B. Titchener was a character; there is no better word for it. Born in England and educated there, he spent two years in Leipzig, Germany, and became German. He spent 35 years in the United States, at Cornell University in Ithaca, New York, and remained a German. His style, his methods, and his psychology were foreign. They were imposing, to be sure, but they were foreign.

His manner was German. He was autocratic, even dictatorial. He lectured in his Oxford gown, for it allowed him, he said, to be dogmatic. He demanded and gained respect from his students. He was like Freud in some ways; he loved a debate of "informed" scholars, but, should their questioning stray too far, should it become not thoughtful analysis but outright dissent, Titchener would stop communicating, separate himself from them, and begin the attack. But he was an invader on foreign soil, and his influence eventually served only as a background for the impressive victories of Watson & Co. Titchener died, unexpectedly, in 1927. The commander of the invading forces was gone, and the invasion collapsed. Behaviorism held the field.

The Introspective Method

Now, with the wisdom of hindsight, psychology is beginning to recognize what Titchener brought to the study of humankind and to understand what he was trying to say. So what if he seemed pompous and autocratic? Who cares if he looked funny, flapping about in his gown? He was, in spite of it all, one of the Great Ones.

Titchener's psychology was Wundtian. Wilhelm Wundt founded the very first psychological laboratory, in Leipzig, Germany, in 1879. Titchener was then 12 years old. In 1890, 11 years later, Wundt welcomed a new student, age 23 years. Titchener spent two years with Wundt, and he took his doctorate in Leipzig. He hoped to return to Oxford, where he had studied philosophy, but Oxford was not interested. He came instead to America, to Cornell, in 1892. Add them up: 23 years in England, 2 years in Germany, 35 years in the United States. What kind of man is this? A German. Titchener was peculiar.

The Stimulus Error. Titchener's method was *introspection.* In his view, if one wanted to study the workings of the mind, one should do it scientifically. The method common to all science is observation. Therefore, if one wishes to study the workings of the mind, one must observe the workings of the mind; one must introspect—look inward.

Introspection, in Titchener's view, was not an easy task. When we are observing our mind at work, we are prone to many errors. One of the most prominent is the *stimulus error.* Consider yourself looking at a 50-watt light bulb. What do you experience? What do you see upon introspection? A sensation of light. Now a second 50-watt bulb is turned on. What do you experience? Is the sensation of light twice as strong as before? No. We know that for a fact. But you might answer "Yes," thereupon making the stimulus error. You base your report not on the inner experience but on the outer experience: twice as many light bulbs. The distinction is not always an easy one to make. Titchener used only highly trained introspectionists, and he refused to study children and abnormal subjects because they could not be expected to introspect properly. Animals? Don't be ridiculous!

The Basic Mental Processes

As we said, his psychology was Wundtian, focusing on "mental chemistry." What are the "chemical elements" of psychic life? Titchener decided, on the basis of introspective evidence, that there are three basic mental processes: *sensation, images* (or thoughts), and *affections* (feelings). Each of these has at least three attributes: *quality, intensity,* and *duration.* Sensations and images both have a fourth attribute of note: *clearness.* This attribute is not shared with affections.

Sensations, Images, Affections. We've just acquired a whole bag full of terminology here—let's pause for a moment and look through these terms again. Three processes: sensations, images, affections. Sensations are just what we might expect—smells, sights, sounds, and such things. The elements of perception. What we take in from "out there." Images are the elements of thought, the internal hunks and chunks that we manipulate when we think about things. Many images are *memories,* the stored-up residue of past sensations. But not all; as we think, we can create new images, new ideas and combinations of ideas. And the third element, affections: just as sensations are the building blocks of perception and images the building blocks of thought, so affections are the building blocks of emotion. Titchener divided all emotions into two categories, pleasant and unpleasant, and the pleasantness or unpleasantness is determined (in part) by the particular combination of affections that make up a given emotion.

Quality, Intensity, Duration, Clearness. Each element of sensation or of imagery or of affection may be described in terms of its *quality.* Sensations have the kinds of qualities we are familiar with in trying to describe things in the outside world: cold or warm, green or blue, fresh or musty. But those qualities don't exactly apply to images or affections (though they may sometimes, partly). Titchener recognized other sorts of qualities that fit all three processes. *Intensity:* is it a strong or weak image (or smell or emotional feeling)? *Duration:* how long does the sensation or affection or image last? And *clearness:* how prominent is it; to what degree does it stand out? Clearness is a special kind of quality, one not possessed by affections. Not, as you might first suppose, because affections are generally muddy and confused. But because, as Titchener pointed out, if you're feeling some affection, some emotion, and you concentrate on that feeling, you find yourself concentrating on the image of the feeling rather than on the feeling itself. Clearness—the quality of standing out in consciousness--is not a characteristic of affections.

Titchener Attacked

The mental chemistry of the conscious mind seemed to Wundt and to his students, including Titchener, the proper object of psychological study. But scientists, as contrasted with philosophers, are a practical lot, and American scientists are and were the most pragmatic of all: what will this theory do for me? Will it work? What's it good for? Titchener's mental chemistry was erudite and scholarly, but it did not seem to have many immediate applications in psychotherapy, education, and the other fields in which psychologists hoped to peddle their knowledge. Titchener, for his part, was disgusted with the interest that North American psychology had in practical applications, and he was forever expounding on the difference between "pure" science (his) and the bastard forms (theirs) that were so heavily polluted by values and utilitarian interests. It was like a theoretical physicist trying to explain the need for atomic theory to a garage mechanic—or, anyhow, that's the impression that Titchener gave. The other psychologists saw him more as a kind of theologian, the weird kind who gets hopelessly involved in trying to argue about how many angels can dance on the head of a pin and other equally pressing questions.

Well, there wasn't much doubt about who was going to win the battle. Titchener was fighting on foreign ground. His most effective weapon was his insistence that his psychology was scientific, for Americans desperately wanted to be scientific. But Watson came along with the perfect criticism, the perfect weapon: he was even more scientific than Titchener. Watson said in effect that Titchener was not scientific at all. Science involves observation, to be sure, but what should be observed? Watson's answer was: publicly observable events. Behavior. Science does not and should not admit into evidence private events, those that can be observed by only one individual. In other words, introspection is not an acceptable method in psychology. The knowledge gained from such a method is subjective, not objective, and only objective information can be considered in a proper scientific theory. Thwack. Crunch.

Titchener's method was discredited on the very grounds that had provided it with its greatest strength. All the facts he had gathered by the method were simply discarded as irrelevant to science. Titchener raged and fumed in awful fury, and the power of his personality alone struck some telling blows, but the battle was lost. When Titchener died in 1927 of a brain tumor, cognitive psychology in North America died with him. Only the growing influence of Freud was an exception. Watson attacked Freud, too, and not without effect. Freud was an introspectionist, too, and as such was subject to the same criticisms. But there was a difference. Freud was useful; Freud was pragmatic and interested in helping people; Freud's view enabled therapists at least to give some structure to what they were doing and to give themselves a high-sounding explanation of behavior that had been previously thought totally irrational. To say that Freud was not scientific was an attack of some importance on this continent, but, to destroy Freud as he had destroyed Titchener, Watson would have had to show that Freud's ideas and techniques had no value, no usefulness in a practical sense. Later, of course, this attack would come; it is precisely the point made by the behavior therapists of today. But for the time Freud was relatively immune. Personology split from the main body of psychology and went its own way. Personology was cognitive; the rest became behavioral.

Behaviorism: Method and Data

Something to Explain

What Watson had wrought in North American psychology was, as we look back on it, beneficial and necessary. There was an emphasis on behavior, both on behavior as something to explain and on behavior as the proper data in a psychological experiment. Both emphases were useful. In psychotherapy, for example, the problem presented to the therapist by the patient is typically some behavior that is not socially or personally acceptable. The question that the cognitive-personality theorists had been trying to answer (and the philosophers before them) was "Why does this person act this way or that?" The answer, it was thought, must lie in how the person thinks about things, so the task became one of exploring the inner machinations of the human mind. Freud asked questions like "Why is this woman paralyzed from the waist down, when there is no physical reason for the paralysis?" The answer: she is hysterical, she is hysterically afraid of what might happen in her life if she were fully mobile, if her legs could part and expose her vagina to any—to all—to him. You had to understand her point of view if you were to understand her behavior. So personality theories quite naturally became introspective. The danger in this approach is that you might forget about what you are ultimately trying to explain—the behavior—and concentrate fully on the explanatory constructs themselves, the workings of the mind. Watson, in the early part of the century, and people like Albert Bandura today, have had a healthy influence in keeping attention focused where it should be.

Something to Study

The second emphasis of the behaviorists was on behavior as data. There is an old example, commonly found in introductory textbooks in psychology, that begins with a question about perception in animals. How can one know what a rat perceives? Or, more specifically, how can we tell whether rats can distinguish one color from another? Animals are good illustrations because very few of them have developed the ability to communicate in English with their human experimenters; one cannot ask one's rat if that color patch looks green. So the researcher is forced to observe other kinds of overt behaior to answer the question. It goes something like this: the rat is rewarded every time it makes an approach response to a red stimulus. When it approaches a green stimulus, there is no reward. Lots and lots of learning trials, so the rat (who is not a dumb animal, by any means) has amply opportunity to learn that red goes with reward and green doesn't. Now the researcher can rephrase the original question: when the rat is presented with two stimuli, one red and one green, will it go to the red stimulus? (Of course, you have to make sure that the hue is the only difference between stimuli. They must be equated in brightness, for example, and size and texture and everything else. The red stimulus cannot be always on the right or always on the left, and on and on. The color must be the *only* difference between the stimuli.) Now, if the rat can distinguish between red and green (assuming it is motivated to gain the reward), it will go consistently to the rewarded red stimulus. If it cannot distinguish between those two colors, if they look exactly the same to it, then it has not basis for choice, and its responses will be randomly distributed between the two colors. Thus one can answer questions about what the animal perceives by observing behavior in carefully constructed situations. To phrase that statement somewhat differently, one can gain quite valuable information about what is going on in the mind of an animal by looking at behavioral data.

The same is true of the human animal. The above illustration is a good one, because color blindness is a common problem in humans. Many color-blind humans are completely unaware of their inability to distinguish between certain colors until they are tested (in a manner not too different from that used with the rat). They think they see reds and greens like everybody else; grass looks green, and the top light in a traffic signal looks red. They are responding not to hue, however, but to subtle differences in brightness, texture, location, and so forth. A behavioral test is necessary; introspection will not suffice. Perhaps you have at one time or another wondered whether the "green" you see is the same "green" a friend perceives. (One of the authors, J.M., was forced to wonder about that, for the final exam in the first psychology course she ever took consisted of one question: "Why is grass green?" Her professor, we might add, had been a student of Titchener's.) Perhaps you have concluded that there is no way to know. In some philosophical sense that may be true, but it *is* possible to determine if you and your friend are responding to the same physical energies when you see, think, and say "green."

A New Cognitive Psychology

As we have previously noted, the advent of Watsonian psychology brought with it an emphasis on behavior. Behavior as method, but also behavior as the proper object of study. Within that framework, there was no possibility of studying "knowledge" or "thought." But today psychologists are returning to the view that the workings of the mind do represent a proper focus of study. The new cognitive psychologists, though, are considerably more sophisticated in the interpretation of data. We use behavior as an indication of mind at work; we even use the verbal report—speech is behavior—that Titchener used exclusively. But the modern theorist does not consider the introspective verbal report as reflecting direct observation of the conscious mind, as Titchener did. Whether we choose to study behavior or mind, the only thing we can *directly* observe is behavior; no one can see into the mind of another. That magic room of personal, subjective experience is closed, in many respects, even to the person who experiences it.

Donald Hebb

Donald Hebb is a Canadian, a professor at McGill University in Montreal. He is a neuropsychologist, which means that he studies the relationship between brain and behavior. He is also a former president of the American Psychological Association, an honor bestowed on few outside of the United States. In short, this psychologist and his views are held in very high esteem. But he is not a personality theorist . . . or is he?

Hebb showed early promise—of dropping out. Perhaps it will be of some comfort to those of you whose college grade-point averages are not the best to know that Hebb's only distinction in college was that he graduated with the lowest possible G.P.A. Like Skinner before him, he desired to be a novelist, but he found writing too painful as an all-day task. By some unknown quirk in the less rigid admission policies of a long-forgotten age, Hebb entered McGill as a part-time graduate student. The other part of the time he was a school teacher; he became interested thereby in cognitive structures and in the changes in them, if any.

A Neurophysiological Approach

Hebb's intellectual development within psychology started with the works of Sigmund Freud. Here, he thought, was a grand and cogent theory, one in need of being made more rigorous. Then he was introduced to Pavlov and the conditioned reflex; perhaps here, he thought, was a way to achieve that rigor. Freud's psychology plus Pavlov's neurology—maybe the winning combination! But he grew dissatisfied with Pavlov, too; there was something missing. By this time, Hebb had begun thinking in neurophysiological terms, and he saw quickly that the simple reflex models of Pavlov were unsatisfying mainly because they were too simple and too reflexive. Even if one remains a physiologist and does not speak of psychology at all, it was clear to him that an enormous amount of *something* occurs between the stimulation of a sense organ (stimulus) and the activation of a peripheral muscle or gland (response). The telephone-switchboard view of the central nervous system that was popular at the time, at least among psychologists like Watson, was clearly inadequate. There had to be some sort of feedback loops and holding mechanisms in the brain, and they had to play some role in behavior.

Psychologists who immersed themselves in studying the brain had (at that time) taken as an unchallenged assumption that brain action was precise. A stimulus comes in, follows some particular pathway, sets off a specific cause-and-effect sequence of neuron activity, and results finally in a particular response. But the physiologist Lashley (with whom Hebb was soon to study) had amassed additional evidence that was disconcerting to all: if you cut out a hunk of the brain—and it doesn't matter much where from—the individual will show a deficit roughly proportional to the amount of brain tissue removed. This evidence suggested that one cannot think in terms of specific links between stimuli and responses, even complicated links with all kinds of feedback loops and holding mechanisms. For, if there are such links, then they should have distinct loci in the brain, and cutting out portions should interrupt them—with resultant effects on observable behavior. This finding destroyed the research young Hebb had in mind, for he had considered only the complexity of stimulus-response connections. So Hebb went directly to the source of his difficulty. He studied under Lashley.

Organization of Behavior

Cell Assembly. In 1949, Hebb published his magnum opus: *Organization of Behavior.* In this and later works, he developed the two key concepts of his theory, the *cell assembly* and the *phase sequence.* The cell assembly is meant to represent, neurophysiologically, a thought or an image. It consists of a brain process that corresponds to some integrated collection of brain cells. The stimulus (for the idea) comes in and triggers one of the brain cells in the collection, which in turn triggers others in its congregation, and the brain process, the idea, occurs. The cell assembly is formed through experience. If one nerve cell fires with another repeatedly, as might happen when both are triggered by the same stimulus, it presumably becomes easier in the future for activity in the first to fire off the second. An assembly is thus integrated on the basis of the ease with which the cells in the group can influence and be influenced by others in the group. Some of the cells in an assembly can also be triggered by ongoing activity in the brain at the time of outside stimulation, so such factors as set, attention, and prior experience can influence the effect of an incoming stimulus. Also, cell assemblies have a number of feedback loops: activity in the assembly can feed back on itself, stimulate itself, and reverberate in a kind of electrical masturbation. This enables the assembly to be active for an extended period of time. Among other features, the feedback loops provide for various holding mechanisms in the brain, so that, when you are instructed to "add" and then are shown two numbers, say 4 and 9, you say "13" and not "5" or "36," which you might have done if you had forgotten the instructions. In other words, given the same stimulus (two numbers), several different responses are possible depending on the previous stimulus input (instructions). The instructions have to be held in the brain somehow if they are to be effective. The feedback and holding mechanism incorporated into the notion of the cell assembly provides for this ability.

Phase Sequence. A phase sequence is an integrated set of cell assemblies, with the integration occurring over a period of time; it corresponds to a stream of thought. Each cell assembly in the sequence can be triggered by sensory stimulation, by another cell assembly, or by both. Again, this theory is quite flexible in terms of the number of sensory and intellectual (memory) influences it can allow and integrate. Moreover, it solves the specific-function or nonspecific-function conflict. You will remember that Lashley's assertion—that a given size of brain lesion causes roughly the same deficit, no matter where the lesion occurs—was pretty demoralizing to the physiological psychologists. But Hebb's model, with its cell assemblies and phase sequences, allowed the neurophysiological basis of thought to be diffused throughout the brain, so that damage to one part need not destroy the mental processes. Voilà! We're in business again!

It is not our place here to describe in great detail Hebb's neuropsychological theory. Perhaps you can sense, from the very definition of the key concepts above, a movement in the area of biological psychology toward a more cognitive physiology. Because of Hebb's speculations, a number of psychologists with training in biological methods began studying the physiology of learning and memory and thinking in general, instead of focusing almost entirely, as they had before, on the simpler mechanisms of sensation and on the simpler mechanisms of the basic motivations such as hunger and thirst. What are the changes in cell structure during learning? What is the nature of activity in various cortical cells during complex perceptions? With Hebb at the forefront, the biological pyschologists moved toward more cortical and less peripheral studies, and something of the brain process that correlates with higher-order mental activities was discovered. Hebb put the complex human brain between the stimulus and the response. The era of radical behaviorism, with stimulus and response and a mysterious black box in between, was over.

Hebb on Memory

Before leaving Hebb, however, we should note two further features of his theory. First, Hebb was one of the earliest psychologists to discuss two types of memory in terms of the duration of storage. The distinction between short-duration memory and long-duration memory stems from the nature of the cell assembly as Hebb understood it. When a stimulus event becomes represented in electrical activity in a collection of brain cells, the information is retrievable only for a short term—only as long as the electrical activity continues. Because of the feedback loops in the assembly, this period can be considered to be much longer than had been previously thought. Hebb was at first thinking of perhaps an hour (at the outside) for short-term memory, primarily on the basis of evidence that an isolated segment of brain, if stimulated electrically, will remain electrically active for about that length of time at the most. But the intact brain is undergoing continuous stimulation, and therefore the duration of any one "chunk" of activity would probably be considerably less, maybe only a few seconds. This is because stimulation in a certain pattern is being continually disrupted and replaced by new stimulation.

Long-term memory, on the other hand, was viewed as some sort of permanent change in brain structure or chemistry, resulting from a momentary activation or from repeated momentary activations. A repeated encounter with a particular informational input will sensitize the brain channels, so to speak, so that a collection of brain cells (now a true cell assembly) is more likely to fire together in the future. This more or less permanent change in structure is seen as the neural basis for the memories we retain for hours, months, and years. The extent to which such long-term memories are formed is primarily a function of rehearsal, if we want to phrase it in behavioral terms, or of repeated activation of the cell assembly, if we use theoretical/physiological terms.

Freud's Mystic Writing Pad. The distinction between two types of memory is a popular one among contemporary memory theorists. Hebb was one of those who brought the distinction into prominence. We said before that Hebb was one of the first to discuss the distinction, which is true enough if by that we mean that he was one of the first of the current lot of psychologists to take these ideas seriously and to study the differences systematically. However, the notion of two types of memory has been around for a long time. William James, writing around the turn of this century, described two kinds of memory, and Sigmund Freud made similar speculations. Perhaps we should be wise to look at Freud's earlier views, as they were spelled out in a paper, written in 1925, entitled "A Note Upon the 'Mystic Writing Pad'."

A Mystic Writing Pad. That's a brand name; you may know it better as a "Magic Slate," a writing surface composed of a plastic-like sheet over a dark, waxy surface. When you write or draw on the sheet with a sharp object, the sheet adheres to the wax, and the writing "mystically" appears. If you then pull the sheet away from its waxy base, the writing "mystically" disappears, and a new message can be entered. Such devices are still commonly sold as children's toys. Freud was intrigued by the similarity in function of this pad to the human memory. In his view, you see, any satisfactory theory of human memory must deal with certain requirements of a memory system. For example, there must be a distinction between conscious and unconscious memories. Conscious memory must have a limited capacity, for consciousness is always limited to a very small subset of the sensory and cognitive events that could, on other occasions, be the focus of attention. But unconscious memory—and here Freud is using "unconscious" in the sense of "not conscious" and so includes both memories that could be retrieved (preconscious) and those that exist and have influence but cannot be consciously examined (the true unconscious)—must have a very large capacity.

Conscious memory must be some sort of system that can renew itself, make itself ready to accept new information, uncluttered by the old information. A piece of solid slate like a blackboard has this characteristic: it can be renewed (erased), and then it is ready to accept new information. But the human memory cannot be like a blackboard, for the latter retains no permanent trace of the information. Once erased, the information is lost. A piece of paper, written on with a pen, retains a permanent trace, but it cannot renew itself; once a page is filled, one must get a new piece of paper. So the human memory cannot be like a pen and paper. The pen-and-paper system, in fact, violates two features possessed by the human memory, that of renewability of consciousness and that of the distinction between conscious and unconscious memories. But a Mystic Writing Pad is a better analogy. It has two systems, one like a limited-capacity blackboard with renewal characteristics and the other (the waxy base) like a piece of paper that retains the impressions for a long time even if they are not visible once the adherence of the sheet to the base is broken.

STM and LTM. Modern theory is still plugging away at two kinds of memory system. We use fancy sets of initials now, STM for short-term memory and LTM for long-term memory, but the basic idea is still the same. STM is considered to be a limited-capacity storage system in which the information decays and is lost unless it is rehearsed and/or transferred into LTM. LTM is a large-capacity storage system in which the information, for all practical purposes, is never lost (although, paradoxically, it is often very hard to find). The theoretical formulations are much more sophisticated now, often using computer analogies, but it is still true that the current views are not far out of line with Freud's image of human memory as a Mystic Writing Pad.

Arousal System

The second feature of Hebb's theory that has gained recent prominence is the notion of an *arousal system.* The history of this issue is a great deal more complicated than that of the two kinds of memory, for arousal became an important issue in the mid-1960s and has enjoyed a kind of fluctuating popularity ever since. So let us again oversimplify a complex issue and take from its history what is important for our purposes.

Libido. There was in Freud's theory of personality the concept of libido—sexually toned energy—that motivated or "drove" the entire psychic apparatus. It was very much like a life force, which is the way Jung saw it, a generalized drive that did little to explain particular behaviors. If the energy, or arousal, construct can be said to aid at all in our understanding of behavior, it would be in the context of such a general driving force. It would help in predicting the vigor of a response, the speed of a response, and the persistence of a behavior over time, rather than the appearance of this or that particular behavior. For example, a very hungry (aroused) person might be expected to eat more vigorously, to get to the table faster, and to eat for a longer period of time than one who had recently finished a turkey dinner.

Freud used the notion of libido (which we are equating, roughly and for the moment, with arousal) to explain the phenomena of puberty. If sexual—libidinal—energy increases rapidly at puberty, it's only reasonable that stronger and more leakproof defenses will be needed to contain it. More of the ego's time and energy will be used for such purposes. And that's exactly what seems to happen. Unfortunately, the libido theory didn't seem to be particularly useful in explaining very many things besides these pubertal changes. Oh, there are a few others: individual differences in the sex drive, the effects of generating and then not releasing sexual energy as in coitus interruptus . . . but, even for these areas and even for puberty, contemporary theorists are finding it easier to explain the changes in purely behavioral, learning-theory terms: stimuli, reinforcements, and the like.

The Big D

The concept of a general energizing drive was brought to a theoretical peak by Clark Hull, one of our major theorists in Chapter 5. His prime formula for behavior, ${}_SE_R = {}_SH_R \times D$ (behavior equals the strength of the bond between a stimulus and a response times generalized drive), turned several thousand otherwise capable researchers to a rather futile experimental inquiry into the sources and the nature of this basic fuel for behavior: Drive, the Big D.

It soon became apparent that Big D was practically useless for explaining behavior. It failed on two rather basic counts: it was not sufficient (that is, it could not by itself account for an observed behavior), and it was not necessary. Wow, there's a real one-two punch! A theoretical construct can survive being insufficient if it is still necessary, and it needn't be necessary if it is sufficient. But to be *neither*—well, that should have taken care of Big D once and for all. We'd better look at that accusation more carefully.

Sufficiency. First, sufficiency. By definition, Big D cannot tell why the rat is running (as opposed to eating or making love). Bid D posits the amount of fuel but not which system the fuel will be used to energize. The habit construct, ${}_{\mathrm{S}}\mathrm{H}_{\mathrm{r}}$, tells us which response will occur. Big D is general; it tells us only that, whatever the response, it will be more vigorous than usual. But Big D is not even sufficient to do this, as the following case illustrates. If rats, from birth, are fed every 24 hours and then observed in a simple runway that leads to food, their running speed will get faster and faster after the last feeding at intervals ranging from about 10 to about 24 hours. But after 24 hours or so, their running speed begins to decline. Now, consider what happens at, say, 35 hours since the last feeding. Big D should be greater than at 24 hours, and speed should be faster. But it isn't: the rat runs considerably slower. The reason, of course, is that the rat was used to eating at 24-hour intervals, and this interval was associated with the most vigorous response. It is something like us humans feeling hunger pangs at the evening hour at which we are accustomed to eat, even if we are not particularly hungry. You yourself perhaps have experienced the phenomenon of missing a meal and noticing that your "hunger" was most intense at the time the meal ordinarily would have been served but lessened as that time passed.

This is not to say that the number of hours of deprivation do not play some role in the vigor of a response, for they must have something to do with it. But it does imply that previous experience or learning plays a very important role in explaining the behaviors that Big D was supposed to have its greatest impact on. One cannot explain the vigor and the persistence of a behavior simply in terms of drive. Big D is not sufficient.

Necessity. But how about necessity? Surely there does have to be some general power, some fuel, to run the system, even though learning experiences may affect the ways in which that fuel is used. Well, not according to some learning theorists. Several have shown that it is possible to explain almost any behavior pattern in terms of stimuli and responses, with no need whatsoever for introducing the Big D. In the case of our run-and-eat rats, for example, the key to understanding is clearly the feeding interval that the animal has experienced again and again; the internal stimuli produced after 24 hours are closely associated with the response of eating, and therefore the most vigorous response occurs at that time. The vigor of the response is explained by the time interval; what need do we have of a construct like Big D?

By 1967, one reviewer found it possible to make the statement that there is

> little support for the hypothesis that all sources of drive contribute in the same way to the organism's motivation . . . but there can be little controversy over the finding that the general drive factor is only a minor determinant of behavior. Behavior is predominantly determined by the specific drive conditions, specific stimulus situations, and specific habit structures that characterize an individual at a given time. Generalized drive has turned out to be a puny fellow compared to the Big D we had expected to find; he cannot carry much explanatory weight.[1]

It is important to realize, however, just what the psychologists were trying to do with concepts like Big D. They were trying, somewhat forlornly, to distinguish between motivation (D) and learning, where learning was seen to be a factor related to behavior in a specific situation and motivation a factor related to all behavior. Motivation was to be nonspecific and learning specific. This, beyond much doubt, is a naive view of motivation, bound to end (as some now claim it has) in disrespect and disrepute.

The MAS. Examples abound of repeated attempts and repeated failures with Big D. We have mentioned the Freudian and the Hullian failures. Another in the Hullian tradition was an attempt to measure individual differences in drive in humans by means of a questionnaire known as the MAS—the Manifest Anxiety Scale. Since most college sophomores, on whom the majority of the ensuing studies were to be conducted, suffer little from extreme hunger or thirst but do on occasion allow themselves a moment or two of anxiety, anxiety was seen as a prominent contributor to Big D. So people who score high on the MAS (indicating that they have relatively high levels of anxiety) are presumed to have a higher level of generalized drive. This assumption was studied in a vast collection

[1]The reviewer who spoke in such funereal terms about Big D was Bolles in his *Theory of Motivation* (Harper & Row, 1967).

of experiments, most of which compared high MAS scorers to low MAS scorers on some learning or performance task. Some researchers reported positive results, some reported negative results, and some reported no results. Or weren't able to find a place to publish whatever mish-mash they wanted to report. The most charitable summary of this voluminous research effort is that it produced no knowledge that could be used to advantage by the police or the military.

The Reticular Formation. Despite the failure of the generalized-drive concept to account for more than, at best, a minute portion of the variability in the behavior of either animals or humans, the discovery of a biological system that appeared at first to have the properties of a general, nonspecific arousal system quickened the hearts of the few psychologists who were still fascinated by the prospect of gaining scientific credibility for old Big D. There is, it appears, a part of the brain stem known as the reticular formation that does little but spray general excitation onto the cortex, where all the important associations are located. Any specific association or cell assembly that is active at the time of spray will be the beneficiary of the electrical storm: it will be more active, more persistent. And, since repetition is the principle of formation in cell assemblies, it will be better learned. Big D is back, in a new, biological dress: Big D has been found in the brain stem.

We really haven't the heart to chronicle the history of another Big D disappointment. Suffice it to say that the reticular formation did not, on closer examination, provide the neat and simple answers that were hoped for. It wasn't a total failure, not by any means. The data are still coming in. But there won't be any single grand enlightenment, any "at last we've found the secret!" coming from the reticular formation. At least, we don't think there will be.

The End of Big D

We're going to stick our necks out here. Either there is no such thing as Big D or, if it has any meaning at all, it relates only to gross conditions such as sleep versus wakefulness. In any case, the explanation of the workings of the human mind will not be greatly enhanced by the use of any such construct. But the construct will arise again, you wait and see. It would be so nice, so tidy, if there were such a thing. And psychologists do their share of wishful thinking, too. Perhaps that's not so bad—it will, at least, be interesting to see what form the next Big D expedition will take. The new form, when combined with the others, may lead us closer to an answer to the question of why humans have this insistent desire to postulate such a factor in behavior.

Of course, we could state some suspicions. Big D may be nothing less than an attempt to explain life itself. That is, the behavior of a dead person in any given situation tends to be quite unlike the behavior of a live person in the same situation, and all must find this a bit puzzling. Why? It will not do to say that one is alive and the other is not. What is the nature of life? How is it different from death? Do some individuals have more life than others? These questions are probably not ones that can be answered by scientific inquiry, no more than the existence or nonexistence of God can be established by such means. But this does not mean that the question will not be asked by scientists, for scientists are human too. Well, most of them. Anyhow, as scientists, they must disguise their theological and philosophical questions and make them look "scientific." Inquiries into the nature and the effects of energy or motivation are more scientifically respectable in the 20th century than inquiries into the nature and the effects of God.

Well, fine. We have come all this way, beaten our brains out over running rats and reticular formations, only to be told that it's a nonissue. What's the point? A fair question, and we'll try to answer it. Most cognitive theorists simply don't worry about what powers the organism. The kind of being that the cognitive theorist studies is lively, active, creative. Why is a person that way? I don't know, says the cognitive theorist, and I really don't care. It's not my concern. The stimulus comes in, and the response, if any, goes out. I want to know what happens in between. What is the nature of the cognitive process that works on the stimulus? What does the cognitive system add? How do the cognitive structures change over time, through experience? What is perception, memory, learning decision, choice, human thought? These are the questions today.

Drive is one of those tempting nonissues that has to be stomped on, hard, or it will continue to distract us. After all, who wouldn't like to find a definitive answer to the problem of the nature of life? It's a siren song, tempting and disturbing. But, if we follow it, we are likely to find (as did Hull and the others) that the beautiful visions melt away and we are left on the shipwreck of our broken theories.

But enough of poetic warnings. For the cognitive theorist, humans are active organisms. That's part of what it means to be human; it comes with the territory. The question is not (any more) why we are active but, rather, what we do with that activity and how we do it. Stimuli come in—okay, we know that. And behavior comes out—we'll let somebody else worry about explaining that part. And in between? Activity, processing, understanding, remembering: cognition. A lot goes on in there, doesn't it?

So much, in fact, that few cognitive theorists have tried to take on and integrate everything. Most have focused on some relatively narrow area of cognitive functioning: cognitive style, for instance, or locus of control. What in the world do those words mean? Funny you should ask; we'll spend all of Chapter 13 talking about them and a few of their friends. For now, though, let's meet someone who did try to tackle that whole cognitive realm at once—and who did, on the whole, a pretty fair job. That someone is George Kelly.

George Kelly

The Theory of Personal Constructs

George Kelly's theory is clearly cognitive; his self-defined focus is on how a person construes his or her environment. By this he means that what a person perceives to be the situation will, by and large, determine the response, if any, that the person will make to it. Behavior is determined by perceptions, and everyone perceives things in a slightly different way. These differences are personality differences; an individual's personality is determined by his or her unique way of perceiving or internally constructing the environment. The theory has a name: the theory of *personal constructs.* From all of this, we could say that, if you understood the manner in which a person processes information from the environment, you would understand a great deal about that person. Such a statement is one that you would make about a cognitive theory of personality; it is the hallmark. It is the hallmark of Kelly's theory.

An Expressly Cognitive Theory. Now we can begin to add the qualifications. Every personality theory is cognitive, so why the big deal? Perhaps two points can be made in answering. First, Kelly's theory was *expressly* cognitive, whereas others claim to be otherwise. Freud's theory was meant to be motivational, and Bandura's theory was meant to be behavioral; both theorists found it necessary to think a lot about cognitive processing of information, but this was not their stated intention. Second, an explicit intention to focus on cognitive variables leads one to quite different lines of thought and research than do other approaches. Just to cite one example here at the beginning, consider the personality trait, long a staple in personality theories (role theorists to the contrary). Generally, the trait is considered an attribute of the person to whom it is attributed. If I say you are very aggressive, people understand me to mean that you are high on the trait of aggression. I may be wrong, but all that my being wrong means is that you are *not* high in aggression.

If I had told George Kelly that you were an aggressive person, his reaction would have been quite different from that of a trait theorist. Instead of observing your behavior in an attempt to ascertain whether or not my assessment was correct, Kelly would have begun studying me! He would have been interested in the behavioral effect of my tendency to see the world in aggressive/friendly terms. In short, a personality trait, which is essentially an adjective applied by one person to another, can be used not only to understand the person to which it is applied but also to understand the person who judges himself or herself capable of making the assessment. At the extreme, the individual who sees almost everything in terms of, say, "for me or against me" will be diagnosed as a paranoid and possibly locked up. But that person's constructions are too global and of little use; mine, when I do that same type of thing, usually slip by unnoticed. Wait—I am offended by the comparison of me with a paranoid. I am objective. Horsefeathers, Kelly would have said; everyone is subjective. The healthy ones are those whose subjective constructions do not diverge radically from the subjective constructions of others.

Projection and Personality. Another point: the fact that personality and perceptions are closely related has long been a basic principle of personality theory and research. Is it not true, for example, that the entire area of projective tests rests on the assumption that, when you describe a picture or an inkblot, you will reveal your own personality organization?

So what's so different about Kelly? The answer is, of course, that Kelly took this assumption seriously and made it the focal point of his theory. In other theories, the projective assumption is an outgrowth, a side-track—interesting, even useful occasionally, but certainly not central to the theory. Moreover, projective tests are even today believed to yield information about the personality dynamics of the test taker, mostly that person's needs and basic desires. Kelly would look at the data with more of an eye as to how the individual construes the environment—how one sees oneself in relation to the world one lives in. (Not to mention the possibility of analyzing the world view of the person who constructed the test!) Again we can use our example of aggression as either a motivational trait or a conceptual category. Kelly chose the latter route.

Kelly did, however, succumb once to the lure of test construction. He devised the Role Repertoire Test. It wasn't exactly a projective test—but yes, it was, sort of. It was intended to map out the subjective categories that an individual uses to describe the world around and within. Now, to understand that statement, we have to back up a few steps.

An Everyday Theory of Behavior

The key to understanding George Kelly's theory (and, incidentally, his personality test) is in the analogy between the scientist and the average person. Very early in his career, Kelly was struck by certain similarities between scientists' methods and the daily-life strategies of plain folks. Far from considering people as being driven this way and that by semi-mysterious forces, Kelly viewed them as reasonably logical researchers who were trying to thread their way through life in the best possible way. When you encounter a problem, you consider the possibilities and form a hypothesis about a course of action and its probable outcome. You might then sample data from the environment in order to provide yourself with a preliminary test of your hypothesis or the wisdom of applying it in this case. Say you face a barking dog. You figure that you must defend yourself or flee; you prepare for the imminent attack. But, as a provisional test, you move your hand slowly toward the dog, saying soothing words. If the dog now approaches with tail wagging, "hostile" dog becomes "friendly" dog, and your original hypothesis is abandoned. If the dog snarls, the original theory—that the dog is angry and about to attack, that the dog could cause you injury, and that some action must be taken—is supported. Should you counterattack? Should you remain motionless, prepared to defend yourself? Or should you back away? You need more information. You back away slowly, a few inches at a time. This test will tell you more about the dog's intentions and inclinations; if the dog moves forward as you move backward, stand-and-fight may be the decision. But the dog stays put, and at a safe distance you can turn and walk away. You glance over your shoulder now and then to gather a bit more data on the situation. Whew. I'm glad we got out of that one.

The average person, like any psychologist, has a theory of human behavior. That theory has theoretical constructs that are related to one another and to behaviors in such a way that one can generate, with more or less facility depending on the situation, predictions about what will happen next. If you are a *part* of the situation, which is usually the case, you rely on your theory of yourself as well as your theory about others and important objects. Your action is based on your predictions: such and such behavior seems most appropriate. The resulting behavior and its outcome are fed back into the theory, as the scientist feeds back data from experiments, and, if the prediction was clearly inaccurate, you make some revision in the theory.

Hostility according to Kelly. Sometimes one's behavior is clearly experimental, as contrasted with coping. As a child, you push buttons, flip switches, and put forks in electrical outlets, not to gain any particular reward, but to see "what happens if . . . " As an adult, you explore your new neighborhood and demonstrate your natural curiosity toward new events and new objects. We are happy when predictions are confirmed and anxious and frustrated when they are not. Kelly defined hostility as an attempt to force confirmation of a prediction that the relevant data seem to prove false. That's a biggie; go back and read it again. Not exactly your everyday, average view of hostility, is it? I make a prediction about how things will be. The prediction looks like it's going to be wrong. So I try to push things around so the prediction will turn out right afterwards—that's hostility. Strange, but in many situations there is a definite ring of truth to Kelly's formulation. Hostilities between parents and children, for example, often arise when one of them behaves in a manner not acceptable to the other. Father, whose theory of family interaction suggests that his son will have taken his (Father's) influence without rancor and integrated it into his own set of principles, finds the son hooked on cocaine and falling prey to the patently socialistic dogma of the Democratic party. Father becomes hostile, not because he wishes to injure his son, but in order to force the son to provide him with the data that would confirm his social predictions about how he and his son ought to relate.

Derivation of Personal Constructs

As we said, the theoretical constructs in an individual's personal theory of human behavior Kelly called *personal constructs.* Like many scientific theories of personality, these constructs are usually trait labels such as kind/cruel, dominant/submissive, or "like my father"/"not like my father."

But we can't just stop there—sure, everybody has constructs, but where do they come from? Kelly said that, in the first stages of construct formation, the person begins to notice general features—similarities—in the events that flow by. This event is like that one in that both made me feel happy. So "happy-making" is a construct, a quality that events may have. Wait, though; there's still something missing here. I can't abstract out the notion of "happy-making" unless I have something to compare it with, something that's different, something that doesn't make me happy. If there is no contrast, then the notion of "happy-making" doesn't arise, because *everything* is that way. Few of us have a personal construct of "person who walks on the ground"/"person who walks on air"; since everyone walks on the ground, we take that quality for granted. In order to build a construct, we need at least three elements: two that are similar in some way, and one that is different. Only through the contrast can a construct gain meaning: if I tell you that Jim and Jane are "worgly," you probably won't be able to guess what I mean, but, if I add that Henry is definitely "unworgly," you may begin to figure out what "worgliness" is.

The Role Rep Test. Kelly's Role Repertoire Test, which we mentioned earlier, is based on this "two versus one" notion. In the Role Rep Test, you are asked to make a list of the most significant people in your life. The tester then arranges these names in every possible combination of pair-plus-one-other. It is your job to indicate, for each combination, how the two paired people are alike and yet different from the third. According to Kelly, analysis of the responses to the Role Rep Test can yield an accurate list of the personal constructs used by a given individual.

And more than just a list: a sense of the organization, the patterning, of those constructs. Constructs, you see, are organized into hierarchies. We don't just shove them into our heads any old which-way, but, rather, we relate them to each other. Some constructs are very general and can be applied to a variety of events. "Happy-making" can fit an interaction with a friend, a walk through the park, a plate of ham and eggs, or half an hour with a good book. "Tastes sour," on the other hand, has a more restricted range. All of an individual's constructs needn't fit into a single hierarchy in a neat and orderly way, though—people are more interesting than that! We often have independent, or even conflicting, construct systems at the same time.

Disorder, Anxiety, and Growth. Indeed, it may well be that *dis*order in our construct systems is a major factor in personal growth. When a prediction (made on the basis of our personal constructs) is disconfirmed, said Kelly, we feel anxiety. Anxiety is uncomfortable, and we tend to shift around, to change our perceptions of what has happened, or to revise our constructs, until things fit again and the anxiety is reduced. Conflicting construct systems are likely to bring about inaccurate—or even conflicting—predictions, so it is within such systems that we might expect to find the most anxiety and therefore the most growth and change.

Kelly, being a cognitive theorist, focused on the cognitive side of human functioning, trying to build a theory that would encompass rational human behaviors. He took care of Big D by postulating a basic human need to predict and control. He integrated perception and activity in the process of construct validation: we both perceive and behave so as to improve our predictive ability. Feelings, in Kelly's view, are a side effect. They don't run the machinery; they come and go as we pursue our construct-building goals, rather like the clicks and whirrs and drips of oil that may accompany the workings of a complex machine.

You don't like it? You think "love" and "hate" are more important than clicks and whirrs, maybe even more important than predicting events? Perhaps you aren't cut out, then, to be a cognitive theorist. But you can still use the insights of the Kellys and the Hebbs, you know. You don't have to buy into the whole thing—but understand it, sort through it, extract what's useful to you. Every story has its own truth. Kelly's story has a lot of truth, a lot of validity, for a good many human situations.

Chapter Summary

We began this chapter with the story of another phase of the ongoing battle between the behaviorists and the rest of the world—in this case, the rest of the world being represented by the introspectionists, headed by E.B. Titchener. Titchener brought a small chunk of Germany to the United States and lived in it for 35 years; he even invited others in occasionally. From it he pontificated and philosophized about the elements of *mental chemistry,* the building blocks from which thought is constructed. He also hurled thunderbolts at the behaviorists, who were, in his opinion, far too practical and down-to-earth to be truly scientific.

The thunderbolts, though, turned out to be duds. They didn't destroy Watson and the behaviorists; Watson blew Titchener right out of the water. What's scientific about sitting in a chair and thinking about how your head works? That's not science at all! And the pragmatic Americans ate it up. Watson took a few potshots at Freud, too, using the same argument, but it didn't work so well there, maybe because Freud was helping other people to find out how *their* heads worked, too.

Meanwhile, back at the lab . . . the neurologists and physiologists were actually *looking* at the insides of heads. Well, at least they were worrying about physical structures and nervous pathways that housed—constituted? determined?—thought. That's pretty scientific too; it went down well in the New World. Donald Hebb, a Canadian, worked out a whole set of notions about *feedback loops* and *cell assemblies* that looked like it might make sense out of all that complicated mental machinery. That's what the mind is, a machine; all we have to do is map out the circuitry, and we'll understand the nature of thought.

But there was another riddle, hiding inside the riddle of thinking. Even if we explain *how* people think, we still don't know *why* they think. What starts the whole thing in motion? What is the fuel that makes the machinery go? *Arousal, drive, the Big D.* Posit a generalized motivator, an "all-purpose fuel." Find a physical mechanism in the brain that works to "arouse" the system. A neat idea, great if it can be done. But so far nobody has succeeded, not even Hebb. It may be a blind alley.

So back to the drawing board. *Memory,* which is surely a part of thinking, isn't all that simple either. It comes in at least two varieties, short term and long term. The two work in different ways and are probably grounded in quite different physiological processes. Freud anticipated the idea; Hebb worked on the physiology of it. From the notion that people may be defined as cognitive creatures—as creatures with brains that process ideas and remember them and actively deal with their environment—it is only a step to the theory of personal constructs. That's George Kelly's term, his baby. People do create, construct, the worlds they live in. And, being people, they do so with infinite and wonderful variety. Each person's world is a little different, because we don't construct them in exactly the same way. And the differences are differences in personality! Forget about drives, and feelings, and traits; the way one perceives the world determines one's behavior. What you see in and believe about your world is equivalent to what kind of person you are. If I understand your system of personal constructs, I will be able to understand and predict your behavior.

It's a neat idea, an excellent springboard to the exploration of a host of more narrowly defined aspects of thought and perception. The "narrower" theories—some of them, at least—are waiting in the wings, ready to make their entrance in Chapter 13. Kelly's theory appears to be (so far) the only one that can accommodate all of them. With Kelly, we seem to have come full circle: back to Descartes, perhaps the very first cognitive psychologist, who said "I think, therefore I am." Kelly transposes it: I am, therefore I think—I am *what* I think.

Suggested Readings

E.G. Boring has written the classic book on the history of psychology, titled (appropriately) *The History of Psychology.* You'll get a good sense of Titchener's place in the scheme of things from sampling selectively in this book. In fact, the whole book might be well worth your while; it will give you a picture of the ebb and flow of psychological thought over the years. It's written from a strongly experimental point of view and isn't exactly what you'd call chatty in style, but digging in can be a really fascinating experience. You'll begin to understand the ins and outs of the whole behaviorist/introspectionist conflict in much greater detail than we've dealt with it here.

Koch's several volumes of *Psychology: A Study of a Science* (McGraw-Hill, 1959) are likewise excellent sources of more detail and background than we've had room for in these pages. Hebb's chapter in Volume I of this series will give you a good jumping-off place for the neurophysiological approach. For an overview of the whole memory-encoding problem, look into Melton and Martin's collection of readings, *Coding Processes in Human Memory* (Winston, 1972). The "Big D" issue is dealt with in a very interesting way in several of the chapters of Weiner's *Cognitive Views of Human Motivation* (Academic Press, 1974); Bolles' introductory chapter gives an excellent historical overview, and the discussion and comments chapters at the end of the book provide a rare opportunity to observe some high-powered theoretical sniping from the battleground itself.

If you want more straight cognition, then of course you must read Neisser's *Cognitive Psychology.* It's somewhat out of date, but it's the big picture, the overview. Neisser's more recent *Cognition and Reality* (Freeman, 1976) would make a nice chaser.

Kelly's big book is *The Psychology of Personal Constructs* (Norton, 1955). It's readable and well organized, and it makes you think.

Notes and References

Boring's *History of Psychology* and Koch's *Psychology: A Study of a Science* are the basic sources for the ideas presented in the early part of the chapter. Additional information about Hebb was drawn from his 1949 book, *The Organization of Behavior* (Wiley) and from his *A Textbook of Psychology* (Saunders, 1966). An excellent survey of the work done on the neurophysiological aspects of behavior up to the middle of this century, including Lashley's work on localization of function, can be found in Boring's chapter entitled "Brain Function."

Freud's "A Note Upon the 'Mystic Writing Pad'" is published in Volume V of the Basic Books edition of the *Collected Papers* (1959). You will also find his theory of libido spelled out in detail in chapter 3 of *Three Contributions on the Theory of Sexuality,* first published in 1905.

Taylor's original report of the development of the MAS was published in Volume 48 (1953) of the *Journal of Abnormal and Social Psychology* (pp. 285–290). A further exposition of the relationship between work with the MAS and the whole Big D concept is found in Spence's article "A Theory of Emotionally Based Drive (D) and Its Relation to Performance in Simple Learning Situations" (*American Psychologist,* 1958, *13,* 131–141).

Neisser information came, as mentioned in the Suggested Readings section, from his *Cognitive Psychology* (Appleton-Century-Crofts, 1967) and *Cognition and Reality* (Freeman, 1976). Similarly, much of the discussion of Kelly is from his *The Psychology of Personal Constructs,* mentioned in the Suggested Readings. A short discussion of the Role Repertory Test is also found in Anastasi's *Psychological Testing* (4th ed., Macmillan, 1976).

13

Tinkering with Ideas

I do not want to discourage anyone from the pursuit of the psychological Holy Grail by the use of the Skinner box; but as far as I am concerned, there will be no moaning of farewell when we have passed the pressing of the bar.

Harry Harlow

In the study of the interface between cognition and personality, psychologists have surely gone beyond the radical behaviorism that insists on ignoring everything that can't be counted, weighed, or measured. Rather, many researchers are now recognizing how necessary it may be to take into account those very real events that occur inside the organism, beyond the reach of our most sophisticated observational tools. Cognitive psychology has come into its own.

We've just finished looking at some theories of cognition and at one theory that is a cognitive theory of personality. Notice, though, that we said *a* cognitive theory, not *the* cognitive theory. There is no such thing in psychology today as *the* cognitive theory of personality, as there is *the* psychoanalytic theory or *the* individual psychology of Jung or *the* Gestalt approach. Cognitive theory is more like a jumble of ideas and approaches, all interrelated, some overlapping, many suggesting contradictions and confusions. Maybe they'll all come together some day into a neat, integrated, unified theory. And maybe they won't—and maybe they shouldn't. After all, the inside of your head isn't exactly neat and orderly and unified. If it were, you'd be a computer. Our minds are more disorderly than orderly, more jumbled than neat. We leap from one idea to another; we are stewed and steeped in emotional eruptions; we slog painfully through the muck of a problem only to find ourselves—how?—caught up, halfway across our mental world, in a solution that seems to have come from nowhere. As scientists, we scarcely dare admit it, but more than one of us takes secret delight in the creative disorder of the mind, recognizing it as the source of most of what makes life worth living. Don't find out too much, we are tempted to say; don't clean out the cupboard all the way. The magic show isn't fun any more once you know the secret.

We probably don't have to worry too much, though, about explaining away the secrets of the mind and thus destroying its magic. Those secrets that we have "explained" have only led us further into the maze and revealed new bits of "magic" that are at least equally intriguing. As we learn more and more about how people construct their reality, we see boxes within boxes, puzzles within puzzles. Will it end? Probably never—we are not likely ever to be able to explain or understand ourselves fully. We keep trying, and we come closer and closer, but there will always be some mystery. Only the Worm Oribouros can swallow itself completely.

But we do keep trying. Mainly because it's fun. The ideas in some areas are less jumbled and confused than in others. We usually do the easier things first, follow the promising trails as far as we can before going back to hack our way through tangled underbrush.

Cognitive theories of personality are, right now, a kind of tangled underbrush. Or, a more accurate analogy might be that of a spill of partly built Tinker-Toy constructions, some old and some new, some using others as subparts of themselves, some with pieces missing. You can visualize the thing for yourself. In this chapter we're going to explore some of the bits and fragments that have been built up into theories or at least mini-theories of their own. We won't try to integrate them or bring them together into some grand, overarching cognitive personality theory. You will notice, though, as you meet each one, that they all build on the idea articulated by Kelly: *humans create and construct their own reality.* That's the unifying theme, the basic assumption.

The Dissonant Leon Festinger

There is an interesting phenomenon that has been (unwittingly) demonstrated throughout this book and that becomes more and more apparent as we move into the cognitive domain. Over and over, we have presented some interesting example of behavior and then introduced a theory, or an extension of a theory, to explain it. We're fascinated by the confusions and contradictions of behavior—the "magic"—and we can't seem to leave them alone. Just as the audience at a magic show struggles to figure out how the tricks are performed, so we are driven to resolve the contradictions and tidy up the confusions of human behavior.

The Theory of Cognitive Dissonance

A man named Leon Festinger noticed this tidying tendency, shining like some kind of fixed star through the murk of everyday human activity. He picked it out, polished it up, and established it as the basis for his theory of *cognitive dissonance*.

Now Festinger is one of those scientists who carried a reputation around with him. He was hated, he was loved; he was a man to be reckoned with. His students—some of them, and most of the better ones—found that he inspired them to work harder than they ever had before, to do things they didn't think they could do. He inspired loyalty and love in them, and he could destroy them with sarcasm. Festinger could get away with much and could be forgiven much, because he had done much. He was forever exploring new territory, getting excited about a new topic, building bridges from here to there. Festinger noticed things—about other people, about students and colleagues, about himself. He deserved his reputation.

In building what came to be the cognitive-dissonance theory, Festinger wasn't especially interested in explaining why psychologists build theories. But psychologists are people too (at least most of the time), and they act like other people. As scientists, and as lovers or tennis players or gourmet cooks, they try to resolve confusions. Stripped of all its trimmings and embellishments, that's what Festinger's theory says: people are uncomfortable with things that don't seem to fit, and they will construct and reconstruct their internal worlds so as to make things more consistent with one another.

Dissonance, said Festinger, occurs when a person contemplates two or more cognitions—beliefs—that contradict each other. If I believe, for instance, that all people are fundamentally the same, regardless of the color of their skin and, at the same time, believe that Blacks are less trustworthy than Whites, than I am in a state of dissonance; both of these things cannot be true. Likewise, I might have a picture of myself as a good and loving mother but concurrently be aware that I occasionally feel a very strong dislike for my child. The loving mother who is fed up to here with her child feels uncomfortable. The inconsistency has created a state of dissonance.

Dissonance Tends to Resolve Itself. It is hard to find good examples of dissonance, because dissonance, by its very nature, is a fleeting phenomenon. Festinger, in his original statement of dissonance theory, said that the presence of dissonance gives rise to pressures to reduce that dissonance and that the stronger the dissonance is, the greater will be the need to reduce it or do away with it. What this means, of course, is that people struggle to avoid awareness of contradictions in their belief structure, but, if they are forced to recognize such contradictions, they immediately move to change the situation in some way and thus reduce the dissonance. They reconstruct their internal world so that it is consistent or consonant again.

How is Dissonance Created? Dissonance is created when you realize that you are holding two inconsistent or contradictory beliefs. But what does this imply in terms of real-life situations? How do people acquire and then become aware of such contradictions? Essentially, every time we choose to do something, to believe something, to feel a particular way, we create the possibility of dissonance. In choosing one thing, we have rejected one or more other things. If these alternatives are also attractive, we are aware of two facts: (1) I would probably have enjoyed or benefited from that; and (2) I gave it up. Usually we minimize the dissonance by telling ourselves how much better was the choice that we did make; again, it's difficult to observe a dissonance state in any example because we are so very efficient at dispelling dissonance quickly. Indeed, there is some evidence that we may begin the job of dissonance reduction *before* we actually feel the discomfort of dissonance, just because we anticipate that we may feel it soon.

Dissonance also commonly arises when some new knowledge or perception interferes or conflicts with an old and well-established belief. It is disruptive to throw out our beliefs, to admit that we have been wrong. It is also difficult to deny the reality of a new perception. A child who "knows" that tomatoes taste bad will usually reject the opportunity to learn otherwise; or an old-timer who grew up believing that "painted women" had no morals may experience dissonance when faced with the evidence that today's makeup-wearing females may still adhere to a strong moral code.

What Affects the Degree of Dissonance? Festinger and his students have done a great deal of research aimed at defining the various factors that affect the way, or the degree to which, dissonance is created. They have found, for example, that, when one chooses among various alternatives, the more attractive the rejected choices, the greater the dissonance arousal. If a choice is quite clear and the things that must be rejected in order to make that choice are things one doesn't care much about, then dissonance is usually no problem. But, if one must choose only one of a number of desired alternatives, one experiences dissonance. Let Jimmy Jo choose one piece from a plate of candies. If there is only one kind of candy that he really likes on the plate, he will not experience dissonance. But if, in taking one kind, he must give up another sort that he likes, he will have difficulty choosing and will feel tension and discomfort. Similarly, the more negative characteristics possessed by the *chosen* alternative, the greater the dissonance. It is just as hard to choose among punishments you must endure as to choose among rewards you may enjoy. Did your mother ever ask you whether you would rather wash the dishes or tidy up the living room? Yrrrch—dissonance!

Conflict between behavior and belief is also a source of dissonance. When I do something that is inconsistent with the kind of person I think I am, it makes me uncomfortable. I'm generally warmhearted and generous, but I refused to buy a box of cookies from the Girl Scout who just rang my doorbell. What's wrong? Immediately I begin to search for a reason, to try to find information that will allow me to reconstruct what happened in a way that fits with who I think I am. The fewer reasons I can find to justify what I do, the greater will be my dissonance. In particular, the more I must believe that I *chose* to perform the dissonance-producing act (as opposed to being forced into it by circumstances), the more uncomfortable I will feel.

Resolving Cognitive Dissonance

The word *cognitive* in cognitive dissonance implies that dissonance is usually a conscious phenomenon. When we experience dissonance, we should be aware of experiencing it. But that isn't necessarily so. The conscious element may exist, but it may also be true that our "awareness" is merely a recognition of discomfort. The ability to recognize the *source* of the discomfort and to pinpoint the discrepant cognitions that cause it is probably the exception rather than the rule. Moreover, even if we are aware of dissonance, we are often unaware of the means we use to deal with it. And those means are what the cognitive personality theorist is especially interested in—they are actual restructuring techniques. They are world-creating rules. Let's look at some of them.

Repression. One common strategy is to repress one of the conflicting ideas or beliefs—to refuse to recognize that it exists. If you have decided to study this afternoon, you simply don't admit to yourself that you really wanted to do something else. This self-deception may work reasonably well for a while, but as a rule repression is a rather unsatisfactory weapon against dissonance. Sooner or later, the repressed idea begins to force its way back into recognition, and then there are *two* dissonances to face—the original one, plus the conflict between the idea struggling to be known and your need not to know it.

Giving Up or Altering a Cognition. More common ways of dealing with dissonance are to give up one of the conflicting ideas or to alter one or both of them so that they no longer conflict. Additional information that will lessen the amount of inconsistency can also be gathered. Consider Alicia, a young executive who believes herself to be a hard-working, industrious person (cognition #1) but finds that she is taking coffee breaks eight or nine times a day (cognition #2). These two cognitions are clearly in conflict. What might she do to lessen the resulting dissonance?

First, she might give up one of the conflicting cognitions. She can develop a new, less industrious self-image, or she can stop taking all those coffee breaks. Second, the nature of one or both of the cognitions might be changed: "Sure, I take lots of coffee breaks, but I need them to function as well as I do the rest of the time." Finally, she might utilize new information about the situation. Finding out that most of the people in the office take as many or more breaks than she does allows her to interpret her own work patterns within the boundaries of acceptability for that particular job. But all of this restructuring is a whisker-flick-quick kind of process. It is often more a part of the perception itself than a matter of "see it, feel that it's wrong, then change it." Whichever strategy is chosen, it is utilized so immediately that it is almost impossible to capture the state of the person between recognition of the dissonance and the attempt to reduce it; indeed, such a state may not really exist.

Restructuring—but not exactly. Because the structuring happens in the very act of perceiving. Perception is a creative act; we become aware not of a world that is "out there" but of the world as we create it, out of a multitude of possibilities. And we continue to create, to rebuild, to make the new fit with the old. To make the behavior consistent with the beliefs, to alter the beliefs to fit the behavior. Since we can never be completely aware of all that we do and feel and believe (even if those things would hold still long enough for us to deal with them all, which they won't), the process is never done. Festinger's rules describe how dissonance is aroused and how we deal with it, but they are artificial because they deal with discrete chunks of behavior and perceptions—microscope-slide sections, frozen in time, of what is essentially an ongoing, interactive process. But, artificial as they may be, they still give us some new insights into how we are and how we construct ourselves to be.

The Stylish Herman Witkin

Make a rectangle out of four long sticks, and mount it on a machine that will tilt it in any direction. Then mount another stick in the middle of the rectangle, and fix it so it can be tilted too, independently of how the rectangle is being tilted. Finally, ask people to sit across the room from this apparatus, darken the room so that all they can see is the rectangle and the stick inside it, tilt the apparatus in all sorts of combinations, and ask them to tell you when the stick is straight up and down.

This is a personality test?

Cognitive Styles

At least one psychologist, Herman Witkin, says that it is. It provides another way of finding out how people create the world they live in. And Witkin ought to know, because he worked with the Rod and Frame Test (among others) for more than 30 years. His reasoning goes like this:

Some people, when they observe the world around them, tend to zero in on the main thing they are looking at. They are straight-line thinkers. They focus on what they are after; they don't often get sidetracked or allow themselves to be influenced by peripheral issues. Others tend to operate more globally: to them, things must be seen in context, and an object is what it is (at least in part) because of its relationship to other objects. The Rod and Frame Test discriminates these two kinds of people. The straight-line thinkers will recognize that the stick is vertical when it is, in fact, vertical, regardless of the position of the frame around it; the more global thinkers will be more likely to say it is vertical when it is tilted to match the position of the frame.

The Perception/Cognition Process. There are two things that we need to notice right away about Witkin's logic here. First, he is assuming that the way people perceive "out there" things corresponds to the way they think about things; that one's general patterns of structuring the visual world are somehow parallel to one's general patterns of structuring the world of thought. Neither one necessarily causes the other; rather, they are both a part of some overall "this is how I apprehend reality" in each of us. That's not new; Festinger appeared to make the same assumption. It is, in fact, a basic assumption of the cognitive theorists: perception and cognition are both parts of the same process, the world-creating activity of thinking/seeing/being. Second, Witkin assumed that individuals are consistent in the way they tend to perceive and think about things. We aren't "focus-in-ers" one day and global thinkers the next. Our way of seeing and thinking about the world is an integral part of our selves, and it changes only gradually, over time, if at all.

Field Dependence/Independence. The Rod and Frame Test, Witkin believes, taps a stable dimension of the world-creating process that underlies all human behavior. The two ways of behaving on the Rod and Frame test represent the two extremes of a continuum. Let's give those two extremes their proper names, now, within Witkin's theory: those who focus in on the immediate task, regardless of what else may be cluttering up the perceptual field, are called *field independent*, and those who are more influenced by the extraneous stimuli are *field dependent*. Field dependence/independence, if it is a major factor determining how we structure and react to the world around us, and if it is also a relatively stable characteristic of each individual, certainly qualifies as a dimension of personality in anybody's book. But especially so for a cognitive theorist.

The degree to which one tends to be field dependent or independent is a kind of style of thinking and perceiving. This notion has provided the catchphrase that describes a whole area of research: *cognitive style.* Cognitive style doesn't really "belong" to any one subspecialty within psychology. Learning theorists have been interested in the effects of different styles on learning; those who study memory have been similarly intrigued. Social psychologists may rightly ask about the relationship between cognitive style and interpersonal behavior; counselors and clinicians may find that therapeutic success is affected by the cognitive style of both client and therapist. And personality theorists have explored cognitive style *itself,* not as it affects some other process, but as a true dimension of personality, worthy of study in its own right.

Cognitive Complexity. There is, as might be guessed, more than one cognitive-style continuum. Indeed, one of the problems with cognitive-style research is the unfortunate tendency theorists have of popping up with new style dimensions—rather like the classic multiple personality that keeps creating and displaying new "faces"—rather than sticking with one or two major ones until we understand how they work and what their implications may be. A few major dimensions, though, have emerged over the years. A great deal of work has been done by numbers of people on field dependence/independence, the granddaddy of them all. In addition, a dimension called *cognitive complexity* has attracted some attention. Cognitive complexity has to do with the degree to which we prefer (and are able to deal with) complex rather than simple stimulus patterns—and, by extension, complex idea structures. The cognitively simple person feels most comfortable with simple, neat, tidy percepts and functions best in situations that are clear and uncomplicated. The cognitively complex individual, in contrast, likes more variables, more complicated relationships, a more chaotic visual field.

We must bear in mind, throughout all our discussion of cognitive-style dimension, that we are defining styles in terms of their extremes. We are describing caricatures, overdrawn examples that probably don't even exist in real life. You and I are not clearly cognitively complex or cognitively simple; we are not either field dependent or field independent. We are somewhere in between. But each of us leans in one direction or the other, and it is that leaning that flavors our behavior, that is a part of our personality.

Cognitive Tempo. A third dimension of cognitive style that shows real promise is the impulsivity/reflectivity dimension, also known as *cognitive tempo.* We each have a preferred tempo, a rate of responding with which we are most comfortable. People who are more impulsive are quick off the mark, impatient with long deliberation. They may be sharp, witty, incisive; they may also be blurters, forever doing and saying the wrong thing and bemoaning the fact that they can't seem to stop and think before acting. Reflectives are just the opposite: they are the long-pausers, the peaceful-puff-on-pipers, the slow-and-steadys who often win the race.

It's very difficult for reflectives and impulsives to get along with each other. To the impulsive, the reflective seems unbearably deliberate if not downright dull and stupid; to the reflective, the impulsive may appear an irresponsible mental lightweight. Impulsives can't understand how a reflective can take so interminably long to answer a simple question like "Would you like another cup of coffee?" Reflectives are often grossly annoyed by the pokings and proddings of a gadfly impulsive. Marriage counselors take note: cognitive-style incompatibility may outweigh infidelity as a root cause of divorce!

Cognitive Style: The "How" of Behavior

Although it seems quite clear now, looking back over the work of several decades, that cognitive style is, indeed, appropriately considered an aspect of personality, this was not always the case. Cognitive style was for a long time a sort of poor cousin, living on the fringes of the more traditional areas of psychology, not quite accepted by any because it didn't seem to fit neatly into any single place. Witkin maintained all along that this quality of "not fitting" is a strength rather than a weakness: that it is the pervasiveness of the concept that makes it valuable and valid as a way of looking at personality. One's cognitive style affects not only how one sees the world and how one thinks about that world; it also affects how one relates to other people. If you are field dependent, you are sensitive to background stimuli in a perceptual sense; you are also sensitive to the subtle messages you get from other people in interactions, as those messages serve as "background" to the central, overtly communicated message. Field dependence/independence, if it can be measured accurately, can help explain one's world view, one's typical approaches to problems, and one's social-interaction style.

Cognitive style, Witkin insists, is not a "thing," a construct that a person either "has" or "doesn't have." It is, rather, a process, a way of doing things. Knowing a person's cognitive style doesn't tell us what the person thinks about or whom the person interacts with, but it does tell us something about *how* the person will think or interact. Moreover, knowing one's own cognitive style can provide new insights into one's ways of thinking and interacting. People tend, for the most part, to be peculiarly blind to the fact that cognitive styles can differ—and especially that their own cognitive style may be different from that of their neighbor. Because I have always been this way and "this way" is the only thing I know, it simply doesn't occur to me that someone else could be any different. It is the unusual fish who knows that it is wet; wetness is an integral fact of its existence and, as such, is neither questioned nor noticed. Similarly, it is an unusual field-independent person who is aware of his or her field independence. The only way I can know how other people think and perceive is by analogy to me, and the things I don't notice in myself are not likely to be contrasted with others. Being made aware of cognitive styles other than one's own, then, carries a double benefit: not only is one better able to understand (tolerate, benefit from) people whose styles *are* different, but one is also introduced to the possibility of change in oneself. Maybe I *am* too analytic, now that I think about it; maybe I should try to let go, to let ideas just come flowing in from wherever. Maybe I do tend to respond too quickly (or too slowly), and maybe I should experiment with changing my tempo. You mean there are really people who *enjoy* complicated, confusing situations just because they are complicated and confusing? Wow, maybe I could learn to do that, too. Thus, in recognizing that differences can exist, we open ourselves to the possibility of new modes of experiencing and interaction.

Stability of Cognitive Style. Two other characteristics of cognitive style, said Witkin, are also important. One is its stability. We have already mentioned this—one's style doesn't fluctuate a great deal from task to task or from day to day but tends to remain pretty much the same. So, if you know what my style is in a laboratory test, you can predict with some accuracy how I will behave in the classroom, at a party, or in an argument with my spouse. And cognitive styles are bipolar; that is, they arrange themselves on a continuum ranging from one extreme to another. A cognitive-style dimension is not (like, for instance, IQ) something you have a lot or a little of. You tend in one direction or the other; if you are very analytic, you are not very global. Each extreme of the continuum has some advantages and some disadvantages, but there doesn't seem to be any "best" style, any more than there is a "best" color of hair or a "best" sense of humor. Cognitive style isn't an ability, a thing we have more or less of; it determines *how* we do things but not how *well* we do them.

Changing Cognitive Styles. This is not to say, of course, that all cognitive styles work equally well in all situations. Being a reflective may be a great handicap for a race-car driver; being an impulsive is not so good for a school child. There are, in fact, some rather interesting research findings on that latter point that seem to point to a relationship between impulsivity and anxiety. This is the way it works. Children in school are frequently expected to respond to questions. When we try to answer a question, we generally have to sort through a pile of mental odds and ends to find the right answer. What is the capitol of Illinois? Chicago? No, that isn't right. What's that other city—Peoria? No, that's the one they make all the jokes about. Wait, it's like another city back East—Springfield! That's it, Springfield. Reflectives, who can tolerate pauses and conversational gaps, find it easier to take the time to sort through possible answers until they are confident that they have the right one. Impulsives, on the other hand, want to move quickly, to spit out an answer right away. They are less likely to sort through a long list of possibilities, more likely to say the first thing that comes to mind—and, therefore, more likely to give a wrong answer. And to be told that it is wrong. Now, if you have a history of being told that you are wrong, you are likely to become anxious in a question/answering situation. The impulsive child, having given wrong answers more often in the past (other things being equal), is more prone to anxiety in this kind of situation than the reflective child. And what does anxiety do to one's tolerance for pauses and silences, to one's ability to relax and think things through? None of us needs to be told; we've all been there ourselves! So a vicious circle is created: the more impulsive I am, the more times I'm likely to be wrong. The more often I'm wrong, the more anxious I become, and the more anxious I am, the more impulsively I act.

Can a teacher change the cognitive style of a child? Or a therapist change the cognitive style of a client? Can I change my own cognitive style? The answer seems to be a qualified "yes." There is some evidence that cognitive styles can be changed, by a number of different methods. One way is a very straightforward and simpleminded "tell them to change." Particularly in the case of impulsive (as contrasted with reflective) children, their answers can be slowed down noticeably just by reminding them to take their time, that they don't need to hurry. Field-independent people will be much more sensitive to the background of whatever problem they are working on if that background is simply called to their attention. Since one's cognitive style acts very much like any other habit, though, the tendency is to fall back into the preferred mode as soon as the immediate reminder is removed. Somewhat longer-lasting results have been obtained through *selective reinforcement*, rewarding a person every time he or she shows evidence of having operated within the desired style framework. The danger, particularly with children, is that we don't yet know very much about why people operate within their preferred styles. Is it an inherited tendency? Is it learned throughout childhood, through watching the behavior of significant others in the environment? Does my particular set of styles meet some needs of which I may be relatively unaware? Is there a developmental process, perhaps unique to each individual, such that operating within a given style at a given time is a necessary step toward optimal functioning later on? Until we have answers to these questions, trying to switch someone from one style to another may be a pretty risky operation, particularly if the someone is a child.

Measuring Cognitive Styles

So far, we have been talking about various cognitive styles as if they were relatively straightforward, easy-to-measure characteristics. Indeed, we began our discussion by describing a test for one dimension of cognitive style. There are, however, some serious problems that arise when we begin to look closely at measurement of cognitive style, and the solutions to those problems may have an important effect on our understanding of the very nature, and the implications, of the cognitive-style concept.

Tests That Push. The great majority of cognitive style tests appear to "push" for one kind of answer. That is, they ask questions, or pose problems, that have a right and a wrong answer, and if one gets the right answer then one is seen as leaning toward one end of the style continuum. In testing Henry for field dependence/independence, for example, we ask him to indicate whether or not the rod (shown in its frame) is vertical. If he is able to answer the questions correctly—to say the rod is vertical when and only when it really is, regardless of the position of the frame—then he is assessed as field independent. Another test of field dependence/independence involves finding a particular figure that is "hidden" within a field of other lines and shapes. Again, the person who succeeds more often at this task is seen as field independent.

The "Right" Style. This kind of equation of "right" with field independent imposes an inadvertent value orientation on the dependent/independent dimension. People are expected to do as well as they can (get as many right answers as they can) on a test, and there is an underlying assumption that, in some way and to some extent, you are good (competent, respect-worthy) to the degree that you do well on the test. Which means, in this case, that the more field independent you turn out to be, the "better" you are. Although Witkin denies vehemently any such theoretical orientation, pointing out that, in fact, people who are field dependent tend to have superior skills in interpersonal relations, the implication of the testing methods themselves can't be ignored. Until some field dependence/independence tests are developed that have no "right" answers or in which getting the "right" answer requires behaviors more characteristic of field dependence than of field independence, the problem is likely to remain.

Typical versus Possible Performance. Related to this "pushing" issue is the question of whether tests of cognitive style should measure what one is capable of doing or what one habitually, or most comfortably, does. Tests developed to date tend to measure what one is able to do and, as we have seen, may look rather exclusively at how far to one particular end of the continuum one is able to function. But when we think of cognitive style as a personality characteristic, it doesn't make too much sense to think in terms of how field independent, or cognitively complex, or impulsive one is *able* to be. After all, when we talk about other, more traditional personality characteristics, we don't do that. We talk about how aggressive or how dependent a person is most of the time, is under certain circumstances, or would like to be. It might make sense to develop measures of how aggressively a person is able to act when encouraged to do so, but the characteristic thus measured would be quite different from what we ordinarily think of as "aggression." When it comes to cognitive style, though, we tend to think in one way while we test in another. We discuss cognitive styles as though they were typical personality dimensions, with the typical flavor of habitual or preferred functioning in a particular way, but we test people for how *able* they are to be this way or that. Not only does this create a certain inconsistency between the "label" and the thing it represents, but it also doesn't leave room for the person who is able to switch styles, to be complex or simple, field dependent or field independent, as the situation changes. And that ability to switch, to change styles to meet the demands or the possibilities of the moment, is perhaps the thing we have said doesn't exist. It is perhaps the best style of all.

Cognitive Style: In Summation

What can be said in summary about cognitive style? Certainly the area has its problems. There is little agreement about what dimensions of cognitive style are most important or even which ones are valid. Some dimensions, whose proponents seem to claim them to be independent, have undeniable overlap with other "independent" dimensions. Some are well researched, and others are almost ignored. There are serious inconsistencies between the ways in which they are used conceptually. But the field is still extremely promising and exciting.

Witkins' "old original" style dimension, field dependence/independence (which he has lately begun referring to as "articulated"/"global," in an effort both to expand the scope of the concept and to divest it of some of its value connotations), has mellowed with the years and is being shown to have relevance to many areas of human behavior. "Articulated" people and "global" people not only see their worlds differently; they also attack problems in different ways (we can caricature these differences: "this leads to this leads to this" is comfortable for the articulated-style people, while a more intuitive "let's shake it around and see how it feels" is typical of globals), and they behave differently socially. Field-dependent, or global, people tend to have a well-functioning social-radar system, sensitive to nuances and unverbalized messages from others; field-independent, or articulated, people, in contrast, are more likely to go full-speed-ahead on whatever topic is ostensibly the subject for the day, ignoring off-the-subject social cues.

As we learn more about dimensions of cognitive style, and how different dimensions work together to form patterns of social and cognitive functioning, we may see a whole new vista of predictability open up. Cognitive-style research may shed light on other aspects of personality and the ways in which personality interacts with ability in determining behavior. There's a lot to be learned. Witkin and his friends have only just begun.

The Balanced Fritz Heider

Another piece of cognitive construction (remember those Tinker Toys scattered all over the floor?) comes from the work of an itchy-footed Austrian named Fritz Heider. Heider, as a youngster, was one of those people who couldn't quite seem to settle down. He was interested in too many things; all of those "practical" careers that seemed so appealing to his father (who was, after all, financing his education) were restrictive and—well, yes, they were boring. When he finished high school, he thought it would be fun to be an artist. But his father put his foot down; Fritz had to have a "real job." How about architecture? That was related to art . . . sort of. So Heider dutifully tried architecture. Fizzle, flop. Now what? Well, said Father, how about a government job? (Steady work, pay coming in regularly, get this kid off my back!) Okay, said dutiful Fritz, I'll study law and go to work for the government. Flop again; law was just as boring and constricting as architecture. Father must have been at his wit's end by this time; he just couldn't understand what Fritz was talking about when Fritz said he wanted to go to college just to "learn things." What in the world was he doing while he was supposed to be studying law and architecture? But it wasn't the same, Fritz insisted; he wanted to learn things he was interested in. What's a father to do? Heider Sr. gave up; he lent Fritz the money to go to college and study whatever he wanted—with the stipulation that the money would be repaid as soon as Fritz graduated. There was even a plan for how this was to be accompished: Fritz was to take over the management of a small farm owned by his father and raise pigs for fun and profit until the money was earned.

Fortunately for us, Heider's dutifulness apparently did not extend to the point of actually carrying out that agreement. His early interest in painting had led him to study problems of perception in college, and this in turn eventually led to a doctorate in philosophy and psychology. Colleagues and teachers in graduate school weren't particularly impressed with his work. They thought he was simply restating the obvious, getting excited over trivial facts that everybody had always known about anyhow.

Heider Meets Lewin

Undiscouraged, Heider bounced off to Berlin, to live with his uncle and study more psychology. He met Kurt Lewin there, and the two of them became lifelong friends. Lewin was busy trying to define the "life space" and determine the relationships that affect the way one moves about in one's life space, and that was beautifully complementary to Heider's interests. But even the excitement of working with Lewin couldn't keep Heider in one place for very long. Off he went again, this time not to stay with an obliging relative but simply to wander, through Germany, Italy, Czechoslovakia. . . . He supported himself by doing odd jobs here and there, and he also had a small monthly allowance from a cousin (one wonders what this tribe of aunts and uncles and cousins must have thought about their peculiar relative, who was so different from most young people of his day, but yet somehow so—what was it?—so *something* that they couldn't just wash their hands of him).

Finally, in 1930, Heider decided it was time to stop this butterfly business and find a place where he could really get down to work. There were several opportunities, one in Vienna. Ah, Vienna—the music, the rich food and wine, the Gemütlichkeit. . . . But a friend warned him that, if he did go to Vienna, it would just be more butterfly; he'd spend all of his time sitting in coffeehouses and dancing with pretty girls. So, firm in his resolve, Heider turned his back on fun and frolic and took a job at Hamburg. Where he met Franz Koffka, one of the founders of the Gestalt school of psychology. Also fascinated with how people perceive and organize their worlds. Also sympathetic to young Heider. Koffka went off to the United States shortly thereafter, and some time later he invited Heider to join him in setting up a research department in a school for the deaf. Research in a school for the deaf—who ever heard of such a thing? It was just far out enough to appeal to Heider, and off he went. Thus missing the Hitler regime, with all its nastiness. And beginning a series of appointments in U.S. schools that ended only with his retirement in 1968 as Distinguished Professor at the University of Kansas.

Organizing the World: The Balance Principle

The overarching question of how people understand and organize the world around them is the theme of Heider's professional career. The early influence of Lewin, with his strange geometry of people being pushed and pulled about by various forces in their lives (Heider described, many years later, standing at a bus stop with Lewin, watching as Lewin excitedly traced diagram after diagram in the snow with the tip of his umbrella), and of Koffka, fascinated by the interaction between the seer and the thing seen, was no less important than his own experience as an artist. As an artist he himself had struggled with the problem of abstracting a chunk of the world, of organizing it somehow so that it would be meaningful. He had experienced, in his own eyes and with his own fingertips, the way in which people see the world as a set of *units,* rather than as a crazy, shifting pattern of stimuli. And it occurred to him, as it does to few others, to ask "why"—why do we organize as we do? What governs the way we set some things together as units and keep others separate?

And not just "things"—people, too. In fact, especially people! Because people move about and interact with one another and are categorized in terms of those actions, they are ever so much more interesting than simple objects. So we come to the question that best characterized Heider's contribution to psychology and to personality theory: what are the rules that govern the ways in which we understand and predict relationships among people (including ourselves)?

Language as an Organizing Element. But where to start? Well, people are interesting because they interact. And how do they interact? There are clusters of words in our language—the language of "naive psychology," as Heider put it—that describe some of the relationships that people have with things and with other people. These clusters include words like "trying," "causing," "wanting," "belonging," "being affected by." Words like this are particularly interesting because they not only describe what people do but also tend to link people and things, entities, concepts, together. They are unit-forming words. When we say, for instance, "the girl is trying to open the window," we have linked the girl and the window together. We don't think of simply a "girl" but, rather, of "a girl who is trying to open a window." The girl and the window and the effect she is trying to have on that window are linked into a conceptual unit. The activity is a part of our perception of what is out there.

Of course, these "activity relationships" aren't the only basis for linking things together. Many theorists have worked on the problem of association (including Koffka and the Gestaltists) and have taken great pains to show how closeness in space or in time or similarity of appearance tend to make us group things. But, for personality theorists, concerned with how people act and react, it is the activity relationships that are of special interest.

Similarity, Like, and Dislike. Heider noted that some actions toward or feelings about things tend to make us link the actor (or feeler) with the thing, while others tend to make us separate the two conceptually. And some feelings and actions tend to go together, to create a *balanced* unit, while others create a sense of imbalance or tension. If A sees himself or herself as similar to O, for instance, he or she is inclined to like O. And if I believe A and O are similar, I tend to expect that they will like each other. Conversely, dissimilarity goes with disliking (and, Heider noted, it is probably no accident that the same word, *like,* is used for both the positive sentiment, when it is a verb, and the quality of similarity, when it is an adjective). The relationship works in reverse, as well: two dissimilar people are expected, other things being equal, to dislike each other. "It's not like Harry to be so quiet and withdrawn" means that the speaker sees Harry's usual behavior and the quiet and withdrawn behavior as very dissimilar; it further implies that Harry ought not to enjoy (like) acting that way. At a party, introducing two people with the statement "You two ought to get along well, because you are very much like each other" carries the tacit assumption that similar people will be drawn together—will like each other.

Proximity. We tend to make the same kinds of assumptions about liking and proximity. If two people spend a lot of time together, we assume that they like each other, and, if they like each other, we assume that they will try to spend time together. And, conversely, if they avoid each other, we conclude that they dislike each other; and, if we know that they dislike each other, we expect them to avoid each other. These are balanced relationships; they fit, they make sense. But what about the people who we are told are good friends but are never seen in each other's company? There's a tension here, a not-right-ness, an imbalance. We must add something to the equation: either we were misinformed, and their friendship isn't that great after all, or they are constrained by some external forces from being together and are probably unhappy about it.

Familiarity, Ownership, and Benefit. Familiarity with, ownership of, and bringing benefit to another entity follow the same rules of association. We tend to like the things we are familiar with and the things we own and to dislike that which is unfamiliar and that which doesn't belong to us. We like the things that bring us good and the things that we can bring good to; we dislike the things that bring us evil, as well as the things we mistreat. A standard children's story involves a boy who wants to be friends with a classmate, but the classmate will have nothing to do with him. The boy takes his problem to a wise person (his father, or his grandmother, or a kindly neighbor or teacher) and is advised to let the classmate do him a favor. The boy doesn't understand, and he decides to ignore the advice. But events transpire so that the classmate is, in fact, forced to help him (he falls through thin ice into the pond, for instance, and the classmate pulls him out). And, lo and behold, as a result of having done the boy a good turn, the classmate is now drawn to him in friendship. The boy is delighted, but he still doesn't understand. He has obviously not read Heider's principles of balanced relationships!

Components of the Balance Principle

We are now nearly ready to state this balance principle in a general way. First, though, we must classify the possible relationships among entities (objects, people, concepts) into two major groups. First, there is the *sentiment* group. These have to do with a person's evaluation of something: I may like it, admire it, reject it, condemn it, and so on. Sentiments are either positive or negative; they aren't neutral. Second are the *unit* relationships, the things that make us tend to categorize two entities as belonging together: similarity, causality, ownership, proximity. If we next define a unit-forming relationship (such as similarity) as positive and a unit-dissolving relationship (such as dissimilarity) as negative, we have the basic elements of the balance theory.

Which is, for any pair of entities: balance exists if all the relations between the entities are positive or if they are all negative. Imbalance (a sense of wrongness, a tension to change something, to "balance things out") exists when some of the relations are positive and some negative.

An Example of Balancing. Try it out for yourself. Choose one possible unit relationship and one possible sentiment relationship. Imagine two people, or a person and a thing, who are potentially in interaction with each other. Then apply to those two entities each of the four possible combinations of positive and negative sides of the two relationships. Here's an example to get you started.

Sally K., a person. Buster, a dog. Two entities. Let's take ownership as the unit relationship and approval as the sentiment relationship. Two positives: Sally owns Buster, and Sally approves of Buster. Fine, no conflict. Same with two negatives: Sally doesn't own (or want to own) Buster, and she disapproves of him. But try a plus and a minus together—Sally owns Buster, and she disapproves of him. It's hard to even assimilate that without immediately adding something to improve the balance: she disapproves of how he acts, so she's taking him to obedience school, or she disapproves of him in a kind of fond and teasing way. What about the other possibility, that she doesn't own him and she approves of him? There is again an immediate, almost-a-part-of-the-perception-itself kind of subtle addition: she doesn't own him, *but she'd like to.* Or, she doesn't own him, but *she approves of his being owned by someone else.* We choose an explanation that makes sense to us and that balances the relationship.

The Unbalanced Relationship. We are so used to balancing up unbalanced relationships that we are hardly aware of doing it. And we are intrigued by ideas or stories or proverbs that imply serious imbalance:

they pique our curiosity, they challenge us to "understand what they mean" (which translates to "find a way to balance them"). Consider Oscar Wilde's famous line "Yet each man kills the thing he loves . . ." Tremendous imbalance! And we are drawn to probe the meaning of the line, to question the author's definition of "kill" or "love." Our experience insists that the statement can't be objectively true, that it doesn't make sense; and yet, in a different way, from a different perspective, is there a glimmer of truth, a subtle profundity? The imbalance won't let us go; it demands resolution, it is an itch that must be scratched.

Balancing a Triad. Dyads, balanced and unbalanced (especially unbalanced) are interesting. But the fun really begins when we look at triads: relationships in units composed of three entities. The kinds of triads that Heider studied were those involving two people and some third, impersonal entity toward which each of the people has some sentiment. In general, a triad is balanced when all three of the relations are positive or when two are positive and one is negative. Let's look at Sally and Buster again, but add Danny H. to the unit. Sally owns Buster, Sally likes Danny, and Danny likes Buster. Everything nice; everything balanced. If Sally, owning Buster, dislikes Danny and knows that Danny hates Buster, that's balanced too. But if Sally likes Danny and Danny, in turn, can't stand Buster, there's an imbalance. Something will have to happen. Either Danny will learn to like Buster, or Sally will get rid of Buster. Or of Danny.

In examining triads and the relationships among them, we must choose one of the (human) members as the focus person and define the pluses and the minuses in terms of that person's point of view. Remember, Heider's whole theory has to do with how people perceive relationships, and that's not necessarily the same as how they "really" are. A triad may be balanced from the point of view of one observer and not balanced according to someone else. Consider the hypothetical case of Bob and Betty Wilson, for example. They have been married for five years, and Bob has recently taken a job with a high-powered advertising agency. Bob and Betty are my friends, and as far as I know everything is fine: Bob likes his new job, Betty is very pleased about it, and the marriage is working. My behavior toward Bob and Betty will be determined (in part) by my perception that the situation is in balance. In private, though, Betty is very unhappy about Bob's new job. She has never told anyone, but she really has no respect for the advertising industry and regards advertising people as social parasites. She still loves Bob, and she knows that he is excited about the job. For her there is a serious imbalance (two positive and one negative relations), and she will experience tension and discomfort until it is resolved. Now, from Bob's point of view, things are different still. He is pleased about the job, all right. He is aware of Betty's real feelings about it. But he is also having an affair with a co-worker, and he's planning to ask Betty for a divorce. He sees the unit as composed of one positive relation (between him and the new job) and two negative ones (between him and Betty and between Betty and the job), and so for him things are quite consistent and balanced.

Leveling and Sharpening. Balanced situations are stable and comfortable. They tend not to change until some new element is added, upsetting the balance. Unbalanced situations, in contrast, are not stable. Usually, there is great pressure to balance them. If the situation is one of which I am a part, the pressure is to change me or one of the other members of the unit. If I am merely an observer of an unbalanced unit, there is pressure to shift my cognition, to redefine one or more of the relationships, to search for additional information that will balance things up. Heider calls this tendency *leveling*. Leveling—changing one's perception of a situation so that it appears to be more balanced—is most likely to happen when things are only a little bit out of balance to start with. Strangely, when things are very unbalanced indeed, there is a tendency toward *sharpening*—exaggerating the imbalance still further. Sharpening an unbalanced situation is like drawing a caricature: we remember it better because we have underlined its strangeness, heightened its peculiarity. A college professor of ours whom we liked and respected once gave a failing grade to a student who was (so we thought) one of the smartest people in the class. Here was an unbalanced situation: the teacher was good (plus), the other student was good (plus), but the teacher failed the other student (minus). Looking back on the event now, we see that there may be have been reasons for the failing grade that the rest of the class weren't aware of. But in memory—the cognition of the situation—we don't attempt to balance things by providing or inventing those reasons. Instead, we sharpen the picture, by highlighting the imbalance. In this example, the positive relation between us and both of the other people was strengthened by exaggerating the respect and liking we had for them, and the negative relation was quite possibly strengthened as well (did he really flunk? Maybe the grade was only a C . . . but it makes a better story if it was an F). Balanced situations may be comfortable, but they also can be boring. Imbalance is the stuff of anecdotes and adventures.

The Impact of Heider's Theory

This is, of course, only the barest skeleton of what Heider has worked out in his psychology of interpersonal relations, but it does at least convey some of the flavor of what he was trying to do. It remains for us to reemphasize the relationship between all this and what is traditionally thought of as "personality." Which isn't really difficult; there seem to be three major ways in which Heider's work impacts on the whole personality question.

First, like all the cognitive theorists, Heider is trying to make a statement about how people construct their worlds. His notions of balance and imbalance aren't some remote, laboratory-bound theory; they are a fundamental aspect of everyday life for all of us. I don't interact just with individuals and with objects but with *units*, with groupings of people and things and ideas that shift kaleidoscopically as my focus moves this way and that. And those groupings are not "given" in reality; rather, I construct them myself. It is my own perception that determines who and what go together into which units. Since the way I see units and relationships affects in turn the way I will feel and act (toward others and toward myself), the process of construction then must be pretty important. In trying to delineate what goes on as people form and reform relational units, Heider sets up a theoretical structure that cuts across all sorts of behavior. He is giving us one view of how people *are*, of what sorts of processes lie at the very roots of personality.

But he's giving us more than that. In positing the existence of pressures toward balance, of leveling and sharpening tendencies, Heider provides us with a predictive and analytic tool. Personality theories, in general, are concerned with the analysis and prediction of behavior, with making statements about what people will do under given conditions and why. Heider has done that very thing; he has told us how we will behave *cognitively* in specific kinds of situations. Cognitive-personality theorists believe that cognitive behavior is important, both as it influences other, observable behaviors and in its own right. Personality manifests itself in cognition as it does in other behaviors; personality is also shaped by cognitive events. The way I behave is a function of how I see my world, and I see that world as I choose to construct it. (Choose? Am forced? Whatever.) The *way* I construct it is a part of my personality. Perhaps it is the basis of my personality. To the extent that Heider's theory helps us to understand that construction, it is another relevant part of personality theory.

Finally, Heider's work has been a seminal force in the exploration of all sorts of other cognitive phenomena. Research that started with or was inspired by his theories has pursued many directions and often has gained so much momentum of its own that the original connection is hard to trace. But it's there, and Heider deserves the credit for pointing many of us in very promising directions. Take the general field known as "attribution," for example. From asking "How do we see the fit between relationships among people and things?" some students moved to "What do we see as *causing* the relationships among people and things?" This gradually shifted to "In general, why do people think things happen?" and "To what, or whom, do people attribute the events of their lives?" and, finally, "What are the consequences of attributing causality to this or that?" Attribution research has come a long way from Heider's rules of balanced and unbalanced triads—but that's where it got its start.

And, as long as we've brought it up, let's take a look at what attribution theory can tell us about personality.

The Attributed—Who?

Unlike many areas of personality research, the study of attributions is not primarily the domain of any one person. There is no father figure in attribution research, as Heider is the father figure in balance theory or as Witkin is in cognitive style. Rather, a whole collection of researchers have interacted with each other—and continue to do so—in building up a body of knowledge about how and why people attribute causality in their lives. Names like Harold Kelley, Edward Jones, Richard Nisbett, Stuart Valins, Bernard Weiner, and David Kanouse appear again and again in the literature. Because their work tends to be so interactive and interdependent, it is difficult if not impossible to give credit for each specific part of the theory to a particular individual. We will present some of the major ideas about attribution as a more or less unified whole, without reference to the specific source of each bit of information; we hope this liberty will be forgiven by those on whose work this section of the book is based.

Attribution Research

One of the most universal questions asked by people in constructing their world is "Why do things happen?" We want to know how events are caused, either to increase our ability to predict and control future events or out of simple curiosity. We need to know, in order to construct a rational environment. But, of course, we can't know such things directly. We can only infer them on the basis of the events we experience and hear about from others. Causal inference goes on all the time; it too is an integral part of our perceptual process. Like so many universal behaviors, this constant cause seeking is such a commonplace event that it was for many years quite ignored by psychologists. It's the old wet fish phenomenon all over again: you tend not to be aware of things that are always there, because there's nothing to contrast them with.

Why We Ask "Why?" When Fritz Heider began teasing out the rules governing such "obvious" behaviors as the tendency to balance social relationships, he kicked off a flurry of activity in other "obvious" areas of behavior. "What other things do people do that we have been taking for granted?" psychologists began asking themselves. And, all of a sudden, a great deal of attention came to be focused on the whole problem of "why" asking. If people do spend a lot of time asking themselves why this or that occurs—or, even more interestingly, making assumptions about those "why's"—then psychologists had better look at how they do it: how they ask and how they answer the question. And thus attribution research was born, the study of how people attribute causality, how we structure our world into cause-and-effect units.

Unitizing Behavior. And structure it we do. No doubt about that. Some truly fascinating research has been done to simply nail down the fact that people do "unitize" their ongoing experience. Subjects have been asked to watch all sorts of behavior sequences and indicate when the behaver stopped doing one thing and started doing another—in other words, to carve the stream of behavior up into logical chunks. People show surprising consistency in this sort of task, both with their own previous assessments (performing the same analysis on the same videotaped sequences, after a several-week interval) and with others doing the same thing. The delineations become quite precise, with many subjects feeling quite certain about specifying the exact fraction of a second when the observed behaver began a new unit. One subject, watching a videotape that he believed to be a live television performance, was even convinced that the experiment was deceptive and that he, the subject, was actually controlling the actor's behavior. This subject had a theory that, when he pushed the button signaling the end of one unit and the beginning of the next, the actor on TV was trained to respond by actually beginning some new activity. He had, in fact, tested his theory out, he reported triumphantly, and it worked!

Unitizing behavior makes it more understandable, more capable of being ordered. It also makes behavior more amenable to the attribution of causality. "Why did that happen?" or "Why did he do that?" are much more reasonable questions when "that" is a finite chunk rather than a long, unbroken stream of occurrences.

Having established, then, that people chunk behavior and then ask questions about what causes the various chunks, we come to the heart of the attribution problem: how do they, in fact, answer those questions? And (the scientist's own attribution question, which could, if we let it, lead to an infinite, box-within-a-box series of further questions) *why* do they answer them as they do?

Logical Attribution of Causality

One of the more reasonable answers is that we attribute causality—reasonably. After all, people are pretty rational most of the time. When we try to make sense of our world, we go at it fairly logically. We look at what things tend to go with other things, and, if there is a consistent relationship, we take that as good evidence that the one may have caused the other. If the shingles on the barn roof always lie flat when there is little wind but stand up straight when the wind is high, we are likely to assume that the wind causes the shingles to stand up. If people smile at me when my hair is bleached and ignore me when I'm a brunette, I will probably conclude that my bleached hair is the cause of the extra attention I get.

We also act pretty logically (most of the time) in attributing causality in situations where there are several possible and plausible causes of a given event. In one study, designed to illustrate what happens when people have to deal with more than one possible cause of a particular behavior, subjects were asked to watch videotapes of men applying for jobs as submariners or as astronauts. The subjects were given descriptions of the jobs that implied rather strongly that a particular personality type (an introvert, in one case, and an extravert, in the other) would be best suited and were told that the job candidates had also read the job descriptions. Some of the candidates (actually confederates of the experimenter) acted, in the interview, in ways consistent with the job description, and others took on the "undesirable" personality characteristics. In other words, some of the candidates behaved "in role" and some behaved "out of role." Later, the subjects were asked to indicate why the candidates behaved as they did. Subjects who watched candidates acting out of role attributed the candidate's behavior to personality characteristics much more often than did those who watched an in-role candidate.

Dispositional versus Situational Attributions. We have, in this experiment, a situation in which behavior can be attributed to either of two major causes: either the candidate acted as he did because "that's just the kind of person he is" (dispositional attribution) or because "that's what was expected of him" (situational attribution). For the in-role candidates, both the personality and the situational causes were plausible. But for the out-of-role candidates, only the personality attribution made sense; the situation was no longer a plausible cause. And, as predicted, the role of personality was considered much less strong a factor when there was another reasonable explanation for the behavior.

What about a situation where there are conflicting "causes"—that is, where there is an obvious logical reason for doing something but another obvious reason for not doing it? For instance, we see Walter acting generously in a situation where generosity will cost him a great deal—where he has to sacrifice something that he really wants. Here again there are both situational and personal "causes" to consider. We may attribute the generosity to his personality; it's reasonable to say that he's a "generous" sort of person. The situation is not a reasonable cause; in fact, the situation would tend to push him in the opposite direction, to make him *less* likely to act generously. Gosh, we say, he must *really* be generous, because he overcame the "push" of external circumstances and shared his resources even when he probably didn't want to. If we compare attributions of causality in these kinds of instances with attributions of behavior where both personality and situation appear to push in the same direction (behaving generously when to do so costs a person little or nothing), we find that people are much more likely to say that behavior is caused by personality factors when there is a push in the opposite direction from the external situation than they are when either personality or situation could reasonably have caused the behavior. It's as if we have a little adding machine inside us, weighing the positive and negative forces that might affect someone's behavior and helping us to decide what is probably going on.

Freedom to Choose. Another element in this kind of decision making—and again, a quite logical one—is that of freedom to choose. If I see Janice as doing something on her own, as choosing to do it when she could just as easily have chosen to do something else, I will be likely to see her as doing it because "that's the kind of person she is." If I think she "had to" do it (she studied hard for the exam because she was afraid of flunking out of school, or she took part in the robbery because her companions threatened to beat her up otherwise), I'll blame the situation, rather than her personal characteristics, for the behavior.

The Scientific Method. The general principle that can be extracted from all this takes us right back to our old friend George Kelly: people tend, in attributing behavior to this cause or that, to act like scientists conducting experiments. We look at all the possible reasons for (and against) a behavior, we consider the past history of such behaviors and the "causes" that have or have not been present when they have occurred before, and we come up with a working hypothesis about which of those causes is most likely to be operating. It's all very logical, very reasonable.

Attributions to Self, Attributions to Others

But once we've cleared away the "obvious" part, we find some not-so-obvious things left over. And here's where it starts to get interesting. One of the first of these not-so-obvious attribution tendencies was discovered when scientists found that the way in which people assign causes to their own behavior is different from the way they assign causes to the behavior of others. In general, if you ask people why someone else does something (with no additional information, just the statement that it was done), they are likely to give a "dispositional" reason: He did it because he wanted to, or she did it because that's the kind of person she is. But if you ask them why *they* did something, they'll give a situational reason. That fellow put a bumper sticker on his car because he likes bumper stickers or because he believes in the thing the bumper sticker says. I put a bumper sticker on *my* car because my roommate gave it to me or because there's a radio station that gives away prizes to people riding in cars with bumper stickers. You laugh at a TV show because you're easily amused; I laugh at it because it's funny. You are writing a book because you are a scholarly person; I am writing a book because I need the money.

Differences in Attention. Apparently we pay attention to different things when we are explaining our own behavior than we do when we are trying to explain someone else's behavior. Different things are more *salient:* they stand out more, are more important, or appear more relevant. One early study illustrates this point quite clearly. Subjects in the study watched other subjects solve problems on an "IQ test." What the subjects didn't know was that the "test takers" were really confederates of the experimenter and that they were deliberately getting some of the problems right and getting some of them wrong. In general, the confederates' "answers" fell into two patterns: some people would get most of the early questions right and do badly on the last part of the "test," while others would get the early ones wrong and do very well at the end. The real subjects—those who watched the others take the "test"—were then asked to estimate the confederates' intelligence and predict how well they would do on another, similar test. There was a clear and consistent tendency for these observers to weigh early performance more heavily than later performance: test takers who did well at the beginning of the test were judged more intelligent and were expected to do better on later tests than those who did well at the end of the test. But that's not the end of the experiment! (These social scientists are very sneaky people. . . .) Another set of subjects took similar tests *themselves,* and this time the tests were arranged so that the subjects would themselves do well on one half of the test and badly on the other half. Afterward, the subjects were asked to predict how well they would do on a second test. And here the predictions were just the opposite: those who did well at the beginning and badly at the end expected to do badly on the next test and vice versa (see Table 13-1).

Table 13-1. Differential predictions of future performance (given knowledge of past performance), depending on whether one is evaluating oneself or someone else.

	Good Early Performance, Bad Later Performance	*Bad Early Performance, Good Later Performance*
Prediction of Other's Future Performance	Will do well	Will do badly
Prediction of One's Own Future Performance	Will do badly	Will do well

In this (and similar) studies, then, it is clear that we pay attention to different things when we try to explain someone else's behavior than we do when we try to explain that same behavior in ourselves. When we are watching other people take tests, we tend to form an impression based on the first things we see them do and then interpret everything else in the light of that first impression. But the most recent things *we* have done or experiences we have had are the ones we are likely to use in explaining what we are doing or predicting what we will do next.

Differences in Information. Okay, why? As students of personality, we are attributors, too. We aren't content with just saying that this or that describes behavior; we want to know the reasons for that behavior. And (in this instance, at least) we needn't be disappointed: students of attribution have come up with some fairly sturdy hypotheses that explain and predict the differences in attributions to self and attributions to others. In the first place, the actor and the observer have different information available to them. There are two general kinds of data about any behavior, data related to the cause of the behavior and data related to its effect. Cause data include relevant aspects of the situation and relevant internal motivations of the actor, while effect data have to do with what was actually done, what the environmental outcomes were, and how the actor felt about the behavior. Let's look at those data with reference to a particular act—say, pulling the cat's tail. Kevin pulled the cat's tail, and Corey watched him do it. Both Kevin and Corey know what was done, and they know the environmental outcome—the cat screeched, scratched, and scatted. They both know what the external situation was before the act occurred. But only Kevin knows what was going on inside Kevin before he yanked (he was feeling grumpy and hungry) or how he felt afterward (still hungry but not quite so grumpy). Most important, Corey has no way of knowing the long-range history relevant to that act (Kevin usually pets the cat and often sits with it on his lap) or the long-range intent (Kevin wondered if the cat, a very fat and placid beast, was really capable of moving fast). Not knowing these internal factors, Corey can only infer what is going on; and, in the absence of contrary information, he is likely to infer internal factors consistent with external behavior. Kevin, in contrast, knows what is going on internally; he also knows the past history of his behavior in similar situations and is more likely to call on the situation to explain why he did this thing at this particular time.

Differences in Focus. There is also a difference in the focus of attention for an actor and an observer. The actor, in the situation, is focused outward. I look at the things with which I am interacting, at the external environment. For you, the observer, in contrast, that environment is merely the background against which the activity occurs; your focus is me, the actor. It seems quite natural, given these differences, that there should be a tendency for each of us to weight more heavily that with which we are more immediately concerned: for me, the actor, the situational factors, and for you, the observer, my characteristics.

Attributions to Enhance or Maintain Control

There seems to be another general principle that affects how we explain our own and others' behavior, and this has to do with our need to feel in control of what happens to us. The feeling of helplessness, of being out of control, is usually a very unpleasant feeling indeed and one that we try very hard to avoid. Therefore, there is a strong tendency in most of us to make attributions that enhance our sense of control. If we are trying to make something happen, for instance, and it does happen, we aren't likely to consider the possibility that our trying had no effect, that the thing may have happened just by chance. A psychotherapist, seeing improvement in a patient, credits the improvement to successful therapy; Dr. Clark doesn't usually suspect that Pleasing Polly would have done just as well on her own. Clem the Crapshooter believes, against all reason, that throwing the dice harder will help him to get the point he needs. If you study a long time for an exam and do well, you aren't likely to think you'd have still gotten the A with no studying at all.

Credit and Blame. Even in attributing causes of other people's behavior, we tend to overestimate our own power, at least in those instances where things go as we want them to go. The group leader takes credit for the group's successes but is likely to blame failure on the ineptness of other members. In a study of teacher behavior, teachers were allowed to believe that some students improved their arithmetic ability while others stayed about the same. The teachers believed that their own efforts were responsible for children's improvement but blamed lack of improvement on lack of ability or "not trying" on the part of the students.

It's easy, in looking at these tendencies in others, to shake our heads and smile about how vain or self-centered many people are. But before we do that, let's realize that we, the scientists, are also observers. In making a judgment of "vanity," we ourselves are fitting right into the predicted pattern: we are making a dispositional attribution about someone else's behavior. How likely would we be to say that our attributions about our own influence were caused by personal vanity? Hmmmm . . . maybe we'd better look a little further.

Errors of Attribution. Several different sorts of errors of attribution can increase our sense of personal control. First is the tendency to assume that, when things happen at the same time, one of them causes the other; when I root for the home team, for example, and they win, I have somehow helped them (even if I was watching the game on TV). Second, we often exaggerate our ability to control things that are, in fact, out of our control—again, the TV rooting, or the crapshooter's belief that he can somehow influence that fall of the dice. And, finally, we tend to *under*estimate the degree to which our own behavior may be controlled by something or someone else. I want to believe that I determine my own life and am not buffeted around by chance or manipulated by other people.

Reciprocity and Personal Freedom. What all this suggests is that we use our explanations of people's behavior as a means of preserving or of restoring our sense of personal freedom. Stephen Worchel and his colleagues have carried out a series of studies to try to dig out this relationship and clarify the rules that govern it. They begin with the assumption that there is in our culture a norm of *reciprocity,* that, other things being equal, we expect ourselves and others to reciprocate behaviors, to do unto others as they do unto us. Ordinarily, this general pattern works pretty well. But what happens when you don't *want* to reciprocate, when your freedom to do as you wish is threatened by the social pressure to treat other people as they have treated you? As long as you believe that someone has done something to you because he or she wanted to behave that way (dispositional determinant), the norm to reciprocate will be relatively strong. But if the person did it only because the situation required it (situational determinant), then you don't have to reciprocate. You can argue that he or she would have acted otherwise if it had been possible, so you can act toward the person as he or she would have acted toward you under "ordinary circumstances." Do you see where this is leading? To a neat, testable prediction, which makes experimental psychologists lick their chops and grin with satisfaction! If (a) dispositional attributions (of someone else's behavior) push us to reciprocate the behavior but situational attributions don't, and if (b) we use attributions to maintain our sense of personal freedom, then we can expect that (c) people will make dispositional attributions when they want to reciprocate someone's behavior toward them and make situational attributions when they don't want to reciprocate that behavior.

Now, let's see how we can test that hypothesis. We'll need to set people up so that some of them will want to reciprocate a behavior and others won't want to reciprocate that behavior; then all we'll have to do is ask them why the other person acted that way toward them. If the hypothesis is right, the don't-want-to-reciprocate subjects will say that the other people acted as they did because they wanted to or because that's the kind of people they are.

Expectations and Attributions. Worchel and Andrioli led subjects (female college students) to believe that they would be working in pairs in either a competitive or a cooperative task. When a subject arrived at the experiment room, she was told that her partner was late and that the experimenter would go ahead and explain the task anyhow. Then she was asked if she would mind alphabetizing a stack of IBM score sheets while she waited for the partner to arrive. When the partner did arrive (actually, of course, the partner was a confederate of the experimenter), she either offered to help with the alphabetizing task or made critical remarks about the subject's behavior ("Boy, that's a really stupid thing to do. They can get some people to do anything in these experiments").

Now, let's see where we are. We have some subjects who expect to be cooperating with their partners and some who expect to be competing. And we have some who experience cooperative and friendly partner behavior and some who experience hostile partner behavior. If our hypothesis is correct, those whose expectations of future behavior are consistent with what they received from their partners—that is, those who experienced cooperation and who expect to cooperate in the experiment and those who experienced hostility and who expect to compete in the experiment—should attribute the partner's behavior to dispositional factors. Those who experience inconsistent expectations and partner behavior should make situational attributions. And that is exactly what happened. After the alphabetization of the IBM sheets and before the "main" part of the experiment (which, in fact, never took place), all the subjects completed a questionnaire in which the first question asked why their partner had acted as she did. People in the hostile/expect-cooperation condition and in the friendly/expect-competition condition said that the partner either helped or didn't help because of the nature of the situation (anyone would have acted the same way under the circumstances), whereas those in the hostile/expect-competition and the friendly/expect-cooperation conditions said that the partner helped or didn't help because of some trait or traits that she had (she was a nice person; she was aggressive and unpleasant).

In general, we tend to attribute the behavior of others to dispositional factors—to "the way they are." But, as Worchel and his colleagues have demonstrated, maintaining our own sense of control, our personal freedom, can override that tendency. When a dispositional attribution forces us into behavior we'd rather not engage in or makes us feel uncomfortable about how we are acting, we are much more likely to attribute the other person's behavior to the situation.

Summary on Attributions

We have only begun to describe the various approaches that attribution theorists have made to the study of assessing causality, and already it begins to feel overwhelming. But there are a few general principles that can be extracted from the confusion. In general, it appears (1) that people do (at some level and seldom consciously) weigh a number of factors in deciding why they and others behave as they do; (2) that many of these decisions are made logically and rationally, on the basis of available data; (3) that differences in attributions made by actors and observers may be due (partially) to differences in the data available to each; but (4) that we tend to distort the data in order to make attributions that will enhance (or at least not interfere with) our sense of personal freedom or control. Moreover, we tend to assume that other people operate pretty much as we ourselves do, so that people who are (or see themselves as being) situationally determined will make situational attributions of other people's behavior and vice versa.

Effects of Attribution Theory. Another complication. We tend to think of psychology as explaining behavior, as a means of satisfying our curiosity about how people act. We seldom realize the extent to which psychology, as a scientific discipline, has *changed* that behavior. This doesn't mean, now, the kind of thing you see in psychotherapy or in a classroom behavior-modification scheme, where a particular theoretical approach is being actively applied in order to accomplish a specific purpose. We're talking about the simple existence of a body of knowledge, the coming-into-the-culture of a set of beliefs. What we believe about our actions can change, is changing, and will continue to change the very actions we are theorizing about. And nowhere is this more true than in attribution theory. People's whole understanding of motivation, of causation, has been turned upside down with the advent of modern psychology. Freud got the ball rolling, and just about every psychologist since seems to have given it another shove.

So that's great. As we learn more about what makes us tick, we can tick more happily and more efficiently. Or can we?

One of the bad legacies that Freud & Co. have left us is a whole lot of cocktail-party conversation about unconscious motivations. All of which, of course, are undesirable, unflattering, unadmittable, and generally horrid. The woman who enjoys her work is probably sublimating some sort of disgusting sexual proclivity. If a man has a dozen girlfriends on the string, that's probably a reaction formation and he's really a latent homosexual. Liking children means that one is afraid of being around adults and/or harbors strong inadequacy feelings. And so on and so on. Not only are these kinds of suspicions and assumptions thrown around about others—which is bad enough—but we frequently turn them on ourselves, with potentially disastrous results. As, for example, in the case of the woman who began to experience painful stomach cramps every night at bedtime. Being a good product of our modern culture (and, no doubt, with the enthusiastic help of a well-meaning friend), she began to suspect the cramps were an excuse to avoid sex. She must really be a very frigid person. Fortunately, a perceptive doctor was able to intervene before she had done herself serious damage and suggested that a tomato allergy might be causing the cramps. The woman eliminated tomatoes from her diet, the cramps disappeared, and her sex life was fine.

Back to Personal Control. The point here is that attributions, beyond being an interesting part of behavior in and of themselves, can and do have effects that spread throughout the whole behavioral spectrum. Some behaviors (both internal and external) may appear quite inexplicable until we understand these spreading effects. Why is it, for instance, that so many people who have experienced a personal disaster (having cancer, being raped, losing a loved one) feel guilty? How can a person possibly feel guilty about getting cancer? The principle of making attributions so as to maintain a sense of personal control may hold part of the answer: I feel guilty because I attribute some (bad) thing to me—I have caused it to happen. If I have cancer, it's my fault; it's because of something I did. As painful as that belief may be, it is still (at least for some people) less painful than the sense of being out of control, of being helpless. If I can attribute this disaster to my own activity, then at least *I did it;* I was in control.

Taking the blame for bad things that happen may, in a strangely contradictory way, ease the discomfort of those kinds of situations. Taking credit for the good things that happen is also a way of asserting and maintaining a sense of personal control and is thus also a generally comfortable kind of attribution. In general, feeling in control of things—especially of oneself—tends to accompany other feelings of well-being, the absence of depression, and even physical health. There is some risk, of course (there's no such thing as a free lunch). If I take personal credit for every good thing that happens to me, I'm likely to get pretty overconfident, and I may come down pretty hard when things don't go right. But overall, whether things are good or bad, we seem to be better off when we think we have at least some control over what is happening to us.

Let's push that a little further and ask about the implications of our attributions about other people's behavior. Behavior on the part of another person, if it is psychologically meaningful to me, falls into one of two categories: it helps me (I like it; it is consistent with my well-being) or it hurts me (I don't like it; it interferes with my well-being). Behavior that makes me feel neither good nor bad is not really a part of my space. I don't get involved in it. If I do get involved, the first thing I do is relate it to myself, in some way or another.

If I like your behavior, it's more comfortable for me to believe that the behavior is dispositional, that it's caused by some characteristic of yours. That means it's predictable, and predictability gives me some degree of control. If the cause must be situational, I will tend to see myself as a (major) part of the cause. Again, this gives me some control.

If your behavior is uncomfortable or punishing to me in some way but is clearly caused by the situation, then I can believe that you didn't really want to act as you did but were somehow forced to. You would have acted differently if you could have; you really aren't "that kind of person." This allows me to believe that, ordinarily, I would like your (dispositional) behavior, which I can usually predict, because I know what kind of a person you are. Again, I have some degree of control. But if your punishing or uncomfortable-to-me behavior is dispositional, caused by the kind of person you are, then I will be inclined to reciprocate, to do something punishing back to you. We can predict, then, that an individual will behave more punishingly or aggressively in a situation in which she or he is punished by someone and attributes that punishing behavior to dispositional factors in the punishing person. If there is some plausible situational reason for your bad behavior toward me (if you "couldn't help it" because of some rule you had to obey or some inadequacy or inability of your own, or if I somehow deserved to be treated that way), I am not so likely to respond aggressively to your behavior.

Attribution as a Personality Variable. Attributions, then, cut across all of our other activities. As with cognitive style, attribution doesn't seem to "fit" into some neat category like learning or abnormal behavior or child development; it is a true personality variable in that it is a basic aspect of "how we are." It is an especially powerful determinant of behavior in that we are so seldom aware of the attributions we make or the ways in which we make them. But make them we do, about other people and about ourselves.

It is perhaps easier to accept the idea that we make attributions about other people's behavior than that we make them about ourselves. Finding an answer to "Why did they do that?" is a bit closer to consciousness; we are more aware of that kind of cognitive activity in ourselves. But "Why did I do that?" is a question we ask, too. Or, if we don't ask it, we at least *answer* it, without being aware that it's a question at all. Attributions about those behaviors and events that have an immediate impact on our own lives are, of course, the most immediate and interesting ones to us. We're involved in them: we can't just sit back and take an impersonal, objective view. The special importance of such me-and-mine attributions is perhaps one reason why they get a section here all to themselves. Coming up now, our next feature attraction, in wide-screen technicolor, full of suspense and human interest: Locus of Control, starring you and me and everybody. . . .

The Controlling J.B. Rotter

In 1966, J.B. Rotter wrote a monograph (formidable sounding word, "monograph," and Rotter's was indeed pretty formidable) entitled "Generalized Expectancies for Internal vs. External Control of Reinforcement." Whew! But, if we dig through all the fancy language, we find that Rotter's basic idea was relatively simple: when something happens to me, either I believe I caused it to happen or I don't believe I caused it to happen. Or, using the language we got used to in the preceding section, I *attribute* the event to myself or to something outside me. And—here's what makes Rotter's thesis interesting—those attributions don't depend so much on an accurate perception of what really caused the event as they do on my general tendency to see myself as the cause of things or to see myself as acted on by the outside world. Each person locates the majority of life-controlling elements either inside or outside himself or herself. If you believe that you can decide for yourself what you will do or be, that you are the "captain of your soul," you locate your control internally; if you believe that what happens to you is largely a matter of luck or that it depends on the decisions of others, you are locating your control externally.

Rotter, you notice, didn't start out to be an attribution theorist. He wasn't particularly interested in how people deal with the "Why did they do that?" question. What he was after was how we handle "Who's in charge here?" questions. Some good things happen to me, and some bad things happen to me. Why? Do I make them happen, or does somebody (or something) else pull the strings?

Internal versus External Locus of Control

It's very important, right at the beginning, to point out one important characteristic of Rotter's work. Rotter is *not* interested in who *really* causes things to happen. He isn't looking at whether or not people are actually in control of the events in their lives. That's one for the philosophers, and so far their batting average on that question isn't all that good. What turned Rotter on was whether or not people *think* they are in control, and how, and why, and what happens when they do or don't think so. Also, as is the case with the other cognitive variables we've looked at, locus of control is a true continuum. Very few people are *all* external or *all* internal in this dimension. Most of us lie somewhere in between the two extremes. We'll continue to talk about "internals" and "externals" because using extreme examples makes it easier to illustrate differences between the two orientations. But we must remember that these examples represent special cases and not (for the most part) real people. Got it now? Good. Let's go.

Locus of control is another one of those central concepts that cut across all sorts of behaviors. My locus of control can affect the way I perform in school or on the job, the way I interact with friends, the kind of person I believe myself to be. It may even affect the kind of results I get when I do psychological research; there's some evidence that experimenters who see themselves as being in control of what happens to them are more likely to get significant results in their research than those who see themselves as externally controlled. A highly suggestive can of worms, that, but one that we'd better not open or we may have to go back and write this book all over again. . . .

Consistency of Control Orientation

Anyhow, Rotter's data suggest that people are pretty consistent in the way they assess the control element in their lives. People who say that they are in charge in a particular situation, that they caused this particular event to happen to them, tend to take personal responsibility for most of the events of their lives; people who blame outside forces for some things tend to do so for most things. In other words, locus of control appears to be a true personality variable, relatively stable within a given individual and cutting across all sorts of life situations and activities. Externals, the people who think outside forces are responsible for what happens to them, are consistently external; internals believe that they are in control of most of their experiences.

We might note parenthetically that, as of a few years ago, the average position of young people on the internal/external continuum appeared to be shifting toward an external orientation. The literature of past generations suggests that people value taking responsibility for their own behavior and see it as a good thing to be able to control one's own life. That value doesn't seem to have changed, but the degree to which young people feel that way appears to be lessening. And, as we'll see in the next few pages, such a shift may have ominous implications.

Differences within External and Internal Orientations. It appears fairly clear that there is, in fact, a locus-of-control continuum onto which people "fit" and by means of which their perceptions of a given situation can be predicted with some accuracy. Some researchers, though, have suggested that this continuum is not sufficiently descriptive. Externals, say some, are not just externals; there are important differences between those externals who believe that luck or chance determines what happens to them and those externals who believe that powerful others are in control of things. At the other end of the continuum, researchers have developed a test that distinguishes between the internal who takes responsibility primarily for successes and the internal who blames herself or himself for failures. These two types of internals have been shown to follow different developmental courses and to behave differently in competitive and goal-setting situations.

In spite of these possible subdivisions, though, most of the work on locus of control still looks at overall internal/external differences. Most of the locus-of-control tests differentiate on just the one main dimension, and most hypotheses deal with those same differences. It's analogous to a literature professor saying "Sure, we know that there are lots of different kinds of fiction and lots of different kinds of nonfiction, but we are still primarily interested in the overall fiction/nonfiction differences." Which seems reasonable. But, as we look at what the researchers have to say about the main internal/external sorts of differences, we should stop once in a while to remind ourselves that there may well be more subtle distinctions that could be important, too.

Children and Locus of Control. So, what are some of these major differences between internals and externals? Well, first, there is a clear and consistent relationship between locus of control and age, at least among children: the older a child is, the more internal that child is likely to be. This seems a logical enough reaction to the reality of the child's life situation. Small children do, in fact, have less control over their environment than do older ones; they are less capable of influencing events, and they are also less able to understand why things happen as they do. As you grow up, your area of control expands. You learn to handle your own body. You begin to move about and manipulate your physical environment. Gradually you develop skill in interacting with and influencing other people. You change from a relatively helpless receiver to an active doer and initiator. It isn't surprising, then, that your sense of being in control should reflect the objective truth of your growing abilities.

Parental Influence. But age alone can't account for all—or even most—differences in locus of control. Children within any age group show a broad range of internal/external scores, and the relationship of locus of control to age breaks down almost completely when we get to adulthood. Before we move away from locus of control in children, though, let's consider one other factor: how do the attitudes and behaviors of parents affect a child's locus of control? If one's perception of locus of control is based in part on external reality, we should expect that children of highly controlling, authoritarian parents would be more external than children reared in more permissive environments. And this seems, in fact, to be the case. In a study done by Pruitt in 1971, teenagers who described their mothers as behaving democratically tended to be more internal than those who described them as behaving autocratically; and the teenagers' descriptions of their mothers reflected the mothers' actual behaviors quite accurately. Even more interestingly, the internal/external scores of the mothers and their children tended to correlate with each other: internal mothers tended to have internal children and external mothers have external children. It looks suspiciously like a continuing cycle: parents who, as children, were very controlled and have come to think of themselves as powerless tend to use the same sorts of child-rearing techniques on their own children.

Locus of Control and Relationship to Others

What about the ways adult internals and externals act with other adults? Do locus-of-control differences relate to differences in the kinds of friends one chooses and how one treats those friends? You, Internal, believing that you are responsible for the events of your life, would expect to be able to control other people. You would want to control other people, in order to confirm your view of yourself. Given this kind of orientation, we might expect that you would seek out people who allow themselves to be controlled, that you would prefer externals for friends rather than other internals. On the other hand, there is a tendency for people to like people who are similar to them; if this is true, then you should prefer the company of other internals, and externals should seek out other externals. Two conflicting predictions—and the data don't seem to be able to show clearly which is true. Instead, there appears to be a preference on the part of *both* internals and externals to have internals for friends. Externals seem to be torn between being drawn to other people who are similar to them and enjoying the company of assertive, successful, self-confident people. Remember, though, that most of us are both internal and external, though we tend to lean one way or the other most of the time. We have both internal and external needs, and we select a friend (who is also a mixture of internal and external) to meet those differing needs. There is also a strong social-desirability factor operating here and cluttering things up. In our culture, people are "supposed to" be successful, self-confident, and so forth, and we are "supposed to" get along with such people. It's likely that primarily external people, even though they might feel more comfortable in the company of other externals, would rather be seen (and see themselves) as preferring friends whose descriptions fit this socially acceptable pattern.

Confusing things still further is the fact that we frequently make mistakes in assessing the personality characteristics of others. Being an internal or an external influences what I believe about *your* locus of control. Internals tend to see other people as more external than they (that fellow isn't as much in control; he doesn't take responsibility like I do). Externals, though, don't exaggerate others' internality; it is as if the external, seeing herself or himself as acted upon by the environment, believes that others feel pretty much the same way. The social perceptions of the internal have an almost arrogant flavor, as if the need to control and to feel in control demands that one see oneself as slightly above (or at least apart from) the herds of sheep-like others. In contrast, the external doesn't see lack of control as due to personal inadequacy; that's just the way the world is. Internals are likely to feel drawn to, but also somewhat threatened by, other internals (even though they're somewhat irresponsible, they're at least less so than externals). Externals seem to be drawn to internals, too, but they are less able to say why.

Externals, who like to be around internals and who see themselves as controlled rather than controlling, might be expected to be relatively conforming people. They are likely to prefer to be followers rather than leaders. Internals, on the other hand, actively resist being controlled. No manipulation for them, thank you! If you are an internal, I may ask you nicely to do something, and you may do it—or you may not, if you have a good reason for refusing. Put pressure on you to do it, and you're likely to go out and deliberately do just the opposite. There may be a moral here: if I'm going to try to manipulate an internal, I'd better be sure that the internal doesn't find out what I'm up to. Internals can be conditioned, or manipulated, like anybody else, if they aren't aware of what's going on. But let them get one whiff that they're being pushed around, and—that's all, friends.

Internals, then, want to control things and resist influence. Indeed, they try to take over the influencer role. Externals don't believe they *can* be in control and thus are less likely to try to exert power. Notice the self-fulfilling nature of these contrasting beliefs and behaviors. Sarah doesn't think she can control things, so she doesn't try, and, sure enough, things happen to her that she can't do much about. Lilly resists any external effort to influence her behavior and in so doing demonstrates to herself that she can, in fact, control what happens to her. It's no wonder that one's locus of control tends to be pretty stable: confirmation of those beliefs, whatever they may be, are built right in to the belief system itself.

It's hard, in talking about internality and externality, not to make internals sound like suntanned superheros and externals like sniveling weaklings. Part of the problem lies in the social-desirability patterns of our culture, which we referred to earlier. We are trained to value assertiveness, success, and self-confidence; we tell our children to "get control of yourself" or to "show them that you can do it."

Locus of Control and Emotional Adjustment

Even if we try to be as objective as possible, however, the evidence does seem to suggest that internals have a psychological edge over externals. Internals tend to be happier with themselves and their lives, better able to cope with problems, and less anxious and depressed than externals.

Anxiety. Anxiety, in particular, appears to be more common among externally oriented people than among internals. Externals tend to focus on the bad things that the environment may do to them—logical enough, really. If you're liable to be dumped on at any moment and there isn't much you can do to prevent it, you can at least try to be ready for it when it happens. On the other hand, externals do seem to have some advantage over internals when it comes to dealing with failure situations. Internals get very upset about failing. Since they are in control, they must take responsibility for failure. It's their fault; they did it. The external, though, can see failure as just another of those things that happen. Some are good, some are bad; sometimes you're lucky and sometimes you're not. The consequences of the failure may be just as bad for the external, but at least externals escape the guilt trip that internals lay on themselves. And, since externals believe that success and failure are both largely a matter of luck, they don't see a present failure as a signal that they are now likely to continue to fail. For the internal, a failure may look like a sign of not being able to handle things any more, that one is no longer competent, that one is—horror!—not in control. For the external, it's just one of the breaks of the game.

Defensiveness. Anxiety and defensiveness are the "terrible twins" of the personality; one is seldom seen without the other. One of the classic ways of studying defensiveness is through the use of a tachistoscope, a machine that presents visual stimuli by throwing an image on a screen for only a fraction of a second. As the exposure time becomes shorter and shorter, it becomes more and more difficult to recognize the stimulus. Theoretically, this situation gives the defenses more of a chance to come into play; if the stimulus is a threatening one, the defensive subject can simply fail to recognize it. Externals and internals differ significantly (very obliging of them, don't you think?) in their responses in this sort of test; externals fail to recognize threatening words more often than do internals. This fact fits the theory nicely: externals don't go out and conquer the threats in their environment but prefer to use more passive defenses. Their way of coping with threat is to deny that it exists. "Wait a minute!"

you say. "Didn't you just tell us that externals focus on the bad things that may happen to them, so they can at least be prepared to be dumped on?" You're pretty sharp, there. It does seem like a contradiction. But it really isn't one. The things the external focuses on are the occurrences, the events, that are unpleasant. It's a kind of Eeyore-like "Yup, here we go again, no sense getting my hopes up that things will be any better this time." In the tachistoscope situation, though, the "threat" is out there, away from the viewer. The only thing that will make it a real threat, that will bring it home, is recognizing it. By ignoring it, we keep it from happening at all. It would be perfectly possible, and perfectly consistent, for the external to sit in front of the tachistoscope and wonder "What sort of unpleasant thing will be done to me now" (focusing, you see, on the possibility of being dumped on by the universe) while at the same time steadfastly not seeing those threatening words being flashed on the screen.

Denial. Externals use defensive denial to deal with their own behaviors as well as with outside threat. In situations where success is valued and generally thought to be a function of one's own ability and hard work, the experience of failure tends to make externals devalue success. Unlike internals, for whom failure can be a spur to greater effort, externals don't believe that working harder is likely to help much. And since they have little control over whether they will get the reward—and they tend to remember best those instances where they didn't—they deny the value of the reward. Like the fox who decided that the grapes were too sour after it found that it couldn't jump up and get them, failing externals tell themselves that the promotion wasn't important, that going on dates is a waste of time, that a college diploma is really just a worthless piece of paper.

Defensiveness, and particularly denial, are ways of avoiding knowledge about what is happening. They are anti-information-seeking behaviors. Can we assume, then, that internals are in general more likely to seek out information about themselves and their interactions with the world than are externals? Rotter hypothesized that this would be the case and described the internals as more sensitive to those parts of the environment that provide information relevant to their own behavior, as alert individuals ready to take advantage of any new information that comes along.

Depression. But what if information about the environment isn't readily obtainable? What if the environment yields confusing or contradictory cues? An environment that doesn't lend itself to predictions, that appears to be uncontrollable, may force people to behave, to think, to feel like externals. Can we go so far as to say that it forces people to become externals? And what is the result when an otherwise internally oriented person is pushed into being an external? While prizing the ability to handle oneself, to exert control over the surroundings, one must now submit to being controlled. A growing number of personality theorists are coming to recognize these conditions as precisely those that lead, almost inevitably, to depression. Depression, according to this view, is caused by seeing oneself as unable to affect or change the environment. For externals, too, a sense of powerlessness leads to depression when things are going badly. In fact, given that things do go badly, externals will be more susceptible to depression than internals, since they chronically feel helpless to control or change events. Being trapped in a losing game, even when it's not your fault, can get to be a drag.

Worse than a drag, in fact. Depression is exceedingly debilitating and painful. Unlike anxiety, which may facilitate certain behaviors if it is not too strong, depression facilitates nothing. If depression and externality are linked in some way and if externals are more susceptible to depression, then to be an external is indeed a precarious and undesirable state. Yet here again, the degree to which one is trapped in one's externality seems a critical factor. It is the extreme external, the external who resists all pressures toward a more self-responsible orientation, who feels at the mercy of a hostile world and is a prime candidate for depression.

But extreme internality, too, can lead to problems. The highly internal individual who fails in an important task is likely to fall prey to self-blame or guilt. Focusing on external forces may be healthy if it is the result of accurate and objective assessment of reality. In other words, an external orientation based on a realistic appraisal of the power of others is psychologically different from the "Nothing I do matters, it's just a question of luck" attitude. People who are in fact blocked from achieving their goals by circumstances beyond their control are better off if they can recognize what has happened than if they take full responsibility for the failure. "I will work harder" isn't a useful philosophy if it leads one to ignore real limitations imposed by one's social or physical environment; it may be better to enjoy the limited goodies on this side of a wall than to break your head trying to beat the wall down.

Another Personality Variable

And where does all this leave us? Like attribution, the locus of control that Rotter introduced isn't a complete personality theory. It's a minitheory, a descriptor, a notion, a bit of information about how people function. Knowing whether or not I see myself as being in control of things (as attributing causality to self rather than to external forces) helps you to understand a little better some of my behaviors, some of my attitudes, some of my hopes and fears. It helps you to predict how I will react, what I will do in a problem situation. It's an inside-the-head thing that relates to outside-the-head behaviors, and elusive, intangible *something* that is nevertheless intrinsically and inescapably human.

Chapter Summary

We began this chapter with the promise that a number of partly completed "minitheories" that all fall under the general heading of cognitive approaches to personality would be presented. Now the task is completed (or nearly so), and it's time to write the closing section. And we're finding that very difficult to do: how do you summarize and pull together so many diverse bits and pieces?

Let's start with a basic question: what do all the minitheories have in common? That's easy enough; they're all *cognitive.* We agreed in Chapter 12 that a hallmark of a cognitive theory of personality is its concern with how people process information from the environment. That's essentially what each of our minitheories is getting at. They differ in what sorts of information they deal with and in what sort of internal processing they focus on.

Festinger's *cognitive dissonance* and Heider's *theory of balance* both concern themselves with discrepancies. First, what *is* discrepancy? Under what circumstances are we likely to feel that things are wrong, that they don't fit? And when that happens, what do we do about it? Festinger was most interested in discrepancies within the actor; he looked at the consequences of believing two contradictory things or of believing one thing but acting differently. Heider, in contrast, looked at people as observers of others. How do we perceive relationships outside ourselves? Even for someone who is a part of the dyad or triad that is being "balanced," Heider's theory has a flavor of standing to the side, observing oneself, rather than churning around internally. But the two approaches are quite compatible; neither one contradicts the other. It's just a matter of what you want to look at most closely, of which perspective you want to take.

Then come Witkin and all the cognitive-style people. Surely the whole concept of *cognitive style* was developed in an effort to explain differences in the ways that people process information. But here is a major contrast between cognitive-style research (and locus-of-control research, too, for that matter) and the work done by Festinger and by Heider: Festinger and Heider were interested in finding universals, in describing ways in which *everybody* processes information. Witkin and his cognitive-style folks, as well as all the locus-of-control researchers, were looking for *individual differences,* for consistent characteristics that could account for Sarah Smith seeing things one way and Jack Jones seeing the same things quite another way. Witkin and students found a number of such traits, such dimensions, and used them to shed light on a whole variety of behaviors. Rotter and the locus-of-control theorists did the same, but they focused on only one dimension, the "who's in charge" belief that each person has. *Locus of control* and cognitive style are both trait theories. They both posit the existence of stable, predictable tendencies in an individual, tendencies that differ from one person to the next, that persist over relatively long periods of time, and that can account for corresponding differences in a variety of externally observable behaviors.

And, last but not least, *attribution theory,* another attempt to describe how people process information. This time, information about why things happen as they do, about why I (and others) act this way or that. It's a huge question, maybe too huge. One part, the who-controls-my-own-rewards question, has already split off into its own subspecialty. Perhaps still other aspects of attribution theory will split off as the work goes forward. At any rate, our look at attribution research should be valuable in giving us a glimpse into an excited, ongoing, *live* area of research.

Attribution may turn out to be a new foundation stone for personality theory—or it may turn out to be a dead end. We're in the middle of it now, and we can't tell.

What does seem certain is that the cognitive approach is here to stay. It probably won't turn out to be the only trick up the sleeves of future personologists, but it will be a major one. We are finally past the adolescence of our science, in which Watson and his crew boisterously threw out everything they couldn't see and measure, and the behaviorists reigned supreme. We have "passed the pressing of the bar."

Suggested Readings

For a good, solid, thorough grounding in the whole area of modern cognitive personality research, you might start with Bernard Weiner's *Theories of Motivation: From Mechanism to Cognition* (Rand McNally, 1972). Be warned—it doesn't exactly read like a novel. But it will put things into perspective and provide you with a lot of detail as well.

Now, for specific reading on the various minitheories:

1. Festinger's *A Theory of Cognitive Dissonance* (Row, Peterson, 1957) is an oldie-but-goodie.

2. Witkin and friends have a chapter in the 1977 *Review of Educational Research* entitled "Field Dependent and Field Independent Cognitive Styles and Their Educational Implications" that will give you a good start in the cognitive-style area.

3. Heider wrote *The Psychology of Personal Relations* in 1958. It states the essentials of the balance theory and an awful lot more, for those who want to really dig in.

4. The best introduction to attribution theory that we know of is published as a "learning module" by General Learning Press. It's written by Bernard Weiner and a number of colleagues and is entitled "Perceiving the Causes of Success and Failure" (1971). Another excellent module in the same series is "The Actor and the Observer: Divergent Perceptions of the Causes of Behavior" by Edward Jones and Richard Nisbett (1971).

5. For locus of control you can, of course, start with Rotter's monograph (*Psychological Monographs: General and Applied*, 1966, *80*(2), 1–28). However, our recommendation would be that you begin at the other end (historically speaking) with Phares' relatively new volume, *Locus of Control in Personality* (General Learning Press, 1976). This will allow you to use his extensive bibliography to follow up any interests you may uncover.

Notes and References

Festinger's cognitive-dissonance theory is best and most completely described in his *A Theory of Cognitive Dissonance* (Row, Peterson, 1957). Brehm and Cohen's studies of sufficient and insufficient justification, typical of many on which the conclusions and generalizations of this chapter are based, are found in their book *Explorations in Cognitive Disso-*

nance (Wiley, 1962). The various strategies used in dealing with dissonance are explored in a 1968 paper by Hardyck entitled "Predicting Response to a Negative Evaluation" (*Journal of Personality and Social Psychology,* 1968, *9,* 128–132).

Material on the field-dependent/field-independent dimension of cognitive style is taken largely from the following sources: Witkin and Goodenough's unpublished paper "Field Dependence Revisited," circulated as an Educational Testing Service Research Bulletin; and Witkin and associates' "Field-Dependent and Field-Independent Cognitive Styles and Their Educational Implications" (*Review of Educational Research,* 1977, *47,* 1–64). The original work on cognitive complexity was done by Frank Barron and was described in an article "Some Personality Correlates of Independence of Judgement" in the *Journal of Personality* (1967, *7,* 111–116). More recent findings are reported in Altmann and Conklin's article "Further Correlates of the Barron Complexity Scale," in *Perceptual and Motor Skills* (1972, *34,* 83–86). Jerome Kagan and associates, in a monograph entitled "Information Processing in the Child" (Psychological Monographs, 1964, *78,* Whole No. 58) report work on impulsivity/reflectivity. And Kagan, in his book *Cognitive Styles in Infancy and Early Childhood* (Erlbaum, 1976), provides a good update and overview of the whole cognitive-style research area.

Heider's balance theory is best articulated, of course, in his own *The Psychology of Personal Relations* (Wiley, 1958). A number of applications of the theory are found in Cartwright and Zander's *Group Dynamics* (Harper & Row, 1960).

Both the Weiner and associates and the Jones and Nisbett papers on attribution (referred to in the "Suggested Readings" section) can be found in *Attribution: Perceiving the Causes of Behavior,* by Jones and associates (General Learning Press, 1971); the book contains a number of other articles describing research and applications of learning theory. More recent work in the area is detailed in *New Directions in Attribution Research* by J.H. Harvey, J.W. Ickes, and R.F. Kidd (Erlbaum, 1976). The Worchel and Andrioli study, dealing with reciprocity, is found in the *Journal of Personality,* 1976, *44,* 294–310, entitled "When is a Favor a Threat to Freedom?"

Rotter's 1966 monograph has been cited in the preceding section. A more recent article, "External Control and Internal Control", (*Psychology Today,* 1971, *5,* 37–42, 58–59), restates and updates his position. The Pruitt study, in which students describe their mothers' child-rearing techniques, is reported in an unpublished doctoral dissertation done by Pruitt in 1972 (*Dissertation Abstracts International,* 1972, February, *32* [8-B], 4869). Evidence of the shift to a more external locus of control is discussed in articles by Steger et al. ("Reply to Wolfe and Egelston," *Psychological Reports,* 1973, *33,* 312) and by Schneider ("College Students' Belief in Personal Control, 1969–1970," *Journal of Individual Psychology,* 1971, *27,* 188). Recent reviews of research on this topic are found in E.J. Phares' book *Locus of Control in Personality* (General Learning Press, 1976) and in Lefcourt's *Locus of Control: Current Trends in Theory and Research* (Halsted Press, 1976) and from J. Moursund's *Us People* (Brooks/Cole, 1972) and *Learning and the Learner* (Brooks/Cole, 1976).

14

The Last Word

Very often it is difficult to understand what a personality theorist is saying, especially what a humanistic or an existential theorist is saying, if you are approaching his or her theory from the point of view of traditional scientific methodology. What is the operational definition of "being" or of "nothingness"? Carl Jung once said that a theoretical proposition should not be accepted as true unless the *opposite* of that proposition could also be accepted as true. What kind of logic is this? Even Freud and his followers bedeviled their critics by insisting, for example, that, when people say that they love their mother, the statement should be taken to mean (1) that they love their mother; (2) that they hate their mother; or (3) both the above. The last is the most likely. Surely this is a bowl of Jello; how can one criticize a theory that covers all possibilities?

Psychologist/philosopher Joseph F. Rychlak pondered these questions in his 1968 book, *A Philosophy of Science for Personality Theory.* In the constant arguments between the "hard" scientists, mostly learning theorists, and the "softies," mostly humanists but including Freudians, Rychlak saw an age-old debate being reenacted. The underlying question, rarely recognized by the debaters, was: which is better, dialectical reasoning or demonstrative reasoning?

Dialectical reasoning is characterized by oppositions and contradictions and by logical analysis and synthesis. In its best known dress, dialectical reasoning can be seen as a three-step process: thesis/antithesis/synthesis. A statement (thesis) is made and immediately suggests a contradiction (antithesis); the paradoxical truth of both the thesis and its antithesis results in a synthesis, a new, higher-level statement that somehow combines the truths in both thesis and antithesis. This synthesis becomes a new thesis, suggests a new contradiction, and is itself synthesized into a still higher-level understanding. It is a self-perpetuating, never-ending sequence that can lead to remarkable insights. Many of these insights, however, turn out to be worthless products of the thinker's remarkable imagination. Like the unicorn. And therein lies the danger of dialectical reasoning.

I love my mother. I hate my mother. I am ambivalent. But I am not ambivalent. I must be. . . . Shakespeare drew pictures of people reasoning dialectically: "To be or not to be" (Hamlet), "I am not what I am" (Iago). Our legal system is at least partly dialectical. One attorney argues one position, and the other argues the opposite.

Demonstrative reasoning, on the contrary, is characterized by the choice of one proposition as "more true" than its opposite and the logical pursuit of the implications of that truth. Science, as a method, is one way to establish a proposition as true. For example, "if a hungry rat is given food when it presses a bar, the likelihood of future bar pressing is increased." This statement is based on a wealth of research, and, were we to assert instead that food would result in a decreased probability of future bar pressing, most psychologists would cast us out into the cold, calling us names as we went. The same names, by the way, are sometimes used against reasonably respectable personality theorists and theories—"philosopher," "science-fiction writer," "nonscience and nonsense," "magician," "artist."

The last—artist—is used, of course, in a derogatory fashion, but it is illuminating to note the real affinity between artists and personality theorists. The writer, the painter, the sculptor, the composer, and even the comedian all rely on the dialectical tension of opposites and incongruities for their emotional impact. "To be or not to be. . . ." That psychologists trying to understand the workings of the human mind in a therapy setting, from which many personality theories have emerged, have come up with theories that look very much like art is no accident. People can and do reason demonstratively at times, but they also reason dialectically. Any observer with any sensitivity at all can see that humans do not consistently think one proposition is true; we have minds full of contradictions and opposites, thinking one thing one moment and arguing the reverse a moment later. The human is an artist as well as a scientist. Rychlak argued that theories of personality that deny the dialectical character of much human thought will ultimately fail to explain or understand much of human behavior.

Let's rephrase that last statement. As we look at the "behavior" of a machine—say a computer—we find that we can set down certain "laws" that relate what goes into the machine on one side to what comes out of the machine on the other. But imagine a dialectical computer. You read in "A is B," and the computer responds with the possibility that A is not B, oscillates between the two possibilities, and explores the implications of each. You ask "Is A the same as B?" The computer expresses the opinion that it might be. Our dialectical machine also makes mistakes. Some of these mistakes would be remarkable insights—creations of speculative machinery. The ability to create, said Rychlak, is the ability to make mistakes. The dialectical computer might also respond to your question by telling you a joke or by admonishing you for unethical practices. An interesting machine, but who could build it? And, once built, who would buy it?

But *people* are such machines. Could we possibly understand a person by seeing that person as a demonstrative computer, as an empty organism, as an object whose movements are determined by external events? No way, said Rychlak.

The problem with dialectical reasoning is that it can be horribly wrong. Thus many dismiss it as bad for science. The human mind is capable of coming up with several logical reasons for believing that Woodrow Wilson is now President of the United States, but the facts show otherwise. As a means of theory generation, dialectical reasoning desperately needs the tempering effect of direct observation and systematic experimentation—in short, the traditional research method—to prevent the (personality) theories so generated from slipping into absolute absurdities, like the unicorn. Personality theories should be science, not art. Like Fitzgerald's Great Gatsby, dialectical theories tend to take flight, to become high-hatted, high-bouncing lovers, with relevance to nothing real in life. Cold, hard facts are mundane and unappealing, but they are relentless; hopes are ultimately dashed if they are forlorn, and fantasies cannot be maintained if they are incredible.

There can be little doubt that many high-bouncing personality theories—like those of Freud, Rogers, and Maslow—are objectively wrong in some respects. Research is still needed to find out exactly where and to what degree. And here we come to a problem, for it is difficult to come up with operational definitions of many of the dialectical constructs that are embedded in humanistic theories. Point me to an "id" or to "self-actualization." The request hardly makes sense. Research on dialectically phrased theories is difficult, but it must be done.

Demonstratively phrased theories have an easier time of it. An S-R theory of personality—like Skinner's—lends itself readily to experimentation in terms of independent variables affecting dependent variables, and advocates of these theories are quick to point out this fact. It is a virtue, indeed. And as Rychlak points out, if we were studying rocks and not people, S-R or other demonstrative theories might suffice. But people create new realities for themselves. For instance, they take ethical positions. Sometimes they even behave in accordance with those positions. No rock has yet been known to acclaim a single God or to express a desire to achieve the greatest good for the greatest number. Ethics cannot be established demonstratively.

We have seen many examples of dialectical constructs in the theories discussed in this book. Freud is considered a genius primarily because he accepted his patients' false statements as true. Sounds ridiculous, doesn't it? But, when he discovered that his patients were lying about their childhood sexual traumas, he could have easily dismissed these lies as irresponsible nonsense, as most other therapists of his era did. Freud sensed the truth of the lies, not in the real world but in the equally real mind, and psychoanalytic theory was born. What is false is true. What better statement of dialectical thinking can we find?

The structural theory of an id, a superego, and an ego is like a thesis, an antithesis, and a synthesis. The id wants and the superego prohibits; the ego compromises. Throughout Freud's theory one can see the tension of opposites. The conscious and the unconscious battle to control behavior, and synthetic behaviors emerge; slips of the tongue, dreams, and symptoms. The neurotic personality is conceptualized as two dissociated parts of the whole in conflict, carrying on a dialectic, a Socratic dialogue in which the winner now becomes the loser later, back and forth, back and forth.

It is not difficult to pull similar dialectic themes out of many of the personality theories you have studied or will study. And we think it's helpful to recognize such themes, to understand the basic incompatibility between the dialectic and the demonstrative models.

But there's another way, perhaps even more important, in which recognizing dialectical processes can be useful to you. Every good personality theorist, you see, is a dialectician—whether his or her theory is dialectic or not. The whole purpose of studying other people's theories is to help you in building your own. And (to some degree, like it or not) you must use dialectical reasoning to carry out that task of construction. One theorist says this. But a second theorist says that. Both can't be right. But wait—if I interpret one's theory like this and bend the other's theory just a little bit in that direction, don't they begin to fit? And, in fitting, don't they take on a new richness, a new meaning, a heightened explanatory power?

That's the process; that's the dialectic. We all use it to create our own theories. The theories may not be—usually aren't—full-blown, star-spangled models ready for simultaneous publication in three psychological journals and the Reader's Digest. But they are theories nonetheless. They are sets of beliefs and observations and conclusions that we use to help us understand how we and others behave.

To study personality theory, really study it, is to create your own personal theory. If you don't do that, all you will achieve is a collection of unrelated fragments of ideas bouncing around inside your head. And creating your own personal theory must inevitably involve you in dialectic. Don't fight it! There will be time enough for scientific testing later, when you have a synthesis that's firm enough to be worth the trouble.

So here is one final bit of advice. Argue with yourself. Posit the impossible. Search for new syntheses, and then let them dissolve again in their own contradictions. Nothing can be kept unless it is let go.

Name Index

Subject Index

Subject Index